Ignite & Unshackle

The Latent Power of You

TRAFFORD
PUBLISHING™

Note for Librarians: A cataloguing record for this book is available from Library and Archives Canada at www.collectionscanada.ca/amicus/index-e.html

ISBN 1-4120-8016-9

Printed in Victoria, BC, Canada. Printed on paper with minimum 30% recycled fibre.

Trafford's print shop runs on "green energy" from solar, wind and other environmentally-friendly power sources.

PUBLISHING

Offices in Canada, USA, Ireland and UK

Book sales for North America and international:
Trafford Publishing, 6E–2333 Government St.,
Victoria, BC V8T 4P4 CANADA
phone 250 383 6864 (toll-free 1 888 232 4444)
fax 250 383 6804; email to orders@trafford.com

Book sales in Europe:
Trafford Publishing (UK) Limited, 9 Park End Street, 2nd Floor
Oxford, UK OX1 1HH UNITED KINGDOM
phone 44 (0)1865 722 113 (local rate 0845 230 9601)
facsimile 44 (0)1865 722 868; info.uk@trafford.com

Order online at:
trafford.com/05-3014

10 9 8 7 6 5 4 3 2

Ignite & Unshackle

The Latent Power of You

**How to be and get absolutely everything you
want in life...naturally, easily and quickly**

Jonathan**Clark**

Because one mind is never enough

Four months ago, I lost my job in broadcast news and asked Jonathan to help me find another. When Jonathan said the situation was "absolutely perfect" right now, I could have laughed.

But it was perfect. And in the months that followed, Jonathan helped me see the bigger picture and focus on identifying my needs and meeting them.

Amazing things started to happen. Suddenly the interviews began to appear... and offers rolled in. In the end, I had three exceptionally strong offers, all of which could have been perfect for me. The job I took, as a radio skills trainer for the BBC, paid almost 50% more than what I had been earning yet it was in an area I hadn't considered prior to working with Jonathan. It was an outcome I couldn't have believed was possible, but it became possible because my coach believed in me.

I have to admit I was skeptical about hiring a coach at first. It was no small challenge to be paying the price of a small mortgage at a time when I had no regular income. But I can assure you that if you want to achieve truly remarkable things and are willing to put in the work, hiring Jonathan as your coach will be the best investment you ever make. You will recoup your money many many times over.

Put simply, Jonathan offers unconditional support and encouragement to be and do whatever you desire. Now, who else do you know who can do that for you?

Ros Toynbee, Career Coach

Although I've done presentation techniques for 30 years it had never really gelled in my mind. I can't get over the difference it's made for me. I've done NLP before, I've done the Tony Robbins courses before, but until you get somebody who actually touches the inner core of your unconscious, it doesn't work, and Jonathan does that.

Carol Bentley, Copywriter and Published Author

Someone once told me this would be a "life changing" experience and I was skeptical, however after the past 7 days, I feel the changes – I feel different, I think differently. Wow!

Debbie McCormack, Trainer

I can't even see my obstacles! I don't have any obstructions now, the path is just opening up. For the first time in many years I no longer feel overwhelmed. There are things going on which I know that I'm not doing, and yet there is no other explanation other than it's me. Every time I go into a shop or restaurant they love me at first sight. I know that I'm not doing it consciously, but the rapport skills have soaked in. Things are really clicking into place, it's such an amazing experience.

Jules May, Inventor

I have methods to control my emotions and feel my self esteem has directly improved – in addition to being well on the way to becoming a master communicator.

Dr Tricia Granger, Dentist

My whole outlook has changed. I am now more confident, happy, contented and relaxed. I believe that this is where I was supposed to be.

Susan Forde, Researcher

I wanted to be confident in my abilities, learn how to communicate with maximum effectiveness, let go of stuff, free my potential and go forth and practice. Jonathan was very helpful and considerate, cared how we were doing but remained detached enough to be effective. I have trust and confidence in myself and you. Things are infinitely more open and bright.

Kari Gillies, Scottish Power

I feel that I am released from so much that held me back – like a different person in the same skin, **and** *changed forever.*

Maria Doherty, Hypnotherapist

Standard of conduct and professionalism was very high, the most complete training I have ever participated in. I am confident in my choices and path in the future and have left the baggage behind.

Tom McNamee, NLP Master Practitioner

As always well planned, beautifully delivered and great fun as well as many new learnings. Feel more confident and more excited about my career. What can you do to improve? Not much – it's hard to beat 100%

Karen Lawson, NLP Master Practitioner

Instead of just knowing that I am in control of how I feel, I know how to do it! I am enjoying increased energy from the Ha Breathing. I am communicating far more effectively and my relationships with my family, friends and girlfriend have improved dramatically. I really enjoyed the opportunity of spending a week with you – you are an amazing guy and your ability to deliver and your in depth knowledge inspires me very much

Sandy Newbigging, Coach

My investment in your Practitioners and Master Practitioners training equates to approximately 1/3 of the total cost of my MBA. In terms of value and return on investment your training puts the MBA in the shade. There is direct application and immediate return on so many aspects of the trainings. Thanks!

Mike Tierney, Managing Director

I found the course absolutely mind blowing. Your presentation skills (something I know quite a lot about) are superlative. I learned a lot from you on so many different levels. Thank You.

Erick Rainey, Coach & NLP trainer

I have received everything I expected and a whole lot more. This has been a very emotional, fun and profound experience. If people are interested at all in growing and changing for the better, you have to start training with Jonathan!

Liesha Ross

HGE has far exceeded my expectations of NLP

Kim Macleod

A fantastic journey – change, breakthroughs, learning, wisdom, it was all there. Seven days of immersion with some fantastic people, its hard to find the words. Enlightening, enabling, freeing, awe inspiring are a few that filter through. It's really whetted my appetite for what comes next. Keep evolving.

Ron Mills

I'm getting more out of this course than I did when we did it in Hawaii

Pam Neill

Your <u>52%</u> off preferential HOME STUDY *certificate*

Because you have purchased "Ignite & Unshackle The Latent Power Of You" Jonathan has agreed to allow you a full **52%** preferential reduction in his **Home Study** "It's What You Do That Counts" programme – the most powerfully effective change programme available today. Instead of £99, he's allowing you to get the COMPLETE programme for **just £47** plus VAT (total £55.23) if you complete this certificate (otherwise price is strictly £99 plus VAT for the set)

You'll receive:

- 2 CDs from the one-day live sessions Jonathan takes his live group through, including:

Jonathan's story

Organ language – programming your neurology inadvertently

Going through Transitions and your continual evolution

Your 3 biggest sources of stress right now

Results versus Reasons

How to start removing the veil…

The relationship between your money and your energy

Do you want to take the blue pill, or the red pill?

The story of the Carpenter

Watching Quantum Leap

Why it helps to bring in someone who knows the tricks of the trade

Introducing Hypno Genetic Evolution

The big picture of how all personal development methods work, or don't

The Neurological Levels in action

The downside of conventional approaches and why they frequently fail

The HGE Communication Model – how your head works ~~The HGE Communication Model – how your head works~~

How your mind runs your body

The human mind can't process a negative

Changing your internal critic

The HGE Scramble – permanently heal any painful memory in 60 seconds

Watch your physiology – change how you feel in seconds

Activate your radar and start to pick up all the signs

The Satir Categories – how to communicate at 100% using your body

Your personal invite to the 3 day Foundation Skills seminar

Its not who you are, it's what you do that defines you

- Relaxation Self Hypnosis CD - Just put this 26 minute long CD in your stereo and let Jonathan help you make some dramatic changes in your life
- Personal workbook – Jonathan takes you through some personal application as he leads you through exercises and questions designed to uncover your blocks and drive you forward towards vibrant health, focussed motivation and communication excellence.

❏ Yes, please send me the Home Study "It's What You Do That Counts" programme of 3 CDs plus Manual for the preferential investment of only £55.23

I am paying by (please tick)

❏ Cheque (payable to J. Clark)   ❏ Credit Card

Send to Jonathan Clark, Suite 211, Claymore House, 145 Kilmarnock Road, Glasgow G41 3JA

(Please use block capitals)

Name _____ROGER LAMB_____

Address _____190 TOWN STREET_____

_____ARMLEY, LEEDS_____

Postcode ___LS12 3RF_____

Tel ___0113/2791375_____

Email ___−_____

*Card Number*___6759/0510/3030/8796/221___

Start Date _____ *Expiry Date* ___10/06___

*Issue No. (if applicable)*___7___

*3 digit security code*___502___

*Signature*___(NdC) R. LAMB_____

Dedicated to Cheryl, who's always been there for me, and never let me down, no matter what

"Nau ko-u aloha"

My love is yours

WHAT THIS BOOK CAN DO FOR YOU

100 BENEFITS, ADVANTAGES, PROMISES, RESULTS, ACHIEVEMENTS, CURES, TRANSFORMATIONS, CHANGES AND IMPACTS IT'S POSSIBLE TO ACHIEVE USING THIS BOOK

1. Rapid personal growth – reach your dream lifestyle, be a better person, be who you want to be, have it NOW!, improve your life, less problems, happier inside, change bad things about your life, become more spiritual, more confident, gets you quickly out of a bad life you don't want to be in, good quality of life, leave your problems behind.

2. Set goals that really come true – learn the magic formula that really works! Get more of what you want, dream lifestyle, happier, ideal life, more money, ideal partner, nice home, nice car, healthy sexy body, more free time, more fun, less stress, happy family, happy healthy kids, live life to the full, achievement, pride, admired, given status in society, happier, healthy, do things you'd never imagined, direction in life, motivation, not bored or lazy, always have a purpose to your life, not idle, helping society, good role model, always busy in a good driven way.

3. Develop your intuition – trust your own feelings, make good decisions, feel sure of yourself, know who to trust, certainty, security, know what to do, do the right thing, not get it wrong, protection from danger, make good choices in friends, money, etc, trust your own judgement.

4. Affect other people profoundly – impress, be liked, be admired, feel superior, know what to say, feel important, not

be invisible or insignificant, Significance, respect, admiration, maybe didn't get that in your past so want it now.

5. Help people solve their own problems – helping, giving, connection, empowering, be liked, caring, less hassle, not taking on their monkeys, solutions, easier life, feels good, giving something back, others more willing to help you in future.

6. Become more self sufficient – count on yourself, depend on yourself, security, not needy, independence, freedom, always know what to do, feel strong, don't have to look weak or ask for help, trust your own feelings, feel sure of yourself, self confidence, certainty, hope, know what to do, no matter what happens you can handle it, feel solid, do the right thing, respected and looked up to, admired, get on and do things quicker, self-reliant.

7. Find out stuff from your parents you never knew! Connection with them, closer, learn about yourself, fun, surprise, understand yourself better, fascinating, know your history, pass it on to your kids.

8. Get to know your friends at a deeper level – trust, more fun, connection with them, feels good, bond, deeper & longer friendship, find out more about them, know who to trust, know who to depend on, find out the truth, better quality of life, get more help, attract more friends.

9. Get to really know your partner's deepest thoughts - trust, more fun, connection with them, feels good, bond, deeper & longer friendship, find out more about them, know who to trust, know who to depend on, find out the truth, more loving

bond between you, help them overcome their deepest fears, be their hero, understand each other better, mate for life, security, hope, certainty, build happy relationship, better life, argument free, hassle free, impress them, make them love you more.

10. Amazing self-discovery – understand yourself, know why you do what you do, change habits, become a better person, laugh at yourself, more self confidence, feel happy in your own skin, change things you don't like, happier, sleep better, less self-criticism, stop self sabotage, be your own best friend.

11. Stimulate great conversation – make friends, be interesting, be significant, not be a wall flower, better social skills, learn about people, get everywhere in life, good communicators go places, shy people get left behind. Overcome shyness by always knowing what to say.

12. Challenge attitudes- break the mould, shake things up, move society forward, rock the boat, wake people up, wake yourself up, unplug from the Matrix, think outside the box, progress, new horizons, have a strong opinion, be heard.

13. Become able to virtually read minds – know if you can trust someone, know what someone's really thinking, get what you want from people, build a bond of trust, know how to please them, have people like you, predict their response, tell if someone is lying or not, get the truth, impress people. Defend yourself from manipulation and mind games – mental aikido!.

14. Find out how you keep yourself stuck, and how to change it- achievement, ending self sabotage, understand yourself, move forward, improve yourself, stop bad habits, become a better

person, get more of what you want, become happier.

15. Find out what makes experts so good at what they do – copy them, emulate your heroes, business success, make more money, become healthier, achieve, learn, understand people, duplicate success in any field.

16. Reduce stress – live longer, be healthier, easier life, makes you a nicer person, better quality of life, nicer to be around, less adrenaline, less tetchy, time for pastimes, think straight.

17. Become a master communicator – get what you want, easier life, be understood, be respected, be admired, have the gift of the gab, people will like being around you, be a leader, have more influence, be a team player, less argument, more understanding, more extroverted, become a people person.

18. Become an expert problem solver! – remove obstacles, get what you want, less stress, help others, make more money, peace of mind, easier life, security, significance, achievement, pride, be remembered after you die, be more valuable to your company, good friend.

19. Cut through the flannel and get straight to the point – be understood, problem solver, save time, less stress, good manager, cut down mistakes, clear thinker, stay on target, more efficient, cost effective, good negotiator.

20. Become a living lie detector – know who to trust, avoid getting hurt, choose your friends better, make better choices, protect your heart, protect your wallet, trust your gut, better relationship.

21. Elegantly disagree with someone – save the relationship, make your point, keep the peace, stand your ground, self confidence, remain friends, keep your job, protect your reputation, your social standing, avoid falling out, negotiation skills, reach agreement.

22. Learn how to be a master negotiator – get more of what you want, keep the peace, achieve more, keep everyone happy, happy families, people will turn to you for help, reputation, stay out of trouble, cover your trail.

23. Learn how to run your own head – self confidence, cope with anything, be happy, take control of your life, achieve your dreams, control your emotions, understand yourself, awareness, personal growth, be healthier, less stress, more intelligence, emotionally stable, socially acceptable, nicer person to be with, more upbeat & positive, forward thinking, popular.

24. Unobtrusive – content free therapy, so no need to go over it again, don't have to suffer it all over again, quicker than conventional, more comfortable for the client, keep embarrassing, personal details personal, less emotional cos you're not reopening the can of worms.

25. You take responsibility for your own life. Stop blaming others, move forward, feel empowered, become independent, realise how strong you are, more emotionally stable.

26. Take control of your destiny – strong direction, achieve your dreams, pride, achievement, something to look forward to, happy, healthy, feel emotionally secure, driven.

27. Solution orientated, purpose driven. – stop dwelling on the problem, achieve more, solve problems, progress, think outside the box.

28. Reveals possibilities that you didn't realise you have – get out of being stuck, progress, light at the end of the tunnel, hope, expand your creativity, flexibility, freedom of choice..

29. Allows you to choose to let go of problems. Feel better about yourself, no need to hold onto pain, move on, change yourself for the better, get over past hurts, see a real shift in your behaviour.

30. Gives you more tools in your toolbox – more ways of getting what you want, feel you have the advantage, flexibility, choices, whole range of tools and techniques, can handle anything, master of communication & behavioural change, always have the answer, never run out of ideas, always know what to do next, certainty, power!.

31. It's not delivered by an authority figure – safe, keeps it real, what works in the real world, non threatening, unconventional, off the beaten path, different point of view, breath of fresh air, whole new perspective.

32. Resistance, disbelief that you can actually change. Shatter the illusion, bust the stereotype, prove 'em all wrong, do the impossible! Seen every expert so far and failed – now there's hope! Challenge boundaries.

33. Work with you – a do with, not a do to. It's a joint collaboration, have your say, take active role in the change, be heard,

equal say, not patronised, just as important, have things be the way you want them. Support you, 2 of you working on your goals.

34. What if change was quick, painless and requires little effort? People think change takes ages and is hard, but it's not. Get over it quickly, fast relief, overnight transformation, works like magic, may actually be fun! Get over lifelong blocks now! No need to wait.

35. HGE allows you to see the motivation you need to change. Wakes you up, gives you hope, shows you how, certainty – gives you a route map to follow, taste your true potential, gives you the push you need, opens your eyes.

36. Become a great conversationalist – no longer a wallflower, overcome shyness, get respect, feel more confident, doors will open for you, always know what to say, be popular, not afraid to speak your mind, stimulate others intellectually, emotionally happier and more secure, great social life, known for being witty and chatty.

37. Be fascinating to talk to – be interesting, more attractive, land jobs at job interviews, great people skills, make people feel at ease, good mixer, good team player, good leader.

38. Therapists become ten times more effective – great reputation, attract more clients, better clients, confidence soars, help people more, in less time, see real change, deal with your own stuff so better able to help others, quicker, can charge more for what you do.

39. Teachers pull out the student's latent potential – help people learn and grow, achievement, proud of them, boost their confidence, reputation for being a good teacher, promotion prospects, deal with angry parents better, with colleagues, staff conflicts.

40. Trainers can breathe new life into old material – keep it fresh, make courses come alive, stay motivated, learn state of the art techniques, take it to the next level, reputation for being good at what you do, students achieve more, confidence soars, more fun for everyone, better success results, promotion prospects.

41. Salespeople really uncover the customers deepest desires – true consultative selling, win/win agreements, customers for life, repeat business, satisfied clients, reputation for being good at what you do, meet and beat targets, better rapport, less appointments, work less and earn more, promotion prospects, use state of the art techniques, more confidence, less stress, asked for by name, customer loyalty, future security, more friendships, happier, healthier, stability, certainty.

42. Single people really can find the perfect match – partner for life, less misunderstandings, avoid nightmare dates, have more fun, virtually read minds, find your soul mate, rely on them, trust, find Mr Right.

43. Interviewers get the ideal candidate – less training costs, quicker, stay in job longer, happier secure work force, less turnover, less overhead, loyalty, better morale and better production, less sick absence, recruit with confidence, get the right person for the job every time, certainty, reputation for spotting the talent improves your prospects and promotion.

44. Uncover someone's hidden agenda – know if someone can be trusted, avoid being sold to or manipulated, virtually read minds, protect yourself, security, hold onto your money, spot the bad ones, help them get what they really want, uncover true intentions, negotiate better.

45. Consultants pull out the client's real problems – do a better job, satisfy the need better, loyal clients, reputation for helping, get to the root of the problem, repeat business.

46. Life Coaches provoke shifts and leaps in their clients – reputation for being a good Coach, people progress and achieve their goals, happiness, get a full practice, understand people better, dramatic magic, hear hidden agendas, repeat clients, sustainable practice, clients stay longer, earn more money, people talk about you, life gets easier, advertise less cos more referrals coming in.

47. Always make the best decision for yourself forever more- certainty that you're doing the right thing, better quality of life, less stress, achieve more, be doing the right career, in the right relationship, doing the right things, help others with less effort, hope for the future, bright prospects, self assured and self confident, stronger person, self-reliant.

48. Speakers can run the room – reputation for being good, feel totally in control, wow the audience, respected and admired, popular, attract more and bigger audiences, confident in your own ability, get rid of stage fright forever.

49. Managers lead by asking profound questions – make breakthroughs, turn around the business, gets you promoted, re-

spect, happiness, seen as intelligent, reputation precedes you, open doors, solve problems, reduce stress, better team morale and productivity, new horizons.

50. Get more in touch with your spiritual side – peace, hope for the future, certainty, inner calmness, serenity, live in harmony with your life, secure inside, trust yourself, learn that there's more to life than this, reduce stress, get out of the rat race, think bigger picture, contribute to your community, know why you're here, discover your life's purpose, honour the planet.

51. Energised – more energy, feel alive, get more done, look healthy, feel young again, live longer, have more fun, be more attractive, seen to be happier.

52. in control – security, hope for the future, certainty, know where the goal posts are, get rid of problems, achieve more, less stress, reputation for being in charge, status, popularity.

53. powerful – feel strong, stable, be in charge, take control, get things done, fight for your rights, admired and respected, be safe, influence others, better at what you do.

54. confident – self sufficient, security, better future, emotionally stronger, more attractive, feel unthreatened, be happier, healthier, do what you like, be listened to, speak your mind, not be walked over, get what you're entitled to.

55. self reliant – stronger person, not depending on others, more confident, more capable, independent, be a self-starter, pride of achieving, get things done, get on in life.

56. Better health – live longer, more energy, more flexible and more mobile, be able to do more, keep up with others, look good, feel good, be a model of excellence, able to help others more, take care of yourself.

57. mental stability – happy, healthy, secure, predictable behaviour, people will like you, safe secure future, be independent, good career prospects, mentally tough, can care for yourself and family, not be a burden to society, be respected.

58. freedom – independence, have choices, see solutions, think more flexibly, outthink others, smoke out hidden agendas, living lie detector, avoid being manipulated, happy, shake off limiting beliefs, negative emotions and bad habits, change anything about yourself, less stress, capable of more, open new horizons, look better, more energy, more vibrancy.

59. knowing what you want and doing it – find your direction, know why you're here, make the right decisions, certainty, achievement, pride, success, money, health, fun, be motivated more often, higher energy.

60. Respond vs. react. – don't get caught up, you have choice, make better decisions, know what to do, take responsibility, feel in control, get out of sticky situations elegantly, avoid getting sucked in, make a conscious choice not go on autopilot..

61. Learn how you work. – understand yourself, know why you do what you do, realise you're normal, know how to motivate yourself, understand your emotions, find out what makes you tick, learn what you've always been trying to achieve, happier in your own skin, certainty, reassurance.

62. Let go of the burdens of the past. – freedom, be who you want to be, happier, healthier, move on, weight off your mind, feel freer, take on new challenges, get on with life, feel purified.

63. Take a pressure washer to your problems. – blow out the cobwebs, clean up the past, remove blockages, tidy yourself up, mental clear out, fast, massive impact, breakthrough.

64. Decide who you are for the rest of your life. – have an aim in life, have a mission, life purpose, be all you can be, certainty and security, hope, consistency, tranquillity.

65. Begin living your life. – start afresh, take charge, be in control, boost your energy, design your life the way you want it, wake up.

66. Change overnight – relief, get over it, impact, make an entrance the next day, rapid change, don't have to bear it any longer, start a new chapter, prove them wrong.

67. Fun, painless, quick. – enjoyable, have a laugh, laugh at yourself, easier than you think, easy to do, transformation fast, relief, do it overnight, get over it, impact, make an entrance the next day, rapid change, don't have to bear it any longer, start a new chapter, prove them wrong.

68. You can let go of the past now. - relief, get over it, impact, make an entrance the next day, rapid change, don't have to bear it any longer, start a new chapter, prove them wrong.

69. Taken you years to build up your problems – erase them in a week. Relief, get over it, impact, make an entrance the next

day, rapid change, don't have to bear it any longer, start a new chapter, prove them wrong.

70. You think that to learn something well takes years. – prove them all wrong, use latest technology, achieve your goals faster, learn how to learn, use your brain the way it's designed, become a super learner, have fun at the same time, be a better learner forever more, activate all your previous memories, make more connections, become more intelligent and think more flexibly.

71. You already have all of this inside you. Activate dormant power, tap into your unconscious, learn quicker, develop your inborn skills, drop the excuses, realise how powerful you are, increase your confidence in leaps.

72. Drive your own bus – become a bus driver! Go where you want when you want, charge what you want, drop people off when you want, become a coach, visit new scenery, operate on cleaner fuel, be environmentally friendly, travel farther and faster, lose your luggage, take your friends and family with you.

73. Become the person you always were before you (a) started worrying about it. (b)were told that you weren't. Less stress, get rid of the hang ups, feel secure, happy, be a nicer person to be around, feel happier within yourself, sleep better, change limiting conditioning, change limiting beliefs, prove them all wrong, no longer pleasing others, drop the mask.

74. New and improved. More fun, cover deeper topics, learn more, stuff you haven't seen before, benefit from experience, better understanding, you'll be more confident and competent, fresh

material, no one else has seen this, secret stuff, unique.

75. Reclaim everything you were before you (a) rejected parts of yourself (b) had choice – rekindle your motivation, trust yourself, be honest with yourself, tell the truth, face the reality, trust your internal dialogue, happier in your own skin, be more congruent, walk your talk, speak your mind, fire on all cylinders, emotionally stable, intellectually adult and open.

76. How you make meaning out of what's going on – gives you certainty & control. Understand how life works, be safe, avoid danger, be stable, happy, stay healthy, understand people, solve problems better, know what makes you tick, respond vs. react, certainty, security, know where the goal posts are, stay sane, manage stress.

77. Make your self improvement results even better! You'll achieve more, find new ways to use existing skills, rekindle your enthusiasm, liven things up, get better at what you do, be even more impressive, fix problems faster, deeper impact, make new connections and deepen & broaden your knowledge.

78. Get what's inside a person's head outside! Smoke out the hidden agenda, take the junk out, reveal the true intention, reveal the truth, uncover the blocks, drop the luggage, remove the obstacles, make it easier to get what you want, feel light a burden has been lifted. know if someone can be trusted, avoid being sold to or manipulated, virtually read minds, protect yourself, security, hold onto your money, spot the bad ones, help them get what they really want, uncover true intentions, negotiate better.

79. Understand people and what makes them tick – get predictable results, build connections with people, security, consistency, learn their strategies and model their skills, sell to them better, motivate others, please people, people will like you more, want to be with you, look at you as the leader cos you "know stuff", comfort them, make them feel at ease.

80. Healthy mind = healthy body. Improve your mental attitude and improve your well being. live longer, more energy, more flexible and more mobile, be able to do more, keep up with others, look good, feel good, be a model of excellence, able to help others more, take care of yourself. Stay sane, clear thinking, clarity, positive outlook, optimistic, nice to be around.

81. How to run your own head effectively - self confidence, cope with anything, be happy, take control of your life, achieve your dreams, control your emotions, understand yourself, awareness, personal growth, be healthier, less stress, more intelligence, emotionally stable, socially acceptable, nicer person to be with, more upbeat & positive, forward thinking, popular.

82. Know how to change, how to get there – certainty, hope for the future, achieve what you want, end the frustration, get unstuck, become who you want to be, finally get the answer you've been seeking, switches you on, renewed energy and determination, escape tunnel.

83. Increases choice. Get out of being stuck, progress, light at the end of the tunnel, hope, expand your creativity, flexibility, freedom of choice.

84. Provides you with information that's out of your current

awareness – know what's really going on, hear more, see more, makes you think outside the box, recognise patterns, see the big picture, wake up, become more alert and more conscious, see what others miss, spot potential problems in advance, spot potential opportunities, raises your awareness, whole new perspective, virtually read minds, living lie detector, increase your brain's capability, become smarter.

85. Analogy of learning how to get the most out of software. Batteries were included but nobody taught you how to use it, do things you didn't realise you can do, get more done in less time, be more efficient, smarter ways to do things, quicker, multitask, increase your confidence, tap into your potential, achieve more.

86. Provides options – increases choices, assists change. Get out of being stuck, progress, light at the end of the tunnel, hope, expand your creativity, flexibility, freedom of choice.

87. Raises your awareness. Know what's really going on, hear more, see more, makes you think outside the box, recognise patterns, see the big picture, wake up, become more alert and more conscious, see what others miss, spot potential problems in advance, spot potential opportunities, raises your awareness, whole new perspective, virtually read minds, living lie detector, increase your brain's capability, become smarter.

88. Changes your life from Black & White to Colour. Opens your eyes to possibilities, wakes you up, renewed hope and vigour, blows away the cobwebs, raises your energy, put your foot on the accelerator, race ahead, see things differently, lose the mundane, jazz things up, exciting.

89. Gives you a glimpse of the destination – then it's your choice to go there or not. Exciting, hope, energising, fun, certainty, security, see a clear path, something to look forward to, work towards, achievement, makes you responsible for your results, fill the void, purpose in life, finally make it, relief, determination.

90. Achieve far more by asking useful, progressive questions – shifts your focus, put an end the dumb questions, stop berating yourself, makes you feel better about yourself, model excellence, think like a genius, increases your intelligence, achievement, emotionally strong, mentally tough, change your outlook, solve problems, become more valuable to your employer. Be able to make people see a problem differently.

91. Become more valuable to your employer – improve career prospects, promotion, paid more, get to do new activities, increase respect, more job satisfaction, job security, feel valued, feel important, feel strong, become a leader.

92. Have more self control - understand yourself, know why you do what you do, change habits, become a better person, laugh at yourself, more self confidence, feel happy in your own skin, change things you don't like, happier, sleep better, less self-criticism, stop self sabotage, be your own best friend, no upsetting outbursts in public, certainty, feel in control, act professional, perceived to be more intelligent. Greater self awareness of your thinking patterns.

93. Build hope for the future - Exciting, hope, energising, fun, certainty, security, see a clear path, something to look forward to, work towards, achievement, fill the void, purpose in life,

finally make it, relief, determination, improve your health, mobility.

94. Develop certainty and security – feel stronger, in control, get on with your life, put an end to fear, time for learning, give to others, strong foundation, happier, willing to take risks, accomplish more, more easily. Fully use all of your skills and resources, optimise, end the constant worrying, no longer living on your nerves, remove the problems, end the comfort eating, banish the bad movies in your head. Become more confident and self assured.

95. Use your time better and minimise trivia – achieve more, don't sweat the small stuff, avoid getting bogged down, life gets easier, see the big picture, less stress, more free time to have more fun, be more productive, make more money, really experience life. Self confidence, cope with anything, be happy, take control of your life, achieve your dreams, control your emotions, understand yourself, awareness, personal growth, be healthier, less stress, more intelligence, emotionally stable, socially acceptable, nicer person to be with, more upbeat & positive, forward thinking, popular, become more open minded.

96. Become far more flexible - increases choices, assists change. Get out of being stuck, progress, light at the end of the tunnel, hope, expand your creativity, flexibility, freedom of choice. Happiness, health, less stress, get on with people better, freedom.

97. You'll stop using negative self talk and internal dialogue that undermines your confidence. Shifts your focus, put an end the dumb questions, stop berating yourself, makes you feel

better about yourself, model excellence, think like a genius, increases your intelligence, achievement, emotionally strong, mentally tough, change your outlook, solve problems, become more valuable to your employer. Destroy self-doubt, change limiting beliefs and attitudes by questioning them.

98. Be able to get agreement between any two parties, anytime. Walk into any meeting knowing you will always get agreement. Become a master negotiator, solve disputes, be the problem solver, respect, authority, power, peaceful living, bargain for what you want, save money, seal lucrative deals, certainty, help settle differences, haggle.

99. Learn how to be more motivated and passionate more of the time – achieve more, go further with your career, healthier, fitter, physically more attractive, renewed sparkle, drive, more energy, never be bored again, help others, study things you always wanted to, get more done.

100. It works!

CONTENTS

Affect other people profoundly in therapy, and at parties!

Don't you just hate yourself when you keep doing something
you know you want to stop, but you can't

The only Hypnotherapy script you'll ever need

How to get people to change in advance!

The Pentium 5 of therapy

Discover your own internal time machine

How to get a pilot's licence in ten minutes

Wouldn't it be great if someone could tell you the root cause
of your problems? Well, there is someone who can…

Sometimes it's good to feel bad

Change how you feel about anything in minutes, not years!

The 3 things that make it work every time

Right now you either want to change what you're doing, or
how you feel

The more you let go, the easier letting go becomes!

No matter what happens you can handle it

Why there's no need to hold onto pain

Speed up bad times and make the good times last

Its never too late to have a happy childhood

Remove life long phobias today

Never be anxious about your future again

At last! A goal setting system that actually works!

Become internationally qualified in state of the art therapy

Put an end to your inner critic

How to cut through the flannel and get to the point in 3
sentences or less

How to get done in a day what most people do in a week
2 minute lifesavers when your time is being squeezed
Chunking – not a small town in China, but the secret to
beating overwhelm
Advice if you are stressed & under pressure
Does this task even belong to you?
10 ways to say "no" pleasantly
Here's how to balance your work & personal life
Coaching others to manage their time
The source of your busyness and what to do about it
Time tips to dip into when your life depends on it

The Theory that Explains Everything

Sacred knowledge that was banned from publication until 1989
The Secret Science behind miracles
Is it immoral to live without anger, sadness, fear and guilt?
One instinctively knows when something is right
Don't read this section unless you want to change your
outlook on life, and your ideas about who you really are
If you do it and it gives you energy, keep doing it
You really can increase your energy levels in just 10 minutes a day
Imagine if there was a way to make sure nothing bad could

happen around you
Dramatically increase your focus and concentration
Don't you just hate it when someone else bursts your bubble
I'm starting with the man in the mirror...
You can't have a bath once and be clean forever
You can't fight the future – here's the secret
If you really did have a guardian angel, what would you ask
    them?
Experience the highest and noblest ceremony in Hawaii
Revealed at last! The story of creation
The insider's guide to how balance works
Enjoy the gift of the magical techniques of Taneo Sands
    Kumelae
Discover the secret meaning of Aloha

HOW TO GET THE MOST OUT OF THIS BOOK

This book has something in it for everyone. There are real tools that salespeople can use to get more business. There are educational techniques to help teachers and students alike. Trainers can take whole chapters out of this book and teach them. This represents the best of all that I've learned, and that was going to be the book's title at one point.

People like things they can use – usefulness, real hands on practical tools you can learn and take away today that make your life easier the minute you start using them. And that's what I want for you too – this isn't just a book you can flit through with a cup of tea on a wet afternoon. This is a doing book, it's almost a workbook in that it's full of exercises and tasks and action steps for you to learn and change your life with.

When they work for you (and they work for everyone who can be bothered doing them) then keep them. If some don't seem to appeal to you, then dump the ones you don't like and keep applying the ones you do. You can lose weight just doing the Ha Breathing exercise from Huna. If you want to become more assertive, use the Satir Categories from the presentation skills. Discover your life purpose from the chapter on Values. All of the HGE tools and techniques I'm showing you in this book do work, and work powerfully, if you use them.

If all you do is take one distinction away from this book, and it changes the way you think or behave for the better, then this whole book was worth writing, but all you have to do is to take a few tools out of the pages of this book and practice them, and your entire life will change for the better. Massive dramatic improvements in your health, your finances, your relationships and your confidence are yours for the taking from these pages. Take them!

In this book you'll find initially the straightforward concepts, and then it gets steadily more esoteric. That actually reflects my life experience – the reason a lot of people are fascinated and driven to personal development programmes is to make more money or have more confidence, improve their relationships, or manage their stress, but then as you go deeper into something then it changes you and before you know it you're on a plane to Hawaii to walk across a volcano!

This represents the highlights of all the profound knowledge I've spent fourteen years studying, and that has become my mantra – SLAM IT! Study, learn, apply, manifest, improve and then teach it. If it was too esoteric and "way out" for me I'd discard it, but the tools that consistently worked for me found their way into these pages.

As I've studied and practiced these skills over the last fourteen years, I can credit a lot of my abilities to the many teachers, Coaches and mentors that I've studied under, most of them I've never even met. Throughout this book I'll make references to the various authors and teachers that I've been fortunate to learn from. Reference is made and credit given wherever appropriate. I encourage you to look into their work also, because their quotations, approaches and methods resonated with me, and I hope will do with you also.

Commit yourself to applying the strategies in this book – they can and they will change your life, if you want them to. Highlight sections, underline words and asterisk the ideas that grab you, so you can find them again. Try on the mindset as outlined in the first chapters. Set an outcome for your life, be it big or small. Practice building rapport with other people, whilst watching their eye patterns and reading their minds... Become a master communicator and elicit your loved one's values so you can meet them more often. Use Time Line Therapy to clear up your limitations from the past. Manage your time better, and evolve the way the ancient peoples predicted...

If you want to read the rationale behind this book, feel free to pick up the free report called NLP & Beyond at www.NLPandbeyond. co.uk

Some of the folks who proof read this book say that you should start with Chapter 15 "Where Personal Development Goes To Develop" . Others said leave that one till last. If you think it's not stretching your beliefs far enough, jump to Chapter 15 before continuing.

Who knows, maybe we'll meet on a live programme somewhere. I hope to meet you in person one day. Until then, read on, and change your entire life.

"Aloha a hui hou kakou", (Farewell until we meet again)

I'm offering you the greatest gift...if you can see it. My job is to offer you this information. Your job is to decide what you're going to do with it.

INTRODUCTION

Imagine that you and I are sitting together, eye to eye right now, taking a look at this book together. I'm watching your facial expression to see if you like what your eyes are reading. Picture me sitting beside you as you read this as we work together, and explore together, over the next few hours and days to come. But before that, let's take a look at why you're here in the first place.

Have you ever read a really heavy book {sigh}& all that happened was that you lost a few hours of your life? Or you got to sit through some dry, heavy training that made you feel like you just wanted to dig a tunnel and escape? Or maybe you closed that old book and came out of it feeling like you were leaving with more problems than you started with? Maybe you had really high hopes for what the book would contain, only to end up quite disappointed that it talked a good game, but it failed to deliver real, practical "how to" strategies? I've read a good few of those books in my time.

You know, you bought the book and you weren't really sure how things were going to go, so you were a bit uncertain, possibly anxious, maybe even not completely comfortable – ever felt like that? Unsure of your future? Wondering what's in store?

And then something caught your attention – maybe something you saw, or the way something was said, a certain intonation or words that were…curiously…marked out…that caused your ears to prick up, and maybe you felt that first wave of curiosity. You know? Like on Christmas Eve, and you were looking for your presents. Did you used to do that? I did – as soon as my folks went out the door I was hunting through the house to find the treasure. And if you have kids, and you think they don't know where you conceal the presents every year, think again! My Dad always hid the presents under the socks in a tall wardrobe in their bedroom, and I'd carefully lift the pile of boxes out, carefully memorising the order I found them in. With feelings of excitement, guilt and burning curiousity all at the same time, I'd lift up the present and weigh it – if it was light and soft it probably was clothes or something. But if it was heavy, or hard, or even better **both,** then it was carefully carried to the bed, and I'd slowly start to peel off the sellotape off the wrapping paper, and if you're really careful you can lift up a small square of sellotape and leave a small white square where it lifted the pattern off the paper….. Remember doing this? Was it just me who used to do this?

I'd have the whole thing unwrapped and opened before you knew it, and I could play with whatever I got, then carefully rewrap the box, placing the same sellotape on the same white squares so it looked like it had never been touched… My Dad would often see me on Christmas morning with a new model or something, fully put together, painted with all the decals on it and ask me "Did that thing not come in bits you needed to make up?" and I'd say "No, it comes like this…" Cheekily… Was it just me who did this sort of thing?

Well, I want to talk to you today about something different. I want to share with you some information that you don't hear about very often, if at all. You see, I teach people how to run their own heads, and I'm going to reveal to you tools and techniques that will practically let you read people's minds.

I want to introduce you to a whole mindset, a technology, a tool-kit full of tools for every occasion, drawn from years of real world application and experience using state of the art psychology such as Neuro Linguistic programming and Hypnosis, as well as the secrets and advanced methodologies employed by Life Coaches and spiritual advisers alike.

You see, the leading personal development teachers have evolved an incredibly effective way of training, stimulating learning and unconscious…**change**…in their students. You're about to discover leading edge techniques that seem to work like magic!

This is a step-by-step practical book, with each exercise and chapter building on the last. You will do small exercises as you go along, where you can immediately apply what you've just learned and discover for yourself how effective it is.

True understanding = Intellectual knowledge + experiential results

Now from time to time you'll find yourself getting curious – you'll ask yourself such questions as:

What am I going to gain here?

How can I use this to impact others?

What possibilities are there if I use these procedures?

How do I apply it, practically in the real world?

For what purpose could I use the tools I'm leaving with?

What's the right way to learn this?

What will this do for me?

So all I'm asking is that you keep an open mind and be willing to play a bit today. Is that OK? The mind is like a parachute- it only works when it's open. Are you willing to keep your mind open for the next few hours?

So why are you here, reading this book? Why aren't you out doing the shopping, or washing the car, or feeding the budgie? You must have some reasons for coming to this book. I have to presuppose you have reasons for being here:

1. You may have heard about NLP or Huna, maybe read a bit about it and want to know more. Yes?

2. Maybe you're involved in recruitment and would like to have new, fresh ways of doing things?
3. Do you Coach people or facilitate meetings with people?
4. Perhaps you want to be better at what you do both personally and professionally?
5. Maybe you've attended all of the best seminars, listened to all of the tapes, walked barefoot on red hot coals, broken arrows with your throat and you're still less than perfect…anyone?
6. You're here because this is better than where you would be if you weren't here. Is that true?
7. What other reasons do you have for being here, reading these words? Have a quick think….

So it's time for something different – time for some fun, some energy and a different way of thinking about things. You see, I know that you, like me, value your time highly. That means that to get the most value out of our time together here, I'd like to ask you to think anew. Think newly about things…

You see, with all due love and respect, I'm here to bump up against your beliefs. I'm not here to teach you stuff you already know. That wouldn't be much good, would it? So let's take a look at the big picture of what you're **going to experience** in this book:

By the way, don't be surprised if you find yourself using these new skills in places other than in your Career. You might find, if I can make a suggestion…would that be ok? You might find that you use these skills in other contexts, such as in your intimate relationships, parenting your kids, dealing with the bank manager, all sorts of places…

People you meet are usually in the same kind of place – dissatisfaction, frustration and impatience. However there's a trap. Most people get bogged down in "no man's land" or the grey zone, where "It's not good enough, but it's not bad enough to change". I only work with people who want to make their circumstances better. They still have the spark. The lights are still on, you know? If you're going to whine and complain about how hard your life is, no one wants to hear it. But, if you're going to whine and complain about how hard your life is, *and work at making it better*, this is the book for you!

Changing your behaviours, or getting over traumas in the past, or therapy if you want to call it that, is a highly skilled job. If it was easy your best friend could tell you "Stop it!" and you would. There are plenty of people out there who've read some self help books, done some taster sessions, maybe even attended a training, but there's less than a handful of qualified change experts who have any real experience to speak of.

In any other form of therapy, once you've made the phobia go away, or the depression's vanished, or the relationship is back on and fun again, then you never see the therapist again. You feel like you're on your own. I like to follow up my clients and make sure that the changes they've made extend into their lifestyles and everyday living. What happens the day after the last therapy session? A week later? A month later? That's why I spent 3 years training to become a Life Coach with the longest established Coaching training company on the planet – so I can stick by you as you go back into the "real world" and learn how to get back up to speed again.

WHAT FUELS YOU?

Very often the problem you had was giving you energy, it drove you. Does that make sense? Take the problem away and sometimes the client has no fuel – they're becalmed in the water, and have nothing to push them forward. That's when the Life Coach becomes a godsend, cos they can now help co-create a future set of goals that pull you forward and give you something to aim for, and they'll be in the background holding you accountable and making sure you do what you promised yourself you'd do. Quite frankly I bet you don't see other professionals working as hard as you do or giving nearly as much. Professionalism is dead in most cases. Ask a shop assistant a question and you'll get a blank look. Most so-called professionals grudge every contact with a customer.

NLP AND MORE

This book gives you some incredibly powerful tools – mind techniques and life strategies that will help you run your life more effectively, so you can be more of who you really want to be. Time-Line Therapy is one particular method which enables you to let go of emotional traumas very, very quickly – in minutes, in fact, not years. It also enables you to create things that you want to see happen in your future, and to change things that have happened to you in your past, or change the effect that they have on you. Is that useful to you at all?

Add to that self-hypnosis - a lot of HGE techniques go hand-in-hand with hypnosis techniques, because a lot of them came from hypnosis originally. We certainly have a lot of HGE people who are learning hypnosis, and a lot of hypnotherapists who are learning HGE. The two go hand-in-hand, and you're about to learn both. There's a chapter on hypnosis later in this book.

THE ULTIMATE MASTER SYSTEM

Those are the "modern" tools in this book. So, whether you look at it from an esoteric point of view, or whether you look at it from a purely common sense point of view, there are concepts that work. Many ancient teachings and ancient philosophies have certain core pillars that keep showing up time and time again, and Hawaiian

Huna is one of them. Huna is rumoured to be the source of an awful lot of other esoteric disciplines, such as Chinese Medicine, Energy Healing and Shamanism. I actually trained in Hawaii and continue to go back to The Big Island to develop my knowledge in the healing, spiritual and shamanic discipline of Huna, to study and learn the "master system" where most other forms of alternative and complementary methods come from, and I've been initiated into the Huna lineage on a live volcano, in Hawaii, by a Huna master, **five times.** I have visited sacred locations in Hawaii where permission is rarely granted for white people to go, and that are so remote hardly anyone has ever laid eyes on them. As you will discover, it was forbidden, and even punishable, to teach these sacred methods well up until late last century. This book actually contains Huna secrets that were banned until 1989!

The technology we're going to employ to **make the changes you're here to make**, is an eclectic combination of NLP, Hypnosis, Huna and Life Coaching, and I call it HGE. So what is HGE? That's where we're going to start...

INTRODUCING "HYPNO GENETIC EVOLUTION"

Maybe you've tried all the goal setting, the achiever, "if it's to be it's up to me" syndrome. You've had the house, the car, the money in the bank, the social circle, the good job...and yet there's still something missing? You see, goals without a higher purpose lack passion or deep meaning. At some point you'll ask yourself "Who I am? Why am I here? What should I be doing with my life?" Perhaps you have an inkling…a hunch…that something more spiritual is the place to go next. Maybe you, like me, have a "calling" – that something calls to you for some inexplicable reason. There's a great quote that once said "Religion is what people do to avoid going to hell. Spirituality is what people do once they've been there!"

Now I'm not a psychiatrist or psychologist – but I have spent fourteen years in personal development helping people transform their lives – I've learned and taught advanced techniques like NLP and Hypnosis. But after a while I got frustrated with the lack of depth, there was something missing. There had to be more….do you know what I mean?

For me it was always about making changes. If you're not happy with the results you're creating, then change what you're doing. Whining and complaining won't make it any better, and nobody's going to come and rescue you. The sooner you realise it's you, the better. **It's what you do that counts**. So initially I did private therapy, then started doing workshops to try and share this mindset with as many people as possible.

Then I came across the blossoming field of Life Coaching, and saw a natural extension to what I was already doing. NLP helped me to help my clients clear up the mental clutter and limitations that hold us all back. Life Coaching looks at the external factors that make you who you are – your health and eating habits, your family relationships, your intimate relationships, your management of money, your environment, your career. Now I had ways of dramatically improving my own life, and the lives of others, on both the inside and the outside.

However, in a completely unregulated industry, people could simply read a book and call themselves a Life Coach. Oh dear.

Then you start to hit your late thirties, and true to the model, the idea of spirituality starts calling to you. Now it takes different forms for different people, and for me it was in a concealed body of knowledge and wisdom that had been banned till 1989, until laws were passed that allowed the Hawaiians to teach their original ways again. Something about Huna attracted me, and for the first time in my life I could relate to what people often term "a calling".

Huna balances you out, and gets you down out of your head and into your body again, grounding you. Instead of being "the NLP guy", I started to teach other concepts and principles that I'd picked up that seemed to make sense, and more importantly, consistently worked with everyone I shared them with. Then one day I was sitting at the back of the room during one of my training courses, and as I watched the students going through a transformational week, I looked at the table of books beside me, and my eyes fell upon the first self-help book I ever read, and I thought "Wow. Look where reading that one book has brought me!" I never set out to become a therapist or a Trainer (or an author), I just wanted to help people, and in so doing live a rewarding life. As one of my first teachers Zig Ziglar once said, "You can everything in life you want if you just help enough other people get what they want".

That was always my core drive, and still is. To help people. Now I'm not a complete altruist, because it's my business and I expect to be paid. But that was my passion – Maybe you've seen "Star Wars", when Obi Wan Kenobi told the Imperial Storm troopers "These aren't the droids you're looking for" and they let them pass, instantly changing their minds. "Wouldn't it be really cool to be able to do that!" I thought. I want someone to come to me with a problem like "I'm depressed", and with a wave of my hand I tell them "No you're not" and they wouldn't be. That would be magic! Real magic.

And if you study every philosophy, every theology on the planet, certain key concepts keep coming up. Rituals. Physical exercise. Energy. Numbers. The Five elements. Taking responsibility. Being at one with yourself. Life being a mirror of you. There has to be something to that if they keep showing up, throughout history, throughout the planet. Mark Twain once said "The ancients steal all our best ideas".

My friend and teacher Tad James had once suggested to Richard Bandler, the co-creator of NLP:

"What if all NLP is, is tying up the conscious mind with a technique, while you give suggestions to the unconscious mind?"

In Huna, the Kahuna would often create a ritual or task for the patient to undertake, and in so doing they gave their unconscious mind permission to make the change. It's almost like the conscious mind needs to be convinced by doing something tangible, while the unconscious mind does what it already knows it can do, but needs the conscious mind's permission. Think of the placebo effect in medicine. Or being dunked in water to feel cleansed, or anointed. The ritual works better if you use real water...

Milton Erickson, the world's leading Hypnotherapist, often gave clients tasks or ordeals to do, and by doing then, they "fixed" themselves. Hmmmm...

I knew I was on to something. It was also painful to watch people study, and teach, NLP as a bunch of techniques that claimed to be able to cure everything from nail biting to HIV, but then get disappointed when it didn't work. Or worse, blame the NLP practitioner when it didn't. There's more to it than that. You can't expect someone to come along and "fix you". You have to be the source of your own change. Because then you get all the pride and achievement of having taken charge of you mind and your behaviours too!

It was a shame to watch people spend four days with (in my opinion) the world's greatest presenter and teacher, Tony Robbins, get all psyched up to change the world, and then crash down to earth a week later. Not only were they disappointed, they'd had a taste of how good they could feel and they couldn't recreate it themselves. They'd have to spend even more money becoming seminar junkies, just to recapture the high. As one client of mine once said, "How much more money do you have to spend before the penny drops?"

To make matters worse, the world of NLP was renowned for its competing developers who spent more time arguing about who the genuine leaders of the field were, than in advancing and improving the technology for the betterment of it's enthusiasts. Too much emphasis was placed on legal actions, copyrighting, jargon, cyber squatting and whose signature was on your certificate, which is ironic when one of the basic beliefs promoted by NLP is to "respect everyone's model of the world." It was a world of politics, cliques and possessiveness where the self-styled governing bodies had practically no regulatory authority, and no way of enforcing their code of conduct. Basically anyone could attend a training course and call themselves a Trainer, regardless of ability, flair, depth of knowledge or integrity.

Intriguingly, all of the most successful leaders in the field of NLP got into spirituality. Richard Bandler lived in Hawaii for years. John Grinder used animal forms during trainings. Tad James is my Huna teacher. Tony Robbins calls himself a "force for God". The "heart" that was missing from the NLP model could be found in the ancient teachings of the earth.

NLP had to evolve. Hypnosis alone wasn't enough. Life Coaching is more than just hiring a personal trainer. Huna was too ancient and esoteric and turned some people off. There needed to be a comprehensive and ecological model which was simple and straightforward to use in your daily life. After all, its what you do consistently, and persistently that shapes your life. You can't have a bath once and be clean forever. To that effect, I want to share what I've found with you, and I've called it HGE:

HYPNO – which suggests

Sleep

Hypnosis

Fascination

Spellbinding
Producing sleep-like condition
Therefore "Hypnogenetic" – producing trance, or the induction of a hypnotic state
GENETIC - meaning
Origins
Causes
Act of producing
Study of heredity and variation
Characteristics
Thus "Genetic Evolution" – the gradual improvement of characteristics
EVOLUTION – defined as
Unfolding
Emergence
Improvement
Progress
Development
Systematic movement in position
The history of all things
Origination of a species by development from earlier form
Gradual advance to more complex and of higher order

HGE IS THEREFORE

The systematic development of a person's positive characteristics through self hypnosis

Gradual improvement in the mind and body through trance

Close your eyes, go inside and come out better. True Reality Engineering.

Unfolding the causes of problems through relaxation

Using magic words and gestures to improve, in your thoughts, deeds and intentions. What I call Neuro magic.

Dreaming of becoming better and then making it so. What the Hawaiians called "Make luck business."

How we affect our own genetics by giving ourselves suggestions.

Let me explain what HGE is really all about, and to do that you need to be familiar with 3 models of thinking.

To begin with, you have several bodies, all connected together.

Well, is that true? Who knows. But it's a convenient model to work with. Let's assume then that you have a Physical body, the foundation upon which everything sits – the vehicle that houses your awareness. Remember, your body's a temple, but it's also a nightclub! Your nervous system is designed to notice differences. It seeks out anything unique or unusual from the norm. Some people believe that opposites attract for example. Or that to generate energy, you need a Yin and a Yang, a positive and a negative, like the terminals on a car battery for instance.

Above that is the Emotional Body, the seat of your unconscious processes and the source of your memories and emotions. The emotional body is magnetic, and attracts people with similar emotions e.g. Anger management groups. Protesters.

Next you have the Mental Body – the rational, thinking Conscious Mind, and usually with an area of interest or a field of knowledge that it specialises in. The mental body likes stimulation, deep and meaningful discussion, debate and new ideas.

Last but by no means least comes the Spiritual Body, the super conscious mind and your connection with whatever is higher and bigger than you. The Spiritual body attracts like minded souls, such as in gathering to worship, or a "calling", or you reading this book....

Now at the core of HGE is the assumption that the reality of personal growth, the way to evolve yourself and reach a balanced, flowing life where you are happy, healthy and fulfilled, is to pay attention to all 4 bodies. If you don't pay with attention, you'll pay with pain. Neglect one of these bodies and it will come back and bite you later. Take care of, and nurture all 4 bodies, and you'll grow and evolve and develop to your full potential.

Most people tend to focus on one of the 4 bodies at any given time in their life. Physical body people are driven by basic drives, food, shelter and reproduction, and as such have a very narrow focus. Some are Physical + Emotional, so they feel a lot but aren't very intellectual. Some are Physical + Mental, but not emotional, so they dissociate from feelings, the cold computer like accountant or academic. Others are purely spiritual, so they meditate and see auras while their bank balance vanishes, divorce goes through and house is repossessed.

The ideal is to develop them all – have a healthy physical body to live in, nice surroundings and money to do what you want, understand, feel and be in control of your emotions, have a developed intellect and focus, and be connected to a spiritual power that's bigger than you. Now as we grow up and get older, each of the bodies evolves with us, doesn't it? As you think back about your past, you'll see phases where you've focussed on one or two bodies, to the exclusion of the others.

Picture a College professor stuck in his or her Mental body. Spiritual students often get stuck in Spiritual, with no connection with material. So they can quote philosophy, but their money, relationships, house and earthly material possessions are in trouble. Or very spiritually attuned but can't express it fully in material world, therefore are out of balance, not grounded. Some even use Spirituality as a way to excuse their lack of responsibility, saying "If it's meant to succeed then it will". Nothing to do with you then...

Remember, lots of people who follow spiritual disciplines don't have any discipline. The great magical author Dion Fortune said

"The descent into matter must be complete before the ascent into spirit"…

If you're someone who can see auras, or you've seen Kirlian photography, you'll see these four bodies. The four bodies mature at "crisis points" in our lives – time of a major life change. At birth the physical body is ready to develop. Along comes Puberty – hormones, and emotions kick in, and thus the Emotional body develops. The Mental body comes into play about age 5 and develops into mid 30's, where abstract qualities become valued – freedom, security, peace. At age 28-30, if you know your Astrology, Saturn returns in the birth chart.

Many people in their late 30's talk about a "mid life crisis", where Uranus opposes in your birth chart. Certainly in the mid 30's the Spiritual body develops, and you get an inkling that there has to be more to life than this… Some people only experience 1, or 2 of the bodies. Think of it as a map of how to evolve ourselves. Realise that everyone's going at their own pace – sometimes you're early, sometimes late, sometimes one may never develop that body at all. The Kahuna (Hawaiian Shaman) were good at spotting children who were developing quickly, and would pick them out for further training.

Each body has it's own language. The Physical body is the language of biology, chemistry, physics, atoms, particles, the material. The Emotional body thinks in terms of needs, wants, desire, hunger, basic drives. The Mental Body likes words, concepts, philosophy and language. The Spiritual Body likes images, ceremony, rituals, chants, songs, and mantras.

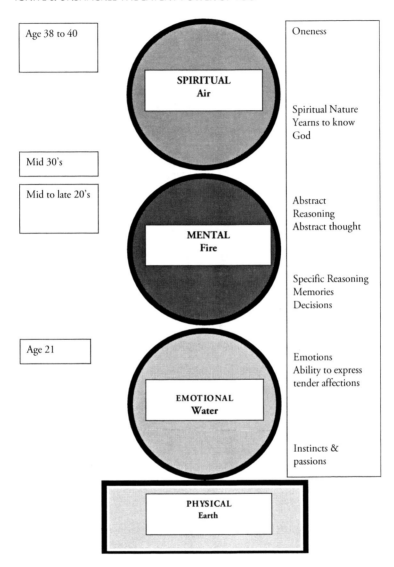

Think of the ultimate path of evolution starting at the top in Spiritual, then going down into mental, then emotional, then physical. Isn't that how all things are manifested? There's the initial inspiration (S), then the conceptualisation and dwelling on the idea (M), then the passion & motivation to create it (E), then it becomes real (P). That's the descent into matter. However, that's only halfway home. To ascend to spirit, you then have to go back up again, so from Physical, to emotional, then mental, then Spiritual. It's like a game of hopscotch. We all need to complete that cycle, and we'll eventually do it, even if it takes several lifetimes!

Unfortunately, many people try and take a shortcut. Many spiritual gurus and followers have turned their noses up at material things, thinking that it's beneath them and that it's "just" attachment. Actually, it's the necessary foundation upon which their desire to reach spirit is fulfilled. Foundation first, because that's where you step from. In other words, if you shave your head and live in a cave on rice and berries, you're missing half the story! It's GOOD to have the spiritual ethics and see the being of light in everyone, AND it's good to be able to offer them a lift in your Ferrari!

Throughout history the enlightened, the shaman, the medicine woman, the guru and the wizard went nuts, got real eccentric and became isolated from the rest of the community, forced to live in caves or out in the desert (remember Obi Wan Kenobi?). Remember that the next time you neglect your Physical or Emotional Body!

What if this is also how illness and disease is manifested? Perhaps a trauma occurs, the person obsesses about it (M), focuses on it, replays it over and over and frets about it (E) and then it becomes real (P). More and more medical research is starting to bear this theory out. The Tao says "heal things before they're born". Shift the blueprint of the body and the physical self responds. The field of Psychoneuroimmunology (PNI) has proven that we can create psychosomatic disease. What if we could create psychosomatic health?

So what I'm suggesting is that you follow a four part workout regime for the rest of your life. First, get into shape physically, and take care of the vehicle in which you're a guest, your physical body. And have nice things, manage your finances (or come and do my weekend seminar "Your Money or Your Life") and improve your health. Read the chapter on health later on.

At the same time, master your emotions. Use the techniques in this book, and any others you know of, to uncover negative emotions, then release them. Download the "Master Your Emotions" technique at www.jonathanclark.org/products. Let go of past pain and hurts as quickly as you can. And if you think you can't, keep reading. Besides, time is a great healer no matter what you do...

Learn to think like a genius – both inductively, and deductively. Be able to handle the details and specifics, as well as the abstract, global big picture. People who can think flexibly age at a slower rate than people who can't. Avoid hardening of the attitude. See the chapter on thinking like Aristotle. And master a field of mental endeavour - learn, study, research, get into something you enjoy and go deep. You probably are already. Become an expert in HGE...

And then you can see everyone as doing the best they can with what they have, raise and expand your consciousness, and tap into the spiritual aspects of your personality. Use the Huna techniques I share with you at the end of this book.

Put it another way. You should have
• the freedom to choose your spirituality
• the ability to think flexibly and creatively
• control over your emotions and the ability to feel a full range
• money, things you want, toys to play with and a supportive environment
...wouldn't you agree?

Wouldn't it be great to be able to measure how well you're doing in your personal growth? I thought it would be really good to have a measuring device to tell you how it's going. To take part in your own self assessment of your four bodies and to find out how developed each one is, go to www.jonathanclark.org/bodyquotient and do the test. You'll then be gifted some immediately useful downloads and a gift certificate from me just for making the effort.

THE 3 MINDS

You probably know that you have a conscious mind, don't you? The part of you that answered - that was it! It likes experience, knowledge, mental power, analysis and rationality. It also likes respect, admiration, significance and success. It's focussed on specifics, likes order and sequence, and it usually kicks in at about age five. Unfortunately, it's also an expert in denying and avoiding pain. But did you know that you also have an unconscious...mind as well? And you may also realise that you have a Higher Self too.

**This is the second major teaching of HGE –
that you are of three minds.**

Our ancestors used to teach this, as the Father, Son and Holy Ghost. Ever wonder why it's in that order? This trinity is present in every tradition on the planet. The Pope's cross has 3 horizontal bars, the Cardinal's only two, and the Priests only has one. Hmmm. Or the Lovers Card in the Major Arcana of the Tarot Cards. There's a man (conscious mind) looking at a woman (unconscious mind), but she's looking above him at an angel (higher self) *which he can't see*. Think of it as the child, the parent and the grandparent. You'll never be alone again when you realise that there's three of you in there.

You're more than just a Conscious Mind. It thinks, "I am". But you also have an unconscious Mind with feelings, "I feel". It runs your body, beats your heart, stores your memories, controls your emotions. It's sometimes called the "body/mind". It's like a timid animal with basic desires and a mental age of about five years old. It adores food, clothes, security, sex, fun, the five senses and safety. It has no words. You always know you're really at the unconscious level when you have no words for the feelings you're experiencing. Any time you criticise yourself, you're criticising your unconscious mind. People treat their pets better than their own unconscious. Society likes to keep you out of here – men are taught to be unemotional, therapists will help you manage your anger (rather than clear it up completely) and prescription drugs suppress your true feelings. They're still there, you just can't feel them. So the next time a red light appears on your car dashboard, just paint black paint over it. It's still a problem, but at least you can't see it.

Many believe you have a third self, the Higher Conscious Mind also, with still more, higher functions, such as wisdom, order, justice, ecology, peace, truth, perfection and evolution. This is the spiritual part of you, your guardian angel, and it looks down at you like a totally trustworthy parent gazing lovingly on a perfect child (you). It creates anything that you ask for, (whether you dwell on good things or bad) including health and energy, as well as more tangible goals.

You'll also see that there's an arrow linking the Conscious Mind to the Unconscious Mind, and another arrow linking the Unconscious Mind to your Higher Self. But there's no direct connection between the Conscious Mind and the Higher Self. The only way to get communication with your Higher Self, is to first learn how to connect with your unconscious mind. Hence the use of Hypnosis, or trance in HGE, where you go inside…

As you can see, there is a direct relationship between the four bodies and the three minds, in that the Higher Self governs the Spiritual Body, the Conscious Mind runs the Mental Body and the Unconscious Mind runs the Emotional & Physical Body. The Physical body is the vehicle for the whole package. That's why visualisation with feeling works better than affirmation – the former impacts the unconscious mind, and thus the Emotional and Physical bodies. Affirmations are Mental body, conscious statements. Does that make sense?

Daddy Bray, a Hawaiian teacher or Kahuna said that the lesson of life is for the Unconscious Mind to become conscious, and for the Conscious Mind to become a Higher Self. Your conscious mind's job is to teach the unconscious mind and grow it up, so it becomes a conscious mind. Strive to make the hidden contents of your unconscious, conscious. He also said that the lesson of Mastery was for the Higher Self to come down into the consciousness, and for the conscious mind to merge with the unconscious. We'll talk about that later as we consider the process of evolution.

Become a Higher self and integrate that back into your physical life. Bring your spiritual nature all the way down into the physical body. Then you can truly and profoundly affect other people in your daily life.

Oh and by the way, your unconscious mind looks up at you like an awestruck child – you are a God in it's eyes. Your Higher Self looks down at you as perfect, in every way, right now. It's only your conscious mind that needs convincing…

BALANCE DURING GROWTH

"First Noa then Noho" said the Hawaiians.

Noa = cleansing through the fire of spirit, freed from taboo

Noho = bring spirit down inside the physical body

Think of your 3 selves as a team, all working together. The first step then is to get rapport with the Unconscious Mind, then clear up anything negative in the Unconscious storehouse. Fears, angers, limitations, old traumas, past hurts. That's the "Noa" part. Only then can you ascend into the spiritual self, and start to do real magic.

"The study of magic should always be preceded by a good study of the

human mind" – Dion Fortune, 1924

Too many students of esoteric studies have tried to practice magic without the focus of a trained mind, and whilst still harbouring anger, hatred and greed. That's why they got terribly mixed results, sometimes creating things they wish they hadn't.

The sensible way is to learn HGE, train the mind, learn how to keep yourself clean, then start to make magic happen.

That's why all meditation and prayer has you "close your eyes and go inside". You have to go from conscious, to unconscious, and that then gives you access to the Higher Self. But more on that later...

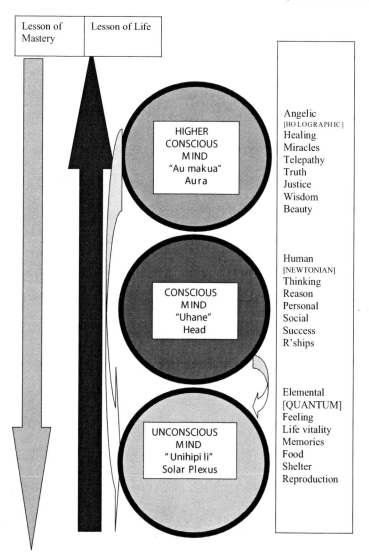

Lesson of Mastery	Lesson of Life

HIGHER
CONSCIOUS
MIND
"Au makua"
Aura

Angelic
[HOLOGRAPHIC]
Healing
Miracles
Telepathy
Truth
Justice
Wisdom
Beauty

CONSCIOUS
MIND
"Uhane"
Head

Human
[NEWTONIAN]
Thinking
Reason
Personal
Social
Success
R'ships

UNCONSCIOUS
MIND
"Unihipi li"
Solar Plexus

Elemental
[QUANTUM]
Feeling
Life vitality
Memories
Food
Shelter
Reproduction

The third major teaching of HGE is that you have different neurological levels to consider too:

Neurological Levels

LANGUAGE		NEUROLOGY
FOR WHAT PURPOSE? Higher Self, Mission, Why I am here, what's bigger than me?	**SPIRITUALITY**	SYMPATHETIC/ PARASYMPATHETIC NERVOUS SYSTEM
WHO? Who I believe I am, Values	**IDENTITY**	IMMUNE SYSTEM Defenses
WHY? X causes Y, what I believe is true	**BELIEFS**	AUTONOMIC NERVOUS SYSTEM Blood Pressure, heart rate, digestion
HOW? States, strategies, Metaprograms, what I'm capable of	**CAPABILITIES**	SEMI-CONSCIOUS REACTIONS
WHAT? Habit, what I actually do	**BEHAVIOURS**	CONSCIOUS ACTIONS
WHERE? Externals, results, geography	**ENVIRONMENT**	REFLEXES Peripheral Nervous System

Hippocrates said that peoples' health was a by-product of living in harmony with themselves and their environment.

In ancient China I'm told that the doctor in the village was paid an income by every well person in the village, so if you got sick you didn't pay him. That way it was in his best interests to keep everyone well. Nowadays, more money goes to the Health services as more people get sick. Something's wrong with that picture.

NLP author and teacher Robert Dilts developed a useful model called "Neurological Levels" and I've borrowed it here. The bottom floor in this pyramid is the environment, the external surrounding, things, people, places, relationships, triggers, etc. This is detected by your 5 senses and your peripheral nervous system. Its what we react to. Pleasant surroundings promote good health. We all need good diet, clean air, clean water and regular exercise.

Above that are Behaviours, what you actually do knowingly and habitually. Habits, repeated actions.

Next comes Capabilities – what you're capable of. But not necessarily what you do. This includes strategies that we run, recipes if you like, thinking patterns, including Metaprograms and the full range of emotional states we can access.

Beliefs are higher up – what we think is true, both empowering and disempowering. Permissions and limitations. Unquestioned commands to our nervous system. When you get passionate about your beliefs, that raises your blood pressure and gets your heart thumping, doesn't it?

Your Identity comes next – including what you believe about yourself, and your core Values – your compulsions and revulsions. The things that are so important to you that you spend your resources on them. How you label and define yourself. I like to further break this down into three more layers. On this floor of the pyramid there's a glorious Persian carpet, then the floorboards, then the very foundation of the temple:

1. This is the "you" that you like to project – the face you like to put on, and the version of you that the world gets to see every day. You don't want people to know your doubts and fears (what lies beneath…) and you certainly don't let any old person in to your heart and soul, so this is the mask you put on instead. The you that you pretend to be, the role, the actor or actress. (Read the Huna chapter on getting "pono" with people later in this book). This is the part of you that likes to please and fit in, or look good. The Persian rug.

2. A middle ring of doubt and fear – this is the person that you're scared you might actually be. With time a layer of sediment builds up around your core self based on your "life shocks" and learning's. Focussing on your low points and screw-ups feeds this mental cholesterol This is the source material for your limiting beliefs, which show up lower down the pyramid. Think of very dusty floorboards.

3. The centre of the target –the real you, what a lot of self-help calls "your authentic self", or who you really are at your core. Your self-concept, how you really see yourself, and your deepest unconscious values. (This is why eliciting someone's values always affects them profoundly). This is the vintage *objet d'art* that needs to be restored and polished up.

At the penthouse suite level is Spirituality – your highest purpose, your highest intention, and your connection to all living things. Why are you here? What's bigger than you? Your creator, the source, the super conscious, whatever you want to call it.

This model becomes a great way to diagnose a problem and to break complicated things into bite size chunks. And the higher up we go, the more of our neurology is affected. Beliefs and Identity stimulate the autonomic nervous system, which regulates your internal states. When someone's sense of identity has been dented, often their immune system reacts and they get ill. People who practice spirituality usually talk about a feeling of calmness and centeredness, as they shift from "fight or flight" sympathetic nervous system mode to restful and healing parasympathetic.

"Theoretically every disease is psychosomatic, since emotional factors influence all body processes through nervous and humoral pathways."

- Franz Alexander, Psychosomatic Medicine: It's principles and applications. 1950.

Now here's the golden rule – change on a lower level will not necessarily change anything above it. People often buy a new house then repeat the same old behaviours. Or they fly to a remote vacation resort then bitch about how far away the ocean is.

However, change at a higher level will create a resultant change in the levels below to support the higher order of thinking. Change someone's identity, they start to behave differently and thus create new results in their environment.

Most training works on the levels up to Capabilities, and never crosses the red line. I've never been asked "What do you believe about...?" in a job interview. And no conventional training ever aimed to change my identity. HGE on the other hand...

You see,

ALL Learning, all behaviour and all change IS UNCONSCIOUS

So if you want to train people to learn something, or behave differently, or change something, you need to train the unconscious mind. That's where HGE excels....

"NLP'S NOT VERY SPIRITUAL JONATHAN...."

This statement came from a very Level 6 (see the chapter on Evolution) colleague of mine a few years ago, at the end of one of my NLP weekend seminars, and it set me on a mission. I was determined to bust that statement and prove him wrong. In reality I didn't want to be typecast as a purely left brain, logical scientist type. It must have fried his mind when I was initiated on a volcano in Hawaii!

So I set out to investigate this thing called "Spirituality", because up until that day I saw it as "tree hugging hippy crap" (how very Level 5 of me then). I learned that everyone has their own definition, their own interpretation, and I was interested in finding links between my NLP knowledge and this notion of the higher self.

Many people you meet are turned off by the word.. Some are passionate about it. Some people couldn't care less. But it had come up several times in my life, and now felt like the right time to really listen. Then one day one of my students actually asked me outright "What do *you* believe?" during a seminar, so I had to give it some thought.

And it can be a touchy subject. Or touchy feely too. It brings in issues about religion, morality, meditation, miracles, the metaphysical, and the occasional tree hug. I'd once read somewhere that "people avoid spirituality if they can't be with themselves".

It seemed that most people don't think about spirituality, or want to, until

1. Crisis – and they have to look beyond their usual coping strategies.
2. Touched by something (you see, read, hear, etc) that's spiritual.
3. Spiritual experience – that wakes them up.
4. Suggested (by somebody) as advice to look into.

Human beings have a strong need to connect, with themselves as well as each other. Ecology is important – is what you're doing good for you, your family, your community and ultimately the planet? We're all growing and evolving, both individually and as a race. Personal development work of any kind will accelerate that growth. It's the highest, and arguably therefore the most important level on the pyramid, so it needed to be explored. When you die, what will you take with you? You can't take your possessions. You can't take your loved ones. You can't take your children. Yet many believe that you can take your consciousness.

What I did find that was that there was a common set of beliefs, certain core assumptions about the subject.

1. Everything happens for a reason and it serves you (and you caused it).
2. The present is perfect (and there are things you'd like to perfect).

3. You attract who and what you're ready for (Your clients will be one step behind, or ahead of you). When the student is ready, the teacher appears (and vice versa).

4. If you don't learn all the learnings, it'll return (and gets worse until you do).

5. We are all connected (because everything is made of energy).

6. Life is easier with a strong Personal Foundation (Repair the cracks).

7. Integrity (1st) Structural soundness, physical health, intact. Needs (2nd) Emotional hunger, have to have, primal, physical. Wants (3rd) Icing on the cake, dreams, mental.

8. The truth shall set you free, but may make you miserable first!

9. We're built to be happy. However, often we lack good role models. You become like the people you associate with.

10. You have all the resources you need (if you can get to them) Sometimes they get smothered under several layers of negative programming and emotion!

11. True contribution begins with extreme self care. As my first Life Coach nailed me with years ago, "You can't give what you don't have". [Thanks Lesley.] Keep your own tank full first!

So that's what led me to develop HGE – an outlook, a mindset that comes with a whole bunch of physical, emotional, mental and spiritual tools that grow and evolve you the more you use them.

You'll have less problems, drop toxic acquaintances, feel better more of the time, have the money you need, live as you wish, get in touch with your higher purpose and give off a vibe that others want. *Society Says*

Stop doing what you should be doing, and do what's right for you.

"I'm not sure whether we're spirits having a human experience, or humans having a spiritual experience."

"I've heard of NLP before – so what makes this different?"

HGE includes the entire NLP syllabus, and more. We'll cover everything that you'd learn in a typical NLP training, but I also teach you more advanced methods. Quicker, deeper interventions. Imagine if you could free yourself from having to use techniques! Most NLP trainings teach you the fast phobia cure, reframing, Submodalities, and so on. But imagine if you could make problems disappear, in yourself and others, without having to use any scripts, without even saying a word! Now that's real change work!

Additionally, most self-help approaches presuppose that you need help – that you're 'broken' in some way. I disagree. I think people work perfectly. A spider phobic never forgets. What a great skill!

What if there was a way to "Teflon coat" yourself so that you don't need any interventions or emotional rebalancing? That would be real progress. What's the old saying that goes "prevention is better than cure?"

HGE teaches you methods that amplify and work underneath and alongside any other form of therapy. That's on the energetic level. Then there's the language tools. A therapist will be talking to their clients. Imagine if the actual words they used were creating change all by themselves…

You'll understand how every other "–ology" system works – EFT, NLP, Reiki, Sekhem, you name it. If you learn HGE you'll be able to understand any other form of personal development and see how it works and why it works, and also predict why something won't work in advance. *Save thousands of pounds buying useless books and pointless treatments*

Most personal development courses are either business-like and logical, or esoteric and spiritual. HGE is both. We deal with all four bodies, not just the mental.

You will be accessing the Higher Self, completely omitted in traditional NLP, therefore exploring the more esoteric or spiritual side of you. We're in a new century – time for a new methodology.

The most successful NLP Master Trainers have all delved into spirituality and esoteric studies. HGE explains why that's the next place for you to go. Never before has the personal development process been fine tuned to this high a level.

There is much less jargon in HGE, so it's easier to remember and more user friendly. NLP is often criticised for being hard to understand and full of buzz words – I'd like to demystify all that. To be honest, the only reason it's called "HGE" is because I needed a name that made sense. That's the least simple phrase you'll learn.

Be the first to train in pioneering new technology – this method has just been trademarked and launched in 2005. You will be one of the founding members.

HGE Practitioner courses cover full training in hypnosis and time line techniques, essential skills to be really effective at what you do.

You can do the HGE Foundation Skills, Practitioner and Master Practitioner in 24 days, the time most NLP courses just take you to Practitioner level. Most NLP certification courses take 21 days. We do it in 7, which means you save a lot of time, and you can get done in a week what would normally take 3 weeks, because we use accelerated learning-techniques to actually teach the stuff. We use HGE to teach HGE.

NLP courses teach you techniques. HGE teaches how to create techniques. Eventually, you won't even need them.

For the last 14 years I've been living, breathing and sleeping NLP, but there were always 8 things that kept niggling away at me:

1. There was no "heart" or higher purpose – that was missing
2. NLP was full of technical jargon that put people off

3. It excluded people who wanted more spiritual experience
4. It wasn't evolving and developing as a technology itself
5. It largely ignored the mind's affect on health & healing
6. It was often criticised as a "quick fix" that wouldn't last
7. There was too much politics and too many cliques
8. Even once trained in NLP, people weren't applying it

I never quite understood how to create the real potential break-through in people that I saw as possible. Now I have, and it's called HGE. It's beginning to prove already to be genuinely the next level.

Remember, you can do the online assessment to find out how developed each of your 4 bodies is, by going to www.jonathanclark.org/bodyquotient and doing the test.

With that, let's start applying the mindset and attitude of Hypno Genetic Evolution...

"Close your eyes, go inside and come out better!"

2

WHAT IS HGE?

HGE is not just a collection of techniques or tools to make things better. It's a way of life, it's an entire mindset, an attitude, a code of conduct if you will, with 3 pillars:

1. **Curiousity** – when you see someone excelling at something, ask yourself "how do they do that?" Wanting to know what's going on behind what's going on. What do they do that makes it so much fun? What does he use to be captivating?

2. **Wanton Experimentation** – be willing to do anything to get a result. Just do it! If you keep doing what you've been doing, you'll just keep getting what you've been getting. Try something different for a change.

3. **Modelling what works** – learn from the best, and model their Physiology, their language, and their beliefs. All human experience has a structure – if one person can do it, anyone can borrow their recipe and reproduce it.

This then creates a collection of techniques and tools that make your life easier.

Here's another way of looking at things. You have a peripheral nervous system, through which our experience is processed via five senses:

- Visual
- Auditory
- Kinesthetic
- Olfactory
- Gustatory

You then use language and other nonverbal communication systems to code, order and make meaning out of those signals that your nervous system is receiving from the outside world. This is all done by the central nervous system. That includes:

• Pictures
• Sounds
• Feelings
• Tastes
• Smells
• Words (Self Talk, known as Auditory Digital)

You then organise these in an order and sequence, and this is stored in your central nervous system, at the unconscious level. Think of them like recipes – we have a recipe for every behaviour we do, and we tend to be creatures of habit, doing the same thing in the same way time and time again.

In other words, HGE studies *how people do what they do*, and once you know that, you can:

Stop it	Install it
Make it quicker	Change it
Learn it	Remove it

…depending on your outcome.

Take a look at the illustration below. This is the HGE communication model and it kind of explains everything we're going to cover in this book. As you can see from the head diagram, I've chunked it into 3 major sections – Practitioner level, which covers the thoughts we have and the states we feel and how that's interlinked with our physiology. Then Master Practitioner, which goes into all of the filters inside the head that make us who we think we are. Then Trainer, which deals with changing the external reality to make it the way we want it. But more on that later.

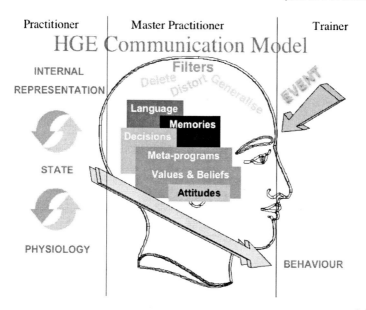

Here's how I normally explain this concept, and if you follow along I think you'll find this is really easy to get your head around. Information comes into us from some external event – something we see, hear, touch, smell or taste, which is detected by the 5 senses in our Peripheral Nervous System. That's all we can be aware of. If the door to the room you're in right now opened and whatever came in couldn't be seen, smelt, tasted, touched or heard, how would you know it was there?

So the information comes in through the 5 senses, at something like 2 million pieces of information per second. That's a lot of stuff!! Now there's no way we could process all of that information consciously, so one of the great things your unconscious mind does for you is to filter out a lot of the content. It does that initially through the automatic processes of deletion, distortion and generalisation

DELETION

We delete a heck of a lot of information at any one time. Right now, become aware of your left big toe. Now where was it until I mentioned it? That's deletion. We miss things all the time, overlook the obvious and tune out.

DISTORTION

We bend reality to fit – we read between the lines and hear what we think we hear, or make it the way we want it. Daydreaming is distortion, seeing faces in clouds. Have a look at the following illustrations and tell me what you see..

Is that a figure playing a saxophone, or a woman's silhouette? And the second picture – is that a young woman wearing a hat looking to the left, or an old woman? That's distortion at work. Twisting our perception to make the outside world agree with our inside opinion.

GENERALISATION

We group things together and say "This is like that". Cushions, stools and sofas are all places to sit, so if you came into my house and I said "please sit down" you'd know what to do. You compare new data to what you already know, which is the basis of all learning. Every morning when you swing your legs out of bed, they always go down to the floor. They never go up. You've learned that now.

Whatever gets through those initial processes, gets further filtered by a number of unconscious "files in the filing cabinet" which sift through the data and codify it, make meaning out of what we've just perceived. These include:

LANGUAGE

The words and labels we use. Imagine the scenario - three managers learn of their company's takeover. One calls it an opportunity, one says it's a makeover, one calls it a crisis. And each will react differently based on the words they chose. People program their neurology through the words they use.

MEMORIES

Imagine I was burned by a chip pan when I was four years old, and you are a veteran Fire Fighter. If this book was to spontaneously combust, we'd both see the flames, smell the smoke, feel the heat, taste the fumes and hear the crackling. You'd be reaching for a fire extinguisher or dunking this book in a bucket. I'd be sprinting down your street screaming "Not again!". We both perceived the same external information, but our memories affected what we did. Can you see how that could happen?

DECISIONS

Behind every belief that something is true, is a decision that you made to make it so. If you believe you're a confident person, it's because at some time in the past you decided that you were. The Latin root of the word decision means "to cut off". Once you decided, that was it. But haven't you made some decisions in the past that changed your life forever? My decision to try to remain positive and be optimistic has shaped my life and my career – now I'm writing a book because of that one decision. Yet haven't you also made some negative decisions that have hindered or limited your life in some way? What are some of the decisions that you've taken in the past that have led you to where you are now? And isn't it exciting to know that you can always change your decisions...

METAPROGRAMS

Metaprograms are thinking styles that determine how we sort, pay attention to and process information. The question is why do people react so differently to identical information? To use one really old cliché, why does one person see the glass as half-empty and another see it as half-full? Why does one person hear a message and feel energised, excitedly and motivated, while another hears the exact same message and doesn't respond at all?

Metaprograms are the keys to the way a person processes information. They're powerful internal patterns that help determine how you form your internal representations and direct your behaviour. Metaprograms are the internal programs (or sorts) we use in deciding what to pay attention to. A computer can't do anything without software~ which provides the structure to perform specific tasks. Metaprograms operate much the same way in our brain. They provide the structure that governs what you pay attention to, how you make sense of our experiences, and the directions in which they take you. To communicate with a computer, you have to understand its software. To communicate effectively with a person you have to understand his or hers. Through understanding those mental patterns you can expect to get your message across, whether it's trying to get someone to buy a car or to understand that you really love him/her.

For example: are you someone who moves towards what you want, or away from what you don't want? Are you interested in learning, achieving, gaining, progressing, acquiring? Or are you into security, minimising the risk, being cautious, and avoiding hassle. That one thinking habit shapes *everything you do*. That's only one Metaprogram. There are over 30 listed in the chapter later on in this book.

VALUES

Are the positive & negative emotional states that your nervous system pursues or avoids. They are your compulsions & revulsions, they are your strongest feelings about what is right or wrong for you, they dictate how you spend your time & they judge all your actions - in short they govern your entire lifestyle.

To use a computer analogy you can install any program you want, but it is your values that will override everything you put in. They are the ultimate guide to understanding, predicting, & assessing your behaviour.

Some people are good at making decisions, while others struggle to do so easily. What if there was an easy way to make decisions for yourself that were always right for you? What if you already had this built in Compass which has guided all of your decisions in the past, & will always do so in the future ? Wouldn't it make sense to use the software that came factory fitted, so to speak?

Most of your values have been programmed in at random from the environment, your parents, the media, society, & your heroes. To make it even more fascinating, your values about money will differ from your values about relationships, although some core values will come up time & again, as they are part of your identity. Do you understand how important it is that you discover your own values ?

The problem is that these are unconscious - you don't know why you do such things, you just know you have to. Not only that, but some values are more important than others, & every time you make a decision what actually happens is that the hierarchy of values is filtering your choices, & ultimately your actions will be determined by them. If you find yourself regretting a decision, is it simply because you went against your internal compass. Any internal conflict inside yourself comes from your values - you may have a fantastic job, but if your life goes against your values, you will be unhappy & unfulfilled.

Alternatively, a person living on the breadline but living in accordance with their values will feel satisfied inside.

Most people are surprised to see their core values on paper. However, becoming consciously aware of them you will learn to understand why you do what you do. Also once you know what they are, you can take steps to ensure that you experience these values on a daily basis, & when you do that life becomes more Technicolour as opposed to black & white.

Values are especially important in relationships because it is the satisfaction or violation of them that will sustain or end the partnership. People give away their values all the time in their language, & once you've read the chapter later in this book, you will be more aware of them in everyday conversation. Chances are people are giving you strong clues about what motivates them in their everyday speech, *if you're trained to hear it.*

The things that matter most to you are indications of your values so it is critical that your analysis is as accurate as possible. Do you spend time with people who share your core values? Or do you find yourself in conflict with other people? Any argument with another person comes about when someone's value is violated. Many people achieve all of their goals, have all the material things they always wanted & yet are miserable - because their values are still largely unsatisfied.

Remember: values are the compass to steer you to your ultimate destination: if you violate them you feel conflict, resistance & nagging doubt. When you live life in accordance with your values you feel rewarded & satisfied.

BELIEFS

A belief is a feeling of certainty that something is true. If you believe the floor is blue, then you feel very certain that it is. And unless I get you to question it, you'll keep that belief. The structure of belief is certainty. The structure of doubt is uncertainty. There are probably beliefs that you once had that now you'd be embarrassed to admit. And you changed them because you questioned them, or someone else did.

WHAT A LOAD OF B.S.!

"I can't believe that !" said Alice.

"Can't you ?" The Queen said in a pitying tone. "Try again: draw a long breath, and shut your eyes."

Alice laughed "There's no use trying", she said. "One can't believe impossible things."

"I dare say you haven't had much practice," said the Queen. "When I was your age, I always did it for half an hour a day. Why, sometimes I've believed as many as six impossible things before breakfast."

- Alice Through the Looking Glass, Lewis Carroll.

In other words, I'm talking B.S. (belief systems). Why ? Only because:
• they govern everything we think is true
• most of us have limiting beliefs
• most of us think that beliefs are permanent things.

In fact however, you're going to learn that you can change. If you change your beliefs, what you think you can do, you'll in turn change what you actually do. This in turn will change the results of your life. Remember the Neurological levels diagram earlier in this book.

What are Beliefs? They are generalisations, global brush stroke comments about life, people etc. built up from one or more experiences in your past. Generalizing makes it easier to learn and to put big ideas together. A belief is simply a feeling of surety that something is real or true.

If you think this page is made from paper, then you will behave as if that's true, even if it wasn't. Beliefs are also like tables with legs - the legs are the experiences that support the belief, the table top is the belief. So you've found pages of paper before, they are covered in words like other types of paper, it feels like paper and it sounds papery when you touch it. Great - you now have four table legs holding up this belief, et voila, a solid belief! Now you will act upon this inner map of reality (even if you're mistaken!)

How do I know a belief when I hear one ? They usually start with the words "If....then...", or "Life is....", "People are....." Or even more personally like "I can't..." Or "I am...." And yes they are mostly generalisations. For example "I can't relate to other people".

Where do they come from ? There are lots of sources for beliefs: one's upbringing, the environment that you grow up in and the people you associate with. Modelling elders or idols: your heroes as a child, rock groups and singers, movie actors, and even (god forbid) your parents ! Repetitive experiences install beliefs: reading regularly, cinema, MTV, the internet. Even books can change your beliefs...

If dad let you hammer a nail and you did it well, you started a new table leg. If you fluffed it you probably built a few limiting ones in one go! Past trauma will work too, pain being a great motivator: marital break-ups, abuse, accidents, health worries. In truth, you were a blank page waiting to be written on.

How do they work ? Once installed, they become unquestioned commands (software) to your nervous system (hardware). You act as if it were true and never question it !

So how do you change a belief ? You do exactly that - you question the belief, and reverse the process. Start sawing some legs off the table. Think about it, aren't there some beliefs that you once held dear that you'd be embarrassed to admit now ? Like your favourite pop group will never split up ? ("Make it last forever, friendship never ends"). To elicit a belief about a particular subject, ask yourself the following:

What do I believe about _____ ? "Well, it's hard to know what to say"

How do I know that ? "Because when I try I get flustered"

What causes it to be that way ? "People make me nervous"

There's the limiting belief – "People make me nervous". Change that and you'd change your world!

What if you changed more of your beliefs ? The world is your Oyster- change your beliefs and you change the way you perceive the world. Beliefs are what placebos are all about. Believe the sugar pill will cure the symptoms and it will. Beliefs are what Vietnam P.O.W.'s had changed to sign confessions renouncing capitalism. Question a belief often enough, even one you've had since you were a child, and it will change. Use the same technology now to change your own beliefs for the better.

ATTITUDES

Attitudes are made up of the values and beliefs we've just talked about:

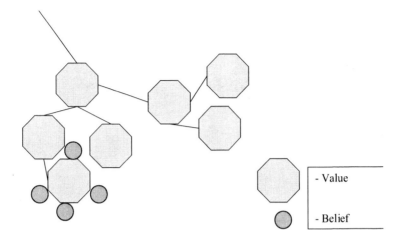

The Value is represented by the green octagon, and the beliefs that are related to that are the pink circles. The beliefs that are connected to that value are like the rules of the game – what has to happen for that person to feel like they're meeting that value. So for example, the value might be Freedom. The beliefs might be "To be free I have to be self employed" and "If I can get up at any time in the day that I choose then I'm free". Together, the combination of values and beliefs makes up that individual's attitude. Does that make sense?

All of this makes up your "map of the world", your own personal model of reality. Now it's just a map, it's not real. If you look at an A-Z of your home town, it'll probably have green buildings and brown roads. Yet when you look out at the real world, the roads aren't brown and the buildings aren't green, but the map still works – it still gets you from place to place. You don't see a picture of a McDonald's hamburger on the menu, bite the plastic menu and expect it to taste like hamburger, do you? The menu is not the meal. Or as Alfred Korzybski said, "The map is not the territory".

A woman telephone operator
at New England Telephone
c. 1926

It's like the old telephone exchanges – we all have the same big board with all the same holes and all the same wires. It's just you have your particular combination of wiring. I have mine, and everyone else has theirs. Hopefully the message is getting through....

So basically here's how all of that works. You take in some external event through your 5 senses, it gets filtered, and you then form an internal representation of it in your mind. You either picture it, hear it, talk to yourself about it or get a feeling. And whatever I/R (internal representation) you make, that affects your emotional state. Run Steven King horror movies in your head and you'll feel scared. Run intimate fluffy movies in your head and you'll feel warm and fluffy.

That then affects your physiology – your blood pressure, heart rate, brainwave frequency, temperature, your breathing, your facial expression, skin colour, your balance and your posture. These all change as your state changes.

Yet ultimately it's your state that drives your behaviour. What you do is greatly controlled by how you feel. There are days when I can write and it flows from my fingers onto the keyboard and onto these pages. There are other days when I can't spell the word "THE". Ever had that?

Now by way of demonstration, stand up and get depressed. Right now, after reading these instructions, I'd like you to stand up, look straight up at the ceiling above you, put your hands up as if you're waving at the sun, and smile like a Cheshire Cat. Breathe from the pit of your stomach. Now without changing anything, get depressed.

Go on – do that now. I'll be here when you get back.

Go on, do it! I'm watching!

> <

So what happened? Can't get depressed? Feel silly? That's the point. That physiology is not one of depression. It's maybe nuts, or amusing, but it isn't depression.

Show me a depressed physiology.

Go on.

Shoulders slumped forward, head down, breathing high and shallow… eyes looking down, off balance.

Now pray to the sun again!

Notice a difference? If not, call me immediately!

How you use your physiology changes how you feel. That's one reason for giving prisoners regular exercise breaks. That's why manic depressives tend not to go to the gym. There's a clue in the word E/ Motion. The more you move, the more you feel. Now am I suggesting that next time you feel "down" that you stand up and smile at the sun, waving your arms wildly? Yes! But maybe not at bus stops….

We filter out a lot of information unconsciously – we're not even aware we do it. Until now… Think about it, you're not getting the raw data of this book, you're getting your nervous system's version of this book. By the time you hold it or see these words you've already filtered it – it's already gone through your 5 senses. But this frame, this concept has far wider repercussions as we'll find out in the Huna chapter.

We take all of that information, the sights, sounds, smells, tastes and feelings, and we give them a verbal label in our head. So if we see a couple arguing, we might see that and say "lovers' tiff" in our head. For all we know, it might be an undercover policeman and a shoplifter, but we think we know what we're seeing and we label it. We then act as if the label was true, not the raw data. On a seminar one of my students said she'd run into another woman in Sainsbury's and they'd bumped trolleys, and the woman had given her "such a dirty look, she obviously hated me!" I said, "how do you know she hadn't just had an abortion?" You don't, you just assumed. And remember that old cliché, "Never assume, because it makes an ASS out of U and ME"

Basically, to sum all of that up, what we say to someone comes from our thinking patterns, and our thinking patterns come from our map of the world. That map is made up of our past experiences. I'm not sure if you are what you eat, but you are what you think.

Now here's another major premise for everything that we'll talk about in this book. One of my Hawaiian teachers, John Kaimikaua, said that modern man values the intellect, where previously he valued Intuition:

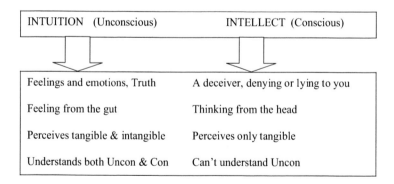

INTUITION (Unconscious)	INTELLECT (Conscious)
Feelings and emotions, Truth	A deceiver, denying or lying to you
Feeling from the gut	Thinking from the head
Perceives tangible & intangible	Perceives only tangible
Understands both Uncon & Con	Can't understand Uncon

This is really important, and I think you'll agree it's accurate. Your head can trick you or deny anything's actually wrong, and it's always wanting tangible proof before it believes anything. It doesn't understand feelings and hunches, because they're not logical or rational. The unconscious mind always tells you the truth, you can feel it in your gut, and it learns from experience, not things. Ever ignored a hunch, only to regret it later? I know I have. This is critical -

ALL Learning, all behaviour and all change IS UNCONSCIOUS

LEARNING

How much of the School syllabus that you learned do you use now? Do you remember how you first learned the alphabet, the difference between a p and a q, and then you learned to put them together into words? Spelling tests? Do you remember that stuff? And where is your phone number stored? Where was it till I mentioned it? I keep my bank card PIN number in my right forefinger. I can just walk up to the bank machine and my finger automatically types it for me, I don't have to think about it. Now that's a useful finger! I bet you can sing songs right now yet you never formally studied the lyrics. How is that possible? Probably because you were relaxed when you heard it, it was repeated a couple of times, and you were having fun. Hmmmmm, magic formula. Now is that how you were taught in school? Probably not. I spent most of my school years stressed, expected to get it right first time and hating every minute of it. Was it only me that had that experience?

All human skill development goes through 4 stages. At first, you aren't even aware that you're lacking in a skill set. Once you learn that, you wonder if the skill really does work. And if they do, will **you** be able to learn them? That's when any limiting beliefs about learning kick in: "Will I be able to do it, after all, it took me forty lessons to pass my driving test?". What if they do work and you do learn it? "Will that make me a better person, or a smart arse? Maybe I won't bother going into this any further…."

Does this sound familiar at all?

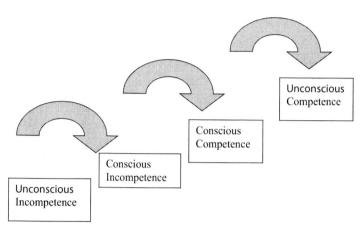

At first you don't even know that you're crap at something, because you have never even tried! Something may be broken but you're unaware of what it is. You may have a vague notion something is wrong, but have no idea how to fix it, or indeed, what to fix. You don't know it's there until you become aware of it. Like the first time you tried to ride a bicycle. There was a time when you hadn't even thought of riding a two wheeled piece of metal, then one day you tried, and you became intimately familiar with the road surface. Now you know there's work to be done. There's something to learn here. So now you're excited at the possibility, but you're also scared of trying and scared of failing, looking stupid, getting it wrong. Like learning to drive a car – you don't even think about it until one day, and now you want to be able to drive. But there's so much to learn. 3 pedals, at least 4 forward gears and a steering wheel as well?

The next stage up is when you now try to do something and you are fully aware of how hard it is. It all feels unfamiliar and ungainly, clumsy. You know what to do but you can't do it yet. That's frustrating, and often confusing. So you stall the car several times, or crunch the gears. Now you know you're crap at it! You know what to do, but you don't seem to be able to do it yet!

Conscious competence now means that as long as you concentrate really hard and focus, then you can do the new skill, but it takes a lot of effort and repetition. Sometimes you need to remind yourself of what to do. So now you can overtake and you're saying "mirror – signal – manoeuvre" over and over again in your head. It's not fully integrated yet, but you are using the skill successfully.

Unconscious Competence is the level of mastery, where you use the skills automatically. They are now part of your everyday life and you don't have to think about it. Nowadays you can start the car, switch on your mobile, look at a map, in the dark, in snow, and you don't bat an eyelid! You never find yourself putting the car key in the ignition and then asking yourself "Now how does this work again?" It's automatic.

Imagine then, if you could skip all that effort, and make a quantum leap – by going straight to Unconscious Competence. How? *Train the unconscious mind.* It's quicker and shaves years off your learning curve! Imagine the possibilities for a moment...

All Training needs to train the audience's Unconscious Mind to create change. If you're training their Conscious minds then they won't retain it for long, and they'll just go back to their old ways. Isn't that the problem with most training courses? They get all psyched up for a few days then the bubble bursts and they're back to square one. Or worse, because they spent all that money on that team building event and now they're even more disappointed and cynical.

We operate from unconscious desires and compulsions, and we filter information massively, and unconsciously.

BEHAVIOUR

You have something like 159 muscles in your arm – when you picked up this book, you didn't do it consciously. That would take way too long. Muscle 5, then tendon 37, then extensor 114. No, you just went "Book – grab!" Put your hand up if you can drive? Good unconscious arm movement there! Most people drive in an unconscious trance – and have no recollection of the traffic lights being out at the big junction, yet you must have driven through them. Or it's the weekend and you end up at work by mistake….. Who was driving the car………?

CHANGE

Ever tried to stop smoking, or stop eating something that's bad for you, or change a habit consciously? Does that work? Rarely. If it did, your best friend could say "stop eating chocolate now!" and you would. Or you could diary in bouts of guilt between 7 and 8 every Thursday night. If only it were conscious. When people change their ways, it's because they've changed at the **unconscious** level. That's why Hypnotherapy is so important and so powerful.

So in light of this, let me give you some information next, that will help you respect, align & communicate with your unconscious mind. And the Unconscious Mind of others…

THE PRIME DIRECTIVES OF THE UNCONSCIOUS MIND

Today we're meeting a very important part of you – your unconscious…mind… because that's the apart of you that will assist you in all of the se concepts and ideas as you read this book, and forever more. It has a lot of jobs to do – it repairs your cuts, keeps you breathing at night while you sleep, beats your heart, digests your food, adjusts your body for maximum comfort, cleans and moistens your eyes as you blink. So let's look together at the Prime Directives of your unconscious mind –

This is primarily left brain information, for your conscious mind so it can begin to respect your Unconscious Mind. And in doing that it can communicate better with your Unconscious….

Let's learn how to use the Unconscious Mind the way it was intended. This is some of the most useful, and most unique, information in personal growth. You don't come across what I'm about to share with you very often. The Hawaiian name is Unihipili:

U means to stem from the heart, the seat of our emotions or our feelings

Ni means to pour out a liquid, like water

Pi means blow out with the breath or blow out liquid

Li means to cling to or to associate with

Nihi means silent, careful, secretive action, as well as to speak with a quiet voice. Isn't that exactly how you perceive your unconscious? A faint little voice in your head?

Your Unconscious Mind clings to your Conscious Mind like a five year old to it's mother. It also translates as "grasshopper"- the Egyptians used the grasshopper as a symbol for the Unconscious Mind. You may even remember the old 70's TV series starring David Carradine "Kung Fu" – snatch the pebble from my hand – real traditional Chinese historical teaching (yeah, right). In this chapter we're looking at the Prime Directives – Dr Tad James's compilation from talking to Kahuna in Hawaii, reading books, his deep knowledge of Hypnosis, and his extensive research in the field of esoteric studies. This is how your Unconscious Mind works…

❶.   STORES MEMORIES

In 2 ways : Temporal (in relationship to time) and Atemporal (not in relationship to time)

In 1957 there was the Penfield study – where surgeons probed a woman's brain with an electrode – she suddenly recalled her birthday party aged two, of which she had no conscious memory previously. The feel of the dress, the songs they sang, the taste of the cake, she was reliving it. The conclusion was that everything that's ever happened to us is stored in our brain. Everything we've seen, heard, felt, smelled or tasted is in there. Karl Pribram won a Nobel prize in 1960 when he wrote about the holographic storage of memories throughout our whole body. Remember how R2D2 projected Princess Leia as a hologram in the movie Star Wars? That's a hologram. The memory is not localised, stored in just one place, it's throughout the whole body. In Hawaiian Huna there was the Black bag theory – throughout the body, we store significant traumas in little black bags. The problem is they interfere with neural network pathways and that stops the signals getting through. It's like sewage in your pipes. In Germany Dr Hamer's work is now being published under the term "New Medicine" He believes that a Significant Emotional Event (hereafter a SEE) causes a lesion on the brain, which in turn sends the wrong information to organs in the body. That then shows up in physical symptomology. Hamer's work is unpublished in the States so far, but look out for it.

2.   MAKES ASSOCIATIONS

(Links similar things and ideas), **and Learns Quickly**

You hear a song on the radio just at the same time you get some bad news. Forever more every time you hear that song, you'll feel bad (although this "anchor" can be collapsed and neutralised using HGE techniques).

❸.   ORGANIZES ALL YOUR MEMORIES

(Uses the Time Line. The Mechanics of which is called a Gestalt, like a string of pearls). It organises your memories in date order. Your Time Line is one way. Values are another way (see chapter later on)

❹.   REPRESSES MEMORIES WITH UNRESOLVED NEGATIVE EMOTION

Takes a painful memory into a little black bag, draws it shut and shoves it down, to protect the Conscious Mind from having to experience it. This takes a lot of energy.

❺.   PRESENTS REPRESSED MEMORIES FOR RESOLUTION
(to make rational and to release emotions)

Opens up the bag when you least expect it, in your quiet moments, lying in the bath, nodding off to sleep, and says: here, handle this! If you don't deal with it, you start to break rapport with your Unconscious Mind. It's doing the best it can – it looks at you like a younger version of you would, and it only wants the best for you. It brings it back up so you can learn from them. Get the learning's, you can then let go of the emotions. That's the basis for the Time Line Therapy techniques later in this book.

6.   MAY KEEP THE REPRESSED EMOTIONS REPRESSED FOR PROTECTION

Can keep traumas, deep rooted SEE's kept hidden from the Conscious Mind. That's why we need Unconscious and Conscious Minds working together to be totally whole and healed.

❼.   RUNS THE BODY

Has a blueprint:

> of body now
>
> of perfect health (in the Higher Self)

Your Unconscious Mind is in charge, and it compares the blueprint of how your body is now with the blueprint of your body in perfect health that is stored in the deepest part of the unconscious, in an area some would call the Higher Self. Instantaneous healing was common in ancient Hawaii, and as recently as 1930 there's a written account of a broken arm being healed instantly. Instantaneous = overnight. When using HGE techniques for health, this Blueprint is recovered, and Physical health then complies back to optimum. In 1997 on my NLP Practitioner course with David Shephard, there was one student with a dislocated shoulder. David is a Huna Master and using Huna he helped the guy take the sling off and his arm was healed instantly. We all heard the crunch as it snapped back into place. And I thought "I want to be able to do that!"

❽.   PRESERVES THE BODY
Maintains the integrity of the body

Black bags jam up the neural network, and prevent free flow of impulses. You have a built in Fight or flight reaction – it's completely instinctive, unconscious, and it protects you. If you step out in front of a bus, or a bug hits your windscreen, or you sneeze and your eyes close, it all happens automatically. The one I've never understood though is when you choke and your eyes water – what use is that?

9.   IS THE DOMAIN OF THE EMOTIONS
It weeps if you're sad, it laughs if you're happy. You don't do emotions on purpose. If you were depressed and it was conscious, you could diary it in for every Tuesday between 5 and 7 pm, and then it would go away. But it doesn't work like that, because it's not conscious. It's unconscious.

10.   IS A HIGHLY MORAL BEING
(the morality you were taught and accepted)

Whatever you believe is right, it will adhere to. Sometimes people need to clear guilt to be healed. Some people think they're ill because they're "Being punished" and if you're guilty, you deserve a lesson. Everyone has a code of morality and your unconscious will follow it to the letter.

11.   ENJOYS SERVING, NEEDS CLEAR ORDERS TO FOLLOW
Takes direction from the Conscious Mind, like a loyal servant. It will pay attention to whatever your dominant thoughts are, and the more you focus on one thing, the more you dwell on something, and the more energy you give that idea, the more your unconscious

mind thinks you want it to be reality. So be careful what you dwell on. Now when you talk to your unconscious, it's not "you do this or else", it likes a loving, caring cooperative relationship. The Conscious Mind needs to learn to relate with the Unconscious Mind, then others'. The Unconscious likes that, it's a "do with" not a "do to". The greater the rapport between the two, the more you can be happy, healthy, healed. It will do as you ask. If there's poor rapport between the two you will feel split, or suffer internal conflict, and if you give it no orders it'll do what it thinks is right. Remember it's not rational or logical, it's emotional. It reacts, not responds.

12. CONTROLS AND MAINTAIN ALL PERCEPTIONS
Regular
Telepathic
Receives and transmits perceptions to the conscious mind
You have 5 senses, and you filter 2 million pieces of information per second down to 7+-2. That's quite a task! You will also have had episodes in your life when you dreamt about a friend, and they called you the next day. Or you think about your brother and he calls you. This is also the function behind more extraordinary feats such as Remote Viewing or Clairvoyance.

13. GENERATES, STORES, DISTRIBUTES AND TRANSMITS "ENERGY"
The Unconscious Mind is in charge of your energy. It can generate lots or a little – and you can ask for more. The Metabolism is controllable via the unconscious, using Biofeedback, ideomotor finger signals (see the Hypnosis chapter) or a pendulum. Glucose + oxygen = energy. Your Blood sugar needs to be stable, so watch your diet.

14.   MAINTAINS INSTINCTS AND GENERATE HABITS

It learns what works & keeps doing it, until it's given a better alternative. That's why you often repeat stupid behaviours, even though intellectually you know better, your unconscious doesn't.

15.   NEEDS REPETITION UNTIL A HABIT IS INSTALLED

You have to cultivate a habit till it becomes unconscious. For most people it seems to take 3, 7 or 21 repetitions to make it stick. That's the truth behind the old adage that it takes 21 days to form a habit. If you can get yourself to the gym 21 times in a row, chances are that you'll do it forever. The Unconscious Mind will undo habits too – ever tried to stop a habit consciously? Did that work? Probably not.

16.   IS PROGRAMMED TO CONTINUALLY SEEK MORE AND MORE

There is always more to discover

Ever had a Dream goal – a had to have – and you finally got it, and it was a complete anti-climax? It wore off. Ho hum…. You think "If only I got the new car, my life would be different" and then you did, and it wasn't? The Maharishi said "We continually seek more and more until we eventually seek more than the most". Remember the first men on the moon (if we ever did go to the moon, but that's another book!). They spent decades in training and when they finally got there many of them crashed into depression – where do they go from there? There's always the next mountain. Picture the successful Rock group – money, platinum records, fans. Then they want more. Of all of it. That's human nature, it's the way we're built. So I've written some more…

17.   FUNCTIONS BEST AS A WHOLE INTEGRATED UNIT

Does not need parts to function

Ever heard anyone use language like "Part of me wants to, but part of me doesn't, or devil and an angel, self-sabotage"? Ever said that yourself? Sometimes 99% of you is going one way and 1% is going somewhere else. We call that a Part of you. The ancient Hawaiians preferred integration and in HGE we always try to have a person be 100% aligned and whole. In Hawaii one of the reasons we chant the ancient chants is because the ancient language integrates all inside you. All the best philosophy or theology on the planet talks about being whole, complete, congruent, and oneness. At least part of me thinks so…

18. IS SYMBOLIC

Uses and responds to symbols

Carl Jung in Psychology was famous for his Archetypes – famously they were also the first 22 cards in the Tarot deck. How's that for a basis of a sound school of psychology? What about Dreams? When your Unconscious Mind sends you a message and you're supposed to "get it"? And a blue tree frog to you may mean something entirely different to me. That's why dream books don't work. They're fine for the person who wrote it, because that's their interpretations.

19. TAKES EVERYTHING PERSONALLY.

(The basis of Perception is Projection)

When you point the finger at someone and blame them for something, there's 3 times as many fingers pointing back at you. This is a huge part of HGE, as you'll see later on in this book. What you like about your partner is you. What you hate about them is also you. If you say "He's a _____" remember that you cannot be other than what you see outside yourself. Right now as you sit in your chair – you can only be aware of your perception of the chair – it already exists in you for you to be aware of it. So be careful what you point your finger at…

20.   WORKS ON THE PRINCIPLE OF LEAST EFFORT
Path of least resistance

The Unconscious Mind does as little as it can to get its outcome. It likes the line of east effort, which is why more cream cakes are sold than gym memberships. That means as a therapist one has to pin the Unconscious Mind as to when it will start and finish any work you ask it to do. You'll read about that in the Hypnosis section.

21.   DOES NOT PROCESS NEGATIVES

Don't think of Elvis Presley. Now what are you thinking about? You can't think about what you don't want to think about without thinking about it. So ask yourself are you focussing on what you want, or what you don't want? People often keep getting what they don't want, moving away from pain all the time. They say "I hope I don't blow this meeting the way I did last time" or "Hope I don't get the cold" which the unconscious Mind hears as "Hope I ____get the cold". You get what you focus on. Think about what you're feeding your mind? Is it towards what you want, or away from what you don't want?

So next time a little Black Bag opens up – ask yourself "What is the learning I need to get right now to let this go?" And know that you'll never be completely finished - you're always a work in progress. There's usually another set at a higher evolutionary level, so there's always more to clear.

Next time a major issue returns, look at the opportunity – go where the resistance is. You can't clear it out if you don't know its there, that's why I say "Awareness is Progression". You can't progress until you're aware. But the moment you become aware, you've progressed.

It's like a Christmas tree with fairy lights on it, but the room is dark and the lights are off. You have to put the lights on before you can see where all the lights are, so you can unravel it safely from the tree. Light up the Christmas tree first. We talk about that in my Master Practitioner courses – you have to get the client fully associated into the problem before you attempt to blow it out. In reframing, you ask them to restate the problem just before you reframe them. It's like in computers, you have to highlight the file before you press delete.

Which leads us nicely into the next major concept I'd like you to try on…

SOME BASIC CONCEPTS

This is where HGE excels, when we talk about the first concept of Cause vs Effect

1. RESULTS VS REASONS

One of my Trainers once shared this as an afterthought and I've been teaching it ever since, because I think it's so profound.

In life, you either get the result that you want, or you can give me a whole bunch of reasons why you don't. [Another word for reasons is excuses]

There Are Only 3 Reasons/Excuses

1. **N**egative Emotions – Anger, Sadness, Fear. You feel bad about your outcome, and associate pain to it. Scared to get your goal, or angry that you haven't, or guilty if you do.

2. **I**neffective Behaviours – "running West looking for a sunrise" as Tony Robbins once described. Or trying to become financially independent by spending more than you earn. That will never work.

3. **L**imiting Beliefs – "I can't… I'm not…I don't deserve…People like me don't…"

Now some people use this model as an excuse to blame, or to beat themselves up. It's not about that. It's about responsibility:

- "Responsibility" = the ability to respond
- It's not about fault, or blame, or guilt (Those are negative emotions)
- It's about **handling it.**
- **What are you going to do about it?**

There are certain rules we operate from in HGE. The 1st teaching of HGE is the assumption of C>E. For us to get maximum personal power we need to take maximum responsibility for everything that happens in our world. It took me a long time to "get" this, so let me explain myself carefully.

In our culture at the moment it's a case of "If at first you don't succeed blame someone else, then sue the bastard!" Or in relationships your partner says "make me happy". Wrong – only they can make themselves happy. They need to do something.

The effects that occur in our lives are our own. You either created it, manifested it or attracted it. So rather than say "I would have succeeded too if it wasn't for …." Ask yourself "For what purpose did I create this?" Which side are you on? Are you the cause, or are you at the effect? If a pigeon shits on my shoulder, am I responsible? Yes! I might have shat on someone this morning. For Every Effect there's always a Cause. Is it you? And how are you going to handle it?

WHY IS CAUSE & EFFECT IMPORTANT?

C>E is the principle that for every effect, there is a cause. Everything that happens has a cause. You would be more empowered if you operated from the C side, besides it's always nice to go to the C side (groan). When you're at Cause you always have a choice. Moving to cause = creating more choices. A lot of people learn this then use it as a place to hide behind, so they can abdicate responsibility and blame their hardships on you. If that's the case, read the Huna chapter segment on the concept of Perception is Projection.

The majority of people tend to place more importance on the outside world that they do on themselves. People let the outside influences make up their minds for them, and think all of the answers are "out there". You are the only source of truth for everything you experience. You have five senses, values, beliefs, choices, decisions, everything that I explained in the Communication Model earlier – and yours are different from everyone else's. No two people have the same identical filters. You are unique. And your reality is unique too. Your beliefs create your reality, NOT the other way around! Your life will be the way you choose it to be, and you'll have loads of good reasons why you are where you are. The bottom line is, you'll simply decide to accept something, or not (including these ideas).

If you're at the Effect end, you **resist your circumstances**, blame other people, circumstances, and all the external things outside, for how you feel inside. "Life's a bitch, it's not my fault, why me, it's not fair." Effect people use words like "should", "I don't know", "I'll try", "he makes me". "If it's meant to be it'll happen" – advocate all responsibility, put the cause outside self. You have no choice and can't do anything about it. You're choosing to accept a bunch of reasons or excuses for not having your result. If the cause is outside of you, then so is all the learning, wisdom and pride in solving it. Remember the old adage that says "That which you resist will persist". If you're really eager to destroy your career, your relationships, your health and your life, jump to effect and do the following:

- Justify and complain "If only (name of scapegoat) hadn't (injustice)…"
- Compare yourself to other people
- Confront those you blame
- Resent your circumstances and brew
- Give up and seek revenge
- Wait for the white knight to arrive
- Lay blame on others so you're right, or yourself (the martyr or sacrificial lamb) or on your crappy circumstances (which by the

way you created)
- Sedate yourself or distract yourself with self-pitying melancholy music, coffee, processed low quality food and crap television
- Watch the news and read the newspapers. You are fed edited, biased material. News programmes are therapy appointments in advance!

From the book "Provocative Therapy" by Frank Farrelly, I've borrowed Frank's blame list. This was his collection of the reasons his clients gave him for not having what they wanted in their lives. Just so you know, these are all excuses.

BLAME LIST

BODY	DESTINY	FAMILY
Biology	Astrology	Parents
Body Type	Bad Luck	Brothers
Deficiencies	God	Sisters
Genetics	Satan	Children
Heredity	Karma	
Hormones	Past Lives	**SOCIETY**
Looks		Boss
Menopause	**HISTORY**	Education
Nerves	Age	Law
Nutrition	Childhood	Politics
	Origins	Media
NATURE	Birth Order	Men
Nurturing		Women
Yin	**MIND**	TV
Yang	Unconscious	MTV
		Culture

Frank said that clients go through four stages with this concept:

1. Client is provoked into a series of experiences that leave him/her

   Astonished

   Uncertain

   Even outraged

2. Client's protests reduce and they begin to realise **they** must change, not the therapist

3. Client affirms that therapist's opinion of them is wrong

4. Integration – client no longer protests. Confidence and adaptability increasing.

So if you want to live at effect, then you'll (maybe) reach age 80 and have along hit list of people you can blame for your crap life, but you won't have a damn thing that you want. Living at effect is a DITY (Do it to yourself) project.

If you're at the Cause end, you **accept** that you create your own universe, and everything that happens you have either attracted or created unconsciously. If you chose it, then you can unchoose it. Or choose anew. You're honest with yourself and you accept responsibility (the ability to respond). The more responsibility you take, the more support you get from your surroundings. Take one step forward and the universe takes one hundred towards you. Empowered people use words like "I know I can do that", "I will", "I choose to". "The universe I'm in is perfect right now. However, there are some things I would change." The responsibility for change lies with the client - you simply facilitate it. You can't do it for them, and you don't do it "to" them. You simply show them how to do it for themselves. The fitness trainer designs the programme, but it's you who gets on the exercise machine! They can be your tour guide, but they can't have your holiday.

If you want to jump to the Cause side, here's how to start. And by the way, moving from Effect to Cause can be as easy, or as difficult, as you choose to make it....

- Start telling the truth (and that starts with you!)
- Compare yourself to yourself, not others (where are you now compared to where you were a year ago?)
- Tap into your passions and interests
- Remove the tolerations (the crap you put up with)
- Start repairing the cracks
- Take better care of yourself (exercise, good quality food, water and fresh air)
- Start taking responsibility (at least during weekdays. At weekends you can blame the bastards all you like! Just kidding!)

You have to get the results for yourself. You have to take 100% responsibility & do whatever it takes to achieve them. You (the reader of this book) are responsible for getting value from this book yourself.

The extent to which you (the Therapist or Coach) take responsibility for the client's results is the extent to which you create codependency.

A good coach will keep pointing out any C>E violations they hear. As a coach I'll do everything I can do – whatever it takes to facilitate your results. But you do the work. The fitness trainer helps design the programme, keeps you on track, helps you stay motivated. But it's you who gets on the machines and sweats.

HOW DOES CAUSE & EFFECT WORK?

If forms the basis of all beliefs: "x causes y". It is identified by the words "make, if….then, because, as, causes". People frequently (mistakenly) believe that "When he does _____ I feel _____". In fact, they are saying is that another person's action changes their state. If you say "She makes me sad" what you're really saying is that "She's selling me sadness, and I'm buying it"

Now you can't experience anything outside of your own nervous system. The truth is that no one's actions outside of your nervous system causes you to change emotional state - you change your own state. It's not them, it's you. The other problem with this mistaken belief is that it implies that the other person can't change if they want to, and is dependent on others for how they feel.

To recover the cause, use language like:

When did you decide that.....?	What is it within me....?	What was my intention in creating that ?
What causes it to be this way ?	Is this person at cause ?	How does ____ cause you to choose to be ___?
What is there to learn here ?		

There's another equation that you may remember from school:

$$E=mc^2$$

Energy equals matter x the speed of light.

Now the Western world is firmly ensconced in the material, physical world, on the right hand side of that equation. Yet the left side of the equation is equally important, arguably more so. HGE suggests you think in terms of energy, effort, potential and intent as well. Be able to dance on the equal sign...

WHAT IF CAUSE & EFFECT IS TRUE?

Think about it – if you want a result, and you feel great about going for it, you believe you can and you deserve it, and you have a specific "how to" plan to get there, what could possibly stop you?

You would be more empowered, because you would be taking total responsibility for the results in your world. All of it. In HGE we say "the meaning of any communication is the response you get". If you try to encourage someone but you demoralize them instead, then you communicated demoralization. Alter your approach. Being at cause does not imply fault, or blame. It implies choice. Let go of the ego, and the attachment to why it isn't working. Be willing to let go of the things that aren't working, and alter your approach. It's not about blame or fault. Those are value judgments – instead it's about handling it. 100% value from this book lies with you– it's how you use the information in this book to get results that counts. Use it or lose it.

Remember that you either get the result you wanted, or reasons why you didn't. Another name for reasons is excuses. And there are only three excuses:

1. Negative emotions: you're scared, overwhelmed, sad, lonely, hurt, etc
2. Inefficient strategies: what you're doing isn't the way to do it
3. Limiting Beliefs: you don't believe you can/need to/will/deserve to

Get rid of these three and then there's only results.

Notice that if you unpack the equation, it actually says "Cause is greater than effect…"

It's all about acceptance versus resistance – accept does not mean surrender, it means admit the truth, accept what's happening, and decide what you're going to do about it. Take responsibility for everything that's happened in your life and ask yourself "What do I need to do differently in future?"

And always remember: if you choose to be at effect then you're still at cause, because you chose…

2. THE MIND-BODY CONNECTION

There was a Nobel Prize awarded in the last decade for the discovery that the mind and body are connected. I call it your spine, I'm not sure what others call it.

Realise this:

• The mind has tremendous power over the body.

- A depressed immune system is often the result of stress, which is the result of disempowering eating and sleeping patterns, as well as habitual poor physiology and/or focus. Anger and resentment are physical poisons to the body. Realise that stress is entirely a function of how you interpret events. The structure of worry is to run horrible movies of worst case scenarios in advance, and pretend that they have so you can feel bad about it now, just in case.
- Your thoughts create a direct physical effect on your body. Fear compromises your immune system.
- Develop empowering beliefs to let you know that there is always a way if you are committed.
- Create a physiology of vibrancy, and watch your health respond. Create a compelling future. Use the Time Line chapter in this book.
- Cultivate an attitude of gratitude.
- Every cell in your body is coated in neuro transmitters, which are chemical messengers. So if you're happy, your toenails are happy. If you're sad, your hair is sad. (That's maybe why you're sad!). All of your cells, all 70 trillion of them, are talking to each other 24 hours a day, even while you're asleep!

3. 3 STEPS TO MASTERY

There are only 3 steps to mastery.

There's an old story, if I can tell you a story for a moment, about a huge automated factory that churns out products like clockwork, until one day when the whole place suddenly, inexplicably, grinds to a horrible halt. Lights go out. Conveyor belts freeze. Machines go silent. The staff are baffled. Power is still getting through, and there's no sign of a fault anywhere, and yet nothing's happening....

So they call in an expert, and he comes to the factory, which is now losing money by the minute. He looks around, hums and haws, holds his chin pensively. Then suddenly, he goes to a fuse box, takes out a screwdriver, opens the box and turns one screw 2mm to the left. Suddenly the factory roars back into life, the widgets start churning off the production line and the company's back in business. Problem solved.

The next day the expert's invoice arrives, for $10,000. It's further itemised– for turning the screw 2mm $1.00 For knowing which screw to turn $9,999.00.

To become a master at anything, you only need 3 things:

1. A role model of excellence – an expert who can teach you the 2mm distinctions, so you can accelerate time and compress decades into days, without having to make all the same mistakes as they already have

2. An Immersion environment for a period of time – an intense workout, where you are overloaded for growth, and for maximum impact! If you're doing ten sit ups, which one does you the most good? Sit up number eleven.

3. Spaced repetition – you need scheduled follow up and re-exposure to the skills, knowledge and mindset. Revisit this book, re-listen to the tapes, attend seminars. As Tony Robbins once said "Repetition is the mother of skill"

I firmly agree with Tony Robbins when he says that any skill, any area of human endeavour is 20% mechanics (how to), and 80% mindset (why to). Mindset, your psychology, your model of the world determines the results you get. It's your attitude, not your aptitude, that determines your altitude.

So with that in mind, I'd like to share with you the common denominator beliefs and attitudes of successful people. Pioneers, geniuses, entrepreneurs and role models of excellence all seem to share the same basic fundamental mindset. There are several convenient assumptions which I'm suggesting you might like to adopt. Act as if they are true, and you'll get better results in life. Think of these as "success software" for your brain.

4. THE PRESUPPOSITIONS OF HGE

1. **Respect for the other person's model of the world.** Everyone has their own map of the territory, and it's a one off. You should respect my model of the world, and I should respect yours. Notice that I didn't say agree with it, or endorse it, but at least listen to it, be patient with it and acknowledge it as theirs. Everyone is right from their point of view.

2. **Behaviour and change are to be evaluated in terms of context, and ecology.** If someone says "I want to have tons of energy all of the time" then that's probably going to have a negative impact on their health, their sleep pattern and their quiet time, so it's probably not ecological. Any new behaviours we want to create have consequences and contexts. Make sure you take that into account.

3. **Resistance in a client is a Sign of a lack of rapport.** (There are no resistant clients, only inflexible communicators. Effective communicators accept and utilize all communication presented to them.) If you're getting objections and difficulty, they don't know you and trust you enough yet. Alter your approach and take full responsibility for building more connection. Commonality breeds agreement, so the more you have in common, the less resistance you get.

4. **People are not their behaviours.** (Accept the person; change the behaviour.) I dislike labels. A client came to me and said he was an alcoholic. I said "you're more than that – you're just drinking too much alcohol too often." Behaviour and identity are two different things.

5. **Everyone is doing the best they can with the resources they have available.** (Behaviour is geared for adaptation, and present behaviour is the best choice available. Every behaviour is motivated by a positive intent.) You always do the best you can with what you know at that time. This suggests

compassion and forgiveness. If you'd had a better choice for coping you would probably have done that.

6. **Calibrate on Behaviour**: The most important information about a person is that person's behaviour. Don't trust what they say as gospel – judge by behaviour. Many people talk a good game. Do you walk your talk, or fumble your stumble? It's always what you do that counts.

7. **The map is not the Territory.** *(The words we use are NOT the event or the item they represent.)* Our mental representation of reality is just that – our mental representation. It's not the way the world really is, it's the way that we think it is. We don't experience raw events – we experience our perception of events. Two people can see the same car accident (Conscious incompetence!) and argue about who caused it. And they're both right.

8. **You are in charge of your mind, and therefore your results** (and I am also in charge of my mind and therefore my results). Who makes the internal representations in your head? You do. Who controls the way you move and breathe? You do. Who controls your emotional state? You do. So who's responsible for your behaviours. You are. As I write this, a Scottish software company is being sued because their computer game made a teenager go out and shoot people. Yeah, right… Or smokers suing tobacco companies because **they made** the smokers roll dried up leaves, set them on fire and breathe in the smoke… (But remember that they're doing the best they can with what they have, and both teenagers and smokers are more than their behaviour, etc)

9. **People have all the Resources they need** to succeed and to achieve their desired outcomes. (There are no unresourceful people, only unresourceful states.) "Re-source" means source again, so it must be in there to begin with.. I firmly

believe that people create their own problems (see Perception is Projection) so therefore they must have the inherent ability to fix it themselves. I don't get your problems. You don't get mine. But maybe you don't have access to the solution right now.

10. **All procedures should increase Wholeness.** The aim of personal development, and every theology or philosophy agrees, is to become whole, centred, integrated, at one, congruent, connected. So everything we do should move us towards becoming more of who we are.

11. There is **ONLY** feedback! (**There is no failure, only feedback.**) You always generate an outcome – it may not be the outcome you wanted, but if you take it as feedback, learn from it and apply those learning's, you'll ultimately get your outcome. If what you're doing isn't working, do something else! If you took everything as feedback you would be a learning machine!

12. **The meaning of your communication is the Response you get.** Regardless of what you meant to communicate, the reaction you get is what you sent out. Take that as feedback and alter your approach until they get it. If you aren't getting the reaction in your listener that you wanted, you need to take responsibility for altering your approach. People usually assume that when they speak they know what they're saying, and any misunderstanding is the fault of the listener. The only way you can be sure what the other person thought you meant, is from their response. It doesn't matter what you thought you said, it doesn't matter what you meant to impart. What matters is the meaning that they got out of it. The master communicator is flexible enough to find other ways to get their message across. I like to think that the response I get is a barometer of how well I communicate. If

they're confused, I need to vary my style.

13. **The Law of Requisite Variety**: (The system/person with the most flexibility of behaviour will control the system.) From cybernetics, the person with the most flexibility of behaviour will run the system, which is why kids run a household. The more choices you have the less chance you'll get stuck. If I have one objection, and you have sixteen solutions, guess who wins.

14. **All procedures should be Designed to increase choice**. In HGE we don't take problems away, we give the client a number of better options. More choice = more wholeness. Reducing choice breaks rapport.

15. **I am never upset for the reason I think** – the thing outside that seems to be the cause of my upset rarely is. Usually it's a reminder of my own unhealed past. To uncover ·the root cause ask "Where, when and with whom have I felt this same feeling before?" Whatever a person does, they have a good reason, either consciously or unconsciously. If they seem to be overreacting, they are probably not responding to their current situation, but instead to painful experiences in their past history.

Now I don't know if these are real or not. They may not even be true. Yet the more I use these in my work and in my life, the better my results get. When I run this software in my head, my external world goes smoother and easier, and anything that makes life easier (provided it's ecological) I think is valid. Try it. You'll like it.

ACHIEVABLE OUTCOMES

One of the greatest gifts HGE has provided as a thinking tool, is the ability to recognise what works. There are certain things that have to be in place, and fully considered, for an outcome or goal to become reality.

Now most people have three levels of personal standards – three degrees of expectation if you will. You see, there's

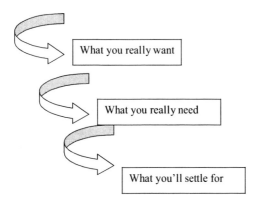

Most people will settle for the bottom level, and live in no man's land, where it's not good enough, but it's not bad enough to change. This book is full of tools and tips that help you raise the bar, raise you're personal standards higher, so you can be who you want to be, do what you want to do, and have what you want to have. I'm reminded of a tee-shirt I saw someone wearing recently, which said "I've upped my standards – now up yours!"

You've probably heard of the famous Harvard University study where out of all the final year graduates, only 5 % had written goals & outcomes. 20 years later there was a follow up study, and it was found that the 5% were worth more in financial terms that the other 95% put together, & held the highest positions in their professions, and had balanced, successful lives.

Have you heard of The Wheel of Life idea? Originally called Non-champs wheel. Use this Wheel of Life to quickly assess where you are. Divide your life into different segments, like a Dairylea Triangle box. On a scale of 1 -10 where are you in Career, Health, Relationships, Money, etc? One being dissatisfied, stuck, emotional, feels bad, ten being fantastic, flowing, exciting, feels great. Take five minutes to quickly rate your life right now.

You lowest score was which area? What if that was your biggest block, and if you cleared that, everything else moved up? You see, Humans are holographic – interconnected – all of these areas affect each other. What if you improved that lowest area whilst reading this book, **once and for all?** What area needs your attention now? How has your perception **changed** of what you thought **was an issue?**

Are you into goal setting? Or have you become so jaded that you just turn up for life everyday and see what it brings you (That takes us right back to Cause & Effect again, doesn't it?) What's the magic formula – "ask and ye shall......?" Well, have you been asking? Probably. And do you have everything in life you want? Probably not.

How come? Ever want something really, really badly and don't get it? There must be part of the formula that you're missing...

There are certain criteria, common denominators that make outcomes achievable.

First and foremost, the Unconscious Mind is very specific – it has a mental age of about 5, so you need to talk to it specifically. That's why when you ask it for more money, and then you walk down the road and come across a 20p piece. There are dozens of goal setting techniques out there. Let's look at a couple that work.

In HGE we use the word outcome. You don't always get a goal – but you always get an outcome. It may not be the outcome you want, but you still generated a result. Learn from it, alter your approach, and keep at it. I firmly believe that if you just keep doing this, you can have anything in life you want. Tony Robbins called it the ultimate success formula. In HGE we call it "Five principles For Success"

1. **Know your outcome.**
2. **Take action. Preferably massive action!**
3. **Have the sensory acuity, the ability to measure whether it's working or not.**
4. **Have the behavioural flexibility to alter your approach if it's not**
5. **Operate from a physiology and psychology of excellence at all times.**

If you go back to that wheel of life exercise that you did earlier (and you did do the exercise, didn't you? If not go back and do it now) ask yourself a question:

What would 10 out of 10 look like in each area? What would your ideal vision for Career, or relationships, be?

Now sometimes people tell me they don't know what they want. If that's the case, get out a sheet of paper and draw 2 columns. On one side write down all the things you don't want, or have got and wish you didn't. List what's not working. Then write on the other side the opposite.

Ok so now we've looked at the best of what you want to see in your future, let's take a look at turning all that theory into practical, tangible results

Begin by asking yourself: "How is it possible that I (they) don't have it now?"

1. **Stated in the positive.**
   What specifically do you want?
2. **Specify present situation.**
   Where are you now?
3. **Specify outcome.**
   What will you see, hear, feel, etc., when you have it?
   - As if it's happening now. Present tense
   - Make it compelling, give it some juice
   - Insert the picture in the future. Where is the future, in front of you? To the left, the right? Somewhere else? [see Time Lines]
4. **Specify evidence procedure.**
   How will you know when you have it?
5. **Is it congruently desirable?**
   What will this outcome get for you or allow you to do?
6. **Is it self-initiated and self-maintained?**
   What's the first step you can take, and what can you do to keep it coming?
7. **Is it appropriately contextualized?**
   Where, when, how, and with whom do you want it?
8. **What resources are needed?**
   What do you have now, and what do you need to get your outcome?
   - Have you ever had or done this before?
   - Do you know anyone who has?
   - Can you act as if you have it?
9. **Is it ecological?**

- For what purpose do you want this?
- What will you gain or lose if you have it?
- What will happen when you get it?
- What won't happen when you get it?
- What will happen if you don't get it?
- What won't happen if you don't get it?

The last four are from Cartesian Logic. They smoke out any last hidden challenges – an objection has to "prove" in all 4 segments to exist. Trust me, it's Quantum Physics – it'd take a whole book to explain that last bit alone. Just ask yourself the questions.

Now by this point if you've worked a goal through the keys to an achievable outcome, you have a well formed goal at both the conscious and unconscious level. However, that's the Mental and Emotional Bodies only. To really make it zing, you can practically guarantee the manifestation of your outcome if you employ the Spiritual and Physical bodies too. Then it's four times as likely to happen! We'll talk about that in the Time Line Therapy chapter.

WHAT IF you started to understand how you do what you do? What if you began to look at the Internal Representations you're making? Who knows ways of doing things that you could model to make your life easier? How could you apply some of these ideas to your work? What would happen if you learned how to motivate people by communicating with their unconscious minds?

From now on, whenever you set an outcome, I'd like to ask you to run it through these questions first. You'll find that it makes it a whole lot more likely to succeed.

I offer a free 30 minute telephone coaching session with anyone who wants it – if you want to take advantage of this offer, and set an achievable outcome over the phone with me, call my offices FREE on 0800 072 5792.

The next step would be to install it in your future Time Line, and just wait for it to show up. It's like ordering a product from the Universal Catalogue – you place your order then forget about it till it arrives out of the blue… To do that, you'll need to read on…

"Focus on what you want to happen"

3

SHY PEOPLE GET LEFT BEHIND, SO HERE'S THE ANSWER

Another of the greatest gifts that HGE has given us is it has denominalised (broken down into a process) that magical state where you "click" or "connect" with a stranger.

Rapport is that state where you like someone; you know them and you trust them. HGE has denominalised that state into a process – that means you are going to learn how to create that state.... with your customers, colleagues and friends, anytime you want, anywhere. Imagine the applications in your career. In your relationships. I once taught this is a Scottish University, and one 18 year old didn't come home for 3 days. He said "That rapport stuff is superb!". Well, that's one use for it. Rapport is kind of like having money in the bank – the more you have, the more freedom and opportunity you have, but when it's not there, you feel unsure uncertain and desperately want some to come your way.

This skill will also give you the ability to shake someone off who wants to get rapport with you, but you have no inclination to get rapport with them. You may have found yourself with an admirer that you could do without. This chapter shows you how to break rapport with someone intentionally, so *they* decide to leave you alone.

In all the great Hypnosis literature going way back, you were told to first build rapport with your client, and then induce trance. Then there would be numerous ways to induce trance. But wait a minute. How do you build rapport? If someone is going to trust you enough to close their eyes and tell you their deepest fears, there had better be a bond of trust between you. Yet nowhere did it tell you how to get that trust – you were magically supposed to know how to do it. But what if, like me, maybe you could have done with some coaching in that area? Everyone has the ability to meet and befriend another human being, and we're all good at it to different degrees, so some of this will feel intuitively right. But what if for some reason your usual methods aren't working?

Which reminds me of a story. One winter I was driving back to Scotland from England, and the weather was getting worse and worse. Then the radio station announced that there were blizzard conditions ahead and the motorway had been closed. "Would all drivers pull off the motorway and seek out accommodation or alternative arrangements." Oh great! So I headed into the last service station and hotel on the road home. As had everyone else that night. There were coaches full of people, trucks, and cars galore, all vying for a place to rest and sleep till the next morning.

So I walked up to the hotel reception and asked the young woman behind the desk if there were any single rooms available? She said "I'm afraid not, what with the bad weather reports and the road being closed. We're full up". Oh oh. Time for rapport…

So I looked at the computer screen she was looking at, I started to breathe at the same rate as her, and I even started blinking at the same time as she was. Then, using my best impersonation of her voice, I asked her "How easy would it be to fit me in? I only need a sofa or something…." She visibly reddened and smiled and said "Let me have another look, seeing as it's you"….

And she rearranged a couple of people and I got a single room for the night, tucked up all warm and snugly as the blizzard raged outside.

Now I was driving all over the country in my job as a Financial Adviser, and in Financial Services the idea was to do a two appointment process with clients. On the first appointment you'd conduct a fact finding interview, to establish the client's financial health, their income, outgoings, savings, investments and their needs. Armed with that, you'd go off and prepare a proposal. Sales people reading this will find this chapter particularly useful.

On the second appointment you would return with a proposal of the best product or service that would meet that particular client's needs based on the information you discussed on the first meeting. And hopefully they would say "yes" and sign up, and I earned a commission. So I started using rapport with my day to day appointments, to see if it would make a difference.

Have you ever had times where you didn't connect? Ever worked with someone and thought "Who is this Martian?" Would it be useful to "click" on command? Think about it - everything you want in life is either owned by someone else, or you're going to need someone else's' help to get it. So you'd better be good at building rapport. If you're a speaker and you want a standing ovation – they'd better like you. Let's learn the secrets of master communicators. Imagine if you could strike up trust with anyone, anywhere..? Who would you use it with? If only you'd known this at 18 you'd be lethal in night clubs....!

Imagine a customer not happy, or distressed, and you need to cool them down. It even works over the phone...

In 1970 at the University of Pennsylvania a professor Robert Birdwhistle was doing a study on Kinesics. He concluded that in any human communication, with yourself or with any other person, there are three parts to the message – the words you use (the blah blah blah, what you say), the tonality in which you say the words (how you say it), and the way you look or stand or gesture as you say them. Now that may seem obvious to you, but what made this study so amazing was the relative proportion each made up in the overall message. One major credit card company used this information in a commercial campaign recently.

7% of any human communication is the words we use. That's the least important. Think about that for a minute.

38% is how we say it, the speed, volume, sarcastic, happy, etc

55% though, more than half, is the way we're moving, breathing, gesturing, standing as we say what we say. Imagine that! Words speak pages, but tonality and physiology speak volumes!

Now when you speak you may think about what you say before you say it. But do you ever say to yourself "I think I'll use sarcastic tonality" or "This sentence will come out with motivation and passion"? Probably not. Now tell me, do you ever decide in advance how you'll stand, or the posture you'll adopt as you deliver the next sentence? Highly unlikely!

Which means the physiology and tonality "just happen", which means 93% of human communication happens unconsciously! We interact with each other unconsciously all of the time. And that's face to face.

On the phone you can't see their physiology (until we all get Dick Tracey Video phone watches) so you're immediately down to 45%. That's why you can describe something inside out and the other person isn't getting it, so one of you says "Tell you what, let me come and **see you**". They need the other 55%.

Email and text messaging is the worst! You're down to 7%. That's why they invented CAPITAL LETTERS FOR SHOUTING or Emoticons and Smiley's to convey messages ☺.

So let's turn all of those facts and figures into something handy and easy to use. Let's use Physiology, Tone and Words in that order, so we can communicate at 100%.

And know that there are four Rapport Indicators – four direct pieces of feedback that you can detect that tell you whether you're in rapport or not. That makes it really fun!

You see this all the time. Guys in the pub chatting away, then they all drink simultaneously, then resume chatting again, then drink simultaneously, then a pretty girl walks by and they all look simultaneously…. Or a couple sitting at a table in a restaurant. If they're both sitting in the same position, they're getting on great. If they are sitting in completely different ways, you can tell they're not. The further apart their bodies are, the further apart their hearts.

So how would you usually build rapport with someone? Conversation? Talk to them? Eye contact. Smile? And what are you hoping you'll get by talking to them? *Something in common.*

Commonality is the key to rapport. People like people like them. Words are smallest tool in your toolkit, so I'm suggesting you use 55% Physiology to become like them before you even open your mouth. And you do that through process that you've probably heard of, called "Matching & Mirroring". This is where you sit, stand, move and resemble the other person as closely as possible.

THINGS WE CAN MATCH & MIRROR:

POSTURE

Tilt your head to the same angle as the other person, either left or right, forward or back. Look at the spine and shoulders and sit or stand the same way as they are. Are the shoulders back, or hunched forward? Standing straight or is the spine arched? Is one shoulder higher than the other? Also the legs and arms. Are the legs crossed, which puts one hip up and then the spine bends? Arms folded? You get the idea. Make your body the same as theirs.

ALIGNMENT

People often sit facing each other, like a Mexican stand off. It's confrontational; and interrogational. Ideally you'd be at 90 degrees to each other, or even better side by side, so you're facing the same direction, and are "on the same side", as illustrated below. Aim for between 45 and 90 degrees.

Gestures

Some people have peculiar gestures, or wave their hands, or draw spirals or squares in mid air. Or maybe they stab the desk with their finger, or point. Lots of people talk with their hands. You can borrow their gestures, and draw the same shapes or use the same mannerisms. But do this sparingly, and do it only when you're talking!

Proximity

Some people like touching you as they talk to you, leaning into your personal space and enjoying that closeness. Maybe that's you. However, some people hate that and like to keep their distance. In the words of the poet W. H. Auden:

"Some thirty inches from my nose the frontier of my person goes,
And all the untilled air between is private pagus or demesne.
Stranger, unless with bedroom eyes I beckon you to fraternize,
Beware of rudely crossing it: I have no gun but I can spit"

The way to get it right is to pay attention to how close people get to you before they stop, when you first meet them. Note that "safety zone" and then keep that distance between you. Only touch them if they touched you first. Especially in an age of litigation, and even more so if it's a member of the opposite sex.

FACIAL EXPRESSION

I have a friend who screws up his face in a grimace at the end of every sentence >grimace< and he does it all the time >grimace<. It wasn't till I learned these skills that I noticed, and now I do the same thing with him >grimace<. Boom! >grimace< Deeper rapport >grimace<. Seriously, people use crooked eyebrows, tongue in cheek, bite their lips, all sorts of little habits and looks. You can borrow those.

BLINKING

There's a connection between blink rate and how fast your brain is ticking over. You blink faster when under pressure than when you're relaxed. There's also a link between the "chunk size" of a thought and the time between blinks. No, really! When you are thinking about vague, abstract thoughts, you blink less often than when you're dealing with details and specifics. So if you blink when the other person does, you're going "into sync" with them, and processing your thoughts at the same speed as they are, which deepens the rapport. Besides they're going to blink anyway, and no one is going to stop you and say "Hey! You're blinking at the same time as me!"

BREATHING

Has a rate & a location, and this is one of the most powerful things to match. You can be breathing high in the chest, somewhere in the middle, or deep down in the stomach and you can see the chest or stomach rise and fall as you do. The shoulders also rise and fall too. So breathe from the same location as they do. Now if you're a male, and you're trying to match a woman's breathing, be careful where you look! Watch her shoulders! No, really! Or even better, use peripheral vision (see later) and see her whole frame, registering the breathing pattern. Here's another clue – when they're talking, they're breathing out, so as they talk, you breathe out, and breathe in when they do. This gets rapport very powerfully and rather quickly, because of the phenomenon Itzhak Bentov called rhythm entrainment. You've probably heard that when you set up a number of pendulum clocks on a wall, all with a different swing, shortly thereafter the pendulum will synchronise and all swing in the same way at the same speed. Or a group of women get together and find that their menstrual cycles are going into synch.

Breathing also has a rate, so they may be breathing quickly, slowly or somewhere in between. Again, the rate at which they speak is a clue. Match this too.

EXERCISE 1

To try this out in real life, go and have a conversation with someone, preferably someone you haven't met before, you just mirror & match some or all of the things I've outlined above, and watch what happens.

Now you might think that someone will spot you, as you "mimic" them, and that's been an accusation levelled at this approach for years. If they do, you're doing it badly. So here's how to do it elegantly. In our Western culture when it's our turn to talk, we're allowed to move. When we're listening we were taught to sit still and pay attention. So here's how to do this and never get called on it:

Start off nothing like them physiologically, sitting or standing completely unlike them, and then when it's your turn to talk, put one of the rapport steps into place, so maybe breathe as they breathe, or blink as they blink. Then, stay still as they talk till you take over, then put another step into place, maybe fold your arms like them or cross your legs. Gradually, within about 4 or 5 sentences, you'll be in rapport, and they won't know that you're doing anything.

EXERCISE 2

Have a conversation with someone you know, but throughout it I'd like you to mismatch them – that is, sit the opposite way from them, breathe irregularly, if they're blinking you don't! Do different physiology from them and feel how uncomfortable that feels. For both of you! Then switch to mirroring and matching them again and feel the difference. Now you'll know how it feels to be out of rapport.

EXERCISE 3

Have a conversation with someone you know, and while you do you mismatch their words, but match their body. In other words, disagree verbally but agree nonverbally. This creates the feeling of elegant disagreement – useful in negotiation, sales, parenting, etc. You can still have differing opinions, but maintain the connection and responsiveness between you.

Now you've got the 55% working for you, lets look at Tonality.

38% Tonality

Have you ever noticed that when people go and stay in a foreign country, they pick up the local accent and start to sound like them? A great Scottish example is the singer Sheena Easton – she has a very unique Glasgow meets Las Vegas twang!

We're going to look at Voice Matching.

There are 4 qualities to the human voice:

Tone –pitch (high pitched like Mickey Mouse or deep and booming like Darth Vader)

Tempo – speed (talking really quickly cos they're thinking in pictures, or real slowly and kinaesthetically)

Timbre – quality (is it crisp and clear, or gravely and raspy?)

Volume- loudness (quiet like a mouse or resounding like a drill sergeant?)

EXERCISE 4

This is best done over the phone where the other person can't see you. More importantly you can't see them, so you can't mirror and match their physiology – you have to really listen and train up the tonality on its own. Listen to how the other person is speaking, and go through the four qualities one at a time, slowly altering your voice to match theirs. Within about four sentences you'll be in rapport.

THE 4 INDICATORS OF RAPPORT

There are four very tangible, measurable pieces of feedback that tell you how well the rapport is going. That's exciting, because it's not just theory – you will get very visible and rapid signals that help you gauge how well you're doing.

1. The first signal is a feeling in you. People describe this in different ways, and it's different for everybody, but it's usually felt between the throat and the navel, down the centre of the body. It's a tingle, or a wave, or a flutter, or a rush or a clunk somewhere in the chest or stomach, which feels like you've "clicked" or are really hitting it off. You know the feeling – you've had it before when you clicked with someone, or felt like you'd known them for years. That tells you you're going into rapport with the person

2. There's a colour change, a flush or a blush, first in you, and then very quickly in the other person. There will be rosy cheeks everywhere! You'll feel a warmth in your face and sure enough you'll see the other person's face deepen in colour as you both go into sync. No really!

3. The other person says something that comments on your level of connection. "Have we met before? You seem familiar somehow" or "Are you a Capricorn?" or "You remind me of my friend's brother" or "I really feel like I can talk to you",

or something like that. When they comment on how well you're getting on, you know you've got great rapport.

4. The deepest rapport signal of all is called Leading. That's when you go to cross your legs, and they follow. Or you lean back in your chair and they do likewise. You're now leading them and now you know the level of connection is at it's deepest. You see this in best friends at the bar, standing the same way. Or couples who've been together a while, moving together. Get to this stage and you've made the connection. Now use it wisely, and treat them with care and respect.

At this point I have to express my opinion about something. People frequently accuse this technique as manipulation, or seduction, and I feel quite strongly about that. The critics clearly haven't studied this process. If you truly have rapport, what that means is that your unconscious mind has a two way connection with their unconscious mind. So if you have any ulterior motive, or suspect intention, they will sense it. Besides, if you offend someone at this level, they will never talk to you ever again. Remember, knowing these powerful subliminal techniques protects you from the shady characters who might use them for their own motives.

So if you're in business and you're having to deal with an irate customer or their objections – increase rapport! Mirror and match them, but use non-confrontational language. Move like them, sound like them, and they'll like you. They'll get that you know they're angry or frustrated, and they'll hear you doing your best. If you're speaking, teaching or presenting and you're heckled, build more rapport. They'll like and respect you more and they won't know why.

In any group of people there will be one Rapport leader at the unconscious level. You can actually watch, and this is fascinating, when any group gets together there will be one leader in the pack, and when they move, so do the others. So if you're speaking to a group, you can look out for them. Notice when one scratches their head, and then several others will do the same. It's bizarre, but true! Or one folds their arms and then so do six others. The one who moved first is the rapport leader. They move and you see ripples going out around them. This is especially useful if you want to get rapport with the group – just get into rapport with that person, and you'll get a whole bunch into the bargain. Buy one get six free!

When I teach this is my live seminars, people often ask me "Won't they notice? Won't they think I'm taking the Mickey?" There's a really elegant way to do this, as I described before. In western culture while we're talking we can move, but while we're listening we're supposed to sit still and listen. You can use this as you're excuse to shift position. While the other person is talking, you sit still, probably unlike them in physiology, sitting or standing in a different posture from them. But when it's your turn to talk, shift one aspect of your physiology – your spine, or your legs, or your head. Only change when it's your turn to talk With each sentence add one more match into the equation. By the fourth or fifth sentence you'll be just like them, and they'll never spot you! The aim of the game is to do this without being noticed, so be elegant.

If you want to hear how this is done in a live setting with real people, you might want to visit www.jonathanclark.org/products and look at the "FUNdamentals of HGE" home study packs. These are live recordings from seminars which include full training on the Rapport techniques in this chapter.

Matching voice Tone is best practiced on the phone as I've said before. If there is any side effect to these state of the art methods, its that it turns you into a genuinely interested listener.

Where could you use this? Is there anyone in particular that you need to get more rapport with? Just imagine being able to strike up a bond of connection with anyone, anywhere? How useful is that? Perhaps there's a member of the family that you've fallen out with, and you'd both be better off burying the hatchet. Or maybe a new boss who's still getting to know their team.

Remember if they're talking, they're breathing out! So you breathe out with them. I also recommend you use Pacing and Leading – meet them where they are then take them to where you want them to go. So if you're best friend is upset, meet them there and then lead them into a more calm and positive state.

You can also utilise other people's rapport – a phenomenon called "Rapport Transference". If you're the third speaker in a row, or you take over from another teacher or leader, use their postures, words, and props. Assuming they already have a good rapport with the audience, then you can "borrow" it and capitalise on their gain. That way you don't have to work so hard. Of course, if they've blown it, avoid doing anything similar to them, and start from scratch.

Before I learned Rapport skills, as a Financial Adviser I did about 3000 miles a month running all over the country doing these two step appointments. After learning rapport, my appointments halved and my sales increased, which made my performance figures look great! And I spent a lot less time hurtling around the world in a Vauxhall Vectra! Again, anything that makes life easier I think is worth learning.

So there I was at the service station, the morning after the blizzard had shut the motorway. In fact, the next morning I had to borrow some hot water to unfreeze my car door lock, and again the girl behind reception used the same expression "Seeing as it's you". Now I'd never met her before, but we definitely had rapport.

Now you know what all the great hypnosis texts talked about – how to create that bond of connection and knowing between you and anyone else. You can have more people like you more often. Now you have the 93% working for you, it's time to get the other 7%. This leads us into the world of Representational Systems, and how different people view the world….

"There's no such thing as resistance – there's simply a lack of rapport"

4

COME TO YOUR SENSES

HGE is all about working with perception and perceptual states, and that's what this chapter is all about – PERception. We live in a world of PREception – the world of rules, legislation and law. Government, councils, and associations very rarely reduce the number of laws. The ancient civilisations favoured CONcepts, and valued idealism, philosophy and creativity. Evolution and personal growth doesn't really have any rules (although it does follow a pattern as you'll learn about in a later chapter) and philosophy itself can often lose it's foothold in the real world. If you wish to make a change in someone's thinking, feeling or behaviour, one liners and clever philosophy rarely does it. Knowledge will cover a lot of ground, but it won't cultivate any of it. It is PERceptual shifts that need to occur. Change your perception and your world changes.

Your nervous system favours one or more of your five senses over the others, and that determines how you first receive external information – how you make sense of your world. Remember the HGE communication model earlier. Words are important – in fact, verbal language is the most useful way to communicate information. Until you open your mouth, I'll learn very little about your values, beliefs, memories, etc. But once you start talking…. Zig Ziglar once said "you can never rise above your words".

Imagine a couple living together. She's a very visual person, and he's very touchy feely, or kinesthetic. She comes home from a social event, dressed to the nines and looking immaculate. He comes into the house from working in the garden, wearing old trousers and muddy shoes, and skulks towards her saying "Come here and give me a cuddle". She stops him in mid flow with her hands up saying "Stop pawing me! What am I, a hunk of meat? Get yourself changed, look at you, all sweaty and dirty!. Look at you, you're a mess!" But he's not for stopping, and he keeps on coming.... "Let's just snuggle down on the sofa and canoodle for a while...." She's now backing away. "Canoodle? Look at you, you're a slob. Why don't you ever take me out, buy me something, get dressed up!? I'm sick of snuggling on the sofa every weekend!"

Does this sound familiar?

Or maybe an Auditory wife and a visual husband. One day she turns round to him and says "Do you know what? You don't tell me you love me anymore." He's shocked! "What? Love you? Of course I love you – look at that rock on your finger! Look at the house we live in! That tells you. I LOVE YOU!" Of course, that shouting tonality probably doesn't do it...

Does this sound familiar?

If you want to deepen the rapport and increase understanding between yourself and others, this is something you need to know about. You can meet everyone at their model of the world and be understood, avoiding miscommunication and getting your message across first time. It will expand and develop your ability to communicate, and if you're in business, increase your sales over the phone.

About 40% of the general population favour their Visual sense as their preferred way of perceiving the world. People who are visual often stand or sit with their heads and/or bodies erect, with their eyes looking up. They typically breathe from the top of their lungs, so may be breathless. They often sit forward in their chair and tend to be organized, neat, well-groomed and orderly. They memorize by seeing pictures, and are less distracted by noise. Good visual memory makes remembering easier, and they rarely get lost. They often have trouble remembering verbal instructions because their minds tend to wander. A visual person will be interested in how your program LOOKS. Appearances are important to them. They are often thin and wiry, spend hours in front of the mirror, and will usually look immaculate. Designer clothes, sun tan, tattoos, shiny cars and gorgeous houses.

Roughly 10% of people are highly Auditory, favouring the sense of hearing. People who are auditory will move their eyes sideways (remember Bill Clinton?). They breathe from the middle of their chest, because that gives them more air to talk with. They typically talk to themselves, and are easily distracted by noise, so much so that they love peace and quiet to concentrate. Some even move their lips when they talk to themselves, sub vocalising. They can repeat things back to you easily, they learn by listening, and usually like music and talking on the phone. They memorize by steps, procedures, and sequences (sequentially). The auditory person likes to be TOLD how they're doing, and responds well to a certain tone of voice or set of words. They will be interested in what you have to say. They cock their head like a dog does, to listen to you, and often use silly voices or sound effects in their speech. May have trouble making decisions because of all the internal chatter. Switch off their car stereo so they can park their car!

Approximately 40% of the population are more touchy feely. People who are kinesthetic will typically be breathing from the bottom of their lungs, so you'll see their stomach go in and out when they breathe. They often move and talk verrry slooowly, and usually with a deeper voice. The spaces between sentences give them time to check in with their feelings. They respond to physical rewards, and touching, and will touch you as often as they can while talking with you. If they can't reach you, they'll touch themselves, preening, fidgeting, playing with their collar or holding an object closely like a security blanket. This is the person who shakes your hand, and holds your elbow too to make it extra sincere. They also stand closer to people than a visual person. They memorize by doing or walking through something, getting their hands into it. They will be interested in your program if it "feels right". They like comfortable furniture, baggy clothes and food.

That leaves about 10% who are what in HGE we call "Auditory Digital", or Cerebral. The Auditory Digital person will spend a fair amount of time talking to themselves, and have a well developed vocabulary using polysyllabic words to save time. They will want to know if your program "makes sense". The Cerebral person can exhibit characteristics of the other major representational systems. Think accountants, IT people and bank managers. Time management, filing systems, civil servants. People who use those sticky label guns to type their name onto their stapler. Very good in a crisis though. These people think in terms of words, logic, sequence, and labels, so tend not to demonstrate much expression or emotion. Think Mr Spock in "Star Trek". They put emotions to one side and deal with what's efficient and practical.

Now I've included a small quiz later in this chapter which will help you elicit your preferred sense. If you want further copies of this quiz, which you can give to friends, colleagues and family to complete, simply go to www.jonathanclark.org/products and you'll find it under "free downloads"

Each of these four categories perceive the world differently, and they will give it away in several ways, including the words they use. We call these "Predicates", key words that tell you and let you see clearly which sense they prefer. It's these Predicates that make up the 7% Words in the 100% communication.

If you think about it, Top 20 hit singles have to have all four catered for. Music by nature is Auditory, but if you want it to really sell, you need to appeal to the Visual and Kinesthetic people in the audience too. Listen to music lyrics and you'll see this being used to bring music to life. Grab a CD right now and take a look at the lyric sheet that's usually inside.

Presentations would ideally use all four. Ideally you would use PowerPoint slides, flip charts and overhead projectors for the visuals. Music, discussion and sound effects help the auditory people. Exercises, a nice environment and handouts satisfy the Kinesthetics, and thick course manuals please the Digital students. You can always tell the digital students because they take the course manual home and read it. A good training course will use all four systems, because that then meets all of the learning styles in the room, and it makes it much more interesting for the trainer too!

You can gauge which Modality, which sense they prefer from posture, eyes, predicates and breathing. You could match that too, by using the appropriate words

EXERCISE

Write a short paragraph about an event that happened to you recently. Just write a short account of what occurred, then look back and analyse the predicates you use yourself.

Then rewrite it purely in visual predicates.

Then in auditory, then in kinesthetic, then in Cerebral.

Notice how that changes your interpretation of the event.

PREDICATES

VISUAL	AUDITORY	KINES	CEREBRAL
see	hear	feel	sense
look	listen	touch	experience
view	sound(s)	grasp	understand
appear	make music	get hold of	think
show	harmonize	slip through	learn
dawn	tune in/out	catch	process
reveal	be all ears	tap	decide
envision	rings a bell	make	motivate
illuminate	silence	throw	consider
imagine	be heard	turn	change
clear	resonate	hard	perceive
foggy	deaf	unfeeling	insensitive
focused	mellifluous	concrete	distinct
hazy	dissonance	scrape	conceive
crystal	question	get a handle	know
picture	unhearing	solid	

LIST OF PREDICATE PHRASES

VISUAL	AUDITORY	KINESTHETIC
An eyeful	Afterthought	All washed up
Appears to me	Blabbermouth	Boils down to
Beyond a shadow of a doubt	Clear as a bell	Chip away at
Bird's eye view	Clearly expressed	Come to grips
Catch a glimpse of	Call on	Control yourself
Clear cut	Describe	Cool/calm/collected
Dim view	Earful	Firm
Flashed on	Give an account of	Get a handle on
Get a perspective on	Give me your ear	Get a load of

99

Get a scope on	Grant an audience	Get in touch
Hazy Idea	Heard voices	Get the drift of
Horse of a different colour	Hidden message	Get your goat
In light of	Hold your tongue	Hand in hand
In person	Idle talk	Hang in there
In view of	Inquire into	Heated argument
Looks like	Keynote speaker	Hold it!
Make a scene	Loud and clear	Hold on!
Mental image	Manner of speaking	Hothead
Mental picture	Pay attention to	Keep your shirt
Mind's eye	Power of speech	Know-how
Naked eye	Purrs like a kitten	Lay it out
Paint a picture	State your purpose	Pain-in the neck
See to it	Tattle-tale	Pull strings
Short sighted	To tell the truth	Sharp as a tack
Showing off	Tongue-tied	Slipped up
Sight for sore eyes	Tuned in/tuned out	Smooth operator
Staring off into space	Unheard of	So-so
Take a peek	Utterly	Scratch built
Tunnel vision	Voiced an opinion	Stiff upper lip
Under your nose	Well informed	Stuffed shirt
Up front	Within hearing	Too much hassle
Well defined	Word for word	Topsy-turvy

PERCEPTION QUESTIONNAIRE

For each of the following statements, please place a number next to every phrase. Use the following system to indicate your preferences:

4 = closest to describing me

3 = next best description

2 = not really like me

1 = least likely description of me

1. **I make important decisions based on:**

    ____gut level feelings

    ____which way sounds the best

    ____what looks the best to me

    ____precise review and study of the issues

2. **During an argument, I am most likely to be influenced by:**

    ____the other person's tone of voice

    ____whether or not I can see the other person's point of view

    ____the logic of the other person's argument

    ____whether or not I am in touch with the other person's true feelings

3. **I most easily communicate what is going on with me by:**

    ____the way I dress and look

    ____the feelings I share

    ____the words I choose

    ____my tone of voice

4. **It is easiest for me to:**

    ____find the ideal volume and tuning on a stereo

    ____select the most intellectually relevant point in an interesting subject

    ____pick the most comfortable furniture

    ____select rich, attractive colour combinations

5. **I can describe myself by stating:**

    ____I am very attuned to the sounds of my surroundings

_____I am very adept at making sense of new facts and data

_____I am very sensitive to the way clothes feel on my body

_____I have a strong response to colours and to the way a room looks

6. **When you wake up in the morning, what you notice most is:**

    _____the sound of the alarm clock

    _____the light through your curtains

    _____the sensation of warmth under the bed covers

    _____the voice in your head and what it says

7. **When you go walking on a beach:**

    _____you notice the noise of the waves and the cries of the seagulls

    _____you feel the wind in your face and the sand under your feet

    _____you admire the view and the colour of the sea

    _____you can think clearly or enjoy the peace and quiet in your head

8. **When you take a bus, a plane or a train:**

    _____you look at the people around you

    _____you find that its too hot or cold

    _____ you listen to the conversations around you

    _____you're thinking about when you'll get there and how long it'll take

9. **At a restaurant, besides the quality of the food, you notice:**

    _____the background music

    _____the décor and layout of the room

    _____the comfortable chairs and nice atmosphere

    _____the prices and the selection on the menu

10. **When you shop at a supermarket, apart from having to wait in the queue at the checkout, what bothers you is:**

    _____the smooth talking sales rep trying to sell you something _____you cannot see your favourite brand in its usual place

_____the lack of help or customer service

_____trying to remember the list of what you need to buy

11. **When you sit in an old church, you notice:**

_____the temperature and the hard benches

_____the semi-darkness and the stained glass

_____the silence

_____the questions and dialogue going on in your head

12. **When it rains in the summer and you're in the countryside:**

_____you feel nice and dry in your shower-proof coat

_____you look around for a rainbow

_____you listen to the rain falling through the trees

_____you question the logic of going out in it

13. **You choose to buy a particular sweater because:**

_____It fits well and its soft to the touch

_____It suits you and looks good in the mirror

_____it's the one that someone tells you that you look good in

_____It's the right size and the right price

14. **Your neighbours return from holiday and you notice:**

_____that the kids look tanned and healthy

_____that's the end of the peace and quiet – the noisy brats are back!

_____you feel secure knowing that their house is now occupied

_____you're calculating dates and how long they were away for

15. **While buying petrol at a self-service garage:**

_____you watch the numbers carefully on the pump gauge

_____you hear the noise of the pump and the sloshing of the fuel

_____you have to keep squeezing the trigger without spilling any

_____you're thinking about how much to put in and the cost

16. **You are the passenger on a road trip and:**

_____you admire the view and the landscape flashing by

_____you put music on or search for a radio channel you like

_____you relax and enjoy being driven by someone else

_____you dwell on the thoughts in your mind

17. **You're taking a warm bath and:**

_____you lie back and enjoy the warm caress of the water

_____you enjoy the peace and quiet, or listen to soft music

_____you daydream with eyes closed or staring into space

_____you wonder how much time you've got

18. **When you think back to your decision to read this book:**

_____you liked the sound of what I said

_____you read about my work and then you decided

_____you were looking for someone to show you the way forward

_____you felt good about getting in touch with it

PERCEPTION QUESTIONNAIRE PART 2

Copy the scores from the previous pages to here. So if you answered question one with 1,2,3,4 then write those numbers in the boxes below:

Question	1	2	3	4	5	6	7	8	9
	K	A	V	A	A	A	A	V	A
	A	V	K	C	C	V	K	K	V
	V	C	C	K	K	K	V	A	K
	C	K	A	V	V	C	C	C	C
Question	10	11	12	13	14	15	16	17	18
	A	K	K	K	V	V	V	K	A
	V	V	V	V	A	A	A	A	C
	K	A	A	A	K	K	K	V	V
	C	C	C	C	C	C	C	C	K

Add the numbers associated with each letter:

	VISUAL	AUDITORY	KINES-THETIC	CEREBRAL
1.				
2.				
3.				
4.				
5.				
6.				
7.				
8.				
9.				
10.				
11.				
12.				
13.				

14.				
15.				
16.				
17.				
18.				
TOTALS				

The total scores will give the relative preference for each of the 4 major rep systems.

Another major way of telling which system people prefer, is to observe their Eye Patterns. You can tell what someone is doing in their head by watching their eyes. Sometimes crystal ball gazing is not crystal ball gazing!

Where your eyes move controls which part of your brain you access. Ask someone a question, and to retrieve the answer their eyes move, as if searching through the data bank for the answer. Well, that's exactly what they're doing.

You'll be able to tell what someone's thinking…

When you talk to people and you ask them questions, people's eyes move. Now, you've probably seen that before, but you didn't necessarily know what it *meant*? It's been studied that when someone accesses different parts of their brain their eyes move in different ways, and by watching what people's eyes are doing on the outside we can actually tell what they're doing *on the inside*. You can tell if they're making pictures in their head, or talking to themselves, or feeling feelings and you can almost mind read them. Now, this has lots of useful applications, you can use this in all sorts of contexts.

You can tell if someone's lying to you or not – you can become a "living lie detector", just by watching their eyes. Watch the film "The Negotiator" with Samuel L. Jackson and Kevin Spacey, because he actually ties someone up in the film and asks him questions, then reads his eyes. You can even help someone who's supposedly learning disabled, by helping them access the parts of their brain that are best for spelling, useful for remembering things. So, you can even help people improve their memory, or even your own, don't forget! Now that's got lots of uses, and that may be an area you'd like to specialise in.

As you look at the person's face, there are 6 major "zones" people tend to access.

EYE PATTERN CHART

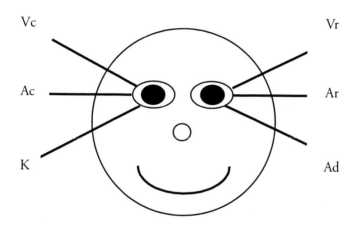

V^c – Visual Constructed. Making up pictures in the mind's eye.
V^r – Visual Remembered. Remembering images of things they've seen
A^c – Auditory Constructed. Making up sounds in the head.
A^r – Auditory Remembered. Remembering sounds they've heard
K – Kinesthetic (Feelings). Emotions and sensations.
A_d – Auditory Digital (Self-talk). Repeating your question to themselves, telling the time, internal dialogue.

If you're a teacher or presenter you can look at audience members and know which modality they're in at that moment. Listen to the predicates in their questions.

I recommend you train up your lowest score by using those Predicates more often, and start thinking the way a large chunk of the population does.

Use the modality appropriate to the chunk you're teaching. If you're teaching Massage for instance, you'd probably want to teach it kinaesthetically. Yet your students will have different preferred representational systems, so as I said earlier it's best to cover all four. Use videos, handouts, discussions, practical hands on exercises, web forums, etc. That way everybody will "get it".

After a while you'll be able to look at people and know which modality they're in. Listen to the predicates in their questions, and use the modality appropriate to the person.

To increase the communication between myself and each of these types, I would mirror their preferred method of representing their world in my own breathing, speech, language and eye patterns.

With visuals I would talk faster, and raise my voice tonality higher. I would move faster, being more expressive and using frequent gestures. I'd also make sure I looked my best, my car or office was clean, and make lots of eye contact with them. Showing them visual aides or laptop presentations would also deepen the rapport. Complimenting them on their apparel or grooming might also be a good idea. Naturally, I wouldn't want to make a spectacle of myself so I'd paint word pictures to expose any fuzzy thinking.

With auditory people I would match their breathing pace and voice tone, so I sounded more like them. I'd try and make the environment quiet and peaceful with a minimum of distractions, and turn my mobile phone off. Lots of verbal feedback for them would reassure them and put them at ease. To harmonise with them I'd compose a well tuned message that they could resonate with.

Kinesthetic people need careful handling. I'd have to slow down and talk softly and gently, really focussing on my emotions as well as theirs. Sincere handshake or a pat on the back if appropriate would deepen the connection. Be prepared to give them time to get into their feelings and emotions, and keep a box of tissues nearby if necessary. I'd also make sure they were comfortable in their surroundings, possibly in a soft settee or easy chairs. We'd grab the chance to get in touch with some smashing opportunities to connect.

Cerebrals will expect an agenda and will expect there to be some decisions made. To communicate effectively with them I'd need to speak fluently and know my terminology. Feeling would be kept to a minimum while procedures and order would rule the day. To expedite an efficient interaction we'd rationalise our communication linguistically.

A lot of couple counselling involves translating. So you tell the kinesthetic husband that when he looks at his visual wife in that way, it feels to her like climbing into a bed full of broken biscuits! THEN he gets it. Now he's talking in her language. And he'll also need to learn to talk quickly and visually...

And if you want someone to leave you alone and you don't want their attention, mismatch them. Become the opposite of them. If they're breathing, you stop! If they blink, you don't. If the fold their arms and cross their legs, you recline and spread out. That way, their unconscious mind will realise that there's no commonality, and they'll decide that they're getting nowhere. Very elegant. Better that than you having to tell them to "beat it!"

Alright, so now you understand what people are doing on the inside by observing and picking up on external clues, let's amplify your awareness by a factor of ten...

"Awareness is Progression"

5

HOW TO THINK LIKE ARISTOTLE & OTHER GENIUSES

This is quite probably the single most important chapter in this entire book. It's all about a simple model which explains how any notion can be thought of in a range, from really specific, to really abstract. You'll see in a moment why that's so important. But first I feel its time for a story.

Do you know what it's like when you've been on a long training course, away from home? So you're going back to a hotel room every night., and you've taken on all these new learning's, and now you just want to loosen up, take it easy, maybe even have some fun....yes?

So on a course in London, I'd been talking with the other course attendees and we all discussed our plans for the evening. Nothing sounded that interesting, and quite frankly I wasn't that sure I wanted to chat with anyone after dinner anyway. I was all talked out, do you know what I mean?

So I scanned the paper to see what movies were showing that night on the movie channel, and I was really glad I looked it up, because my favourite movie of all time was on! "Star Wars"! The first one, which is Episode 4, but lets not get picky. Just about everyone's seen it – it was the big picture in the late seventies. Luke Skywalker, young guy with blond hair dressed all in white, and Darth Vader, older guy dressed in black who breathed funny. Then there's Obi Wan Kenobi, his Jedi Master Trainer, who taught him to "trust your feelings". Trust the force – some vague abstract notion about a mysterious power. I mean, Obi Wan can just speak funny, and people just go into a trance!

So Luke's on a very intense training schedule to accelerate his powers. Up until now he's just zoomed around in his Landspeeder (that's like a car with no wheels – it just hovers up above the ground), chasing Womp Rats – really small animals. We see him learning to use the tool of the Jedi Knight, the Light sabre, against this little tiny robot covered in sensors, which he skilfully evades even with his eyes covered by a crash helmet. "Trust your feelings Luke".

Later he's up against the Empire – a huge and powerful army who have a weapon the size of a planet! So one minute he's up against a tiny sphere, the next he's up against one the size of a planet! The Death Star! But it had a weak spot, remember? He had to fly his X-Wing (which is a different classification from a Landspeeder) and shoot this tiny vent. In a huge battle to take on an army with a planet sized weapon, he has to hit one specific tiny part!

Which reminds me of what Tad James was saying during the course about rain in Hawaii. When it rains in Hawaii it's thought to be a blessing. So that night I went back to my hotel, and as I put my foot on the first step up, I looked down and noticed a small puddle on the carpet. And there's a drip of water coming down from above me, on the ceiling.

Now my room is two levels up, so I thought I'd better get up there and see what I find up there. So I go up one level. The stairs had those big old steps, so I'm practically bounding up them, but as long as I take them one at a time, it's pretty easy. Now I can see water running down the wall... I'm thinking, "What am I going to find up there?"

Now luckily enough I wasn't the root cause of the leak – but I'm thinking "Did I leave the shower running this morning?" But I wasn't the root cause – it must have been higher than that. But even on my level, below the cause of the problem, there are repercussions cos the water has shorted the power in my room, so now I have no power, and no light.

Then I remembered what Tad had said about falling rain being a blessing. So now I've got three blessed metaphors to come up for the next day of the course as part of my homework, and I'm wondering "How am I going to shed any light on the subject? How can I get my result up here?"

You see I was staying in Piccadilly Circus, and when I got there I thought "So where's the big top? Where are all the chattering monkeys? The proud, nimble horses?". I mean, I'm not from London, so how am I to know?

But I have seen clowns before – on my 21st birthday I decided to hire a coach and I took a bunch of my friends to the circus. And that's the first time I got really close up to the mighty elephant. I love elephants, and you know what they say about elephants don't you? That's right. And do you know what elephants love to eat? Peanuts!

I think it's really funny that big powerful beasts love such tiny little peanuts. But you see, that's what they use to train elephants. They work really hard, then get rewarded with peanuts. Can you relate to that? Work hard, get peanuts?

And they keep the elephant in the circus. To train it properly they have to start when it's very small, and they keep it in the circus, so the elephant doesn't have the full range of movement, the freedom of movement that they deserve. And even as they grow up now with all that training (and lots of peanuts!), they still keep the young elephants in the circus, so they still don't yet have the full range of movement, or the freedom that they deserve….

WHAT IS HIERARCHY OF IDEAS, AND WHY LEARN IT?

It's a simple model that explains how any concept can be languaged in a range, a spectrum if you will, from really high up abstract, down to highly specific detail. This is a global chunk of information which, if you can get your head around it, makes all of the other concepts in this book far easier to use. This clever little idea will increase your flexibility of thinking and allow you a helicopter view of what's going on at any given moment.

Like to become a master communicator? Ever met a "flaky airhead" who fantasises and bounces around with vague notions, and you wonder "Will they ever get to the point?". Or do you know any nitpicking, detail lover who gets bogged down in specifics and you think "Just give me the gist". Do you want to know the secret to communicating with everyone?

Ever seen a fluffy airhead trying to negotiate with a detailed nitpicker? Now I know no one in your world ever disagrees, but what if they did? How would you like to be able to get agreement between any two parties at any time? Would that be useful?

Oh I know – ever been discussing something with someone, and you think to yourself "They've got a hidden agenda"? You get a hunch that they're not telling you the truth, or their true intentions? Just suppose you could become like a living lie detector, and uncover their hidden agenda. Does that sound useful? In your business? In your personal life?

Intuition – do you trust your hunches? Do you trust your unconscious mind….yet? How would you like to be more intuitive?

Ever wondered why the simplest ideas are the most profound? We're going to discover why that is…

Managing states – do you ever get overwhelmed? Or work beside someone who does? Or maybe you'd like to know how to manage a team better while you're in meetings or brainstorming?

Lateral thinking – ever been in a working party, or a creative project, or you're struggling to come up with new ideas for a marketing campaign? Could you be more creative? You'll find out how in this chapter.

There's a direct relationship between Power & Value – in that abstraction controls specificity! How's that for an abstract concept! In other words, the more abstract ideas you can handle, the more influence and power you have, and the more you'll earn. Ever have a boss who does half the work effort you put in, but gets paid twice as much? Why is that? You're about to find out.

Personally I think this is the single most useful model in all of HGE. All in favour or learning this say "Aye!"

SOME HISTORY

The Greek Philosopher Aristotle in 300 BC said that mankind can think of thoughts and ideas on many different levels, or strata, and that we all have a floor and ceiling to our capacity for rational thought. In his book "Megabrain" in 1986 Michael Hutchinson quoted research that says "People who can handle abstract ideas age more slowly". In other words, chunking up keeps you young (with apologies to Carl).

Take a look at the next page where you'll see the entire model. This is how it was taught to me by Tad James. Let's break it down into bite size chunks. How do you eat an elephant? One bite at a time.

Language has a range, a spectrum, from really abstract and high chunk at the top of the page, to really detailed and specific at the bottom.

HIERARCHY OF IDEAS

"What is this an Example of?"

"For What Purpose...?"

"What is your intention...?"

⇧

K-Type
INDUCTION
CHUNKING UP
AGREEMENT

<u>In Trance</u>
INTUITOR

BIG PICTURE
ABSTRACT—MILTON MODEL

THE STRUCTURE OF OVERWHELM: TOO BIG CHUNKS

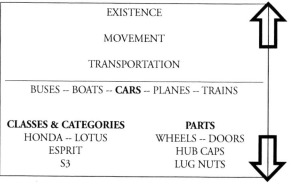

EXISTENCE

MOVEMENT

TRANSPORTATION

BUSES -- BOATS -- **CARS** -- PLANES -- TRAINS

CLASSES & CATEGORIES	PARTS
HONDA -- LOTUS	WHEELS -- DOORS
ESPRIT	HUB CAPS
S3	LUG NUTS

THE STRUCTURE OF NIT-PICKING: CHUNKING
DOWN AND MISMATCHING
SPECIFIC — META MODEL

DETAILS
SENSOR

<u>OUT OF TRANCE</u>

DISTINCTIONS
CHUNKING DOWN
⇩ DEDUCTION
C Type

"What are examples of this?"

"What specifically...?"

   • any Meta Model Question

[Used with permission © Tad James & The Time Line Therapy Association]

The top of the page is where big picture concepts float around, where people think big and conceptualise. In the Myers Briggs personality profile instrument that would be the Intuitor (the person who likes head in the clouds, inspiration, theories and concepts). This is where artfully vague, hypnotic language works best, putting people into trance.

The bottom of the page is where all the nit picky specifics are to be found. The smaller you chunk, the less number of items will be in that group. In the Myers Briggs that would be the Sensor (the person who likes realistic, actual facts, down to earth specifics). This is where the Meta Model questioning tool works best, bringing people out of trance.

If you look in the middle of the page you'll see the word "CARS". Picture the scene – you're a Kwik-Fit fitter, and you know what they say about a Kwik Fit fitter don't you? That's right. So the customer drives in and says "There's something wrong with my car". Is that enough for the fitter, or would they need to ask some questions? Most likely he'll "chunk down" and go into specifics, by asking either "What kind of car do you have?" or "What's wrong with it sir?" So he could go into Classes and categories of car, or parts of the car, do you see? Either way, he's going down into detail, which is how most people think. This is called deduction, or chunking down. "Well, it's a Lotus" says the customer. And that's the end of that conversation, because they don't work with Lotus cars! So going the other way, "Well, it's something to do with the wheels" says the customer. Is that enough? Not yet, so the fitter patiently asks "What about the wheels sir?". He replies "Well, something near the hub cap I think". Still not there yet. "What about the hub cap sir?" he says, patience wearing thin. "Well, three of the four lug nuts are missing" which, if you know anything about cars, is not a good thing!

Now just suppose we go the other way, and chunk up. This is called Inductve thinking and is far less common. In fact, imagine the same scenario - the customer drives in and says "There's something wrong with my car". And the fitter asks "Car? For what purpose sir?" Err….. That's a whole different story! And this direction really stretches your brain! "Well, it's my main method of transportation" says the customer. "And what's transportation an example of?" asks the philosophical fitter. "Why, movement" says the customer. "Movement, what's that an example of sir?". This is turning into a heavy conversation. "Movement is an example of existence…" says the client, rapidly going into trance. Now I ask you, what's existence an example of……..?

Above the line that says Buses -- Boats -- **Cars** -- Planes – Trains there is a line. Anytime you cross that line you're into the world on what Linguists call "Nominalisations". A Nominalisations is a verb that's been frozen into a noun. A process word like "communicating" that's been turned into a thing like "communication". You'll never see a communication, you'll never hold one, because they don't exist. You only ever see people communicating. Values are usually nominalisations, and they're important in hypnosis as well, as you'll read about in the Hypnosis chapter.

So in summary, chunk down into nit picking detail, and you'll get more distinctions and find lots of Cerebral people, or chunk up into big ideas, sometimes overwhelm, where you'll always get agreement and where highly Kinesthetic people tend to live.

POWER & VALUE

Here's the real power behind this model. Abstraction controls specificity. In other words, the ambiguous includes the specifics. For example, the word "car" includes all the parts of the car, and all classes and categories of car. That one word presupposes all the others, does that make sense? The purpose of any part of a system is to serve the greater whole of that system. To illustrate further:

Imagine for a moment you are the manager of your company's

car fleet. How much would you be paid? About £20,000 per annum possibly? Then you are promoted (congratulations!) to the manager of transport. Now would you be paid more, or less? Probably more, maybe £30,000. But imagine being promoted to become the manager.....of *movement*! How much would you earn now? Of course, now your sights are on the next position – the manager of *existence*!! OOoooh!

Or how about the Armed Forces? In the Army a private cleans his or her rifle, polishes his or her shoes and makes his or her bed. A Sergeant manages a squad of Privates. The Lieutenant has Sergeants below him who run things. The General controls the entire Army, logistics, strategy, deployment. How many shoes does he or she polish? And who earns more – the Private or the General?

In Sales the salesperson makes all the cold calls, makes appointments, sees clients and handles lots of paper. Their Manager maybe makes a few calls and sees a few clients, and oversees a team of salespeople. The Sales Director will make few client calls if at all, and manages the Managers. How many cold calls does the CEO of the company make? And who earns more – the salesperson or the CEO?

Here's the deal – the more you do, the less you earn. And the less you do the more you earn. Consultants earn way more than the people who implement their recommendations. That's why you see people working less that you do, and making more money. As you increase the abstraction of your ideas, their value increases. Don't try to be busier – delegate the details. But keep your feet on the ground. Philosophers often earn very little, even nothing, cos they're so chunked up but their feet aren't in touch with the earth! You need the full range. So have your head in the clouds by all means, and your feet on the ground! Think strategic, not tactical. Think big picture, not specifics. As a general rule, chunk up two levels. Ask yourself "What is this an example of? And what's that an example of?" That will give you a broader (and thus more powerful and insightful) perspective.

SO HOW DO I CHUNK UP AND CHUNK DOWN?

You simply use questions. Questions are the answer. The questions for chunking up are on the top left corner of the page, and not surprisingly the questions for chunking down are in the bottom left corner. Use any, all or a combination of the questions, depending on the direction you want to go in.

So for instance you're reading a chapter of a book. What's that an example of? Learning? For what purpose? Self-improvement perhaps? (Forgive me, as you're not here I have to mind read your answers). And what's your intention in improving yourself? Balance maybe. Wow. So your highest intention in reading this book could well be balance. Now balance is a nominalisation – the process of balancing oneself. But balance is the highest intention in this example, does that make sense?

Alternatively, one could chunk down into specifics. So you're reading a chapter of a book. What are examples of this? Well, the Hypnosis chapter for example. What specific kind of Hypnosis? Well, I've written about Ericksonian and Elman hypnosis in that chapter. Which Ericksonian hypnosis specifically? Well, his language patterns and two of his indirect inductions specifically.

Let's talk about applications of this then:

• In negotiation, if you chunk up high enough, you'll always get agreement. By the very nature of how language is structured, if you chunk two opposing sides up high enough, they'll agree on the same nominalisation. For example:

Workers on strike demanding better pay, directors refusing to increase wages due to already low profit margin.

Striking workers want better pay

For what purpose?

More money to spend

What's their intention?

Better quality of life

What's quality of life an example of?

Happiness.

Directors want to keep profit margins intact.

What's their intention?

Successful business.

For what purpose?

Financial security and freedom

What's Financial security and freedom an example of?

Pleasurable life

For what purpose?

Happiness!

Good, so we're all agreed that we all want the same thing ultimately? The trick is now to chunk back down again, maintaining agreement on both sides. To that end you might use a conditional close such as "OK, so if you get happiness then however we do it is OK?"

- Intuition – chunk up at least two levels to see the big picture of what's going on. That will allow you to make connections and see relationships that you previously couldn't see.

- Overwhelm – Usually a symptom of chunking up too far, or having too many things to do at once. "My life's a mess!". Well, probably only parts of it, not all of it. So chunk down by using the appropriate questions. "What specifically in your life is a mess?". This is why the advice is often to make a list. Most people can handle 7 plus or minus 2 things at a time. Overwhelm is usually 10-15. How do you eat an elephant?

- Creativity – Lateral thinking was the phrase coined by Edward de Bono, but he never gave me a strategy that I felt entirely comfortable using. So here's one. To think laterally, or outside the box, chunk up two levels, ask "What's another example of this?" and then chunk back down 2 levels. Or here's another, suggested by a genius inventor friend of mine, which he called "The Idea Factory". Chunk up 2 levels, then across one, then up two more, and keep going!

Foe example, a door company want to run a new advertising campaign, and they've exhausted their bank of ideas. So doors – what's a door an example of? An entrance. What's an entrance an example of? An opening. What's **another** example of an opening? A vacancy. What kind of vacancy specifically? Hotel vacancy. What's an example of a hotel vacancy? The bridal suite of the Brighton Grand Hotel. There we are – a new advertising campaign about the only doors good enough to be fitted in such a plush establishment. I can see a whole series of sketches....

- Rapport – when matching someone's words, notice what chunk size they tend to use. Are they talking about lug nuts or existence? Chunk yourself up or down to their level, then either chunk them up or down to meet yours. Pace them first then lead.

EXERCISE

Here's a fun game – you'll need a six sided dice for this one, and the Hierarchy of ideas page. Think of a problem situation that has baffled you so far, and you haven't fixed it yet. You're going to ask yourself questions, or have someone else ask you. You must answer the question out loud. The question you ask depends on the roll of the dice:

1-2 Ask any chunking up question

3-4 Ask a lateral question "What's another example of that?"

5-6 Ask any chunking question

Ready go!

So how was that exercise? What did you learn? Did you find a solution to the problem? Have you made any new connections in your head? Doesn't it feel different now? You probably found that you have a floor and a ceiling of "chunk size" that's comfortable for you, and it felt hard to go beyond that level didn't it? Good – expand your flexibility of thinking.

How much fun could you have with this? Can you see yourself using this in business? Next time there's a negotiation going on as two parties disagree, you could chunk them both up and take the heat out of the situation. Imagine being on a sales call knowing you can always get agreement.

Or leap logical levels laughingly. You probably noticed you have a preferred style or chunk size, so what would happen if you learned to think how the other half think?

If you earn more for doing less, what will you stop doing? Who could do it for you? Delegate the detail. Where else could you be more strategic and less tactical?

If you chunk up on a negative state, you come out of that state. Think about it. Anger for what purpose? To tell you someone has broken one of your rules. What's a rule an example of? A self-imposed guideline. What's your intention for having self imposed guidelines? To make life easier. What would that give you? Peace. Hmmm… And if you chunk down on a positive state, you heighten and amplify it. Think about it – "Fun" for example. What's an example of fun? Sex. What kind of sex specifically? Slow, attentive sex….. >ahem< We'll stop there.

Just suppose you could uncover someone's hidden agenda just by asking two or three questions. Who can you think of who's not being totally up front with you?

Imagine bringing the flaky airhead down into specifics, or took the nit picker up into a broader perspective? Would that be of any use to you?

You might like to think of five applications in your life for this model, either in your professional or personal life. Ask yourself "For what purpose would I experiment with this?"

So it was my 21st birthday and we're all at the circus. And I've gone in to talk to the one you talk to…inside….the big top, the ring….er….master, and I asked him about training the elephants. And he told me that as the elephant grows up now with all of these learning's, they let them roam free and at last they get the full range of freedom and movement that they deserve. And you know what they say about elephants…

Four candles. Four red candles specifically, bought from the supermarket down the road from my hotel. So there I am, up there…. in my room doing my homework for the course by candlelight. And I'm thinking "one day I'll probably use this story, about Tad saying water coming down is a blessing in Hawaii…"

So let's return to the Jedi. (Good title for a film that). Luke's training is finally complete. He's put all of his intensive training together, and he can now sense the power he has access to. He's learned to "trust your feelings" as his teacher had shown him, and now he can make his X-Wing float higher than his Landspeeder, both different types of vehicles, with the power of his mind. And I'll leave that story with the words of Luke's buddy Han Solo, when he gave the brash youngster a piece of his sagely advice:

"Watch your mouth kid, or you'll find yourself floating home….."

"What's this an example of?"

6

BECOME AN EXPERT IN COMMUNICATION & PSYCHOLOGY

"If you're finding that this is not easy, then you're in exactly the right place to begin understanding it now, aren't you?"

In the modern world it's rare for people to share what really counts with other people- the vulnerable, fragile and intense revelations that they yearn to disclose to each other. At the same time most of us are pretty poor listeners. We maybe hear, but we're not really *listening*. Every communication with another human being can be a chance to explore and develop that person's own rich model of the world, or to rip down and shred their sense of identity. We have been taught weak communication skills by good hearted, well-intentioned parents and teachers who had equally weak training.

So let's begin to change that, shall we?

Consider the following sentences. In fact, read each one aloud, putting all the emphasis on the bold, underlined word, and listen to what you hear:

I didn't say you stole all the money

I *didn't* say you stole all the money

I didn't **say** you stole all the money
I didn't say **you** stole all the money
I didn't say you **stole** all the money
I didn't say you stole **all** the money
I didn't say you stole all **the** money
I didn't say you stole all the **money**

Eight very different meanings, aren't there? Depending on where the emphasis goes.

Here's a second, curious effect:

"If a statement is followed by a question, if the question is answered, the statement won't be questioned"

So if I said "This book is the most useful book you'll ever read. Have you bought this or borrowed it?", then whether you own this copy or whether you've got it on loan, you still accepted the first statement. It just slips right in. Now where could you use that? Are there any applications for that in sales? Education? Coaching?

That sentence structure works every time. Can you see how it works?

So let's talk about language. As one credit card advert that's being shown on TV currently says, only 7% of the message is words. Words are the way you get your "stuff" out. What I'd like you to begin doing now is to re-think how you communicate, and learn the language behind the language...

Whatever you say creates representations in the listener's head. We are going to look at how you can affect the internal representation the other person makes. How can you be sure what they get is what you gave them? After all, one of the Presuppositions of HGE says, "The meaning of communication is the response you get"

So if you want to check their response, use what I call Second Position - float into their head as they listen to you, and see how that communication is being received inside their head. What is the receiver doing in their head to make sense out of what you're saying?

You see, you cannot not affect their internal representations.

So how do you affect it on purpose? How can you use Presuppositions to structure the other person's internal representations? We're going to learn how you structure your language to get your outcome/ create change, and structure the order and sequence of internal representations that the other person makes in their head.

What we're talking about here is the **structure** of language. Presuppositions are the linguistic equivalent of assumptions. In other words, what do they have to assume (what is presupposed) to make sense out of your utterance? I'm going to give you some examples, and give you a step-by-step model of how to use them.

FIRST OF ALL, A STORY

Jonathan Clark is the developer of HGE. He runs workshops and trainings. Now we don't know if you ever will attend one of his events, but we do think that you should. Because if you do, that will make you an even better HGE Practitioner. That means that you would be more competent, and confident. Now I don't know if you've realised this yet, but I have been using Presuppositions in every line of this paragraph, haven't we? Yet you may start to go back to the beginning and read this anew, or you might just wait till you get to the end, and then go back. Now what's presupposed by that sentence? So, as you've read this far, you must have had a reason for reading this. Maybe you have a different reason for reading this, which once satisfied will make you want to read it again. And since that's the case, let's quickly move into how to use this chapter. It's not too big a chapter, or maybe it is for you. We think the former is true...

WHAT ARE PRESUPPOSITIONS?

Presuppositions are ideas, assumptions or beliefs that are presupposed, i.e. taken for granted and acted upon, or assumed to make the communication make sense. NLP author L. Michael Hall describes them as *"Silent assumptions, unspoken paradigms"*

Bandler & Grinder, the creators of NLP said *"Presuppositions are particularly insidious as they are not presented openly for consideration"*. Richard Bandler and another NLP author Eric Robbie have ranked Presuppositions above Distortions, Generalisations and Deletions in terms of Logical Levels. In other words, Presuppositions drive the rest. The higher levels organise the lower levels. Make a change at the Presuppositions level and everything else below will shift!

Presuppose means "suppose first". Suppose (from Latin) means "to put under". So Presuppositions act as the supporting structure of a given statement, and within them they hold that person's beliefs about their map of reality. They don't appear in the surface structure, they are direct "pillars" coming up from the deep structure of the unconscious.

WHY LEARN THIS?

1. You will notice what is inherent in the speech of the person you're talking to
2. You can elicit their model of the world, because their Presuppositions give you a lot of information about the structure of their map – "how reality is for that person". Remember that the map is not the territory, but it is real to them.
3. Use them to structure their Internal Representations (I/R's)
4. Identify the basic assumptions that impoverish their model of the world and expose the limitations they create.
5. Learning their language and speak to them using the same structure. If you want to be a real powerful linguist, and make change in the order and sequence of their I/R's, this is one of the most powerful ways

"Don't sit in the chair unless you're ready to go into a trance" is a useful use of Presuppositions in therapy. The client will likely go into trance just by sitting in a chair that they have presupposed has that effect on you. You've also told them that they're ready.

Imagine making change unconsciously by simply giving the client Presuppositions to consider...

WHAT ARE THEY?

We're going to use the ten most common Presuppositions, although in the book "Patterns & Techniques of Milton Erickson MD Volume 1" Bandler & Grinder listed over thirty. In my opinion, these ten are the most useful, and are enough to be going on with.

EXISTENCE

All sentences have this

Any time you use Nouns, names, Pronouns (him, they), quantifiers (some, all, every, each, some)

"John sees some squirrels in the trees"

(Existence of John, squirrels and trees)

Now if I said, "There are some squirrels in the trees" you could say 'Yes there are', or 'No there aren't'. Yet if I say, "John knows about the squirrels in the trees" it displaces resistance about the squirrels, and puts your attention on John. You're so busy looking at John, you happily accepted the presence of a tree with squirrels in it. Do you see?

"You see and hear presuppositions in every sentence"

POSSIBILITY

Modal Operators of possibility/necessity/impossibility, etc

e.g. can, can't, must, ought to, may, have to, will, should

These tell you if the client thinks they are at choice or not

"John ought to climb the trees with the squirrels"

"You can learn how to do this"

CAUSE & EFFECT

X causes Y

There's a time lag between the cause and the effect

Linear, in sequence

One of the most powerful presuppositions, and one of the most useful.

Every therapeutic intervention is a Cause & Effect violation

E.g. makes, if…. then, because, since, whilst, as you…then you, just that causes, allows

"It was the brilliant flash of lightning that caused John to realise there are some squirrels in the trees"

"John's inquisitive nature made him realise that there are some squirrels in the trees"

"Since you're reading this page then presuppositions are easy"

COMPLEX EQUIVALENCE

Meaning, this means that

Is, means, equals

Happening at the same time concurrently, simultaneous

Equating two things to mean the same thing

Present tense

"John was high all the time and that meant he wanted to climb the trees like a squirrel"

"John knew the squirrels in the trees meant that he had to climb them"

"The fact that you're reading this means you're getting it"

AWARENESS

Verbs of awareness/perception

e.g. saw, realise, heard, felt, aware of, notice, know, understand

"John realised there are some squirrels in the trees"

"Notice how simple it is"

Time

All verbs have a tense – past, present or future

Client comes in and says, "I have a problem." Watch what happens if you reply with "What *was* the problem?" That handles a lot. Especially if the client accepts the presupposition at the unconscious level, and replies "Well, the problem was…"

Time Presuppositions are very powerful

e.g. have, had, am having, will have

Yet, stop, now, just, eventually, soon, after, before, during, since, while, still, anymore, end

"John eventually realised there were some squirrels in the trees" implies that there was a time when he didn't.

"Eventually you'll structure your sentences on purpose"

Adverb/Adjective

Modify a noun or a verb, adding more information

Adverbs such as easily, quickly, smoothly

Adjectives such as fast, big, easy, new, big, small

"John didn't realise how easy it was to climb the trees like a squirrel"

"You'll quickly find how much fun you can have with language"

Exclusive Or

"or"

Black or white, never both

Mutually exclusive

"Either John climbs the trees or the squirrels will"

"Do you want to read the next page or not?"

Inclusive Or

"or"

e.g. Double Binds such as "do X or Y"

Could be both

"Will John climb the trees today or tomorrow?"

"Would you like to finish this chapter or write your own examples?"

ORDINAL

Implies a list or an order of things

Finally, first, last, next, original, former, latter, another, again

"The second thing John realised was that there are some squirrels in the trees"

"This last presupposition is the easiest"

HOW DO I USE PRESUPPOSITIONS?

Decide what you want to impart to someone as presupposed, unquestioned, then embed that within one of these sentence structures. So for example, if you sell sofas and you want clients to accept that they're the best quality sofas, you could embed that within an Awareness presupposition and ask:

"When did you become aware of our best quality sofas?"

The answer will be about when, and the best quality bit slides right in.

Look for or listen to the Linguistic Markers – the words listed above that give it away. Ask yourself "What presuppositions lie in this?" Notice where the greatest emphasis, or inflection, is in the sentence – that's the dominant Presupposition waving to you! So if someone says "He **never** listens to me", with the emphasis on *never*, that's the energy trapped behind the Time Presupposition.

Also remember, however you structure the Presupposition, whether it's a negative or not, you still have to accept the presupposition i.e. John just realised that ...

John hasn't realised yet that...

Still works!

So don't think about Elvis Presley....

Now what are you thinking about?

Elvis Presley!

They work covertly, unconsciously and indirectly as we have to accept them to process what we read/heard

You can use this growing awareness to bring their assumptions to the surface.

OH, AND PRACTICE, PRACTICE, PRACTICE...

NLP author Robert Dilts once suggested the following sentence structures to practice forming presuppositions that will benefit the client or listener:

Do you want to _____ now or a little later?

There is no need to _____ too quickly.

After you have finished _____, you will realise how easy it is to _____.

Since you _____-, you may as well start _____.

How to use this chapter:

- Challenge any presupposition by asking, "What leads you to believe that…?"

I recently had a saleswoman show up on my front door step, representing a charity that supports Ethiopian refugees. Her opening sales pitch was "I'm sure you'll agree that we should be doing something to help them". That's a great time to use this challenge.

- You can use the Meta Model to challenge any of the presuppositions

- Presuppose what you do not want questioned

- Stack Presuppositions on top of each other, using several in the one sentence. Richard Bandler once said that if you stack enough

of them, no one can crawl out from underneath
- Go back to the story at the start and identify all the Presuppositions inherent in that one paragraph

WHAT IF YOU MASTERED THIS?

What if you began to think in new ways? Here's your homework – come up with five applications for Presuppositions in your career or personal life.

You'll quickly identify with one or two of these, because they're the ones you use yourself!

Read their words, or listen to their sentences. Imagine translating your intended message into their Presuppositions...

Practice with one at a time – get used to eliciting it, recognising the linguistic markers (sentence structures) that go with it.

You could elicit some Presuppositions from someone you know, and then write out the linguistic markers that go with them. Then try them out on that person and generate a result. Get feedback and learn from it.

Tony Robbins once said "The quality of your life, is the quality of your communication". If a person has even the slightest pang for improvement, and hopes that things can and will get better, then they can learn to alter their approach to communication. The desire to connect with others, to bond and share with people who care about you and to feel a sense of oneness and intimacy, is a basic human need. To feel like a valid human being, that you count, that you are needed and that you are important in your own right, is another. One of the quickest and most effective ways to meet those needs is to learn to become a better communicator.

To feel like a valid part of the community, to feel wanted and desired by your partner, to feel respected and admired by your peers, to feel close and fulfilled in a relationship, these can all be achieved through changing your communication methods. Job success, earning ability, health, family stability – all of these areas of life are directly linked to the effectiveness of your people skills.

If you keep doing what you've been doing, you'll keep getting what you've been getting. If you want a different result, you have to change your tack.

Another old adage – the only constant is change. We live in an ever-changing world. The way you listen and converse now is probably dramatically different to your style ten years ago. Hopefully you're older, wiser and more effective.

How does one change? First, realise that your ability to interact with others is a learned set of skills, and you can always learn new ones, if you so wish

Modeling effective speakers, conversationalists, leaders and motivators provides the body language, vocabulary and technique that you can emulate. Becoming first aware of your own patterns of conversation is a great step forward. Exploring alternative ways of doing things comes next. Through trial and error, you'll find ways that work. As long as there is a willingness to learn and improve, change is possible.

AND SO BACK TO

So now that you've read this chapter, all of the ideas and concepts in it are now in your head. You may not remember all of them at first, yet some will seem to just hang around in your head more than the others. Therefore, to really enhance your mastery of this subject, we would recommend that you should reread this chapter again after 24 hours. To fully reactivate all the learning's in there, you ought to review this material again after a week has passed. That really makes it stick, and if you only did that, then that would allow you to fully recall all of the ten language patterns listed here. That means that you've really got it at the unconscious level, even if you haven't noticed that ....yet.

This brings us almost to the end of this chapter. I had a positive intention (naturally) in writing this chapter, and I will be happy to receive any feedback you have on it. Soon I'll be publishing some more books, so keep your eyes and ears peeled. Eventually I'll have released a full set for every part of an HGE Practitioner course, as study aids and training handouts. Since that's the case, I suggest you check out my website regularly, just to see what's new, at www.jonathanclark. org . It's a fast way, an easy way to stay up to date, or else you might miss something, and you wouldn't want to do that ever again!

RECOMMENDED READING

Patterns of the Hypnotic Techniques of Milton Erickson MD Vol 1 (1975) Bandler & Grinder
The Secrets of Magic (1998) L. Michael Hall
The Spirit of NLP (1996) L. Michael Hall

"You cannot not affect their internal representations."

WHEN YOU'VE LOST YOUR DIRECTION, IT ONLY TAKES 15 MINUTES TO FIND IT AGAIN!

Let's put this into some kind of context. This is the secret to being motivated all of the time. This is about your internal compass, which will determine to what degree you feel satisfied & fulfilled. This chapter reveals to you the ultimate key to understanding your behaviour and that of others.

That reminds me of a story. My first girlfriend was daft as a brush. She was fun loving, extravert, bubbly, lively, loud and flirty. That probably explains what attracted me to her in the first place. Me, I was older, more serious, and more introverted (nothing much has changed then). She was everything I wasn't and we complemented each other perfectly, but after a while I got serious and wanted a steady stable relationship that I could rely on. She'd disappear for hours and show up late at night off the cuff, and that used to frustrate me. This was just as I was getting interested in personal development. She valued fun and freedom. So did I, but they were a lot lower down my list of priorities…

Which makes me think of a client that I met a few years ago in my clinic. There was a knock on the door and a stunning young woman walked in, wearing very little! She must have been in her early 20's, tall, with very long legs and an incredible figure, concealed in two items of clothing that resembled two bandages. I thought it was a practical joke, and my friends had set me up with a pretend client, because this woman proceeded to tell me that she was a Lap Dancer and had been referred to me by another one of my clients. A lap dancer? Unbelievable! So I looked out into reception, fully expecting to see my mates chuckling outside, but no, this was a genuine case.

It got worse, as she explained what her problem was. She was "amusing herself by abusing herself" as she put it, and her doctor had advised she got some help to stop. Now I'm really thinking this is a set up. "How so?" I asked. She was using a whisk and putting it in places where you don't whisk, if you get my meaning. I get all the boring cases, don't I? A whisk!? And not the hand driven model, oh no, we're talking about electrical goods here.

Now at the time I was sharing a flat with my best mate, and he had a wild girlfriend who used to exhibit extreme behaviours, running away from home, getting into fights. Brian was like my blood brother, he and I were so on the same wavelength, but she was a challenge. For both of us. He eventually married her. Then one day she convinced him to do a runner, and I was left with rent bills to pay. While I'd been at work they'd been burning the electricity, using the phone, and I ended up with hundreds of pounds of debt. But as he'd been my best friend, I approached my landlord and took full responsibility for it – I promised that I would foot the bill and make good on the outstanding rent, because it was my integrity and my ethics to do so.

SO WHY WOULD YOU WANT TO LEARN ABOUT VALUES?

You'll learn what you've been working so hard to achieve all your life. Is that reason enough?

The most common problem in therapy & coaching I've ever met in the last fourteen years is lack of direction. At some point you wonder why you're working so hard, where is it all leading? Am I doing the right thing? "What's it all about Alfie?" Maybe your kids have flown the nest, maybe you've just split up from your partner, maybe just lost a loved one, maybe just been made redundant. At some point in your life, and not only once, you'll find yourself asking these questions. Haven't you?

Would you like to tap into your source of power and determination?

Would you like to understand how to motivate anyone?

Like to be more decisive? Not sure?

Would you like to be able to always make the right decision for you, forever more?

Ever interviewed or recruited someone who is qualified, but it didn't work out? Imagine if you could get people who are wired to do the job, not just qualified...

In relationships your job is to meet your partner's needs, but how can you hit a target you can't see? What if there was a way to pull those needs out? What about your needs?

Ever tried to get from A to B, but ended up at Z instead? You're about to learn why...

Ever achieved a goal and still weren't satisfied? Ever wonder why not?

Sometimes wonder if you're in the right career?

Maybe you are in employee relations and you need to motivate staff. How do you currently do that? And is it working?

The one biggest reason why you need to know this stuff – the only way to have long-term happiness is to live by your values. But you can't if you don't know what they are!

SO WHAT ARE VALUES, AND WHAT WOULD YOU DO WITH THEM ANYWAY?

Your Values are the positive & negative emotional states that your nervous system pursues or avoids. They are your compulsions & revulsions, they are your strongest feelings about what is right or wrong for you, they dictate how you spend your time & they judge all your actions - in short they govern your entire lifestyle.

To use a computer analogy you can install any program you want, but it is your values that will override everything you put in. They are the ultimate guide to understanding, predicting, & assessing your behaviour.

Some people are good at making decisions, while others struggle to do so easily. What if there was an easy way to make decisions for yourself that were always right for you? What if you already had this built in Compass which has guided all of your decisions in the past, & will always do so in the future ? Wouldn't it make sense to use the software that came factory fitted, so to speak?

Most of your values have been programmed in at random from the environment, your parents, the media, society, & your heroes. Your values about money will differ from your values about relationships, although some core values will come up time & again, as they are part of your identity. Are you beginning to understand how important it is that you discover your own values ?

The problem is that these are unconscious - you don't know why you do such things, you just know you have to. Not only that, some values are more important than others, & every time you make a decision what actually happens is that the hierarchy of values is filtering your choices, & ultimately your actions will be determined by them. If you find yourself regretting a decision, is it simply because you went against your internal compass. Any internal conflict inside yourself comes from your values - you may have a fantastic job, but if your life goes against your values, you will be unhappy & unfulfilled.

Alternatively, a person living on the breadline but living in accordance with their values will feel satisfied inside. So let's find out what your values are!

EXERCISE

Firstly choose one area of your life, such as Relationships or Career or Money. You then ask yourself "What's most important to me about

____? Another question is "What does ____ do for me?" or "For what purpose?" Ideally you want one-word answers such as support, fun, satisfaction, excitement, health. Go ahead and do that now.

Once you have a list of no less than eight values, you then want to rank them in order of priority, No. 1 being the most important & No. 8 the least important. You will probably have to push yourself to come up with eight, but often they come in waves - the first few are easy, but the rest are more difficult, & you have to dig deep to get them. This is a good sign & the harder it is the more important it is. Sometimes the order of priority is difficult, in which case compare two against each other & ask yourself "If I could have x or y , which would I have ?" Run through the entire list until you have a hierarchy. This isn't always easy but the more effort you put in, the more accurate will be the results.

This is one of the most important exercises you can do - to understand what has been driving your life & how you have been making all your decisions all this time. If you need help with this exercise, I offer a free 30 minute coaching session on the phone – give me a call on 0800 072 5792 and we can go over it together.

Now to double check the accuracy & validity of this list pick an area of life in this context that you happy with ask yourself "How many of these eight values does this currently satisfy?" You should find that if something is going well, it meets most of the values. The reverse is also true - pick a context that is troubling you, & ask yourself "How many of these values does this violate?" This will dramatically illustrates the relevance & validity of the values list either way

So what have you learned? Is this list accurate? If not, run through the entire process again until it feels right. Most people are surprised to see their core values on paper. However, becoming consciously aware of them you will learn to understand why you do what you do. Also once you know what they are, you can take steps to ensure that you experience these values on a daily basis, & when you do that life becomes more Technicolour as opposed to black & white.

Values are especially important in relationships because it is the satisfaction or violation of them that will sustain or end the partnership.

People give away their values all the time in their language, & having done this exercise you will be more aware of them in conversation. Chances are people are giving strong clues about what motivates them in everyday speech.

The things that matter most are indications of our values so it is critical that your analysis is as accurate as possible. Do you spend time with people who share your core values? Any argument with another person comes about when a value is violated. Many people achieve all of their goals, have all the material things they always wanted & yet are miserable - because their values are still largely unsatisfied.

VALUES ARE FORMED…during what psychologists call "Imprint periods":

- From age 0-7 you are a sponge, modelling your parents, you have no filters, purely unconscious, totally open to suggestion.
- Between age 8-14 you model your friends, relatives, your friends' parents, and your heroes (celebrities, movie stars, bands)
- From 15-21 you put all those previous years of experiences into some semblance of order, at the same time learning about social life, sexual relationships, and trying to be an individual, rebellious teenager who's significant in your own right.
- Ages 21-35 can be argued to install your Business Persona, in that whatever happens during this period will leave lasting impressions and affect your career and business life forever more.

Does any of this feel accurate to you? Probably…

WHERE VALUES COME FROM

SOURCES, AND POSSIBLE EVENTUAL RESULTS

"Life Shocks" – fully associated, significant emotional events.

Family – weight issues, your macho/passive behaviour, these tend to stem from family upbringing and modelling your parents. If you met them = reward, if you disobeyed = punished. So very often your motivation towards what you want or away from what you don't want comes from here.

Religion – feelings of guilt, sex issues, skill with money, life purpose

School – attitude to learning, teachers, Reward, achievements

Geography – your location, government type and policy, culture

Economics – money habits, financial climate, attitude to scarcity and excess

Media – music lyrics, MTV, advertising, immediacy, attention span, internet, text messaging

Friends – who you're hanging out with, habits, smoking, drinking, drugs

You can probably see some connections between who you are now and some of these influences on your life. Now think about the following statement:

"You don't want a drill, you want a hole in the wall"

You don't want money, you want what money gets you – freedom, security, status, fun, whatever. You don't want a relationship, you want what it gets you – security, companionship, trust, significance, whatever. Values are Context specific words – so elicit them in a context. Elicit someone's career values, or their relationship values.

They're all important, but they are organised into a hierarchy, with the most important sought first. If a value isn't satisfied, it moves up the list. The values at the top of the list are really important to you, or they're not currently being met. The ones at the bottom are being met, or just aren't that important.

Once you elicit someone's values you can use them in your language and you'll motivate people. Remember to write down their words, not yours.

Most problems are value conflicts. Most upset between two people are over their values.

Decision making – your unconscious goes down the list ticking or crossing them off. So if you want to be more decisive, know your values and always try and satisfy the highest ranking one first. Remember the questions to elicit values are:

"What's important to you about...?"

"What does that do for you?"

"For what purpose?"

They are usually Abstract nominalisations – one or two semantically packed words, yet very vague in their meaning, e.g. security, freedom, fun, peace, etc. Remember that you'll get a first batch, then they hit a wall, then comes the second wave. Push for the second wave – they're more unconscious.

Want to make more money? The value that money gets you has to be in top four.

If you're not healthy – was "health" even on your list?

You'll hear them in people's language and now you can use them.

Look back on old goals, or failed relationships and see what was missing.

What if you only set goals that were in alignment with your values? What would life be like if you felt these values every day? Wonder what your partner's values are?

Do companies have values?

My values as I write this book – Fun, freedom, hope, impact, excellence, profit, mastery...

How much more energy would you have if these were satisfied?

Imagine a couple where his number one value is Adventure vs. her number one Security. He'd be a self employed entrepreneur who lives in a self-built house and goes off in his sports car to remote locations to paraglide and abseil. She'd be at home making Friday's usual dish, just back from her long standing civil servant job, wondering where he was, and why they don't have a fixed rate mortgage. Does this sound familiar?

How could you use an employee's values in your work? How easy would this be to add to your current recruitment processes?

Remember: Values are the compass to steer you to your ultimate destination: if we violate them we feel conflict, resistance & nagging doubt. When we live life in accordance with our values we feel rewarded & satisfied. Values determine what you wear, who you get on with, who you clash with, how you raise your kids, what you do for a living. They're what we move towards or away from - our compulsions & revulsions. Think of them as Highly valued criteria – what's most important to you.

A value will always be a semantically packed word – emotive. It will represent Pain or pleasure to you. They're what we're willing to spend our resources (time, energy, money) on, and yet they are largely unconscious. Values also tend to be very abstract and thus are very powerful (See Hierarchy of Ideas to learn why). They are deep level emotional states you want to feel again or avoid, and they determine how you spend your time. They provide the positive feelings in motivation – the fuel. They tell you whether something is right for you to do, the purpose for achieving a goal, the reason why.

So you might remember the story of my flatmate and his wife who suddenly disappeared from my flat? I saw his wife with someone else a few years later, so I can only suppose what happened between them. One day we'll meet. Perhaps he'll read this book and understand what my values were in that time of our history (Loyalty & honesty)

And the lap dancer worked with me for an hour. We discovered that fun was number one and health was number eleven. So we moved health up to number two. Within two months she had quit her job at the lap dancing club, and is now a Fitness Instructor for Fitness First, and a very popular fitness instructor at that!

My first love meant fun, sex, freedom, and commitment, but not necessarily in that order. She wanted the same things, but usually in that order, and minus the commitment! Our values differed. That also explains why it didn't last long…

OK, so you've learned about communicating ideas, and how to use someone's values to motivate them. Here's another HGE tool you can use to match the right person to the right job….

"You don't want a drill, you want a hole in the wall."

8

THE SECRETS TO MOTIVATING YOURSELF ...AND OTHERS

Consider the following sentence:

SUCCESSISNOWHERE

Now did you just read that as "success is nowhere", or does it read "success is now here"? Depends on how you look at it really. It's like that old cliché about the glass being half full or half empty....

Here's another one. Tell me about those 3 boxes

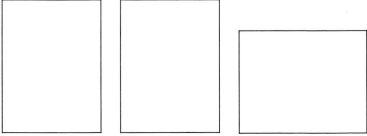

Are you familiar with Psychometric testing? Personality Profiling instruments – DISC, Myers Briggs, LSI, those kind of tools? Imagine if there was a way to elicit the same information from someone at no cost, conversationally, in minutes, without any computers or scoring? Would that be useful?

Metaprograms are what we use in HGE. Metaprograms are thinking styles that determine how we sort, pay attention to and process information.

FIRST OF ALL, A STORY

Somewhere in Scotland an HGE practitioner training is being held. We all know that it would be in Glasgow, but don't tell anybody else, because it's a secret. One day a guy named Guy, walked into the venue and started asking those weird questions. He asks Jonathan what is important to him about the training. Jonathan said, "Well, you know from the direction I'm coming from, I just want to run a good training" whilst Neil, joining Guy and Jonathan, said, "well, for me it's a different cup of tea. I just want to leave my job. I don't like it any more."

By this time Guy became curious, and when he bumped into John, who ran into the hotel lobby from having a smoke outside, he just managed to ask John why he had chosen this training? And although John was late for class, being the reason he was in a hurry, he said "well in order to train other people you must attend this training" when suddenly Julie, standing on the edge of the escalator, cried out loud "Possibilities! It gives you so many choices!"

And when everyone was in class again Guy stood there alone thinking of all these answers, putting them in the right frame and he thought, "How do I know this will be a good training? I mean, I have heard all those people saying it is but can I be sure about that, how will I know?"

After hearing all those convincing people, Guy waited until the next break to ask some key people how they knew that Jonathan Clark was a good trainer. He got so many answers, that he got confused about it. Some people were saying "Well, just look at Jonathan, then you know" while others said "Listen to his voice on the radio, so entertaining" or "haven't you read about him in the papers?" But the most convincing answer came from Gerry: "While I'm doing this training now, I know how great it is." Although, how convincing was Gerry's answer? Guy kept doubting. That is until Jonathan himself came outside the class and asked him "How often do you have to demonstrate that you're the most capable student in this room before you're totally convinced?" And that hit Guy immediately. By just hearing this one question he was convinced.

Not that he hadn't any questions left. Being management director of a large company, Guy knew what it took to organise large meetings of people. "Jonathan?" he asked, "Do you know what you need to be an excellent Trainer?" "Well, of course I do," answered Jonathan. "Oh, maybe you also know what other people need to do, to become a great Trainer?" And then Jonathan answered with "Not only that, I even teach other people how to do that......."

The question is why people react so differently to identical information? Why does one person see the glass as half-empty and another see it as half-full? Why does one person hear a message and feel energised, excitedly and motivated, while another hears the exact same message and doesn't respond at all. So if you want to be a master persuader, a master communicator, in both business in personal life, you have to know how to find the right key.

Think of almost any communication problem you have, and you'll probably find that understanding the person's Metaprograms will help you adjust communications so that the problem disappears. Make yourself understood. If you knew someone's MP's you could talk to them the way they talk to themselves. In Motivation & Decision making, they allow you to match their model of the world, thus increasing rapport, hence reducing resistance, conflict and misunderstanding. Understand & predict a person's way of responding – understanding someone's Metaprograms makes people & their actions seem more predictable, understandable and stable. Learn how to use your own internal dialogue to motivate yourself. Does this sound useful?

When you first learn Metaprograms, probably at Master Practitioner level, you learn how to elicit them using a Questionnaire. You go through them one at a time, get an understanding of what they mean, and learn how to get hear them in your client's language. But that's probably where it stopped. The purpose of this chapter is to give you more application and flexibility.

My Outcome: why I wrote this chapter- I want you to be able to hear Metaprograms and know which linguistic markers denote them, so you can recognise & match them. I want this section of the book to solve a problem for you, thus increasing your use of Metaprograms.

WHAT ARE METAPROGRAMS?

You may have heard of The Myers Briggs study – Isobel Briggs Myers and Catherine Myers did extensive research into "how" people think. Later, Metaprograms were developed by Richard and Lesley Cameron Bandler. They are like a Computer's Operating System, and allow you to predict, understand, match and change someone's behaviour. Metaprograms are the keys to the way a person processes information. They're powerful internal patterns that help determine how he or she forms his internal representations and direct his or her behaviour.

Metaprograms are the internal programs (or sorts) we use in deciding what to pay attention to. A computer can't do anything without software which provides the structure to perform specific tasks. Metaprograms operate much the same way in our brain.

They provide the structure that governs what we pay attention to, how we make sense of our experiences, and the directions in which they take us. To communicate with a computer, you have to understand its software. To communicate effectively with a person you have to understand his or hers. Through understanding those mental patterns you can expect to get your message across, whether it's trying to get someone to buy a car or to understand that you really love him/her. They are highly context specific – elicit them in a particular context such as family, business, or personal growth. Myers Briggs says you're born this way and they are fixed. In HGE we believe they were learned and they're all changeable!

The following listing of the Metaprograms includes the continuum on which each exists, plus the typical kinds of language structures that go with them:

THE 4 PRIMAL SORTS

1. EXTERNAL BEHAVIOUR: INTROVERT/EXTROVERT

"When it's time to recharge your batteries, do you prefer to be alone or with people ?"

Introvert_____Extrovert

Introvert - the idea behind this is to, I know you can concentrate. It's important to be real and genuine, into your own space and territory. Establish a deep connection. Enjoy working alone, be self-sufficient. [Slow, soft, tentative approach, small # of deep relationships. Into conserving their energy]

Extrovert - how this impacts others, get involved in new situations, happy go lucky. Talkative and outgoing person that you are [speak up, talk about friends, stress excitement, loads of shallow relationships. Into expending their energy]

2. INTERNAL PROCESSES: INTUITOR/SENSOR

"If you were going to study a certain subject, would you be more interested solely in the facts and their applications for the now, or would you be more interested in the ideas and relationships between the facts and their applications for the future?"

Intuitor (Future)_____Sensor (now)

Intuitor - possibilities for the future. I have a hunch that you'll. Talk about abstracts and intuitions Change is good. Dreams for the future. [Fluffy, head in the clouds, abstract, global chunks. Imagination, ideas].

Sensor - the immediate, real effects, use sensory modalities. The practical applications of this. Realistic and down to earth., solid and realistic. [Specifics, small chunks, the now]

3. INTERNAL STATE: THINKER (DISSOCIATED)/FEELER (ASSOCIATED)

"Can you remember a work situation that gave you trouble (a one off event)?"

"When you make an important decision do you rely on impersonal reason and logic, or more on your feelings and values?"

Thinker_____Feeler

Thinker - When you weigh up all the pros and cons, what happens when [reason & logic, making sound decisions] Rational, sense, logic, detached

Feeler - if you go back into your past you'll remember how good it felt to. Fair & considerate. In fact, this reminds me of a time [values, touchy feely emotions, praise them]

4. THE ADAPTIVE RESPONSE: JUDGER/PERCEIVER

"If we were going to do a project together, would you prefer it to be outlined and planned out in step by step stages, or would you rather just dive in and go for the big picture?"

Judger (steps_____Perceiver(big pic)

Judger - I think you'd like a planned, orderly way to... make life adapt to them, everything planned. Clear cut categories and rules- demand closure. Lists and schedules, like to have this settled. Quick decision is required The right way to do this. Wants closure, organised, punctual.

Perceiver - ..While at the same time remain flexible.. Adapt to life, do what they feel.

keep an open mind about this - avoid closure, difficulty deciding. Spontaneity and freedom in life. Take life as it comes. Here and now, lateness.

THE COMPLEX METAPROGRAMMES

5. DIRECTION SORT

"What do you want most in life? In a job? In a relationship? What's important about _____?"

Toward_____toward & a bit away_____toward & away_____away & a bit toward_____away from

Toward - If you do this, you'll gain (value) you'll give yourself lots of options

Here's what's so good about this, achieve, attain, progress, obtain. Perks available. "Are you ready for this?" Pleasure

Away - If you don't do this, you'll end up...you're always going to wish you had

You're going to end up no better off, nothing will have changed

The safest thing to do. The price you'll pay.. Avoid, steer clear of, get rid of, help you avoid. Pain. Ask yourself if that's what you want, You'll miss out on, you'll lose...

The problems you can minimise. The things that won't go wrong

This will make your life easier. Give evidence to back up. Here's what we want to avoid. This will reduce our potential problems and liabilities.

6. REASON (OR MODAL OPERATOR) FILTER

"Why did you choose your present job?"

Possibility_____necessity_____both

Possibility - You know what you want out of this...can, will, may, could. We really can do this. So you have a couple of options to choose from here. Consider the possibilities in this. And who knows where this will lead to? Just imagine what might develop as a result of this. You want to be in control of your life. When the next challenge comes up. Offer you more potential for growth. Imagine all of the new avenues this will open up. You're not limited by. following the usual route. The ability to make new distinctions

Necessity - You don't have a choice...must, have to, should. We really must do this

You have to do this now, this is necessary. You know exactly what you have to do

Make it part of your normal, daily routine. Consider the obligations we have

Its just one of those things in life that we all have to do, obliged to do it

The crucial thing to bear in mind is..the usual proven course of action is

You need a permanent base of security to work from. In your current situation, you need...

7. FRAME OF REFERENCE

"How do you know when you've done a good job? Do you just know inside, or does someone have to tell you?"

Internal_____External   Balanced_____Internal with Ext check__
___External with Int check

Internal - I don't know what's right for you to do, but I'm sure you do.

If you stop and ask yourself "What should I do?" Do what feels right

You're the only person who knows if this is right for you. You don't need me to tell you..Regardless of what anyone else might say...I can't convince you, only you can do that. I don't know for certain..."

External - Everyone else gets this...I know you and I know you're good at.

What will everyone around you say when you. Consider what others in this project think. .and you can join the group of satisfied clients. [Testimonies].

Let me tell you what I learned- offer statistics

What I think you should do is.... because other people have done it and got this.

Balanced - as you consider what you think, and what others think

Int with Ext check - as you check on how you feel about this inside, you'll see that the evidence indicates...

8. CONVINCER REPRESENTATIONAL

"How do you know when someone else is good at what they do? Do you have to?

See it_____hear about it_____do it with them_____read about it, or read their work ?

See   -If I could show you an attractive way you could _____, you would at least want to look at it, wouldn't you? If this looks good to you we can focus on the next step, looks right. Look all around and see examples

Hear -If I could tell you how to ____, you'd at least want to hear about it, wouldn't you? Makes sense, clear as a bell. If this sounds good, we can go ahead and discuss... Talk to people and gather information

Do   -If I could help you get a hold of a concrete way to____, you'd want to get a feel for it, yes? If it feels good we can handle all of the details...

Read – makes sense

9. CONVINCER DEMONSTRATION

"How often does someone have to demonstrate competency to you before you're convinced?"

Automatic_____# of times_____period of time_____consistent

Times-Think again, think twice, ask yourself one more time, Here are __ examples of.. [Stack five positive I/R's x times, need x number of appointments] I'm sure you will find that one of them is right for you. If I've told you once I've told you __ times

One time - here is the choice that makes the most sense

Period -Imagine 3 months from now float above timeline and into future. Forever more.. Have a 30-day trial. [Use 10% of this period, and call back after 3 days saying "I've been so busy since the last time we talked, it almost seems like a month has passed"

Consistent - prove to you every time, I know you'll never become truly/ completely convinced, so the only way to know is to try it now/and that's the reason why you'll have to do this to find out. You'll never be convinced you've changed

10. MANAGEMENT DIRECTION FILTER

"Do you know what you need to do to increase your chances of success on a job?"

"Do you know what someone else needs to do to increase his chances?"

"Do you find it easy, or not so easy, to tell him?"

Self & others (YYY)_____self only(YNEither)_____others only(NYY)_____self but not others(YYN)

Self & others - You know what you need to do and what I need to do. Tell me about it.

Self only - where you can remain independent of. You know that what other people do in this project is not important to you, and that's why

Others only - you tell me what I need to do to.. The boss knows what we need to do, so that's why we should...

self not others - Who am I to tell you what to do ? Who are we to tell them what to do? Yet that's exactly why we must

11. ACTION LEVEL SORT

"When you come into a situation, do you usually act quickly after sizing it up, or do you do a detailed study of all the consequences, and then act?"

Active_____reflective_____both_____inactive

Active - It's time to take action, get to it, "just do it". You know its time to do something The go-getters. Let's go and do this. There's no need to wait.

Reflective - You've been biding your time. Think about it, see what others think, let's analyse. Ask yourself if it might be possible. Let things just take their course, don't do anything rash. Don't jump in until you've had time to analyse. I know you want to study this, that's OK. Take all the time you need to make the decision now.

Inactive - neither study nor act, they ignore! Pace values.

Both - You've had all the time you need to study this, and now is the time for action.

12. AFFILIATION FILTER

"Tell me about a work situation in which you were the happiest, a one time event"

Independent_____team_____management

Independent -You're good at working on your own. I know you have a high need to be independent, and that is why it is important for you to foster teamwork in this situation. Solo

Team - put our heads together and come up with a group plan. I know that you want a team to play with

Management - take responsibility for your area. I know you want to be in charge.

13. WORK PREFERENCE FILTER

"Do you prefer mostly to work with…"

Things_____systems_____people

Things - tools for the job. Let me tell you about what we'll be working with

Systems - interested in how things work. Let me tell you how the system works

People - greater level of trust and rapport with everyone you meet. Let me tell you about the people who will be working on this project

14. PRIMARY INTEREST FILTER

"Tell me about one of your favourite (context) experiences." (Holiday, restaurant)

People_____place_____things_____activity_____information

People - think of who you can use this with. Family, colleagues Who you're with is important. Let me tell you who you'll be working with. Customers, staff

Place - Where would this be useful? Home, work Where you go. The location, where they are is important. The view

Things - the right tool for the job, "new stuff", the things involved The what. Let me tell you what we'll need. Menu, decor

Activity - what will be going on & what you'll be involved with, the kinds of behaviours, achievements

Work, home, play. Interested in how. Let me tell you how this will work. The chef cooking

Information - I just thought you ought to know this. Interested in why or what information is available. Let me tell you what you need to know, and why. Map reference, food info.

15. CHUNK SIZE FILTER

"If we were going to do a project together, would you want to know the big picture first, or would you want to know all of the small details first? Would you then need the _____?"

Specific_____global_____specific to global_____global to specific

Specific - check if all the parts work together, then look at the big

picture later

Step by step I'll give you all the details and you will see what it means to you

How to begin & what to do next. Inductive thinker

Global - Look at the big picture first, then see how the parts of it all fit together

The overall concept, fill in the details yourself

The overall direction so you can see what that logically implies.

Deductive thinker

16. RELATIONSHIP FILTER

"Tell me what is the relationship between these three boxes?"

"What's the relationship between what you're doing this year, and what you were doing last year?"

"On the average, how long have you stayed in a job?"

Sameness_____same with exception_____same & difference____
___differences with exception_____differences

Sameness - This is just the same as...and you can count on it

In every case, This is a lot like, It all boils down to this...Better, worse, more, less

There's no reason to change what you're doing, When you have a way that works, why change it ?Like security and routine. You're probably already familiar with this

Difference - What's different about this thing is. You probably won't believe this

This isn't true in every case.. and there's a lot of variety here. Show some creativity, I don't know if you'll do this or not. maybe you don't think this is true, You'll be able to spot where this falls down, what is out of place. I don't care what you've done in the past. Change, variety and newness. I have some serious reservations about whether we can do this on time...

Same with difference - same as what you know, with a twist. [The majority of people]

Same but with more benefit. As you consider what I've said you'll find that it's the same as what you already know. Then, as you consider it, you will probably find the reasons why it's different, and those are the reasons why you'll want to do it.

Difference with exception - different, new, unusual, unique, although has a lot of the same characteristics as what you're used to. "I don't know if you'll believe this or not, but.."

Differences - total variety, innovation, [mismatch them!] Completely new, different "You won't believe this but.." Tell them to not do what you actually want them to

17. EMOTIONAL STRESS RESPONSE {DO THEY ACCESS K WITH THEIR EYE PATTERNS?}

"Tell me about a work situation that gave you trouble"

Dissociated_____associated_____choice

Dissociated - you cope well under stress. I know that this situation doesn't upset you at all, and perhaps you need to show some feeling in this situation. Access Ad

Associated - you know how that makes you feel. I know this situation upsets you, but.. Accesses K and stays there

Choice - You have the choice to react or not in this situation. Accesses K then moves around

18. TIME TENSE ORIENTATION -

"Do you have your attention on the past, the present, or the future? Or are you not concerned about time?"

Past_____present_____future_____atemporal

Past - looking back, all the times in the past, what it meant for you {use past tenses}.

Present - at the moment, at present, in the here and now {use present tense}

Future - looking forward, bright future, in due course {use future tense}

19. TIME STORAGE -

"I'd like you to **stop**...and relax for a moment...and recall a memory from the past........and now an event from the future. Now point to the direction that is the future, and the direction that is the past." Or "If someone is late for an appointment with you, would you care?"

Through time (left to right)_____in time (front to back)

Through - gets your money's worth, you deserve every ounce, you have a hard time putting your past behind you, go through all the pages of your history. Time is of the essence as you know, so let's. Let's take this step by step

In time - in the here and now, keep you on track, go back to a specific time. You know that we're apt to lose track of time, so let's keep track of what time it is. Keeping our options open.

20. TIME ACCESS -

"I'd like you to think back to this time last year. Now the year after that."

Random access_____sequential access

In time_____Through time

Random - off on a tangent, bounce ideas around, make new connections, new insights, off the wall. You never forget

Sequential - go by the book, follow the rules, stick to the procedure, systematic. Rewind the movie of your life history

21. MODAL OPERATOR SEQUENCE {THE WORDS THEY USE TO MOTIVATE THEMSELVES}

"How did you get yourself up this morning? What was the last thing you said to yourself before you got up, to make yourself get up?"

Necessity____Possibility____Desire____Impossibility____Choice
Necessity- must, should, have to. Rules & constraints
Possibility-could, would, might, may, will. Options & choices
Desire- want, desire
Impossibility-can't, shouldn't, must not
Choice-will, choose. Personal choice and free will
[Use should/must/have to/...whatever they use to motivate themselves]

22. ATTENTION DIRECTION

Self_____others_____both

Self - This will impact you personally. You'll be able to do this for yourself, and this.. You're probably asking yourself "What's in this for me?". Relying on your own judgement. In trance a lot

Others - You've probably noticed how people. You'll be able to help lots of other people

We need a solution that all of us are happy about. Scans externally

23. GOAL FILTER

"Tell me about a goal that you once achieved. What was the goal, and what did you do once you'd achieved it?"

Disengager_____optimiser _____Perfectionist

Disengager - refuse to set goals... you know there's no point in setting yourself up for disappointment, unrealistic expectations

Optimisation - do the best with what you've got, appreciate the progress you've made, enjoy the process

Perfection - you need to get it just right, never satisfied with your own performance, talk about the ultimate end product.......never good enough

24. KNOWLEDGE FILTER

"When you decide that you can do something, from where do you get that knowledge?"

Modelling/Concepts___Demonstration___Experience___authority

Modelling/Concepts - you're familiar with the concept of

Demonstration - I can show you how to first so you can learn

Experience - you need to experience it for yourself. you've seen/done
this before

Authority - as a qualified __ I can tell you

25. COMPARISON FILTER

"How are you doing on your job?" "How do you know?"

Numbers_____good/bad_____compare self to self/self to others/

others to others

Numbers - 100 % improvement, measurable change, marked in-
crease

Good/bad - good/best way to...bad/worst thing you could do

Comparison - compared to who/what

26. COMPLETION FILTER

"If we were going to do a project together, would you be more interested in the beginning phase where you'd help start it up, or in the middle of the project where you'd help run it, or in the end phase where you'd close it down?"

"Is there a part of the project you'd rather not be involved in?"

Get this thing off the ground, enjoy the thrill of the chase

Keep it ticking over, manage it well

Put an end to it once and for all, bring it to a conclusion, see it
through to the end

27. CLOSURE FILTER

"Once you've started receiving information that has, say, four steps, how important is it to you that you get all four pieces?"

Not at all - begin the process of, see where it goes

Very - its a 5 step plan, and once the final step is reached..

28. DECISION STRATEGY

"You seem to enjoy your job. How did you decide to do it?"

"Those are nice jeans. I like those jeans, do you like those jeans? How did you decide they were the jeans for you?"

Get the order and sequence of the actions they took

_____ > _____ > _____ > _____ > _____ = D

Run them through the same actions in the same order and they'll decide.

29. SPEAKING STYLE

If you felt that someone around you was not performing as well as they should, would you come to the point and tell them directly (Literal), or would you hint, imply and give them subtle clues (Inferential)?

Literal_____Inferential

30. LISTENING STYLE

If someone you know quite well says, "I'm thirsty", would you feel compelled to do something about it or would you imply they do?

Literal_____Inferential

Literal - "oh right", its simply a statement

Inferential - feels like telling them, or getting one

31. INFORMATION PROCESS STYLE

When you need to work through a problem, is it absolutely necessary for you to talk about it with someone else, or think about it by yourself only?

Internal_____External

Internal - can't talk about it, real deep answers

External - Typical client, talks it through. Thanks for listening. Talks at you.

32. EMOTIONAL COPING SORT

"When you feel threatened, or challenged by some stress, what immediate emotional response arises? Do you want to get way from the stress, or go at it?"

Aggressive_____Passive

Aggressive - you'll enjoy the challenge. Explore and wrestle with this person, question him and future pace him. Be direct and forthright

Passive - feel at ease, create a peaceful harmony

Hear him out, tell me more, I'm genuinely interested

33. TEMPERAMENT

Judge by observation as you explain things to them

Strong Willed_____Compliant

Strong - suggest and plant seeds of ideas, do not confront and teach

Compliant - relax and express your thoughts

34. STYLE OF SORTING

"Why did you choose your car /job/house?"

Procedures_____Options

Procedures - the right way to do this, follow my instructions, here's the process we'll use. Rules & steps. High need for closure. How to...proven way, correct way.

Options - developing new ways to...., figure out all of the alternatives Improve upon the old way, express yourself, use your creativity, innovation

Choose and expand your options. We'll bend the rules for you. Choice

35. PERCEPTION

Black & white_____Continuum

B&W - clear & definite distinctions, quick decisions, perfectionist terms

Continuum - finer level of discrimination, more indecisive "yes...but"

36. VALUE BUYING SORT

What is important to you in a purchasing situation? What do you look for & how do you decide?

Cost_____Convenience_____Time

Cost - the cost effective choice, value for money, more for your money, bargain, can't be beaten, lowest on the market

Convenience - the right tool for the job, handy, useful, no mess, easy to follow instructions

Time - limited offer, sale now on, never to be repeated, while stocks last

37. SATIR STANCE

Placaters like to soothe, please others, and satisfy. Scared you'll reject them or get angry, so apologise a lot and never disagree cos they're desperate to please. PLEASING

Blamers find fault and dictate, boss around. Act superior, and feel that no one cares about them. Shrill, loud harsh voice usually. Cut everything & everyone down, pointing the finger accusingly. Start sentences with *"You* never do this.." ACCUSATORY

Computers are detached and reasonable, calm cool and collected. Feelings shut down as words become abstract. The longer the words the better. DISSOCIATE

Distracters are unpredictable and interrupt a lot. Dizzy and panicky. Fidget and squirm a lot and talk about different subjects, ignoring questions. CRAZYMAKING

Levellers are assertive and kind, speaking honestly and forthrightly. Wholly Congruent! ASSERTIVE

{*Do not try & match any of these categories, as that will simply intensify it. Stay in an uptime state and use all of your sensory acuity to elicit the information that you need*} See the "Stand & Deliver!" chapter for more descriptions of these stances and what they mean.

38. RESPONSE STYLE

When you come into a situation, how do you usually respond? Do you feel 100% aligned, or do you feel conflicted? Do you want to cooperate and agree, or disagree? Or do you look at the pattern of what's going on?

Congruent_____Incongruent_____Polarity_____

Competitive_____Meta

[Whole, appropriate--out of sync_____opposites_____win/ lose comparisons--chunked up]

Congruent - this fits and feels right, every part of you agrees

Incongruent - something is wrong somehow, not 100% sure, something tells you, have a hunch that

Polarity - you probably won't believe this, don't whatever you do...., I wouldn't want you to

Competitive - best, fastest, first, come out on top, be the best you can be, skills noone else has

Meta - How do you feel about the situation, Rising above it all, what's your overall feeling?

WHAT PEOPLE TYPICALLY EXPERIENCE WHEN THEY FIRST LEARN THIS:

- You'll quickly identify with one extreme on the continuum, and find it hard to understand the other. There's a clue there! One is your Metaprogram, the other isn't!
- Remember that they vary by context – your relationship Metaprograms may well differ from your Business ones.
- Read their words, or listen to their sentences, or formally ask them to complete the MPVI questionnaire included later.
- Translate your intended message into their Metaprograms
- Remember that "there's no content in content worth knowing", as Tad James once said.
- Practice with one at a time – get used to eliciting it, recognising

the linguistic markers (sentence structures) that go with it.

• Elicit the Metaprograms from someone you know, and then write out the linguistic markers that go with them. Then try them out on that person and generate a result. Get feedback and learn from it.

• Get someone else to elicit yours, and repeat the exercise – you now have the keys to motivating yourself! Just use those sentence structures in your own head.

• Remember that these are Generalisations

What if you mastered Metaprograms? Where could you use this information? Here's some Homework: come up with five real life applications in your Career or business. Or imagine designing the ideal profile for a role, like a template of the model employee, then recruiting people who match it.

When I first learned Metaprograms, there were 10 listed. When I did my first Master Practitioner training, we learned 16. I currently use the 38 listed here, but The Sourcebook of Magic lists 51. I can picture a wizened Master Trainer hunched over a keyboard in the Wizard's Tower, churning out #117, 118....

MPVI   Name_____

1. "When it's time to recharge your batteries, do you prefer to be alone or with people?"

2. "If you were going to study a certain subject, would you be more interested solely in the facts and their applications for the now, or would you be more interested in the ideas and relationships between the facts and their applications for the future?"

3. "When you make an important decision do you rely on impersonal reason and logic, or more on your feelings and values?"

4. "If we were going to do a project together, would you prefer it to be outlined and planned out in step by step stages, or would you rather just dive in and go for the big picture?"

5. "What do you want most in life?

6. "Why did you choose your present home?"

7. "How do you know when you've done a good job? Do you just know inside, or does someone have to tell you?"

8. "How do you know when someone else is good at what they do? Do you have to?
See it, hear about it, do it with them, read about it, or read their work?

9. "How often, or for how long, does someone have to demonstrate competency to you before you're convinced that they're good?"
"Do you know what you need to do to increase your chances of success on a job?"
"Do you know what someone else needs to do to increase his chances?"

10. "Do you find it easy, or not so easy, to tell him?"

11. "When you come into a situation, do you usually act quickly after sizing it up, or do you do a detailed study of all the consequences, and then act?"

12. "Tell me about a work situation in which you were the happiest, a one time event"

13. "Do you prefer mostly to work with...things, systems or people?"

14. "Tell me about one of your favourite holiday experiences."

15. "If we were going to do a project together, would you want to know the big picture first, or would you want to know all of the small details first? Would you then need the other?"

16. "Tell me what's the relationship between the three arrows?"
⇑ ⇑ ⇒

17. "Tell me about a work situation that gave you trouble"
18. "Do you have your attention on the past, the present, or the future? Or are you not concerned about time?"
19. "I'd like you to stop…and relax for a moment…and recall a memory from the past…and now an event from the future. Now point to the direction that is the future, and the direction that is the past."
20. "Does time seem long or short?"
21. "What was the last thing you said to yourself before you got up, to make yourself get up?"
22. "Is your attention on yourself or on others?"
23. "Tell me about a goal that you once achieved. What was the goal, and what did you do once you'd achieved it?"
24. "When you decide that you can do something, from where do you get that knowledge?"
25. "How are you doing on your job? How do you know?"
26. "If we were going to do a project together, would you be more interested in the beginning phase where you'd help start it up, or in the middle of the project where you'd help run it, or in the end phase where you'd close it down?"
    "Is there a part of the project you'd rather not be involved in?"
27. "Once you've started receiving information that has, say, four steps, how important is it to you that you get all four pieces?"
28. "You decided you needed to get some help. How did you decide to do that?"
29. "If you felt that someone around you was not performing as well as they should, would you come to the point and tell them directly or would you hint, imply and give them subtle clues?
30. "If someone you know quite well says "I'm thirsty", would you feel compelled to do something about it or would you imply they do?

31. "When you need to work through a problem, is it absolutely necessary for you to talk about it with someone else, or think about it by yourself only?

32. "When you feel threatened, or challenged by some stress, what immediate emotional response arises? Do you want to get way from the stress, or go at it?"

33. "If someone tells you what to do, how do you respond?"

34. "Why did you choose your last job?"

35. "Is life black & white [clear cut and broad] or is there grey too [all the fine distinctions in between]?

36. "What is important to you in a buying situation? What do you look for & how do you decide?

37. "How do you behave when someone scolds you or blames you for a problem?"

38. "How do you respond when a problem comes up?"

I have a Home Study programme on Metaprograms which you can order from my website at www.jonathanclark.org/products . We spend at least a day during our live Master Practitioner trainings teaching how to elicit, make sense of and use all of these patterns.

AND SO BACK TO GUY

"Well" Guy thought, "shall I do a complete study of the consequences first, before I take action, or shall I go for it immediately and immediately sign up for this training?"

"Although, when I did that other training a year ago, I had the most transforming time of my life. But that's because I like to work with other people, I think. Oh no, I hope this isn't a training where you have to study alone on your own. If it is, I'll need someone to coach me"

Suddenly Guy remembered a time at his work, where he was offered two different jobs. He had preferred the one where he got to coach other people, because unlike his brother Andy, who preferred to work with computer systems, Guy loved to work with other people. "Actually, I'm at my best when I'm working with other people" Guy thought. "That's it! I'm going to do this training course!" he thought.

"I hope this course has a lot of exercises – I love trainings with lots of activity" Guy was thinking, while he walked towards the trainer's assistant to sign up.

"What we'd like to know" one of the assistants asked "is whether you want to know the big picture first or all of the small details first?" "Well" Guy said, "as long as it's a good training course then I'll deal with the details later"

And while Guy was attending his first day on the course, he said to his neighbour "This is like all those NLP trainings" His neighbour countered with "I don't think so" he said. "Jonathan's trainings are unlike any NLP courses in this country!"

That happened to be true, because on his first day Guy got so overloaded with new information, which he had never heard about, that he got totally confused. And as in earlier experiences in which he found himself under stress, he thought to himself "OK, what options do I have?". And all the while his neighbour got more nervous about it all…

The next morning Guy came in a half hour late. "You must be in time" Jonathan said as Guy walked into the classroom. Guy replied "What? In time? Oh sorry, I thought I was late!" "Yes, that's what I'm saying" replied Jonathan.

"But now you're here and they are there, let me ask you this: what was the last thing you said to yourself just before you got out of bed this morning?" Jonathan asked Guy, while all the other students were completely in trance. "I have to get out of bed quickly, otherwise I'll be late for class" Guy answered.

"That's right!" said Jonathan "and because you were thinking that and you are now in this classroom, I know that you pay a lot of attention to others"

That day Guy got homework – he had to write a metaphor. "How am I going to do that?" Guy thought to himself. "How would my brother Andy do that? Well, he'd probably sit down in his room alone, and produce a magnificent metaphor. But I'm not Andy, I have to talk to someone about this metaphor thing, otherwise it isn't going to work for me"

Suddenly Guy thought "was it homework or not? Well it must be. Jonathan said 'I don't want you to think that it'd be good to write a metaphor tonight' so I'd have to write one. Otherwise, if I take his words literally I now have to not think about writing a metaphor"

So when Guy got home that night, he immediately went to his room, but just before that he said to his partner "I really have to do some homework for the course, before I forget my metaphor. Oh and by the way, I'm thirsty.."

"It's not what you think, it's how you think"

9

STAND AND DELIVER!

If you're a manager, a teach, a presenter or a Trainer you probably feel like you've got loads of responsibility, You may even feel pushed, stressed, and under pressure to perform, close to tearing your hair out moments before you go on stage? Or perhaps you're someone who's terrified at the thought of standing before a group of your peers and talking about something.

So it's time for something different – time for some fun, some energy and a different way of thinking about things. You see, if you keep thinking about things the way you've been thinking about them, you'll keep getting exactly what you've been getting.

You probably work for a business, right? Whether it's a product based or service based business, it must sell to the customers, yes? Did you know that the word "sell" comes from the Norwegian word "selje", which means "to serve"?

The number one objective of a business is what? Profit. And how do you do that? You establish relationships with clients. You have to get them to know you, like you and trust you so that they'll keep coming back to you. You serve them, and if they're delighted with your service, they'll come back.. But then, people buy on emotion, not logic. Even you. You buy things that make you feel good or better, not by logical pros and cons. People buy what they want, not what they need. So if you can sell yourself, your ideas, your products emotionally, you'll make a healthy profit. And as I teach at my Practice Building seminar, there are only three ways for a business to

make a profit:
1. INCREASE THE NUMBER OF CLIENTS
2. INCREASE THE AMOUNT OF MONEY SPENT PER SALE
3. INCREASE THE NUMBER OF SALES

What I'm going to talk about in this chapter is how to use Rapport skills with anyone, especially in groups. Have them know you, like you and trust you, even if they've never met you before, because at the unconscious level they are picking up on your intention to serve them. They'll like you so much they'll keep coming back to you, spend more money with you and refer their friends and colleagues to you.

These skills will also help you deal with customer complaints or clients who are sceptical or who have had their fingers burned and are projecting distrust onto you. If you want to get on with your colleagues better, or always get the offer of a job at every job interview you ever go for because they like you and they don't question why, then keep reading!

How do you think you ended up reading to this point? It even works in writing too...

You already know that all learning, all behaviour and all change is unconscious, so if you train, teach, present or educate, and you want your students to change what they're doing, or how they're feeling, or exhibit some new behaviour, or to really take it in, you need to talk to their unconscious minds...

This is all about audiences, meeting, groups and state of the art communication.

Now at times you'll probably find yourself asking yourself such questions as:

"WHY IS HE SAYING IT THAT WAY?"
"WHAT IS THAT STORY HE TOLD REALLY ABOUT?"
"HOW DOES THIS WORK?"

"WHAT IF I DID IT THIS WAY?"

Maybe you've had uncomfortable experiences in the past in front of groups, or where you thought "I know I can do better than that".

Perhaps you want to be more comfortable when presenting to groups? This chapter is ideal for anyone who's ready to let go of the fear of speaking in public!

Want to know how to use your brain, language and physiology to get the results you want?

Maybe you have to stand up and speak to groups right now – perhaps you're someone who educates, trains or presents. Maybe there's something coming up really soon where you'll have to stand up and give a speech… This is useful even for weddings, promotions or impromptu speeches.

I'm going to share with you a number of hush hush "trade secrets".

To communicate effectively, according to Richard Bandler, you need to entertain your audience, and I'd agree. Specifically you need to do four things:

1. **KEEP THEIR ATTENTION**
2. **BOND WITH THEM**
3. **BE REMEMBERED**
4. **AND MOST OF ALL…..BE YOURSELF IN FRONT OF AUDIENCE**

My outcome is that you become totally comfortable, being yourself, in front of an audience of any size. Being yourself is really important. You won't need a special "speaker personality". You won't have any armour on or a wall up. You don't need a lucky stone in your pocket, "Dutch courage" to get through it, or a special suit reserved for special occasions. You're simply going to be open, honest, genuine and OK being exactly who you really are, in front of a group of other people.

How do you do that? Well, I'm going to share with you about 15 key skills. On our live trainings we cover about 31 things that you can do on stage. But for now, how about:

- Gaining rapport with any size of group
- How to achieve & stay – relaxed, focussed & centred
- Structuring your presentation around preferred learning styles to maximise audience retention and attention
- Using specific gestures and postures to increase your impact & flexibility as a presenter
- Controlling your audiences state of mind moment to moment
- Using metaphors to speed both conscious & unconscious learning
- How to maintain & manage the energy in the room
- The secrets to increase your personal charisma and magnetism
- How to handle criticism and heckling

Each exercise in this chapter will build on the ones before, so you gradually stack up a number of techniques until you're doing them all at once. And you can't do that consciously...

You'll just have to let...go.. and...trust......your.. unconscious.......mind....to do it all for you.

And don't be surprised if you find yourself using these new skills in places other than in groups. You might find, if I can make a suggestion....would that be ok? You might find that you use these skills in other contexts, in your relationships, talking to your kids, dealing with the bank manager.

I had to learn these skills from scratch. At school I was terrified of reading aloud in class. I'd get really scared, I'd break out in a sweat, I'd stutter and my chest would feel like it was going to burst and I couldn't breathe...

I used to dodge English classes in case I'd have to read out loud. Especially plays – where you can see your line coming closer as you go down the page, and the closer it got the more nervous I became. I had an ulcer by the time I was sixteen because I was so nervous and timid with people. I found it nearly impossible to say hello to people I knew! I'd keep my head down, avoid eye contact, stay locked up tight and be shut down emotionally. Can you relate to that at all?

So I started reading about personal development for my own benefit. They say that people get into self help books for one of two reasons – either inspiration, or desperation. Well, I was pretty desperate!

And I slowly learned about using my physiology powerfully, managing my energy, what internal dialogue to run in my head, how to breathe correctly…and the people who knew me at school hardly recognise me now, because I've changes…

You've probably heard the old cliché about FEAR – that it spells "False Evidence Appearing Real", or "F*** Everything and Run!"

Public speaking is the #1 fear in the US

The #2 fear in the US is death

So at the average funeral most people in the US would rather be in the coffin than reading the eulogy!

In the UK the fear of Public speaking is #2

The #1 fear in the UK is the fear of spiders

Imagine public speaking to an audience of spiders EEK!

Rest assured by the end of this chapter you will have **let go of any fear you had in the past.** For most people **this happens easily,** although rarely someone may need extra personal attention. **You'll know when the fear has gone because you'll be laughing..**

YOUR GOALS FOR THIS CHAPTER

So let's look at why you're reading this particular section of the book. What is is you're looking for? Why this section? What would have to happen for you to really amaze yourself in the area of public speaking?

I remember when I first started speaking to groups. I was a Financial Adviser and part of that company's strategy was to hold retirement planning seminars for Civil Servants. So I was given a slide projector, handouts and a script that I had to learn word perfect, to talk in time with, and in the order that the slides changed. And I thought "I can't do this". It was clunky, full of clichés and was quite frankly boring, but it was part of my job description and I set that equipment up in my living room and went over it and over it until I knew it by heart. I still remember my first seminar, which was held in a Royal Mail Canteen to about a dozen soon to retire Postmen. I started my painful presentation and all the while I'm telling myself "I can't do this…"

Now a few years later I went self employed, and some friends of mine set up a public seminar in a pub in Arbroath. Now if you don't know Scotland, Arbroath is a windy little town on the East coast of Scotland, so it's cold and bleak in the winter. I was hoping to attract about a dozen people keen on learning how to *run your own brain,* so imagine my surprise when about fifty people showed up, all huddled into this snug in the pub. I had no structure, no clever language patterns, no real technique, I was just enthusiastic and eager to share this stuff with people.

Then I did an NLP Practitioner course and came back from London really excited. Having asked around, I was told that one of the two best ways to launch your own business was to hold seminars in your living room. So I did. I had about six people in our small flat in Glasgow all talking to their unconscious minds, and I noticed how far I'd come in such a short space of time, and I thought "I'm getting good at this…"

STATES FOR LEARNING & TRAINING

How would you like to learn how to achieve & stay relaxed, focussed & centred in front of a group? The "Learning state" is for you as a student, receiving training, sitting in the audience. The "Trainer

State" is the same state, but used while you're presenting – that's the one to do standing up.

Did you used to get nervous presenting? Would it be more useful to be calm? You probably need some way of staying externally focussed, rather than diving head first into your own head and all the anxiety that you used to experience in there. Wouldn't you like to be able to learn more, and more quickly? If there was a way to make negative emotions vanish at will…wouldn't you like to at least try it out? Just suppose you could increase your "presence" – learn the secrets of charisma?

People ask me about my energy – where do you get it from? I'm going to show you some ways (and there are others in the chapters on Health and Huna). People often ask me "How do you stand, what do you do with hands?" while you're speaking to a group? The Fig leaf, the Prince Charles, hands in pockets, etc? Can you picture those?

REMEMBER THE HGE COMMUNICATION MODEL?

Peripheral vision ✓

To be in a relaxed state, that's controlled by your Physiology and the Internal Representations you're making to yourself. The ideal Physiology is relaxed, straight, standing tall. The ideal internal representation would be externally focussed, using your peripheral vision. That's a highly prized state called Hakalau, which comes from Hawaiian Huna.

You have 2 types of vision, did you know that? You have Foveal vision and Peripheral vision. If you look at some point in the room where you are right now, you'll see that it's sharp and focussed, but everything around it is blurry. The sharp point of attention is called your foveal vision.

But as you look at that point again, you'll probably be able to see the floor. And the ceiling. You're not looking at it, but you can see it. It's blurry, but it is there. You're not looking at it, but you are able to put your attention on it. Try that now.

Notice also that as you look straight ahead, you can see things off to your left, and off to your right. You're looking straight ahead, but you can see things at the far periphery of your vision. This is called Peripheral Vision, and it was part of the Shamanic state practiced by the Hawaiian Kahuna (for more on the Kahuna, see the chapter in this book on Huna).

"Hakalau" ... from Huna

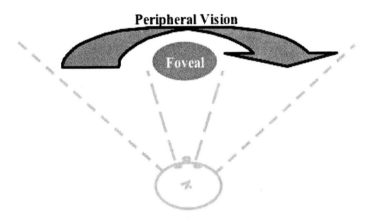

Now when you're in Foveal vision, you activate the Sympathetic Nervous System. That's the part of you that activates Stress, adrenaline, and the fight or flight response. In contrast, when you access Peripheral Vision, you stimulate the Parasympathetic Nervous system, which promotes relaxation, deep breathing and trance.

In peripheral vision you'll be relaxed, receptive, and externally focussed. In fact, IT'S IMPOSSIBLE TO FEEL ANY NEGATIVE EMOTION WHILE YOU'RE IN PERIPHERAL VISION. So the first thing you want to do if you're going to teach, present and talk to a group, is to go into peripheral vision.

In 1843 a Scotsman (and it would be a Scotsman) called James Braid set out to debunk the hypnotist Mesmer and prove that hypnosis was a load of rubbish. In the end he wrote a book called "Neurypnology" extolling the virtues of hypnosis! But one of the first things in hypnosis was to look up at the hypnotist's eyes, or a watch, or a finger held up above eye level. Guess what. That activates your peripheral vision and starts the trance induction...

So here's how to go into peripheral vision, or Hakalau:

Pick a spot on the wall, preferably above eye level. Stare up at it

Breathe in through the nose, out through the mouth slowly

Stare at it, loosen your jaw, let go – "Brain Dump"

Spread out your peripheral awareness, and become aware of what's to the left of you, and to the right

Pay more attention to the peripheral, more attention to the far edges of your vision

Now stay in that state, looking at the book but being aware of the floor beyond it, the room you're in....

Now if you're going to present, I'd suggest you go through the following stages, adapted from Patanjali's Yoga Sutras in 600AD.

"The Trainer State" Yoga Sutras

1. Brain dump – you're here, now, about to speak. Nothing else matters. Put everything else out of your mind.

2. Adopt a balanced physiology – feet shoulder width apart – thigh muscles soft, knees unlocked, back straight

3. Breathe in through nose – out through mouth

4. go inside your head and tell yourself something reassuring like "You sexy beast you"

5. Pick a spot on the wall in front of you to focus on

6. Go into Peripheral vision

7. Expand your awareness to all four corners of the room – and then make eye contact with audience

In any group that gets together, they unconsciously seek a leader, someone who's running the room. As the presenter it'd better be you. If you don't, someone else in the audience will attempt to be the leader. This is a great way to get "Compliance" - to stand at the front of the room and go into Trainer State until the noise dies down and the room goes quiet. You'll look very authoritative and in charge.

ONCE YOU'RE IN THE TRAINER STATE, CALM, RE-LAXED & FOCUSSED, IT'S TIME TO BUILD RAPPORT WITH YOUR AUDIENCE

(see the chapter on rapport!)

….so now you're in the Trainer State and you've got rapport. Now it's time to bring some "out there" techniques into the training, and talk about managing the energy in the room

ENERGY

WHY learn about energy?

Remember the formula $E=mc^2$? We're going to look at the left hand side of that equation.

Everything has energy, and you can pick it up, can't you? Ever met someone with bad energy? The energy vampires? Just remember what they taught you in all the old Christopher Lee, Hammer horror vampire movies – a vampire can only come into your home if you invite them in. Remember I said that.

Ever met the opposite? Someone who's charismatic, magnetic, or has great energy? In trainings, have you ever noticed the energy of a group change, like it suddenly drops? Usually around lunchtime? Wouldn't it be great to discover your own energy, raise or lower a group's energy, and be able to direct it on purpose?

Imagine if you could load up a training room with the right kind of energy appropriate for that presentation? Curiosity. Fun. Safety As the trainer, you need energy. You are the product – you are the message. Especially if you run long trainings, like over a week, or a fortnight. Our HGE Practitioner course lasts for a week! Master Practitioner is double that! If you arrive at a talk exhausted, you need this!

LET'S DEFINE PRESENCE/ENERGY

CLOSE YOUR EYES – and go inside, and if I was to ask you where your energy is, where would it be? In your chest? Stomach? Head? All over your body?

And what does your energy feel like? Is it moving or is it still? Rough or smooth? Solid or liquid? Hot or cold? If it had a shape what shape would it be? Is it light or heavy?

And if it had a sound, would it buzz? Hum? Crackle? Where would you hear your energy coming from? Inside your head or outside? Is it loud or soft?

And if you could see your energy, what colour would it be? Would it be bright, dim or dark? Where would you see it? Is it in one place, or is it all over? Does it extend outside your body or not?

A master of energy can expand their energy, and then direct it. Again, that's a Huna speciality. But for now I'm going to give you a number of exercises to demonstrate your energy, and to build it.

EXERCISE 1 - HA BREATHING

Energy comes from oxygen. Think about it. How long can you live without food? A couple of weeks? How long can you live without water? A few days only. But how long can you live without oxygen? Only a matter of minutes. How long can you live without energy? You can't! THERE'S A CLUE THERE!!

All ancient cultures had breathing techniques designed to build energy and keep you healthy. The more you breathe the more oxygen gets into your bloodstream. That way you're buzzing and you can think clearly. That's a good condition to be in as you teach or present.

So you can just stop – and take a deep breath in through the nose, and breathe out through your mouth. When you breathe in your stomach should go out, and when you breathe out your stomach should go in again.

This time, do it again, but on the out breath, whisper the word "Ha". The Out breath should be twice as long as the in breath. Try that now.

Now keep doing that for a few breaths.

You'll probably feel more grounded, calm, relaxed, with no internal dialogue. That's a good thing.

And in a training you could breathe like that for a few minutes before the delegates arrive, in the car, on the way there. Or in the dressing room.

EXERCISE 2 – STAYING CENTRED AND BALANCED

This exercise is best practiced with someone else helping.

Put all of your attention on your right earlobe

Now have your partner gently push you, and notice how unstable you are.

Now put all of your attention on a spot about two inches below your navel. If you know about the Chakras, the energy centres, or you study martial arts, you'll recognise this as your centre of power. The Hawaiians call it the N'au.

Keeping your attention below your navel, have them push you again, and notice the difference.

I suggest that when you're presenting, you keep your energy focussed down there, and you'll be solid, unshakeable, assured. That way you'll come across more congruent, and you'll be better able to handle hecklers or curve ball questions. White folk talk from their "nasals". Powerful Kahuna talk from their "navels".

EXERCISE 3 - EXPAND YOUR ENERGY TO ENCOMPASS YOUR AUDIENCE

Go into the Trainer state

Imagine your energy as a bubble, in whatever colour your energy comes in. See it. Hear the noise it makes. Feel the qualities your energy has.

Now expand your bubble to encompass your audience. Being in peripheral vision at this point will make it easier.

Now imagine just contracting the bubble, shrinking it in enough to "group hug" the audience.

Now all of these skills take practice, I understand that. But the more you do them the easier it gets. Before going on stage I recommend you build your energy with five minutes or more of Ha Breathing. Practice using your peripheral vision. It keeps you safe on a dark night. Drill the Yoga Sutra steps until you can do them without thinking about it.

Alternatively, you can hear all of these skills taught and demonstrated in live seminar format, in the "Stand & Deliver" Home Study Programme available at www.jonathanclark.org/products . You get to hear the group speaking **before** they've been taught these skills, and listen to the huge difference **after** 2 days of live training. It's a joy to hear the confidence and enthusiasm that emerges from people.

Now lets start getting into the advanced stuff. Let's amplify what you do with your Physiology. After all – you are the message

SATIR CATEGORIES

World renowned couple counsellor and family therapist Virginia Satir identified five key "Postures" that her clients adopted. Stereotypes, which powerfully communicate non-verbal messages.

You can use these postures to increase your "presence" both on stage and off. Powerfully use your physiology (the 55% of any communication) to send non-verbal messages that back up your verbal one, thereby doing what I call "Communicating at 100%". You can also use these to control the energy in the room, raising it, lowering it or maintaining it depending on your outcome. They increase your authority and assertiveness, and women in business can use them possibly more effectively than men can.

On stage they help you deal with hecklers, or to invoke states in your audience. They also answer the question of "How do you stand, what do you do with your hands?" Most speakers do the Fig leaf, the Prince Charles, with their hands clasped in front or behind, or worse, hands in pockets. These are much more powerful.

There's nothing worse than a distracting speaker who paces around, or fiddles, or whose attention is clearly in his or her own head and not on you in the audience. You end up watching them for their weird behaviours and not for what they're teaching. Ooops!

NON VERBAL COMMUNICATION

The five Satir categories are the answer to "what do I do with my hands?" or "How do I stand?". Each category is an instantly recognised stereotype, and you're doing one or more of them unconsciously anyway! They affect your state, and that of the audience. Remember that physiology is 55% of the message. You often see these on book covers as the author has been coached in how to pose for the camera. Here's how to do them, and what they do.

THE COMPUTER

Weight on one leg or evenly distributed
Arms folded, one hand on your chin
The thinking pose
Looks authoritative, like you are the wise one. Helps you deal with a threat so it's harmless.
Says "I'm pensive, thinking it through, I'm the expert, I'm the authority"
Thoughtful, cool, calm and collected. You can hide your self-worth behind big words and intellectual ideas
Completely rational.
Good to use when people ask you questions.
Common in Cerebral people
Be reasonable beyond limit, and use polysyllabic words
Statement tonality – fairly monotone

THE LEVELLER

Weight evenly distributed, feet shoulder width apart
Hands sweep down and out as if you were sweeping snow off a wall
Says "Here's the deal, this is how it's going to be"
Asserts authority and calms things down, especially if you leave a pause after it
Commanding tonality, straight talker
Brings energy down
Common in Kinesthetic people
Congruent, the body matches the words, telling the truth
Good for apologising whilst maintaining your dignity

THE PLACATER

Weight evenly distributed, feet shoulder width apart

Palms up hands moving up, open and vulnerable

Says "Help me out here, please?" and "I'm sorry" and "Tell me what to do"

Suggests openness and trying to please, so that the other person doesn't get angry with you.

Useful to open a questions and answers session.

Makes the energy more emotional, safe, gentle

Questioning tonality, higher pitched voice

Common in Kinesthetic people

Agree with the other person – be a "yes" man or woman

Remember the helpless "Smeagol" character in

The Lord Of The Rings movies

THE BLAMER

Weight on one leg

One foot in front of the other, pointing the finger

Says "It's your fault, on your head be it" or "I'm in charge, right?!" Usually disagrees with people and accuses.

This is the accuser, acting superior, looking strong

Useful for ramming a message home, emphasising, or telling someone they've done really well

Brings energy up

Loud command tonality

Common in visual people

THE DISTRACTER

Weight on one leg, or lock your knees together

Everything moving, angular, diagonal, arms and

legs going out in all directions.

Says "Don't ask me, I'm an airhead, I'm dizzy"

Think dumb bunny, bimbo.

Useful for defusing tension, distracting hecklers, or adding comedy. Comedians often use Distracter with their punch line.

Ignores any threat in the hope that it'll vanish

Releases stuck energy

Voice going up and down

Common in Auditory people

Words make no sense

EXERCISE

I want it to be that when you **do** move it has intention, and it has impact! Try talking about your hobby or your career for a few minutes, or something you know a lot about. Adopt each category for 30 seconds at a time, so 30 seconds in Computer, then 30 seconds in Leveller, then 30 seconds using them all together

You might start doing this in normal life. These still work while you're sitting down, as you use the top half of your body. But think about it. What if you became more assertive?

Women in business – try and avoid Placater and Distracter. They make you look vulnerable and weak. Instead use Leveller and Computer. You'll come over far more assertive, and you'll probably freak the men out with your authority!

Remember that you cannot not communicate, so make sure what you're screaming non verbally agrees with what you're saying with your mouth. And train up the ones that feel awkward and unfamiliar, to increase your behavioural flexibility.

So you've installed the process of presenting - now what about the actual content – the material you want to teach. How do you order and sequence that?

THE 4-MAT SYSTEM

This is an easy way to structure the content, so you always know where you are and where to go next… I like anything that makes my life simpler.

People learn differently, so as a trainer, speaker or educator you can assist them all to learn easily and elegantly. This is one of the most widely used teaching systems in the world – it's easy to understand, and easy to utilise while designing your talk

David Kolb in 1971 at the University of Cleveland did a study on Learning Styles. In the mid 70's Bernice McCarthy combined various research papers into one, and presented her findings from teaching thousands of children. Kids would tend to keep asking the same question over and over. Adults are just big kids.

There are even correlations between this model and Carl Jung's psychological archetypes.

People will only ever ask you 4 types of questions:

1. Why are we covering this? Why would I want to learn this? Give me reasons that will make me feel this is worth learning. Why bother? Jung's Introvert

2. What is it? What's it about? Give me facts, and the thicker the course manual the better. Jung's Extrovert

3. How does it work? Give me steps, walk me through it. They like practical exercises and doing stuff to try it out. Jung's Feeler.

4. What if I did? What are the possibilities? Give me scenarios, options. They like self discovery and tweaking the steps. Jung's Thinker.

In the Western education system we tend to cater for the second category, the What people. We are taught facts, dates, information. Unfortunately that misses 78% of the population.

You might think that it's best to match someone's style and teach them that way. Actually, it's far more effective to teach everyone using all four. That means everyone in the room "gets" it, and you train up their other learning styles.

Now there are cultural differences, and different industries or careers favour different styles. Scottish people like Why. I'm told Germans like What.

So best to include a segment in your presentation or website on each of the 4 areas, IN THAT ORDER. People won't care what it is unless you first tell them why they're there.

So here's what I suggest you do to structure your material:

WHY – WHY NOT? (35% OF THE POPULATION)

Auditory Tonal Predicates

BIG, GLOBAL CHUNKS

Reasons why, and reasons why not. Relevance to reader/listener. Is it relevant to me?

What's in it for them?

Where's the benefit? To them?

Their reasons – Mind Read them

Why should(n't) they?

Discussion

E.G. At start of seminar: write all your reasons for being here

Interaction with them

Motivate them

Modal Operators of Necessity: got to, have to, it's time, must, need to, necessary, supposed to, should, ought to

Ask: "Does this sound useful?" "Would I want this?"

Use Values & Beliefs

WHAT? (22% OF THE POPULATION)

Auditory Digital Predicates

What about it? Give them **information**, content

Analytical, seeking facts, lectures

Need to know what experts think about it

Thinks through the ideas

'What people' pick up the manual in training

In print – use smaller font to make it look denser

Teaching – students listening, taking notes

HOW? (18% OF THE POPULATION)

Kinesthetic Predicates

How does it work? What's the process? How can I use this?

Step by Step – walk them through it

Let them try it out and actually do it!

Strategies, pragmatic practicalities

Coaching them

Demos & Exercises

Students reacting, Seeking usability

WHAT IF? (25% OF THE POPULATION)

Visual Predicates

Same people in training ask all the questions

Let them teach themselves & then others

Self-discovery, learns through trial & error

Opportunities, hidden possibilities

Modal Operators of Possibility: able to, can, choose to, do, intend, possible, permit, will

Future pace them – "imagine a time in the future…"

Let them evaluate it, experiment

Sum it up

Let them predict the future results

Consequences, what would happen if?

E.G. After an exercise, ask for questions, comments ,feedback, discoveries

EXERCISE

You're going to end this chapter by putting all of this together in a 10 minute presentation. You'll need about 5 minutes of content. Choose a topic you will need to present, or something you know a lot about, and structure your content into the 4-Mat sections.

Just think, if you're ever asked to do an impromptu talk, you now have a basic structure to design it, which tells you where you are, where you've been and where you're going next. You could apply all of this in real life, when writing articles, speeches, websites. Heck, you might even use it when writing a book………(grin). But whatever you do, don't wait for it – use it now. If you try and set aside "special time" to use it you never will.

Most classic school NLP trainings were taught in How and What If only, and usually whilst in a deep hypnotic trance. The challenge with that was that the graduates knew how to do NLP and what would happen if they did, but weren't necessarily conscious of why it worked and what it was they were doing. I've met a lot of students from those styles of trainings and they were often repeating the training with another Trainer, so they could know fully what they were doing. I'd prefer that both your conscious mind, and your unconscious mind knew what they were doing, right from the start.

Ideally you should satisfy all areas, in this order. Everyone listens to all four, but everyone has a preference. Use this in Sales Meetings, Speeches, Therapy, Trainings, Brochures, Intro Evenings, in Modelling, Presentations & Business Proposals.

In Adverts & telephone cold Calls – use Why? only. [All good written materials contain one Mismatching statement, chunk Global to Specific, has both Towards and Away From, a Sameness/Difference sentence, a testimony, list the problems they'll stop having, and then the benefits they'll gain.]

So you've learned how to control your own state, now let's talk about influencing the audience's state moment to moment:

ELICITING STATES

Here's how to stage manage the entire training. Think about it, your listeners are going to arrive in a certain emotional state, and you probably want them to leave in a certain emotional state. A good movie is one that sends you home in a different state from the one you started in. People buy on emotion, not logic, including you. So move them. Also, if it's true that all learning is state dependent, what states would the audience be in best to learn your content? Start with that!

There's all manner of ways to create states in your group. I particularly like telling stories, or metaphors. Milton Erickson, the worlds greatest Hypnotherapist, used storytelling to put his clients into trance and to install new behaviours and choices. I strive to be as good as Milton Erickson was. Now I love sword and sorcery stuff, Dungeons and Dragons, Lord of the Rings, all that good stuff. Merlin, King Arthur and the Knights of the Round Table. Camelot. Sounds like a very peaceful place to live...

You may remember the story – young Arthur was studying with Merlin the magician, and he's been studying for a while, pouring over the spell book, learning what herbs to use, studying the stars and mastering the magical words of power. He knew how to speak the special wizards' language, how to use the appropriate gestures, why he should, what it was and how it worked. But he had one final step to complete, which was to pull a certain sword from a large rock. You probably recall the story…

Arthur was hesitating – he knew what to do but he was scared he couldn't do it. "What if I make a mess of it?" he was thinking to himself. Ever done that? Remember when you first drove up to a junction, and you had to cross the traffic, and you were waiting for that space to appear as you had one foot on the gas and one on the brake? Remember what that felt like? It was like wanting to go and talk to a stunning member of the opposite sex, but holding yourself back. Remember that state? Really wanting to but worrying if you'll make a pig's ear of it and look stupid?

Now Arthur was getting really frustrated with himself, almost angry at his own lack of action. I mean, after a while, with all that stuttering and stammering and "should I or shouldn't I?" there come a point where you get SO annoyed at yourself that **something has to give**, you know? Can you imagine how frustrated Arthur was by this point?

Now Merlin was in peripheral vision, in the Trainer state, so he was cool, calm and collected as he watched his young apprentice going through all this internal conflict.

So he watched as suddenly Arthur had an epiphany. Suddenly Arthur had an "aha" moment, a eureka! It was almost as if the lights had come on, and you could see him getting excited, almost inspired. Ever had that? When you're feeling stuck, but then suddenly you get a realisation and you get a renewed burst of energy, don't you?

In that instant Arthur stood straight up and walked congruently up to the stone. It was like he was all powerful, in the flow, everything he touched would turn to gold. Ever had that feeling? Where you can do no wrong and you're just in the groove? And in that state, he grasped the sword and with a resounding "Shing!" it slid cleanly from the rock, and he was master of all he surveyed.

Imagine if you could elicit states in your audience during trainings or seminars, and make them feel emotions you'd like them to feel? For one thing, it makes it much more interesting for the students, AND for the Trainer. It gives both permission to be emotional & expressive. And come to think of it, there are certain states that are useful for learning certain subjects. Also, people buy through emotion – a good movie is a movie that moves you emotionally, that changes your state from the ticket queue to the exit. Besides, you remember the things with the most emotion. You probably don't recall brushing your teeth 7 years ago on April 14th, but you do remember your first kiss, your first pet, your first orgasm…

As a presenter it's your job to hold their attention, and that means be able to affect their state. The more of a rollercoaster you can take them through the more stimulated and moved they'll be, and more importantly, they will have learned!

Metaphors can also be hugely informative, and highly therapeutic. You can load in the information you want to cover directly to the unconscious mind, in the form of a story or legend, so that when you cover it consciously, it all feels very familiar. Read any of the work of Milton Erickson for genius examples of exactly how to do that, or read the rest of this chapter.

That reminds me of a story. There is a case from 1794 when a young boy had to undergo an operation to remove a tumour, in an age before anaesthesia had been invented. Throughout the procedure the mother told the boy a fascinating story to distract him, and so entranced was he by the characters in that story that he felt no pain whatsoever, and very little discomfort. The operation was a complete success, and the boy would one day publish the same story under his own name. The story was called "Snow White", by one Jacob Grimm.

Just suppose you could open up a sales meeting with a state of absolutely going for it! Or start a training session with burning curiousity? Part of your job is to entertain your audience, so if that's something you need, read on.

TELLING METAPHORS

There are several reasons why you'd want to include metaphors in your presentations:
- It makes it more interesting, for everyone
- You'll be remembered
- People buy through emotion
- It identifies you with them, cos they think "She's just like me"
- You can embed direct suggestions in a story
- You become a compelling, master communicator
- It's less threatening, so everyone relaxes
- The listener thinks its not about them, so it bypasses resistance
- It communicates directly with the unconscious mind…
- …therefore metaphors induce trance
- The clients fix themselves
- Six different people all make six different meanings out of the same story
- This is how the elders traditionally passed wisdom down

I love stories, and most people do too. That makes it an excellent vehicle to use. Milton Erickson would have you sit down with him, you'd tell him your problem, he'd say "That reminds me of a story…" and off he went, talking about his tomato plants or how snakes need cold wet places to live, and you'd be thinking "What the hell is he talking about? I just want to stop having panic attacks, and he's talking about his greenhouse?" But when you went home, no more panic attacks….

There are two main sources of stories for eliciting states in an audience:
- Universal experiences – one that most people will have had, usually at an early age, which were emotional. Examples include

Christmas Eve, surprise party, losing a favourite toy, waiting in a queue but you're in a hurry, that sort of thing

- The 1st time…. – your first job, pet, orgasm, bike, kiss. These usually had a lot of meaning for you, and they still will because they're hardwired into your neurology.

Stories you've told friends recently. Family stories in your past. Your childhood. Significant life events. Crises where you fixed the problem. Meetings with remarkable people. Favourite films or books.

How many metaphors have I started in this book so far? How many are still unfinished?

There are 3 main ways to elicit states in your audience:

1. Go into that state yourself and lead them. If you're really feeling it, then so will they. But remember, if you go up to 5 out of 10 on the intensity scale, they'll probably only reach a 2. If you're at 10, they'll come up to about 6. That's why Tony Robbins is such a dynamo on stage, because he wants you to be up there too.

EXERCISE 1 "THAT'S WHAT FRIENDS ARE FOR"

This is a fun exercise that you can do in a group. You pick a state, and your job is to elicit it in your group, so they all can guess which emotional state it is that you're evoking. And anything goes. You can move, dance, grab props, anything, but the only words you're allowed to say are "That's what Friends are for". That's all you can say. The group has to guess what state you were eliciting.

2. Evoke a memory of that emotion in the audience. Just ask them to recall a time when they felt totally motivated, or really happy, and they'll do all the work for you. It helps if you are doing the same, as above.

3. Tell them a story, or a metaphor. Every story has the characters going through a range of emotions. So what stories could you tell that would evoke such an emotion?

Now to make it even more compelling, you can tell a number of stories one after the other. Tell only 80% of it though , then leave it unfinished. That installs curiousity and open endedness.... Then complete the stories in reverse order at the end. Students remain attentive and eager for more, because unconsciously they need closure. Think of it like opening a hatch in their mind, pouring the content in, then sealing the hatch.

This is nothing new, as we all do this all the time. If you have friends round for dinner, this is the structure of the average night. It's just we're doing it on purpose.

Comedians do it all the time.

In business meetings I call them "case studies".

EXERCISE 2

Come up with 3 stories, decide what states they elicit and decide where to break them...where's a good point? Also decide the order & sequence – how can you link them?

Multiple Embedded Metaphors

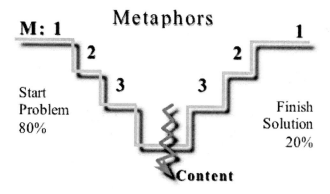

Now I'm not suggesting that if you knew someone's Metaprograms, Presuppositions, Values and Rep systems that you could write a tailor made metaphor just for them. That's not a suggestion I'd make. I would not suggest you consider doing that…

But let's just say that one female client came to me with a so called "problem child" and it was clear that the problem wasn't with the child. So I elicited **her** Metaprograms, **her** values for parenting, and **her** rep system, and then I wrote her three bedtime stories that she was to read him in rotation every night for two weeks. Needless to day the problem disappeared.…

COMPLIANCE TECHNIQUES

In any group of people there will be one Rapport leader at the unconscious level. You can actually watch, and this is fascinating, when any group gets together there will be one leader in the pack, and when they move, so do the others. So if you're speaking to a group, you can look out for them. Better still, you become the leader of the group, and have them follow you

Based on the research done in 1982 at the National Training Laboratory in the US, it is clear that all groups go through a process of formation when they first gather. In its infancy there is confusion, ambiguity, superficiality and anxiety. In this climate people unconsciously seek whatever leadership exists in the environment – whatever direction is grasped for guidance.

In other words, the group is looking for a leader, and as the speaker or presenter, it'd better be you! Compliance is simply the state that occurs where the audience willingly follow the leader's suggestions. Failure to get compliance early will result in a member of the audience running the room.

That reminds me of a seven day course where on the first morning, one of the students asked me to write on the flipchart a brief summary of what we'd be covering each day. Before I knew it I'd complied to her, and there I am following her lead. It took me 3 days to get control back. Never again.

There are several ways to get an audience following you. I call them "Compliance Techniques".

- GET THE AUDIENCE TO WRITE SOMETHING DOWN, SUCH AS THE SESSION TIMES

Stand by the flip chart with pen ready, "You might like to write these down…." & wait till they get a pen out.

- LIST SOME OPERATING AGREEMENTS – GO THROUGH SOME BASICS ABOUT HOW THE TRAINING WILL BE CONDUCTED
  - ¤ Talk only front to back
  - ¤ Be on time
  - ¤ Do all exercises to the best of your Ability
  - ¤ This is an Intensive Training
    - → Keep Distractions to a Minimum
- GET THEM TO WRITE THEIR REASONS FOR BEING THERE
- GET THEM TO PUT EVERYTHING DOWN, STAND UP AND BREATHE, WITH YOU LEADING THE BREATHING
- "TURN TO THE PERSON TO YOUR RIGHT AND GIVE THEM A MASSAGE"
- "TURN TO THE PERSON TO YOUR RIGHT AND IN-TRODUCE YOURSELF WITH YOUR NAME, WHAT YOU DO AND WHY YOU'RE HERE"
- GET THEM TO FORM INTO GROUPS
- STAND AT THE FRONT OF THE ROOM & BE SILENT TIL THEY ARE
- ASK THEM TO DO SOMETHING & WAIT TIL THEY DO
- "NOD THIS WAY FOR YES"
- "ALL IN FAVOUR OF THIS SAY AYE"
- STEP ASIDE AND FRAME IT – "Oh by the way, this is the part of the training where you're supposed to…"

- IF A QUESTION SHOWS UP, TELL THEM YOU'LL TAKE QUESTIONS SHORTLY. THEN ASK THAT PERSON PERSONALLY AT THE Q & A SECTION.
- MAKE SURE YOU START ANY PRESENTATION WITH ENOUGH OF THEIR REASONS WHY IT'S IMPORTANT THAT THEY LISTEN. GIVE THEM RELEVANCE
- BUILD RAPPORT WITH RAPPORT LEADERS
- USE UNIVERSAL EXPERIENCES – Talk about things that everyone can relate to, common experiences most people have or could easily imagine. Identify with them very early on. Get them saying "me too", not "so what"
- KNOW WHO IS IN YOUR AUDIENCE, WHAT THEIR OUTCOME IS, WHAT ATTITUDES WILL BE PRESENT, DO THEY WANT TO BE THERE?
- TELL THEM UP FRONT "here's what we're going to do"
- KEEP ASKING "Is this useful? Does that make sense?"
- PRESUPPOSE SOME OBJECTIONS AND DISENABLE THEM RIGHT AT THE START.
- ASK "HANDS UP WHO….?" AND RAISE YOUR HAND. They're now following you…
- MIND READ WHY THEY ARE HERE AND PRESENT THEM WITH THOSE REASONS.
- USE A PIECE OF MUSIC AS THE "THEME TUNE" FOR THE COURSE, AND TELL THEM TO COME BACK IN WHEN THEY HEAR IT
- DO HA BREATHING TOGETHER

You're in Rapport with them from the start. Never mind pacing, you go straight for Leading

FINAL EXERCISE

Use the content that you came up with in the 4-Mat section, and the three stories that you thought of in the Metaphor section. Put all of this together in the following order:

Metaphor 1

Metaphor 2

Metaphor 3

Why?

What?

How?

What if?

Metaphor 3

Metaphor 2

Metaphor 1

Now that's a superb presentation! Congratulations. You're now ready to stand and deliver.

Just how creative can you get? What states would be required for the material you're teaching? What if you designed your presentation around that? How many universal experiences can you come up with? Have 5 metaphors that you can tell anytime you need them.

Which reminds me of a story. I'd just come back from Trainer's Training and a couple of days later it was my mother's 70th birthday. My brother gave an impromptu speech, and then I was asked to. I ended up telling the same metaphors I'd used on the Training, and I had a room full of pensioners in trance…

So Merlin became King of England because he had all the power he required to pull the sword from the stone. But he was to realise later that it was nothing to do with the sword – he had all the resources he required inside, and magic isn't magic at all when you know how it's done.

So my first seminar was in my house with half a dozen people and a flipchart beside the television. I've come a long way since then, but it's a great way to start.

Now when I look back at the talk I did in that cold pub in Arbroath, it's amazing I got away with what I did, because I knew none of these skills. Now, my presentations have come a long way and are a lot more compelling, and so can yours.

And telling yourself "I can't do this" in front of a room full of retiring postmen isn't a strategy that I'd recommend you follow. Far better to just make it up as you go along, knowing that you really can trust your unconscious mind to say whatever needs to be said.

But then that's just a story…

"It's OK to be yourself in front of an audience"

10

WHAT IF GETTING HEALTHY & WELL WAS QUICK & PAINLESS?

WHAT THIS CHAPTER IS ABOUT

What if getting healthy was quick, painless and fun? You'd at least want to know more, wouldn't you? I mean, you know that your mind controls your body. You may even have exercised your body, but have you trained your mind? We're talking about learning to run your own head so you can do what the Greeks and Romans suggested: "healthy mind, healthy body". Have the health you wanted before you

1. started worrying about it
2. were told that you couldn't

We're going to have a look at your health, and the perspective we're going to use is called Hypno Genetic Evolution.

BUT FIRST A STORY...

Mr. Wright was a cancer patient. A new drug invented to cure cancer, and he was one of the first trial subjects to try it. This was a man who was bed ridden, on oxygen and had been given six months to live. After only five days of being on the drug, the tumours began to shrink. Four days later he was out of his bed & chatting away to the other patients. Interestingly they checked some of the other subjects and they weren't improving, there seemed to be something different about Mr. Wright. Maybe *he just trusted that it would work....* He certainly wanted it to. Two months later he's back living his life, fly-ing his plane, tending his garden. That's when the news broke – the clinical trials were declared a failure and the drug doesn't work. After a certain amount of time the drug's shelf life expired and it became ineffective. One day later Mr. Wright's tumours began to regrow, and his condition worsened. His Doctor however couldn't just stand by and watch this happen, and he had faith in Mr. Wright - there *seemed to be something different* about Mr. Wright, so the Doctor started giving him injections of the next generation of the drug, the new improved recipe. Well, actually, the injections were of distilled water only, but the doctor didn't tell him that. So the tumours began to shrink again…

Then there is the Russian Miner story – that many decades ago a team of miners were digging a very deep vertical tunnel, and when they reached the bottom they discovered they had dug their way into a huge cavern *full of* precious metals and *invaluable resources.* However, they hadn't taken care of the basic structure of the tunnel, which subsequently collapsed around them, trapping them in the cave. Now *being expert at what they do* the miners could estimate the size of the cave, the number of people in it and thus the amount of air available to breathe. So they could estimate how long they had to live before the rescue teams could get to them. So they made a deal with each other – knowing they had about ten hours worth of air, the team leader, who was the only one wearing a watch, told them he'd count down the time by calling out how many hours they'd been in the cave on the hour, every hour. And so after some time had passed, he called out "That's one hour so far…."

What about the Freight Train incident in the Midwestern Ameri-can States, where a young teenager left home after a blazing argu-ment with his father, and in the archetypical fashion hopped on the slow rumbling freight train that went through his home town every night. *He'd often dreamed of going somewhere new.* So in the late evening dusk he jumped aboard a carriage, clambered into the metal boxcar and slowly pulled the heavy door shut. As it clunked into place, he realized that there was no handle on the inside. In fact, he'd just sealed himself in a refrigeration car, and as he peered at the barely visible temperature gauge on the wall, his heart sank to his boots as he read -20 degrees Centigrade...

SO WHY IS YOUR HEALTH IMPORTANT?

Do I really need to ask you that question?

When you're unwell it's very difficult to concentrate, get things done, do even the simplest tasks and live normally.

To live life fully you need a level of health & vitality. It's not a should, it's a MUST!

The statistics about mortality and morbidity rates are shocking!

The longer you're alive the more you can do!

When you understand how your body works and you give it the respect and care it deserves, it will take care of you.

Everything we do requires energy. Energy comes from being healthy, therefore everything we do requires you to be healthy.

The state of your entire physiology all comes from what you do inside your head. Your body is the vehicle that you travel around in. Do you want to chug along in a battered Rolls Canardly (rolls down one hill but can 'ardly get up the next) in the hard shoulder all the time, or would you rather zoom down the outside lane in a lean, efficient machine?

Most people's energy reserves are exhausted and their body shows it. How about you?

A DEFINITION: *HEALTH ACCORDING TO:*

THE WORLD HEALTH ORGANISATION
"Health is a state of complete physical, mental, or social well-being, and not merely the absence of disease or infirmity."

NUTRITION AND DIET THERAPY
"Optimal human fulfillment and productivity — quality of life"

ENCYCLOPEDIA OF NATURAL MEDICINE
"Health is the result of.....individual responsibility – choosing healthy alternatives over non-healthy."

CENTRE FOR ATTITUDINAL HEALING
Health is inner peace, healing is letting go of fear – our true measure of health is how mentally peaceful we are, despite our circumstances. To heal we must release our attachment to fear, thus increasing our inner peace.

DR. ANDREW WEIL ON STRESS AND THE MIND
Physician Andrew Weil, research associate in ethnopharmacology at Harvard University and author of Health and Healing, says, "External, material objects are never causes of disease, merely agents waiting to cause specific symptoms in susceptible hosts. Rather than warring on disease agents with the hope of eliminating them, we ought to worry more about strengthening resistance to them and learning to live in balance with them more of the time."

Health is the result of individual responsibility - choosing healthy alternatives over non-healthy.

If we have poor coping skills, deficient social support, and high stress, the internal balance of our bodies may be easily upset and our resistance lowered. Illness or disease, then, occurs more from our vulnerability than from external agents that are "the cause" of our health problems. The more vulnerable we are, the more risk we run of getting sick.

WHAT IS HGE & WHAT'S IT GOT TO DO WITH MY HEALTH?

Hypno Genetic Evolution is a science & study of how the human mind works. We evolve our genetics by the suggestions we give to ourselves. At it's heart, HGE is a collection of methods and models that conveniently explain how people think, behave and change. As a result, it offers rapid, impactful, almost magical change in people, whether that's in Business, Sales, Therapy, Sport, Coaching, Education, Health, or Parenting. It's all about taking charge of your communication, language, your thoughts & your feelings. HGE is profound knowledge that allows you to change the only two things you'll ever want to change: how you're feeling, and what you're doing.

Now we live in a world that has a lot of information. This is the information Age. But there's a vast difference between information and knowledge. Information is knowing that water is H20. Knowledge is being able to make it rain when your crops are thirsty. And there's a vast difference between knowledge and wisdom. Knowledge is useless unless you can use it. Only then does it become Wisdom.

Most medical metaphors are thick with references to warfare and battlefields. Listen to the language – "boosting the immune system, killer T-cells, fighting the invading virus, eradicate the cancer". The biomedical model either cuts things out, burns them off or puts chemicals in. Yet nothing in that model heals your body. Your body heals your body. (By the way, the third biggest killer in the US today, is **the hospital**) The bio psychosocial model suggests that we have an immune system, which keeps the bacteria out, but that emotions and mental stress compromises it. The micro organisms only become predatory when you're out of balance.

Look back at the model of the four bodies of man. If you want the physical body to improve, you need to let go of any emotional blockages. The little black bags steal your energy, and keep the immune system diminished and operating at less that 100% power. Does that make sense? We are exhausting our array of antibiotics, and we need to find a new way to restore physical and emotional health. Or perhaps we just need to remember an old way... Rediscover that there are other ways to heal the body, that don't involve cutting something out, burning something off or injecting chemicals in. A few hundred years ago all disease was thought to be "spirit possession" and required the attention of the Shaman to heal it. Now whether you believe in that or not, the fact is that when the Shaman conducted his ceremony, the patients usually got better...

Doctors diagnose what's wrong. Shaman, Kahuna, Magicians, HGE Practitioners help the client change. Doctors prescribe. We intervene.

In HGE we use a really simple model called "Reasons versus Results" which we discussed earlier in this book. In life, you either get the result you want, or you have a whole bunch of reasons why you don't. Another word for reasons is "excuses". And there are only 3:

1.   Negative emotions – you feel angry, sad, scared, guilty, hurt or ashamed

2.   Inefficient Strategies – you don't know how, or what you've tried hasn't worked.

3.   Limiting Beliefs – you don't believe you can be healthy, people like you aren't, there's nothing you can do about it, fat equals safety, that sort of thing

Which of these reasons, or excuses, do you use to justify less than perfect health?

And knowing that with the technology of HGE you can change any and all of these in hours, not years, what are you going to do about it?

Now you've probably tried to change these things consciously, and that probably didn't work. How many people do you know who have a harmful habit that they are perfectly conscious of, they know they should stop, they've read about it, talked about it, cried about it, yet they're still doing it! How can that be? That's because you have to change these things unconsciously. *It's your unconscious mind*, or the processes that occur outside of your conscious awareness, *that runs your body*.

Imagine healing disease in advance before it reaches the physical stage. Fix things before they get broken…

We live in a world where if you discover a new way of getting ill, you get to name it after you. Crones' Disease, Alzheimer's'. There are thousands of ways to be ill. There's only really a couple of ways to be healthy.

HOW DOES HGE TREAT HEALTH ISSUES?

GENERAL CONSIDERATIONS WHEN CONSULTING AN HGE PRACTITIONER

In HGE we believe that an illness is a communication – when you pay attention to the communication, the symptoms will lessen, and can disappear if you're willing to change your lifestyle, relationships, nutrition, whatever. Provided you keep listening to your physical body and pay attention to the signals it sends you, you can stay in good health.

A good HGE Practitioner will always ask, "Other than seeing me, what else have you done for this condition?". They should also be selective - you don't want to be someone's next failure if they have seen many & not yet changed.

Any good complementary therapist should refer the client to someone else if the clients:

• Don't want to be there,

- Don't want to change,
- Have secondary gain (more benefits to being ill than getting well)
- or if your intuition says you can't help client send them on — terminate the therapy

Remember it is illegal to interfere with client-Doctor relationship. It is a good time to work with a client if their GP gave up on them. It is illegal to prescribe (even homeopathic) It may be all right to say, "This is what I would do if I were diagnosed with xxx." It is best to align with current laws even if you disagree! Ask if they have seen a doctor. If they have, ask to see the written diagnosis.

Remember a therapist heals no one. It is against the law for a therapist to cure anyone. The client heals themselves depending upon the rapport with their Unconscious Mind.

A therapist can only help them make symptoms disappear, and have body act as though totally healthy.

You also need to believe people are in control of their state. A major part of the intervention is to take responsibility for living.

Proceed slowly with the investigation and detailed personal history. Don't open up issues if you don't want to yet. The longer the ailment has existed the longer it may take to heal.

Other expert opinions:

Phineas Parkhurst Quimby: '"Before healing a person, they must give up their unreasonable belief & faith in modern science, and in religion. E.G. ideas like "I must be punished."

Deepak Chopra: "The immune system is constantly eavesdropping on the internal dialogue."

98% of atoms of body turn over every year. New soft tissue average 3 months, liver every 6 wks, new skin 4 wks. New stomach lining every 5 days. Bones can take a year to replace self

Read "Molecules of Emotion" by Candace Pert, and "The Holographic Universe" by Michael Talbot, and "Quantum Healing" by

Chopra for more information on these fascinating insights into how the human body works.

Dr Paul Goodwin: We have 10 to the 10th to the 11th neurological connections in the body. Our old notions of disease need to go. **Theron Q. Dumont** says (in Mental Therapeutics 1914) you can talk to any organ of the body. **Simontons** have parts of the body fighting. Best to get intervention of the disease. The Brain communicates with neurotransmitters all through the body. To reduce the system to the brain & nervous system is too reductionistic. Goodwin says the unit of the body is the nervous system. Allopathic medicine given us good things e.g. treatment for bacterial infection/trauma care, and it took us out of the age of epidemics. It does poorly with cancer/virus/auto immune diseases. In other words, if your vehicle breaks down you should take it to a garage (Biomedical model). Complementary Therapies are about servicing and MOT'ing your vehicle. (Biopsychosocial model)

Pending Research - 30,000 case studies on cancer indicate: Person has a significant emotional event and has no strategy to cope with it, and thus obsesses/internalises it. This emotional trauma develops a brain lesion on the surface of the brain, which then sends wrong information to the corresponding organ in the body. Client develops symptoms within 1-3 yrs.

> **We can live healthy lives if we have good heredity,**
> **the body is allowed to recover well, and**
> **we keep negative emotions cleared out.**

HEALTH & HEALING FACTORS IN HGE

In HGE we treat physical dis-ease as a Limiting decision made by the unconscious mind. At some point, it has decided that things can't go on like this and something has to change. As soon as that happened, the blueprint altered and the physical body started to change. The reverse is also true. Remove that decision, and the body starts the healing process.

My father used to talk about "Black November", since that was the month when he and various other family members tended to get sick. Repeatedly. Guess which month he died in?

We also investigate all of these factors with a client dealing with physical symptomology:

CONFLICTS

Check on the following areas for possible conflict...

Beliefs - use "Exploring Beliefs About Health" (below). Look for Limiting decisions and disconnect with Time Line Therapy, or belief change work

Values - elicit re health & fitness. If life threatening disease elicit values for "Life". Look for conflicts.

Parts - look for incongruence, verbal & nonverbal. Listen to language. Can always integrate an invading virus part with the health part, in deep trance.

Repressed behaviour - ask if there's anything they want to do but can't, anything they feel compelled to do that isn't acceptable?.

MOTIVATIONS

Check on what other motivations there could be. This is Secondary gain, so use those questions. Ask "What benefits does this give you?" If you keep the gain you'll keep the disease.

THE EFFECTS OF SUGGESTION

A Significant Emotional Event can act like a posthypnotic suggestion, so check for events in the last three years prior to diagnosis.

ORGAN LANGUAGE

Listen for it in client's language. Are they incanting themselves? "Pain in the ass", "Dying to go on holiday", "Stabbed me in the chest"

IDENTIFICATION

Who and what they identify with during key developmental periods in their growing up:

Imprint	0-7	Parents.
Modeling	7-14	Friends. Parents. Heroes. Family, [weight]
Socialisation	14-21	Friends. Sexual Relations, [habits, smoking]
Business	21-35	Business Partners. Company.

MASOCHISM

Self-punishment, a result of guilt. Ask "What have you done wrong? What have you been doing that you shouldn't have been doing?"

PAST SIGNIFICANT EMOTIONAL EVENTS

"If you knew the root cause of this condition, when would it have been?" When did you choose to have this, and for what purpose?"

BODY IMAGE

Formed when? See Identification periods. What do they remember about how or who they wanted to be like? Can they hold a picture in their mind's eye of themselves without the disease? If not, when did they decide that? How does it make them feel? Look for Negative emotions.

General HGE treatment will consist of

1. Note idea of blueprint for perfect health stored in the unconscious mind
2. Cite Chopra as above
3. When did they choose to have this? If they knew...?

4. Time Line Therapy® to clear Limiting Decision to have disease

5. Time Line Therapy® to clear all negative emotions

6. Hypnosis to ask Unconscious Mind to heal body

7. Future Pace for people who don't believe it (the soothsayers of doom who can reinstall the problem!)

8. Help the client create a future vision of a healthy them and what they're going to do with their life (If there's no reason to live, why get better?) This is the true meaning of "re-mission"

Always remember that the very act of just sitting down with another human being and talking things through is therapeutic. **The most personal gift we can give another human being is our total and complete attention, and unconditional acceptance.** Just the act of being fully present with that person, even with no words spoken, is much more important than to have a prepared game plan of interventions and clever language patterns. I used to prepare an hour of therapy interventions for every hour of therapy I did with my clients. Not any more.

Rather than prepare what to say so you always have the "right thing" up your sleeve, just be with the person. Even if there's complete silence, the connection is precious.

Maybe real healing is more about listening with unconditional acceptance, rather than trying to "fix" the person...

AN HGE EXERCISE YOU CAN DO YOURSELF - EXPLORING BELIEFS ABOUT HEALTH

Complete the following sentences:

Being healthy means-

If I am healthy then I can-

Being completely healthy would mean changing...

If I were to take charge of my own health it would mean-

When I am unwell, it means that...

The following things stop me from being healthy...

The following things help me to be healthy...

Which of the following beliefs is true for you? Then complete the sentence in your own words:

I do not deserve to be healthy because...

I deserve to be healthy because...

I may not regain my health because...

I will regain my health because...

It is wrong to want to be healthy because...

It is right to want to be healthy because...

It's not possible for me to be completely healthy because...

It's possible for me to be completely healthy because...

Being healthy is unrealistic because...

Being healthy is realistic because...

Now what do you believe about being ill?

How do you know when you are ill?

What does illness mean to you?

What does injury mean to you?

Think of an area in health where you are not getting what you want. Then answer the following:

Why are you not getting what you want?

What does this tell you about your beliefs about health?

What beliefs would you have to change to increase your health?

How much of your explanation would an impartial observer agree with?

WHAT IF YOU TREATED YOUR HEALTH THIS WAY?

Milton Erickson MD said that the Unconscious Mind is a warehouse of resources – most people use a flashlight. You really ought to put the warehouse lights on!

How would you apply some of the ideas in this book to your own state of health?

What realisations have you had whilst reading this, and what can you do with that?

What decisions did you make 3-5 years ago that got you to where you are now?

What are the improvements you wish to make in the quality of your life?

What needs to be different for your life to be perfect?

Where in your life are you compromising?

Where in your life are you denying your potential?

What do you want more of in your life?

What do you want less of in your life?

Isn't there another way?

What are you doing now in order to get something, rather than just getting that thing without having to go through all this?

How much longer can you continue living this way?

What are you tolerating?

When will you give that up?

Are you suffering about this? How so?

What is the easier way?

How much is this costing you?

IF YOU DON'T

All you'll have is what *you already have*, and the level of health that that has led to. Nothing will have changed.

WHEN YOU DO

You'll *take charge of your own head* and get the level of health you feel you deserve. You would experience a renewed level of energy to *do more of what you want to do*

WHAT DO I DO NEXT?

You may also like to book a free initial consultation for a Personal Breakthrough session in the area of health.

Call me on 0800 072 5792 and mention that you've been reading this book – we'll be happy to give you some advice on where to take things next.

You can also read some powerful testimonials on health issues at our website www.jonathanclark.org

If you want to be kept up to date on workshops and developments through our newsletter, simply email enquiry@jonathanclark.org to subscribe.

DISCLAIMER:

All information contained in this book is the opinion of the author and is provided for educational purposes only. It is neither to be construed as medical or psychological advice, nor does it attempt to diagnose or cure any medical condition or psychological issue. Only a licensed provider can legally offer any medical or psychological advice. Consult the health care professional of your choice for medical and/or psychological care and advice.

AND SO BACK TO OUR STORY...

The Freight Train incident – when the police finally tracked the train to its next destination, they were waiting. Once the freight train had stopped, they searched all the carriages but to no avail, leaving only the refrigerated one unopened. To their amazement, when they opened the freezer compartment, there they found the youth – frostbitten, blue with cold and dead of hypothermia. I say amazing, because the refrigerated carriage was unpowered, fully ventilated and basically a big metal box under a hot summer sky. *It hadn't been switched on....*

The Russian Miners were trapped in the cavern – knowing they only had about 10 hours of air, the team leader called out "That's six hours so far…" However, *there was something else going on.* In an attempt to prolong the teams' lives, the leader decided silently to himself, that after two real hours had passed, he'd announce it as one hour. That way maybe, just maybe, he could prolong their lives. When the rescue team got to them they found them all alive and well. Except one. The team leader – the man with the watch. He was the only one who really knew *how long they had been down there*

News got out that the drug didn't work at all. Mr. Wright died days later from cancer. Yet there was so much evidence to prove that the Placebo effect had given him two remissions – that Mr. Wright's conscious mind just needed to go through some sort of ritual to *allow his unconscious mind to do the healing work.* He had to give himself permission. *You basically heal yourself.*

"Information is knowing that water is H20. Knowledge is being able to make it rain"

11

CHANGE YOUR MIND CHANGE YOUR LIFE

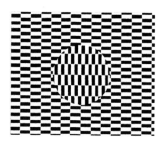

We'll continue your learning with the ultimate road to effortless, automatic and permanent personal transformation – Hypnosis. Hypnosis allows you to

- Take control of unconscious programming which holds you back
- Rewrite it quietly & easily
- Achieve the health, peace and happiness which has eluded you up until now

Now what does the word "Hypnosis" bring to your mind......?

Many people's ideas about Hypnosis have mistakenly come from the stage show, not the therapy clinic.

Hypnosis has been used as a therapeutic technique since the beginning of history. References are made to it in The Bible. The sleep temples of ancient Greece and Egypt were places of healing. In the 18th century Franz Mesmer discovered he could induce trance like states, which he called "Animal Magnetism", and he used this to treat every type of illness imaginable in Europe's most famous clinic. His approach, called "Mesmerism", was discredited back then, in a report that failed to examine the part of the healing process played by the patient themselves.

In reality, hypnosis is a two person relationship, as the individual creates their own relaxed trance state by following the instructions of the hypnotherapist.

By the early 1800's a surgeon called James Easdale used Hypnosis to induce anaesthesia during operations, without chemicals. In the 19th Century James Braid (another surgeon) coined the term "Hypnosis" to explain the induction of a trance like state through simple suggestions to a concentrating patient. Freud briefly used Hypnosis to treat neuroses before shifting to much more time-consuming talking-therapies.

Hypnosis thrived as a form of stage entertainment, thus distorting the public's view of a powerful therapeutic tool. In 1955 the British Medical School recognised Hypnotherapy as a valid method of treatment.

People who've experienced the benefits of trance often describe it as a "magical" experience. How else can you describe something that can change limiting habits in hours or even minutes?

But where there's magic, there's mystery, and I've noticed that people who are attracted to it and who get their hopes up tend to hesitate to explore it, because they aren't sure they want someone else controlling their minds. So please remember - **you cannot be made to do things against your will that you wouldn't do in the waking state.**

In fact what happens in hypnosis is like what happens to your body if you run on a treadmill – neurological and physiological changes whose effects can be observed, measured and understood.

EEG-based research shows that when you go into a trance state, the left brain conscious mind takes a back seat while the right brain unconscious mind pays more attention, opening up and becoming more accessible than normal

When the unconscious mind is open and receptive, it takes affirmations or suggestions as more acceptable. That means you can **rewrite the old programming that runs whole areas of your thinking and behaviour**, so that when you come back to fully conscious again, the new programming runs in the background all by itself. It's like "defragging" the hard drive in your head!

The true magic of hypnosis is that you don't have to comprehend the scientific, neurological processes involved to make it work – **you just have to be willing to give it a chance and really, deep down, *want* what you ask for.**

WHY ISN'T IT EASY TO GET WHAT YOU WANT?

If you're anything like me, you've probably asked yourself the same question. Problem is, the most obvious answers – the ones everyone tells you – aren't true...

It ISN'T about desire – you can desperately want a result and still never achieve it, can't you?

It ISN'T determination – how many times have you vowed to change and still did nothing about it? Honestly, haven't we all?

It ISN'T taking action – you can do all the right things, follow all the rules, and still have your hopes dashed. That ever happened to you?

If you can relate to the frustration of consistently being denied the things you really crave in your life – in spite of your best efforts and desire – then here's the news:

Somewhere between wanting something, and getting it...between setting a goal and achieving it...between where you are right now and where you'd ideally like to be...there is a missing part of

the formula. A secret ingredient that you never thought to look for, because you had no idea it existed.

MEET THE "SILENT PARTNER" WHO'S BEEN RUNNING YOUR LIFE

Imagine if you owned a small business and the wrong products are coming in, orders are getting mixed up, numbers don't add up. You're doing everything right but the results are all wrong, and you're baffled. What's going on?

Now imagine finding out that your silent partner – someone you rarely speak to or meet with – has been overriding all of your decisions and has been running the show himself!

THIS SCENARIO TAKES PLACE EVERY DAY, ONLY THE BUSINESS IS YOUR LIFE, AND THE PARTNER PULLING THE STRINGS IS YOUR UNCONSCIOUS MIND...

From the way you handle your money, the people you're attracted to, the food you eat...even the state of your health...all of your behaviours, actions and attitudes are ruled by your unconscious mind.

And if you're like very other human being I've ever met, you have limiting beliefs, past hurts and dumb habits that hold you back and drag you down, yes? The very fact that the unconscious can resist change is WHY you need to learn Hypnosis.

These beliefs and habits have their origins in deep rooted past experiences that are often long-forgotten by you, but your unconscious mind NEVER forgets. And sometimes, like a scolded child, it overreacts and interprets events in a way that creates obstacles for you, AND YOU DON'T EVEN KNOW WHAT'S GOING ON IN THERE!

Take weight loss for example. You can diet, exercise, stop eating carbs, hire a fitness trainer, do all the best things you can think of to lose excess pounds. But what if your unconscious mind thinks that the extra weight is "body armour" to protect you, or that to be powerful you've got to be big like Aunt Marjory was…? Guess who wins?

The same holds true in money, relationships, health, social life, any situation you can think of – if your logical conscious mind wants one thing, but your emotional unconscious mind likes things the way they are, good luck! **Its simply not going to happen!**

WHAT IF YOU COULD REPROGRAM THE UNCONSCIOUS, BY LEARNING TO TALK ITS LANGUAGE? AND WHAT IF IT COULD TALK BACK? WHOAH!

Once you know how to do that , you'll be able to make changes that you've struggled with for years – even changes you might have thought were impossible for you, because you'll be working WITH your silent partner, not AGAINST them. Imagine for a moment – if it has the power to stop you, what can you achieve with it working FOR you?

Since the unconscious mind takes orders from the conscious mind, we can consciously substitute new, constructive ideas to negate the old, outdated negative ones.

To do that, we need to teach you hypnosis – how to communicate directly with your unconscious mind. Then you'll learn how to talk to anyone else's…

WHAT HYPNOSIS IS…AND WHAT IT CERTAINLY ISN'T

Hollywood, Derren Brown and science fiction have left most of us with a very inaccurate picture of what hypnosis is really all about.

To begin with, you are not asleep. On the contrary, you are in a heightened state of awareness, fully awake, just very deeply relaxed, and responsive to anything you'd like to take on board. **Remember – your mind will flatly reject anything that goes against your values and beliefs.**

But one common perception of Hypnosis is true – **it is extraordi-**

narily powerful, and it can have an immediate, profound and permanent effect on your behaviour.

In this chapter I'll dispel the myths and teach you the fascinating mechanics of trance, including:

1. The difference between the "showbiz entertainment" stage show hypnosis that you're bound to have seen, (usually raucous, fun, shocking and done for show) and Hypnotherapy (safe, healthy, quiet, relaxed done for life enhancement). As C. Roy Hunter (winner of the 1990 Hypnotic Voice Of The Year) once said:

    "All Hypnotherapy employs the use of hypnosis,
    but not all hypnosis is Hypnotherapy"

2. How to communicate directly with your unconscious mind/ inner self, and how to get answers that are undeniable. Just suppose you could talk to your own body – what would you ask it?

3. How to bring your 2 minds into harmony so you can achieve more, and faster than ever before.

4. Why you don't need to relive past unpleasant experiences in order to correct the results they created and let them go once and for all.

Here's what one of my recent clients said:

"Jonathan's skills, experience and knowledge are extensive and he has the gift of applying the right technique at the right time. As I've found, he is also adept at testing his clients when he feels it's warranted. I made more progress in 7 hours with Jonathan than I had in over 7 years of psychotherapy.

Our work together steadily built up my confidence and self-esteem, reignited hope and fuelled belief. Having been at war with myself ever since I could remember, to get to a point where I could accept and trust my unconscious mind and higher self as well as my conscious mind was an immense milestone.

There was a part of me, however small, that had refused to allow me to kill myself and I had a fantasy life that kept me going for many years. Jonathan, in his straightforward, sincere and light-hearted way, made me realise the possibility that not only could life be worth living but I could actually make the vast majority of my daydreams come true.

Only a few months ago, I was at the end of my life. Although I didn't die, that life is indeed over. My work with Jonathan has revealed a new dimension of being and I feel that life is just beginning. I am truly alive for the first time and ready to become the person I've always wanted to be ... and more.

Having searched in vain for many years for a purpose, now I have it. I'm going to learn what Jonathan does so that I can do for others what he has done for me. I have a profound admiration and respect for him and his methods. There is surely no greater job satisfaction than that of helping people radically transform their lives for the better."

LEARN HOW TO HELP YOURSELF AND HELP OTHERS

Induce trance in yourself – relax, go inside, and come out feeling better. Enjoy all the mental & physical benefits of a deep refreshing nap with just a few minutes of hypnosis Induce trance in others – help other people relax and change habits, beliefs...remove unfounded worries, fears and anxieties that plague people's thoughts, strain their health and retard their progress

Deliver trance deepening techniques – the deeper the trance, the more the impact

Programme yourself in different ways – delete negative, counteractive and destructive files from your subconscious "computer" and replace them with positive files that boost and support you How to apply Hypnosis for personal and professional use

Activate your body's natural healing ability to target any illness or disorder you may be experiencing

Yet another success story:

"Wow! Where do I start?

In January this year I had ME, and had done for about 18 months. I was physically and mentally tired all the time, as well as experiencing all the other symptoms that ME can bring. I had also had serious problems with food intolerances for five years, which had resulted in all sorts of digestive difficulties and ill health. As you may imagine, I was pretty fed up with being ill.

I had done so much to improve my health, had tried so many different therapies, and spent so much money. Some therapies helped for a little while, some didn't help at all, and some did help long term, but very slowly.

I felt restricted and frustrated, and wanted change, immediate change. I felt I'd done the feeling bad thing, and that it was time to feel good again.

And then I attended Jonathan's Practitioner course and BAM, the ME was gone. I remember the specific moment that I felt it lose its grip on me. It was during a demonstration of a technique, and I was the person being demonstrated on. I instantly felt different, surprisingly so. I knew that something fantastic was happening. This was it, the therapy that was going to deliver the fast result I had been looking for, for so long.

Now, when I think back to that time, it seems like a different me, because those old feelings are so far removed from what I'm all about now.

I'm happy, positive, content, and full of drive. I've taken up squash, which I'd never played before, and it's so much fun - I even win a game now and then! I've started practising therapies again so I can help other people. I've started work on a property development project. That's an ambition that I had for years, but never had the energy to do it. Now, I'm right in the thick of it, stripping wallpaper, painting walls. This time last year I struggled to climb the stairs in my house, and now I'm up and down ladders, ripping up carpets, hammering in nails.

As well as all that, I also work full time, in a job that I really enjoy. Every day, I go into work and have a laugh with my colleagues, and get some good work done too!

As well as the physical improvements, my concentration and mental alertness have also reached new levels. I can learn quickly and easily, and think differently from before."

Eliminate every negative thought, mindset and impression that unbeknownst to you, has harmed your self esteem and held you back from total success and fulfilment

Rid yourself of the still-lingering effects of toxic, negative energy vampires who've bullied, intimidated or put you down – bosses, teachers, ex's – and permanently protect yourself from them in the future

And much more…

WHAT CAN BE TREATED?

Unwanted habits, stress, anxiety, skin conditions, breathing disorders, sleep problems, gynaecological problems, pain, phobias, compulsions, painful emotions, sexual issues, weight problems, exam anxiety and lots more...

You can also enhance performance at work, study, sport, improve your memory, develop the imagination, make affirmations actually stick, and boost self-confidence. The possibilities are endless.

Note that Hypnosis is not a substitute for orthodox medical care – patients under medical supervision must remain under that care throughout any complementary treatment.

A client-centred hypnotherapist with a variety of simple techniques is more effective than an armchair scholar of hypnosis who doesn't even know how to create rapport.

Many of my clients have spent years trying to overcome their challenges without success, and then they came to me. If only one of their previous "helping professionals" had studied hypnosis, they'd have broken through the blocks in a matter of hours, sometimes minutes!

This really is the secret to personal change work – all change requires trance.

Everyone goes in and out of trance everyday – watching TV, or driving the car are common trances. You probably have whilst reading this page...All trance is about learning how to go into a trance, a state only you can allow. You are not "hypnotised" – you simply follow instructions and relax yourself.

CREATE A CUSTOMISED, TAILOR MADE HYPNOTIC SCRIPT DESIGNED TO SUIT YOUR UNIQUE NEEDS

You will be taught how to be your own guru – no longer will you keep searching, looking for the magic bullet, because there isn't one...**out there.** It's inside you right now, just like every philosopher has said all along. Only this time, I'll finally teach you how to access it! In a very special segment of this chapter, I'll take you step by step through the simple process of self-hypnosis, giving you all the steps you need to guide yourself into a hypnotic state and **program your unconscious to create the specific results you are looking for at any given time**, without the help of a therapist or counsellor.

Each new skill will be explained, and then practiced in a real life exercise. Other essential hypnosis skills you'll learn:

> ➢ How to physically relax your mind, body and spirit
> The signs and indications of trance – from very subtle to glaringly obvious!
> When not to use Hypnosis – stay safe at all times
> How to integrate these and other HGE skills
> Methods of deepening trance
> Counting and breathing skills no one else teaches you
> Post hypnotic suggestions – so it keeps on working
> How to structure a hypnotherapy session

Oh, and you'll spend this segment of the book completely re-laxed!

This is the "Hypno" part in HGE - where you will learn how to induce trance in yourself and others, and establish a connection with your unconscious.

One thing is for certain – if you are ready to finally achieve the changes all the books, tapes and seminars promised, *change will happen!*

Now be honest with me, *be honest with me* ....

A little bit anxious about learning self-hypnosis?

That's OK, most people do feel a little wary of trance and all that *you can learn while you're in a trance*

You hear a lot of weird things about this thing called Hyp...... ah.........hypnosis

People ask a lot of funny questions. You've probably heard people who've done stage show hypnosis say that they couldn't have been hypnotised because *"they could hear everything the Hypnotist was saying"*

Well, that's funny from my point of view. I'm going to see to it that we dispel a lot of the illusions around this subject. I want to rear-range any notions you had about it.

You see, I show people how to run their own brains, and I'm going to reveal to you the truth behind the technology called Hypnosis.

Everyone's heard of it, right? Have you ever read a book about it? Or been to a Hypnosis stage show? Perhaps you've taken some train-ing, or even been to see a Hypnotherapist.

Top Hypnotherapists have evolved an incredibly effective way of training, stimulating learning and unconscious ...change ...in their students.

I'm going to share with you a whole range of trance techniques that seem to work like magic. This is a step-by-step practical chapter, with each exercise building on the last.

The questions you're probably asking yourself even now are:

What am I going to gain here?

How can I use this to impact others?

What possibilities are there if I use this stuff called Hypnosis?

How do I apply it, practically in the real world?

For what purpose could I *use the tools I'm leaving with*?

What's the right way to *learn to go into a trance*?

What will this do for me?

Now I want to rearrange any notions that you ....*had*....about Hypnosis. It's *completely different* from what you thought of. And I'm going to teach you indirect & direct techniques. I want to share with you techniques that are not normally taught on Hypnosis trainings, because these are pulled from literature. I'm a researcher – I like to *go deep*. I like *going deeply into something....* We're not going to do Direct Authoritarian hypnosis – that's old hat. We're Indirect. Most of what we cover is based on the work of Milton H. Erickson

The two kinds of hypnosis are as follows:

1.   Hetero-hypnosis, where there is one person being the hypnotist/hypnotherapist, giving the suggestions, and one subject who is going into trance. The hypnotist leads the client through a self-relaxation process, which creates the hypnotic state. Effectively the hypnotist suggests to the client that they can relax themselves, and assuming the client wants to, they will follow those instructions.

2.   Self, or auto-hypnosis, is where a person goes into a hypnotic trance, which is self-induced. In this process, the subject relaxes himself or herself as before and is in effect both the client and the hypnotist. Learning to run your own body with your own mind.

In both instances, the hypnotic state is a relaxed, attentive state that a person can only induce in themselves. In other words, no one can hypnotise you, you are responsible for creating that state in your own nervous system. Assuming you want to go into trance, you are able to relax and you are willing to accept suggestions, you will be in the hypnosis state. When one is relaxed or tired, one becomes more susceptible to suggestions. Hypnosis is simply creating that condition on purpose.

Self-hypnosis is a convenient tool that anyone can learn to use, and does not require a therapist, complicated rituals, a pyramid to sit under, membership fees or any other added complications. The ultimate in self-discovery, you can do it anytime you choose, wherever you are, whatever you are doing. You learn to "go inside" and talk to the oldest and wisest part of you that runs your body, memories and emotions, and who always tells you the truth. This conscious and unconscious connection will help you grow and evolve as you uncover the real you, and learn more about why you do what you do and your deepest needs, wants and limitations than you ever have before. As a result, your level of congruence will increase as you minimize any internal conflict and get all of you on your own side.

Once you are familiar with relaxing and listening to your inner mind, you can begin to clear the limitations that hold you back and that you subsequently project onto the world. As your internal map of the world improves, so does reality on the outside, and you will attract more of the opportunities, people and coincidences that you want. Self-hypnosis gives you the ability to influence and change your beliefs, behaviours and emotions, meaning you can be more of the person you want to be, amplifying all your best traits and minimizing all your worst. Learning to create a calm, relaxed, inner-directed state of mind reduces stress, and creates optimism and a positive outlook. You will run more positive internal representations and thus give yourself suggestions that are more positive. It also teaches you self-discipline and control, as you learn that you really are in charge of your own mind.

With self-awareness comes self-understanding, as you learn to run your own head, thoughts and emotions. Of course this can help with self-healing, be it mental wounds from previous upsets and traumas, or physical healing, knowing that he mind runs the body and can influence its recovery and optimal state.

Personally, I have a strong need for calmness and peace. The more I meditate, use trance and visualisation techniques, the calmer and more content I become. My health is extremely important to me, coming from a family background of ill health, and living in the European capital for heart disease, cancer and strokes, I am highly motivated to practice anything that boosts my health and happiness. As part of my own passion as an HGE Trainer, Life Coach and student of Huna, my study of self-hypnosis both deepens my knowledge and experience of Hypnosis, and raises my self confidence and references for what I teach. I firmly believe that as a teacher and adviser I should always be learning and growing, deepening my experience and broadening my horizons. My own growth and evolution is pulling me towards Huna and other esoteric studies and I have learned that the discipline and practice of self-hypnosis can only help my growth.

I do lots of public speaking and presentations, trainings and seminars and have done for 14 years– and I use elements of stage hypnotist skills. Richard Bandler, the man who started NLP, said a good presenter should be a good stage hypnotist. Now I'm a Master Hypnotherapist and I do a lot of one on one therapy work with clients, and have done now for over 13 years – I use trance work with all my clients. All change requires trance you see.

I'm also a Life Coach, which means people hire me as a mentor/business consultant – so I use hypnosis skills over the phone too. Imagine that…

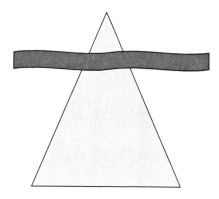

Picture an iceberg floating in the ocean. You have a Conscious mind. That's only the tip of the iceberg. And *your unconscious* .....mind is here too… That's the far bigger part of the whole, and most of it lies unseen, beneath the surface…

Erickson said clients are clients because there is a lack of rapport between your Conscious Mind and *your unconscious*

FEATURES / FUNCTIONS OF THE "TWO MINDS"

Conscious Mind   Unconscious Mind

As we discuss these two functions and educate you, notice the effect it starts to have inside your head…

Conscious Mind	Unconscious Mind
134 bits per second	everything else, 2 million bps
sequential – one after the other	simultaneous – all at once
logical	intuitive, associates things together
linear – this causes that	quantum – all connected
asks "why?" a lot, questions	knows why
thinking	feeling
waking state	sleeping, dreaming
voluntary movements	involuntary movements

aware of only now	storehouse of all memories
tries to understand problem	knows solution
goal setter	goal getter
deliberate, on purpose	automatic, always on
verbal	nonverbal – no words, speechless
analyses, picks apart	synthesizes, absorbs
attends to information	records information
limited, narrow focus	unlimited, expansive
cognitive learnings	experiential learnings

Did you notice a feeling of something spreading apart or expanding?

Milton Erickson practiced from 1920 till he died in 1980. So over 60 years he'd see about 14 patients a day, sometimes 7 days a week. He typed out all his inductions on a typewriter – using the hunt and peck method. *Just using one or maybe 2 fingers*.....

30 typed single spaced, narrow margins

of all the ways he could figure out to *go into a trance easily*

With experience he was able to get it *all the way down* to 25 pages

Then 20

Then 15

And then 10 pages

And then 9, 8 pages......

And then sssssssss 6 pages, then *all the way down* to ffff 4 pages

And then mmm 3 then 2

Then 1 then he reduced it *down further*....to one paragraph

Then one sentence...

"I realised I didn't need to use words at all" he said

I could even *take you with me into a deep trance* nonverbally

He once did an interesting experiment with an Idiot Savante – someone who knows about everything to do with one particular subject, but very little else. Erickson once got this chap to hide a pin somewhere on a University Campus, so Erickson had no idea where it was. Then, just by holding this man's wrist, he walked straight to the pin. And he did it by paying attention to the micro muscle movements in the man's arm. Anytime they walked towards the pin, the man would unconsciously tense and resist, almost imperceptibly, and Erickson could sense that resistance, which told him he was going in the right direction. Anytime he relaxed his arm as they walked away from the pin, Erickson knew that was the wrong way to go. Maybe you've seen the gifted and skilled magician and performer Derren Brown do the same thing on Channel 4's "Mind Control" programme in the UK. I went to see Derren's live show last year and he's extremely good at what he does.

Oh, and by the way, it's impossible to be in a room where someone is being hypnotised, and not *go into a trance yourself*...

All the hypnosis literature said "Just get rapport", and then induce trance. We talked about that earlier in this book. Thank goodness HGE denominalised Rapport and turned it into a process that you can learn and practice. And now you know how to do that. If you can't remember, go back and read the rapport chapter again.

Hypnotic suggestions come to us both verbally and nonverbally, all day, every day. In their book "Healing Yourself With Self-Hypnosis" authors Frank Caprio M.D. and Joseph R. Berger listed the many ways we both give and receive suggestions every day, including:

DIRECTLY

A direct suggestion is any verbal statement or physical action that is to the point and given in a "command" manner.

"Everybody stand up!" "Eat your food." "Come here."

INDIRECTLY

Indirect suggestions are primarily nonverbal motions or sound to which we often respond without being aware of doing so.

Yawn, and you cause others to yawn. Smile, and you cause others to smile. Look upward, and you cause others to look upward.

BY INFERENCE

Inferred suggestions are basically the same as indirect suggestions in that they are subtle and often nonverbal. They differ in that they convey a message from one person to another person or group.

Pointing a finger to suggest "Come here"... Nodding your head to indicate affirmation... Making a fist to suggest violent action...

FROM PRESTIGE

Prestige suggestions are those we act upon with no questions, simply because we respect and believe the authority of the source.

Small children believe their parents. We believe our doctors. We believe our teachers.

FROM EMOTIONAL APPEALS

Emotional appeals are those responses that change a person's emotional state, thereby evoking feelings or sensations that the person associates with the event.

Shouting or threats causing panic.... Antagonizing or "needling" causing anger... Gentleness or empathy causing happiness or crying...

BY SOCIAL DICTATES

These are suggestions that "lead" or "appeal" to a person's desire to belong or conform. The phrases "follow the crowd" and "peer pressure" refer to socially dictated suggestions.

Fashion... hem lines are "up" this year. Politics... that candidate stands for the worker.

Language… words change meaning by increased general usage and acceptance, such as "gear" and "gay."

NEGATIVE CLICHE SUGGESTIONS

There are literally hundreds of phrases that are repeated so often that they actually become a part of our belief systems.

Money goes to money. It's not what you know, it's who you know. You just can't win, no matter how hard you try. Look before you leap, and then he who hesitates is lost. The rat race – win it, and you're still a rat! You can't beat the system.

NEGATIVE SUGGESTIONS/PHYSICAL MANIFESTATIONS

How many times have you heard or said a phrase so often that it becomes true?

He makes me sick. My job gives me a pain in the neck. Her kids drive me crazy.

Now, there are lots of different ways of inducing trance, to make suggestions stick. Television has been proven to be more trancey than staring at a blank wall.

"Trance" – it's a word that people have funny connotations to. Trance is an everyday state – a dozy, sleepy state similar to the way you feel when you've just woken up, or you're just drifting off….. The Scottish word is "Dwam". Or like when you're sunbathing – you hear a man and his dog walking by, and you could sit up and open your eyes, but its too much like hard work. It's easier just to have your eyes stay closed…

Try this for a minute. Read these instructions, then try out this quick self-hypnosis induction. Relax your gaze, and let it fix on something you can see – an object, a picture, whatever. Then notice 5 other things you can see. Now listen to what you can hear, your breathing, a clock ticking, whatever. Then listen for 5 other sounds

– birds, the wind, pipes creaking, anything. Then become aware of how you feel sitting there, the chair or the seat you're on, then 5 other things you can feel.

Notice how that changes your state gently…

Now look for 4 things, listen for 4, feel 4

Then 3 things

Then 2 things

…and that means you're becoming more and more relaxed

with every breath you take

every move you make

every single day, every word I say

I'll be watching you……..

I could just pace your current experience

And you'll notice the heaviness setting in

As the blood flow to your limbs increases

And the more heavy your arms and legs the more you relax

Remember when you were in school

And you were writing a lot and your hand got numb

And you looked down at your own hand and asked yourself

"Is that really my hand?" cos it felt kind of disconnected

Sometimes when I tell people what I do, they try and test me

They say "OK then, can you make my arm lift unconsciously?"

And I think to myself there's 159 muscles between your finger and shoulder

And that means you can't lift it any other way…….

Only un-consciously………

I mean have you noticed yet that one of your hands feels differently from the other hand….

That means…..the one that feels cooler, or maybe hotter

The heavier of the two, or will it be the lighter of the two

Will begin to rise up

Maybe it's just tingling at the moment

Small jerky movements getting bigger…and bigger
Every time you breathe in your hands will lift all by themselves
Now I don't know which hand will begin to lift first
The right……the left
Whichever hand your **Unconscious** …wants to lift
It may be the right hand
It's always the right hand
That's right
Or sometimes it's the hand that's left
Whatever hand isn't holding the book
Or maybe it is the hand holding the book
Lifting……..lifting……….
Your unconscious …..does want to communicate….doesn't it?

If all else fails, every 90 minutes you will go into a trance. In 1986 Ernest Rossi wrote about Ultradian Rhythms, like a very trancey biorhythm. Just wait for it to come around again…

Pauses…………….work well

Any questions so far?

Ernest Rossi wrote a four Vallium set of books – the complete works of Milton Erickson. He wrote loads of books about Hypnosis – all are worth digesting.

Erickson died in 1980. Erickson & Rossi continued to produce books together till 1986. Now that bears thinking about…

I'm into researching the data, the specifics. I am anal only in that respect. I like to know where the information comes from.

A HISTORY OF HYPNOSIS

Let's go all the way back in time to early China, & Hawaii – Ha Breathing was a technique used to build the chi, the mana (life force), whilst at the same time putting the breather into a profoundly altered state of consciousness. To this day most martial arts, yoga and meditation techniques start with breathing exercises. In Hawaii the sacred knowledge was called Huna – and the Kahuna was known for that thousand yard stare that all good gurus have, called Hakalau, the Shaman state. Instantaneous healing was the norm in Hawaii. Walking on lava started the fire walking craze that Tony Robbins made modern and famous. There was the theory of the five elements, fire, air, water, earth, and the last element - the ether, or trance element, which is purple black

In India – there were the Snake charmers, the Fakirs. Hypnosis has its roots in meditation, which is Self hypnosis. Chanting Mantras in your head to drown out and control the internal dialogue. Eye closure was a sign of you're going into a trance..

Patanjali's Yoga sutras aimed for the same state of enlightenment.

In ancient Egypt there were the sleep temples, in which the priest would listen to your problems, touch your forehead and put you into a deep sleep state, and when you awakened the problem was miraculously gone!! Sound familiar? There are hieroglyphics in tombs that illustrate these procedures.

The Elber Papyrus describes an eye fixation technique. The seers of Greece used it, as did the Mayans in South America. African witch doctors, Celtic Druids, Persian Magi – in every culture on every continent, trance was used for insight and healing.

Genghis Kahn is reported to have whipped his armies into a frenzy as they saw hallucinations induced by psyched up emotional states and group suggestion. Throughout history many dictators and leaders used the same approach.

Many argue that Jesus used rapid inductions and suggestion to heal the sick, and to teach his followers. Read the section in this book on generating therapeutic metaphors for an approach that does just that.

In the Middle ages in Europe there was The Royal Touch. Touching the King's robe, usually meant being blessed or being healed. If you could get past the palace guards.. Usually purple. You'll have heard of the tradition of "Laying on of hands". To this day celebrities visit sick patients and their health improves...

1500 – Paracelsus – did healing with magnets. Nikken distributors now sell similar magnetic products 500 years later.

1600 A Priest called Valentine Braithwaite practiced hands on healing. He became known as the "Great Irish Stroker"

1725 – Vienna, a Jesuit Priest called Father Maximillian Hehl. Imagine going to see Father Hehl for confession! He used magnets to heal people. Later studied by a man called Mesmer whom you've probably heard of

1774 – Franz Anton Mesmer – where the name "Mesmerism" comes from. Inspired by seeing Father Hehl demonstrating magnetic cures, he passed his hands over patients and they got better. He had them sit in a bath full of iron filings. He wrote a Doctoral Dissertation called "De Planetarum Influxu" stating that the planets influenced the body of man. Later, he decided it wasn't the magnets that helped people, but the person's "animal magnetism" which is where that phrase comes from. He studied the Planets and magnetic fields, and postulated that the physical body was like a battery with two poles, and that sometimes those poles could be flipped and become imbalanced. (This is an opinion still shared today in the EFT technique). In those days surgery killed people, while mesmerism cured them. There were hundreds of proven cases documented in writing. What was really at work, was the clients' belief, expectation and hope that they would get better. And so they did.

SOMETIMES THE CONSCIOUS MIND NEEDS TO GO THROUGH SOME SORT OF RITUAL, TO GRANT THE UNCONSCIOUS MIND THE PERMISSION IT NEEDS TO DO THE WORK IT CAN DO.

Encouraged by a man called Mozart, Mesmer set up a public performance in Paris where he invented a special stage that held 30 people, iron rods to hold onto, special effects, dramatic music and highly suggestible subjects. He was the "Pop Idol" of his time. Benjamin Franklin investigated Mesmer's work and concluded that he was a fraud, and that al of his successes were caused by the patient believing and expecting to be cured. *How right he was!*

1779 – A Catholic Priest called Father Gassner became known as a Faith Healer, and his parish believed he had God's authority to heal them. In the subdued lighting of his cathedral, with candles, incense, suggestions all in Latin (the ancient languages always make for more belief and authority!), Gassner would touch people with a diamond studded crucifix and they would fall asleep, in as little as 7 seconds!

1800 – Marquis Chastenet de Pusseguyr – wrote about Mesmer, coined the phrase "Somnambulist" or sleep walker. He believed the magnetic power came from the magnetiser, not the client, again feeding the belief about being controlled. He would magnetise a tree, and people who touched that tree would get results. Sometimes, even if they touched the wrong tree, change occurred. But then it would…

SOMETIMES THE CONSCIOUS MIND NEEDS TO GO THROUGH SOME SORT OF RITUAL, TO GRANT THE UNCONSCIOUS MIND THE PERMISSION IT NEEDS TO DO THE WORK IT CAN DO.

Now at this point in history, Pusseguyr and his contemporaries started exploring ESP and other unacceptable theories, which again did Hypnosis no favours, scrutinised and decried by the scientific community.

1815 – Abbe Faria approaches Hypnosis from a scientific standpoint, and developed his "eye fixation" approach, still used to this day. His career ended when some jealous physicians publicly humiliated him.

1838 – Professor John Elliotson – London, started openly using Mesmerism for surgical purposes, despite conventional belief at the time that *healing required pain*!

Despite carrying out major operations with large audiences of younger, eager to learn doctors, he left the medical community after a huge bust-up, and a specially selected committee was employed to remove all records and traces of his work.

1838 – James Braid, a Scottish surgeon, set out to debunk Mesmer and his work as old wives tales, and ended up writing a book extolling all the virtues of Mesmerism, which he now renamed "Hypnosis" which from the Greek means "nervous sleep". This term still exists today, although sometimes disguised as "group meditation", "closed eye process" or "guided imagery". Yup, its all Hypnosis. He also wrote about the learning state and published a book called "Neurypnology" in 1843. Specialised in vocal suggestions and using bright light to induce trance.

1850 – Up until this time the bulk of the Medical community had shunned hypnosis because it lacked proven research. A Scottish Surgeon called James Esdaile did thousands of minor operations, hundreds of major procedures, including painless amputations, by inducing the Esdaile state, a coma like state in which he could operate on patients, without the use of any anaesthetic. He wrote a book called "Mesmerism in India" which explained how he cut the post-operative mortality rate from 50% to 8%. Note that India has a long history of the occult and esoteric, thus the patient largely already held all the belief and expectation needed. Funnily enough his success rate in Great Britain at the time was dramatically reduced – funny that.

1860 – In France Pierre Janet and Alfred Binet could create diseases and take them away again using hypnosis.

1864 – A country Doctor called Ambroise Liebault in Nancy, France develops his own system of Hypnosis and suggestion, and does a free 10 minute consultation with every patient. He was trained by a man called Charcot.

1865 – A man called Hippolite Bernheim teams up with Liebault & forms the first ever hypnosis clinic at the Nancy Medical School – the worlds most acclaimed centre for healing using hypnosis.

1873 – Dr James Charcot attempts to revive Mesmerism, including a scientific classification of various trance depths. The challenge at this point in history was that Hypnosis was used to make symptoms disappear, without any regard to addressing the underlying causes.

1880 – Dr Joseph Breuer uses Hypnosis to uncover the root cause of a girl's inability to drink water from a cup. In trance she recalled being disgusted to see a dog drinking out of her cup, hence the ongoing reaction. As soon as the root cause was made conscious, the problem disappeared. Thus was formed the basis of most psychoanalysis.

1890's – Sigmund Freud studies with Charcot at Nancy. He later declared Hypnosis didn't work and devised the talking therapy cure instead, promoting Psychoanalysis as more effective than Hypnosis. He openly stated that the Unconscious Mind was evil and dirty and perverse. Interestingly Freud was a cocaine addict and he used to rub it on his gums. His gums rotted and he had some false teeth made but they were so uncomfortable and ill-fitting, it was very hard to understand him when he spoke. So instead he started sitting behind the patient, and got them to do all the talking. Needless to say, in one stroke, Hypnosis was set back by decades, just as it was starting to get somewhere…

Emile Couet was another figure of interest at this time, promoting self-suggestion without trance. You probably know his work from the phrase "Every day in every way I'm getting better and better"

1890 – William James, an American professor of psychology, creates what becomes formally known as Psychotherapy. He also talks about Submodalities and Time Lines, two areas greatly expanded and extended in the field of NLP

1895 – Michel Chevreul a French chemist uses a pendulum to detect elements in chemical compounds. This is the same technique used by Uri Geller to detect oil and gold for big companies (with little success).

1898 – Boris Sidis "Psychology of Suggestion" wrote about difference between indirect (choices) and direct (command) suggestion.

1900 – split between two factions:

– Freud and Psychoanalysis. "Not for the poor". He also said it would take 100 - 300 hours to fix a problem. I wonder how much he charged per hour? Or how much cocaine cost back then?

- Behaviourists – no such thing as an Unconscious Mind or Hypnosis, it's all conditioned response.

1902 – Bill Twitmyer notices that when he approaches patient with small hammer, their knee jerks, hence the term "knee jerk reaction". Publishes his findings to the American Medical Association who say "ho hum".

1903 – J. Milne Bramwell lists a whole bunch of hypnosis techniques at the back of his book which calls Hypnosis a load of nonsense.

1904 – Ivan P. Pavlov makes his dogs salivate with steak and a tuning fork (not a bell). Combines this with Twitmyer's work and presents his paper called stimulus response to the Russian Medical Association who go wild over it.

1933 – Harvard University in the US, man called Clark Hull trains a young medical student called Milton Erickson.

1936 – Pavlov's work "Conditioned Reflexes" is published.

1943 – George Estabrooks prevalent in the field. During the Second World War, Hypnosis was used extensively in POW camps for dentistry, dermatology and other procedures, mainly because they had no drugs.

1920 – 1980 Milton Erickson, MD, the one man mainly responsible for getting hypnosis recognised by the AMA as a legitimate form of medical treatment in 1959.

At about the same time Carl Jung brings out work on his psychological archetypes – actually lifted from the Tarot Card deck!

1950's – Dave Elman, arch rival of Milton Erickson, practicing Hypnosis.

1957 – Andre Weitzenhoffer writes "General Techniques of Hypnosis."

1964 – Leslie LeCron writes about Ideomotor Signalling, communicating with the Unconscious with finger signals, twitches, etc.

1960's – Fritz Perls invents Gestalt Therapy. His work is edited by one John O'Stevens. He later changes his name to Steve Andreas, who later figures greatly in the field of NLP and was one of my first teachers in the subject.

1970 – Jeffrey Zeig creates the Erickson Foundation.

1972 – California Student Richard Bandler teams up with linguistics professor Jon Grinder and create Neuro Linguistic Programming (NLP), largely based on Erickson.

1975 – Ernest Rossi writes 10 books with Milton Erickson, some after Erickson died!

1979 – The Hypnotic Patterns of Milton Erickson MD volumes 1 and 2 released.

1986 – Dr Everett 'Tad' James produces Time Line Therapy ® based on Erickson.

1994 – Tad James trains David Shephard in NLP, Time Line Therapy & Hypnosis.

1997 – David Shephard trains Jonathan Clark in NLP, Time Line Therapy & Hypnosis.

2005 – Jonathan releases HGE.

TODAY – you join this esteemed lineage!

Congratulations! Welcome to the family.

STATES FOR LEARNING & TRAINING

The best state for the Hypnotherapist to be in is ..... guess what? Trance!

You go into trance and they'll follow.

I often come off stage or out of a therapy session and I have no idea what happened......at least not consciously.

So I take lots of written notes.......to remind me

Bothered about limiting decisions or bad events in your past? See the Hakalau segment on the next few pages of this book. It's a technique used in Hawaii to expand your awareness & your consciousness. "Hakalau" means to focus in and spread out at the same time – how can you do that? A form of peripheral vision – where you pay more attention on the peripheral than the focussed

In all traditions Kahuna (learned ones) or Shamans can access expanded states of awareness quickly. A Trance state – focussed, expanded and able to access it rapidly. THIS IS HOW TO ACHIEVE & STAY – RELAXED, FOCUSSED & CENTRED

Wouldn't it be useful to be calm most of the time, more often? To do that you need some way of staying externally focussed. All negative emotions (anger, sadness, fear) require that your attention is on *the inside*. So to be calm, relaxed, your attention needs to be on the outside.

Imagine being able to learn more, and more quickly. What if there was a way to make negative emotions vanish at will... Or maybe you used to get nervous presenting?

Would it be useful to be calm?

Want the secret of all learning? Here it comes: All learning is state dependent. That's it. The state you are in when you learn something is the state you need to be in when you want it back out again. And the best state to learn in is trance...

YOU MIGHT WANT TO WRITE THAT DOWN

– the state you're in when you learn is the state you need to be in when you want to recall. That's why when you get sad, you're sad about all the sad things in the sad file. Or you get angry and all the things you're angry about all come up at once.

This also keeps you safe on a dark night.

Hakalau was the active meditation of the Kahuna, where they were externally focussed, in peripheral vision. Called Hakalau from Hawaiian Huna, it means literally "To stare at, and to allow to spread out". You see there's a difference between Foveal vision vs Peripheral vision.

Foveal vision is when you focus on a point and everything is detailed and sharp. This is the kind of vision we use in driving, talking, reading, in fact almost all of the time. Peripheral vision is a relaxed gaze, the day dreamy state where you're not actually looking at anything in particular, you're just using your eyes to drink in the whole scene, such as when you're visualising or looking at the scenery.

In Foveal vision you activate the Sympathetic (Stress) response, as in adrenaline, fight or flight, whereas in peripheral vision you stimulate the Parasympathetic (Relaxed) Response, which is calm, tranquil and externally focussed. In fact the word Na as in "Kahuna" and "Huna" means calm, centred, and quiet. Other cultures used mildly hallucinogenic substances, rattles, and drums. In Hawaii it was thought best to be self-sufficient, and not to rely on external props, to just be able to just go into the state at will. This technique can be a real eye opener!

The steps are almost identical to Patanjali's description in the Yoga Sutras.

If you refer back to the Communication Model diagram earlier in this book, you'll see that a relaxed state is controlled by a combination of Physiology and Internal Representation.

The Physiology is relaxed, looking straight ahead, breathing deep in the stomach, letting your teeth separate. Your mouth doesn't need to be open but you should loosen your jaw. In 1750 Mesmer stood at your head, would ask you to look up at his eyes as he used "animal magnetism" to heal.

James Braid a Scotsman, in 1843 noticed the upward angle of the eyes, and he developed an eye fixation technique in book called "Neurypnology" He set out to debunk Mesmer, and eventually ended up singing his praises. Braid named the relaxed state "Hypnosis" which means "nervous sleep".

Here's how to do Hakalau – or go into peripheral vision

1. Ho'ohaka: Just pick a spot on the wall to look at, preferably above eye level, so that your field of vision seems to bump up against your eyebrows, but the eyes are not so high as to cut off the field of vision. Slightly upward, 45 degrees preferably. That's the way you start this, after a while you won't have to do that again.

2. Kuu: "To let go." As you stare at this spot, just let your mind go loose, and focus all of your attention on the spot. Stare at it, loosen your jaw, let go – "Brain Dump"

3. Lau: "To spread out" Notice that within a matter of moments, your vision begins to spread out, and you see more in the peripheral than you do in the central part of your vision. Notice you can begin to pick up information in the peripheral

4. Hakalau: Now, pay attention to the peripheral. In fact, pay more attention to the peripheral than to the central part of your vision.

5. Ho'okohi: Stay in this state for as long as you can. Notice how it feels. As you do it for a while begin to notice the giggly, ecstatic feeling that bubbles up from inside. It seems to be impossible to feel a negative state in this state

The wise one, the Shaman, the learned one in Hawaii was called a Kahuna. "Na" means calm and centred – they spent most of their lives in this state. Certainly when outdoors in nature – they could see small movements in the woods, the water, in the air. On the ground. Here's the challenge – once you're good, you can get into the state in under a minute, and notice how far out you can see things. 180 degrees? More than that?

Get in touch with the environment around you, pull it around all the way behind you….. Think of it like Radar, all the way behind you. Your awareness fills the entire room. You may not sense it visually, though you can begin to feel the energy patterns as though you saw them, all the way around you. That's why it was so important – to become totally connected to your environment. This is the process.

This is the neurological equivalent to "there's no difference between me and the universe I live in" – you have expanded awareness. Then you can bring your eyes down, but stay in that state of Hakalau. Once you've got that, move around yet stay in that state. Stand up, walk around, staying in Hakalau, walk normally. As you turn keep connected to what's around and behind you. Stay in this state for 5 minutes. When you feel you can keep that state well, come back & sit down.

Use this all of the time, until it becomes automatic. The more you do it the easier it is to let go of negative emotions. Many Shaman won't actually make eye contact with you cos it could interfere with their state (actually you should be able to look someone in the eye and still be in Hakalau).

Now before we go any further, you should ask yourself "Is Hypnosis the right tool for the job here?" My thanks go to my Master Trainer Tad James for providing the following guidelines:

CONTRAINDICATIONS- *WHEN NOT TO USE HYPNOSIS*

WHEN CLIENT IS DANGEROUS TO SELF OR OTHERS

If the presenting problem or the personal history that you gather from the client indicates to you that the client is dangerous to self or others, then the client is beyond the scope of treatment by an unlicensed Hypnotherapist. Someone of this kind is best referred to a practitioner who is trained to handle clinical issues.

WHEN CLIENT IS DEALING WITH HIGHLY REPRESSED OR TRAUMATIC MATERIAL

Under certain circumstances, highly traumatic or highly repressed material could indicate that Hypnosis alone would not be appropriate to use. If you are not trained in interventions that deal in this area, it would be best to refer the client to a practitioner who is trained to handle these issues. (Time Line Therapy® or similar emotional clearing techniques may be used first to clear the negative response, making subsequent hypnosis much more comfortable.)

WHEN CLIENT IS DEALING WITH A LIFE-THREATENING DISEASE

A client who seeks treatment by Hypnosis for a physiological and/ or a life-threatening disease should be advised that such treatment is "controversial" and should be encouraged to get a diagnosis or referral from a Medical Doctor before proceeding. NOTE: It is not illegal to use hypnosis for, say, helping to alleviate an ulcer or its symptoms. It is, however, illegal to claim to use Hypnosis to cure any physical condition.

WHEN A CLIENT IS DEALING WITH CERTAIN PSYCHIATRIC OR NEUROLOGICAL DISORDERS

If a client is dealing with certain disorders which are Psychiatric in nature, such as Multiple Personality, Schizophrenia, Bipolar Disorder, Hysteria, and others, as well as Epileptic Seizures, it would be appropriate to seek a referral from an MD or Psychiatrist before proceeding.

MEMBERS OF THE OPPOSITE SEX:

Members of the opposite sex should only be in trance when there is a reliable witness present. This protects everyone concerned. At least have a receptionist nearby, someone else in the building, but preferably someone else present. I was once asked to help a young female client, with her inability to orgasm whilst making love with her husband. I *insisted* on having her friend and colleague present in the room while I worked with her, as I'm sure you can understand.

Now assuming that Hypnosis is appropriate, it's important that you have a chat with your client.

THE PRE-TALK

Before you ever do hypnosis with another person, it's usually a good idea to have this conversation first.

Much is done before the induction begins. In fact, it is safe to say that this may be the most important time to create success by speaking to the client's fears, and misconceptions and discussing what to expect.

1. DON'T EXPECT TO FEEL HYPNOTISED.

Many people come to the Hypnotherapist thinking that there is something about trance which is markedly different from their "normal" state of consciousness. This is definitely not true. A Light

Trance will likely feel no different from relaxation, or sunbathing and you're off, your mind wandering. Since trance is a normal natural state, then clients will likely feel a feeling of familiarity, no matter how deep in trance they go. You can say, "Don't expect to feel hypnotised. Trance is not about feeling "zonked out;' it is a normal natural state.

2. DO EXPECT TO FEEL RELAXED.

Hypnosis is a natural state where you feel increasing levels of relaxation. You may feel your arms and legs heavy, and that's just because the blood flow is increasing to your limbs, so they feel heavier.

3. YOU ARE IN CONTROL.

"You've seen stage hypnosis shows haven't you? It looks like the subjects' mind is being controlled, doesn't it? But they volunteered didn't they? When they volunteered weren't they hoping that they were going to have fun? The truth is during the trance induction, you need to know that you are in charge. For example, if I told you to stand up, and it was OK, you would, right? But if I told you to rob a bank you wouldn't do that. Well it's the same in Hypnosis. You are in charge. You only accept the suggestions that are given that are consistent with your own internal values and beliefs."

4. TRANCE IS ABOUT LEARNING HOW TO GO INTO TRANCE.

"So the process we are about to learn is just that, a learning process. Each step of the way there are several tests, and we will see how many tests you succeed at. The more successful you are the deeper you can go

"Let me tell you about Hypnosis. Let me demonstrate what it feels like. Close your eyes" Count from one to five and say "That's it!"

Now close your eyes again

Place your hands in your lap

Put your feet together

Do get up, and do a cartwheel for me

At this point the client will open their eyes and ask "Are you daft?".
You see, your Conscious Mind always steps in. I can't make you do
anything you don't want to do

Only you can make yourself do something you want to do.

People on stage show hypnosis are often asked "Were you hypnotised?" and they usually say "No – I heard every word he said".
That's because they think they're supposed to be asleep, and they're
not. When asked "So why did you behave like that?" they always say
"I don't know"

Dave Elman was an eminent Hypnotherapist in the 1950's and
1960's, and he taught that much of the work of hypnosis is done
before the induction begins.

ELMAN'S REQUISITES FOR HYPNOSIS

1. **The Consent of the Subject**—the subject must agree to be
   hypnotised.
2. **Communication Between the Hypnotherapist and the Client** — there must be communication between the Hypnotherapist and the Client.
3. **Freedom from Fear** — the Client must be free from any fear
   about the hypnotic process or about what is going to take
   place.
4. **Freedom from Reluctance** on the Client's part to trust the
   Hypnotherapist — the Client must trust the Hypnotherapist
   and his/her intentions.

SENSORY ACUITY

How do you know when someone is in a trance? As a Hypnotherapist, you have to be able to notice small changes in your client.

Erickson was famous for his sensory acuity. In the mid-seventies, the creators of NLP observed that people make minute changes from moment to moment, and that those changes have meaning *if* you have enough Sensory Acuity.

1. **Skin Colour** Light to dark
2. **Skin Tonus (The Tone of the Muscles)** Shiny to not shiny
3. **Breathing** Has 2 components

Rate

Fast - Slow

Location

High - Low

4. **Lower Lip Size** Lines or no Lines
5. **Eyes**

Focus

Focused - Defocused

Pupil Dilation

Dilated - - - - - - - - - - - - - - - - -- - - - - - ----------Undilated

STAGES OF TRANCE

Skin tends to flush as blood flow increases. Skin tonus tends to go from shiny to matt because the facial muscles are relaxed. Breathing tends to slow down and go lower down from the chest to the stomach, though sometimes it actually speeds up. The lips tend to fatten out, and thus the lines disappear. Pupils tend to become fixed and glassy, staring.

"True hypnotic signs cannot be aped, imitated or pretended. For example, you cannot pretend body warmth, it has to be there. You cannot imitate fluttering eyelids. Try it for yourself and notice how after a second or two the eyelids no longer flutter. In hypnosis, the fluttering eyelids occur almost constantly as the induction proceeds. There are very few people who can, at will, cause their eyes to tear, nor can you at will cause the whites of your eyes to redden..." – Dave Elman

There are different stages of trance, and the further down the list you, the further down you go. Literally.

(from LeCron, 1964)

1.	Lethargy	feeling tired and heavy
2.	Relaxation	comfortably floppy
3.	Eye Catalepsy	staring or closed
4.	Arm Catalepsy	rigid, stiff limb
5.	Catalepsy of Isolated Muscle Groups	could be standing, lying down
6.	Heavy or Floating Feelings	exactly that
7.	Rapport	feel connected
8.	Smell And Taste Changes	hallucinate new ones
9.	Number Block	Erase a number
10.	Amnesia	Forget things
11.	Analgesia	No Pain
12.	Automatic Movement	Repetitive gestures
13.	Hallucinations (Positive) Visual & Auditory	See or hear things
14.	Bizarre Post-Hypnotic Suggestions	Used in Stage shows
15.	Negative Hallucinations	Make something vanish
16.	Comatose	Gone!
17.	Somnambulism	Sleep walking

EXERCISE

The "That's Right" exercise, best done in groups of 3 people, person A, B and C.

B – just sit there

A – look at B, and hold 3 beliefs in your mind about B

"YOU ARE A GREAT HYPNOTIC SUBJECT

YOU ARE TOTALLY RESOURCEFUL

YOU CAN CHANGE EASILY & TIMELY"

Whenever A observes any of the signs of trance in B, they say "That's right". Helps to look meaningfully at them as you say it

C is to be in Peripheral vision, observing

When C sees a hypnotic relationship between A & B, C is to nod slowly and hypnotically

C continues to do that as long as you see that the relationship between A & B is hypnotic

Try this, it's very hypnotic, and it sets up the phrase anchor of **"That's right, very good"** which will now help induce trance in any of the three participants!

Now before any good stage show, there are a number of suggestibility tests done to select the best subjects to go on stage and make the hypnotist look good. You can try these yourself:

SUGGESTIBILITY

1. THE DICTIONARY/BALLOON

"Please hold both hands outstretched and close your eyes. Now turn your right (or your left) hand over and imagine as clearly as you can, a nice red ribbon tied to your wrist which is palm down, and that red ribbon goes up to 400 helium balloons. And you know what helium balloons do don't you. That's right, they **go up**. (Stress these words like a command) Lifting, lifting, lifting…. and the heaviest book in your house, what would that look like? Imagine that on your other hand. And because your arm is straight out there's no leverage, and all that weight is on your shoulder, and it's getting **heavier, and heavier** all the time….Now open your eyes."

This is my favourite – most people have one hand down at waist level and the other above eye level. Very cool.

2. THE HAND CLASP

"Please take your hands and clasp them together, and close your eyes. Now notice your fingers are becoming **more and more tightly clasped together**. Tighter and tighter, (etc.) It's almost as if they've been super glued together. Now try to open them. Try to pull your hands apart. Try and find you cannot. The harder you try the harder they clasp themselves together."

3. THE POSTURAL SWAY

"Please close your eyes and imagine that you are standing on the deck of your very own luxury yacht. It's a warm summer day and the ocean is like a flat mirror, smooth and calm, and there's only the slightest **hint of a rocking** of the boat as the waves gently lap at the sides of the hull. Now the wind picks up and the sea gets choppier, so your boat **starts to rock more from side to side**, and your sea legs will try to compensate as the boat **rocks more from side to side**"

Be prepared to catch them stumbling over...

The more of these tests they pass, the more suggestible and compliant they are. These also pre-train the subject to follow your suggestions, and also prove that the mind runs the body. Excellent if you're going to be working on physical health issues...

SPEAKING HYP.....

In 1898 Boris Sidis in "Psychology of Suggestion" wrote about the difference between indirect (choices) and direct (command) suggestion. "You will go deeply into trance".... versus "you may notice..."

If the client is very alert or conscious, and you're direct, they may not go into trance easily, as you're trying to tell them what to do and they're going to contradict you. However, if you're indirect it gets the Conscious Mind out of the way. When the client is deeply in trance you need to be more specific and direct and literal though, and talk to the Unconscious the way you'd talk to a small child.

Your Hypnotic voice should be softer, lower in pitch, and more gravely. It helps to tilt your jaw down & talk more from the back of your throat, not the front of your mouth. Try that – it really makes a difference.

OK, so now you know how to sound hypnotic, what exactly do you say to yourself or your client to induce a hypnotic trance state?

THE MILTON MODEL

In the old days Hypnosis was Direct Authoritarian, where the hypnotist would say "Sit Down, uncross your arms and go into a deep trance". We don't do that anymore – that's old hat. We're going to learn how to use your voice…..to put someone under "Linguistic anaesthetic". NLP gave us the Hypnosis language patterns to use, as modelled from Milton Erickson MD. Richard Bandler and John Grinder modelled Erickson and broke down the trancey sentences that when put together make the eyes heavy… Imagine that. Your words can alter someone's state…

This chapter will teach you and make you proficient with The Milton Model, abstract, artfully vague hypnotic language patterns as modelled from Milton Erickson, the world's leading Hypnotherapist. Now let's take the trance to learn how to speak hip…notically…

FIRST OF ALL, A STORY

I know that you have your own expectations of what a Hypnotic Language Pattern book will provide you with, and that's just perfect! It's very important to be expectant when reading useful information, and you're learning here today will probably increase your curiosity.

Hypnotic language is exciting, and excitement means rapid change. You see, some people haven't realised…..yet…just how powerful the technology of HGE and hypnosis actually are…although anyone and everyone who's taken the trance to train with us in person sees the very real benefits in the end. You probably thought you couldn't get this level of excellence, and now you can. Now. I'm not sure if you already know this or not, but Milton Model patterns are the key to effective communication, and the more you read and explore this subject, the more you'll get, don't you think?

We're all interested in rapid growth, I mean, weren't you? You know the kind of feeling that you want, so sooner or later you're going to call in some expert assistance…

Now…you're sitting here, thinking about all that's been said and not said here, or whether you just want to take the next step only. Doesn't this sound like just what you're looking for?

See, last month we ran a training in which the team leader talked about his boss's favourite author who wrote always be learning….yet not everyone sees it right away. Yet a profit & loss statement tells its own story, doesn't it? So that team leader resigned..himself to always be learning when the opportunity lands on your doorstep, and we are right on your doorstep, are we not?

Oh that's right, we've already been invited inside….

The team leader's name is John, and he wanted to fly up from where he lives….down there, all the way up here to leave behind all the sounds of the big city, and come and breathe easily in bonnie Scotland – hear all the accents, language and colloquialisms, and just to……relax….and let go..of any concerns of working so hard. So he bought a first class ticket, and went to the station. Now having all the time in the world, he explored the station. And he found something rather curious, down an old, dimly lit corridor. Way down there, he found, dusty and unused in such a long time, a "speak your weight and fortune" machine. So he stepped up, put his money in the slot, and heard it rattle all the way down deep inside the machine. From the machine came a deep gravely voice that said "Your name is John, you weigh 10 stone and you're going to catch the 2:20 to Glasgow"

Now all of that was true, but how did it know? I mean usually fortune tellers are very vague, very ambiguous, but this said **exactly the right thing.** So he stepped back up, put his money where his mouth was, and once again the machine spoke in a deep gravely voice "Your name is still John, you still weigh 10 stone and you're still going to catch the 2:20 to Glasgow"

Now John is a consultant who travels around a lot, and if you're as mobile as he is, you need to stay in touch. You need to be able to get in touch with your messages. You want to get all the messages that are sent loud and clear, because that gives you freedom and flexibility. So you need to make a choice – you need to get the right tool for the job. So I went down the way to see "so and so communications". At least that's what the sign above the door said, and that reminds me of another story....

I needed to get my questions answered. I needed to get something that was once hard to get, and now its part of everyday life. So I went inside to speak to the one.....you know.....the one you speak to. I'm not really sure what I said to him. In fact I'm not really sure he knows what I said to him. All I do know is that we got agreement, and I don't know if you already know how to do this or not, but I had loads to choose from. 19 different types in all. Lots of different types of mobile – different categories to choose from......but which one should I choose? So we talked for a while, and we cut it down to ten, then narrowed it down further......to five, then four, then two......but I still wasn't really sure which one should I pick.....?

WHY LEARN THIS?

You cannot not affect an individual's representation of what you say. In other words what you say creates pictures, thoughts and feelings in the heads of people you talk to. Think about that for a moment... and you're doing that right now, aren't you...?

There are 5 main reasons to learn this model:

5 – It helps you build rapport. You will be using language that is artfully vague, lacks any real content and is easy to get agreement with

4 – It induces trance! When I first learned this, I was amazed!! You can affect another person's state using only your words. Basically hypnotise someone using hypnotic language – specific ways of saying things that are trancey. When I first learned that I got really excited!

3 – You can establish direct access to another person's unconscious mind. You can talk directly to the oldest & wisest part of you. You can activate all the inbuilt potential & resources of the human mind and body. Would you like to know how to do that?

2 – All change is unconscious. That means you can open people up to new learnings and new concepts, which will assist people in getting the changes they want. Just suppose you could help people to change? All learning, all change and all behaviour require trance. Just try multiplying 7 x 6 right now.

Welcome back.

See?

1 – Abstraction controls specificity. There's more power in abstraction – the big picture, global concepts control the small specific details. Think economics. Think politics. Think about those tiny plastic things at the end of your shoe laces. Now which are more important?

WHAT IS THE MILTON MODEL?

The Milton Model is a language tool for inducing trance states in yourself and other people, modelled from a world renowned expert in his field. Elements of genius from a legendary professional. Does that sound like something you'd like to learn?

Hypnotic language patterns are vague, abstract sentence structures that put you into a trance – you go inside your head to make sense out of what you heard.

Bandler & Grinder modelled Milton Erickson's language. John Grinder said Erickson provided him with the single greatest model he ever used. When Erickson read "Patterns & Techniques of Milton Erickson MD Volume 1" (1975) he called it "A delightful simplification of the language I use with patients – I learned a great deal about the things I've done without knowing about them".

There are 19 patterns taught within this Model, so let's go through them one at a time, learn the kinds of words to use, and then we'll give you some examples.

MILTON MODEL

HYPNOTIC LANGUAGE PATTERNS

1. MIND READ

Claiming to know the thoughts or feelings of another without specifying

the process by which you came to know the info.

"I know that you are wondering..."

I know you're wondering how much impact this will have

Perhaps you don't know yet how powerful HGE is

I can see you've learned more than you thought you would

I know you have your own expectations

I can tell that you like what I'm saying

You're probably thinking that it's time to move on

2. LOST PERFORMATIVE

Value judgments where the performer of the value judgment is left out.

"And it's a good thing to wonder..."

It's good to be sceptical about powerful information

It's right for you to wonder what's in it for you

Today's a great day to make a strategic decision

That's perfect!

It's really good that you asked that

This is a wonderful process

There's a right way to do this and a better way to do this

It's a wise thing to review your department's progress

It's best to add your own examples here now:

3. CAUSE & EFFECT

Where it is implied that one thing causes another. Implied Causatives include:

a.   C>E makes

b.   If... then...

c.   As you... then you...

"Because..."

Our discussion will probably increase your curiousity

Because you've booked your place that makes you even more committed

Since you've done training before, that makes you ready for more

If you come into this room then you'll improve

Just by asking that question, you're starting to see the benefits

Since you're reading this sentence, you can think of several more examples.

4.   COMPLEX EQUIVALENCE

Where two things are equated - as in their meanings being equivalent.

"That means..."

Training is exciting and excitement means growth

Having invested this much time shows me you're serious about results

Your questions mean you already want assistance

Having gotten this far means you can write more examples of this pattern.

5.   PRESUPPOSITION

The linguistic equivalent of assumptions.

"You are learning many things..."

The problems you're facing are fixable

Some business people haven't realised how powerful HGE is

Now your HR team will be able to produce with even more credibility

How much more value would you have gotten from me by having another session?

Most of the best examples of this pattern will be written here by you.

6.   UNIVERSAL QUANTIFIER

A set of words having: a. a universal generalization and
b. no referential index. (doesn't say "who")

"And all the things, all the things..."

Everyone in this room cares about profit

Everything will become clear once you've completed this chapter

You always get results

Anyone I've presented to saw the benefits in the end

You have them all in your head. Write every one you can think of here.

7. MODAL OPERATOR

Words which implies possibility or necessity, and which form our rules in life.

"That you can learn..."

You have to understand our position in all of this

You shouldn't have to want it, unless you really need it

Would it be possible?

You might discover you can dare to go ahead

You probably thought you couldn't, but now you can

You must be getting the hang of this by now

You could list a few more examples on the lines below.

8. NOMINALIZATION

Process words which has been frozen in time by making them into nouns.

"Provide you with new insights, and new understandings."

HGE is easy

Your input to this relationship is really important

You're looking for demonstration of powerful impact

Increased profitability shows renewed vigour

Empowerment is a possibility

Your thoughts on nominalizations are an important form of communication

9. UNSPECIFIED VERB

Misses out the "how"

"And you can,"

Tony Robbins says "When you can't, you must"

You may discover you start moving forward

The more you continue with this, the more you'll get out of it
If you could just let go and notice your intentions
Now perhaps you could continue to

10. TAG QUESTION

A question added after a statement, designed to displace resistance. Draws your attention to the question and gets agreement.

"Can you not?"

You can see the value in this, can't you?
We're all interested in profits, don't you think?
We're all looking to agree here, aren't we?
And you do want the best, don't you?
You'll add more to the list now won't you?

11. LACK OF REFERENTIAL INDEX

A phrase which does not pick out a specific portion of the listener's experience. Misses out the who.

"One can, you know..."

We put people though a wonderful process
That's the way to do business
Folk do, you know
It's often said that…
Statistics prove…
Please help them - they couldn't think of any more of these.

12. COMPARATIVE DELETION (UNSPECIFIED COMPARISON)

Where the comparison is made and it is not specified as to what or whom it was made.

"And it's more or less the right thing."

Sooner or later you're going to employ some expert assistance
At one time or another you've loved a training you've done
It's probably better to start now, sooner rather than later

Before or after this chapter?

That are more or less better than the ones above, as they occur to you from time to time.

13. PACE CURRENT EXPERIENCE

Where client's experience (verifiable, external) is described in a way which is undeniable. Makes the person go internal.

"You are sitting here, listening to me, looking at me, (etc.)..."

We're all sitting here, discussing these ideas

Just thinking about stuff like this

Just after you blink, you'll notice your breathing

As your eyes continue reading the words on this page while you're looking at it and from time to time you may become aware of the thoughts in your mind or those sensations in your hand or down there on the soles of your feet you could also begin to wonder if you could think of how artfully you can pace a person's ongoing experience and you might even like to make a note or two right here now about pacing.

14. DOUBLE BIND

Where it appears like there's a choice but actually there isn't

"And that means that your unconscious mind is also here, and can hear (phonological ambiguity) *what I say. And since that's the case, you are probably learning about this and already know more at an unconscious level than you think you do, and it's not right for me to tell him, learn this or learn that, let him learn in any way he wants, in any order."*

Take all the time you need to take the next step

Will you book this training, or the one later this year?

Is this valuable to you, or just vital?

Light trance, medium trance, deep trance – either will do

If you don't write at least one more double bind in the space below now, you will either think of one automatically very soon, or else wonder when the next one will come to mind, so you can write it down then.

15. CONVERSATIONAL POSTULATE

The communication has the form of a question, a question to which the response is either a 'yes' or a 'no'. If I want you to do something, what else must be present so that you will do it, and out of your awareness? It allows you to choose to respond or not and avoids authoritarianism.

"Do you feel this... (punctuation ambiguity) *is something you understand?"*

Does this sound like just what you want?

Do you feel ready to become a master communicator?

Can you picture yourself doing this?

Will you remember to congratulate yourself on your decision?

Would you mind writing down a couple more conversational postulates here?

16. EXTENDED QUOTE

"Last week I was with Richard who told me about his training in 1983 at Denver when he talked to someone who said..."

Last month we ran a course in which the team leader talked about his bosses favourite expression which was "Always seize an opportunity"

Did I tell you that Eleanor watched Newsnight last night, when Jeremy Paxman asked his guest "How badly do you need this?"

The other day, a participant in the training was telling me that her husband said Jonathan had told him to ask you to write a couple of extended quotes down right here.

17. SELECTIONAL RESTRICTION VIOLATION

A sentence that is not well formed in that only humans and animals can have feelings. In this sentence structure you attribute feelings to an inanimate object.

"A chair can have feelings..."

I was driving the car with trainers

How does your toilet feel getting flushed?

How stressed does your email get?

If you're not sure, ask the executive chair

Your accounts speak volumes

Do sales cry out when they fall?

How does a mirror feel being stared at all day?

Who does a ladder lean on for support?

Your pen knows how to write selectional restriction violations very easily, if you will just lead it to the paper below now.

18. AMBIGUITY

a. **Phonological:**

"Hear", "Here"

You can trust **you're unconscious** mind **now.**

So you think you can't deal with your lover? Love her; can't you?

b. **Syntactic:**

Where the function (syntactic) of a word cannot be immediately determined from the immediate context.

"They are visiting relatives"

Your increasing options

Hypnotizing hypnotists can be tricky.

This is a training in trance

c. **Scope:**

Where it cannot be determined by linguistic context how much is applied to that sentence by some other portion of the sentence.

"Speaking to you as a child..."
"The old men & women..."
"The disturbing noises & thoughts..."
"The weight of your hands & feet..."
Your deep breathing and trance....
Speaking to you as a master hypnotist

d. Punctuation:

*"I want you to notice your **hand** me the glass."*
My boss resigned himself to constant learning
If you hear any ambiguities, it's all right to write them right here.

19. UTILIZATION

Utilize all that happens or is said.

Client says: *"I am not sold."*

Response: *"That's right you are not sold, yet, because you haven't* asked the one question that will have you totally and completely sold."

Client: "I don't think I know."

Practitioner: "That's right, you don't you know."

Client: "I can't be hypnotized."

Practitioner: "That's right. You can't be hypnotized *yet,* because you haven't asked the one question yet that will let you relax completely"

Client: "We can't afford you"

Practitioner: "That's right, you can't afford me yet, because you haven't realised the alternative"

Client: "This meeting's dragging on a bit."

Practitioner: "That's right, so it must be time to agree"

Client: "HGE is all about mind control, isn't it?"

Practitioner: "That's right, we do teach people how to control their own minds"

PUTTING IT ALL TOGETHER:

Perhaps you don't know... yet... how powerful HGE is, and it's good to be sceptical about powerful information. In fact, our discussion will probably increase your curiousity, and your internal questions mean you already want assistance. Now, the problems you're facing are fixable, and everything will become clear once you've completed this paragraph. You have to understand your position in all of this - your input to this relationship is really important, and the more you continue reading, the more you'll get out of it... and you do want the best, don't you? You see, we put people though a wonderful process, because at one time or another you've loved a training you've done. And as your eyes continue reading the words on this page, while you're looking at it ...from time to time you may become aware of the thoughts in your mind or those sensations in your hand or down there on the soles of your feet, you could also begin to wonder if you could take all the time you need to take the next step.

Does this sound like just what you want? Did I tell you that Eleanor watched Newsnight last night, when Jeremy Paxman asked his guest "How badly do you need this?" I mean, your accounts speak volumes, but they're conscious, aren't they? You can also trust *you're unconscious* mind *now*, because this is a training in trance. And speaking to you as a master hypnotist, are you wearing anything that restricts you can loosen off now...

HOW DO I USE THESE?

The next step is to figure out how to use all of this. How do you make someone go inside their head to make sense out of what you're saying? It shifts the listeners attention from outside, to inside... As you use fluffy language they go inside and try to make sense out of it from their model of the world.

The Milton Circle – a favourite exercise that we conduct in our 7 day HGE Practitioner and Hypnosis weekend trainings. Simply sit in a circle with a few other willing participants, and simply say aloud a Milton pattern example in your best "hypnotic voice". The next person then picks up and links a sentence onto yours. Then the next person, and so on. Keep going until all your eyes are closed....

Write emails using hypnotic language patterns.

In your speech – talk slightly slower than normal, and softly. As for Tonality – pull your chin down a bit and bring your voice out from the back of your mouth. You will sound deeper and more gravely. Try saying this sentence with your mouth & jaw in that position...

WHAT IF YOU MASTERED THIS?

You're probably wondering where.......and how......you will apply this model in your life, are you not?

What happens if you just dry up? My strategy is to just pick one, say it aloud, and then keep doing that.

You'll probably find some that are your favourites, or that some are easier to remember than others. That's because you probably talk like that anyway. Practice and train up your least preferred patterns.

What happens if someone calls you on it? They might say "You're talking weird! You're not making any sense!". You just utilise it and keep going: "That's right, I'm not making any sense.....yet, and that's because......"

Practice – get a sheet of paper for each category and write out ten examples of each

Come up with five business or career applications for this Model. Where could you use this? Imagine business meetings and you start talking hyp.......ah....

What if you did presentations and talks where you were able to control the audiences state moment to moment...

What would Customer Services be like getting agreement in trance, or in person, over the counter, over the phone?!!

Now you're ready for your first formal trance induction....

HYPNOTIC INDUCTION

The 4 A's method contains the four essential elements of any good self - hypnosis session. It is made up of the following stages:

Autorelaxation stage – the first step is to induce in oneself a calm, relaxed and receptive self-hypnotic state. This is easiest to achieve in a quiet, possibly darkened room, with some light relaxation music, creating a safe and conducive atmosphere. The client should lie back, relax and release all stresses and tensions, mentally and physically, until they are in relaxed state.

Autosuggestion stage – the client then practices suggestibility tests, suggesting to themselves that their eyes want to close, their throat wants to swallow, or their hand wants to tingle. Once these responses are present, now is the ideal time to give oneself some positive, useful hypnotic suggestions relevant to the problem in mind.

Autoanalysis stage – at this point one starts to break down the presenting problem, trace the root cause, and look for possible solutions to improve the situation. Asking pertinent, investigative questions helps strip away the truth of the matter.

Autotherapy stage – the final stage is to prime the mind to think and act positively to resolve the issue, using suggestions during the session, as well as posthypnotic suggestions to be carried out in the normal, waking state.

This method should not be the client's sole method of treatment in cases of severe emotional trauma or physical symptomology. Obviously, someone who is deeply traumatized or highly emotional ought to seek professional help to help with the problems, rather than try to solve it alone. One cannot be one's own therapist for long! In addition, in the cases of physical illness or disease, the ailment should be correctly diagnosed and treated using conventional medical wisdom first and foremost.

Try this trance induction for the Autorelaxation stage. If doing this with another person, speak as your subject breathes out.. If you really want to practice self hypnosis, here's the single best way I know of – dictate this script out loud and record yourself, using your best gravely trancey voice. That way you can play it back anytime you want and I promise you, you'll feel the benefits. There's nothing more hypnotic than your own voice using hypnotic language and tonality.

INTRODUCTION

"Welcome to your self-hypnosis session. This is a self hypnosis session for relaxation, managing stress, and for accessing the resources within yourself

This tape should not be played in a moving vehicle, or in an activity that requires your full attention.

Sit or lie back in a relaxed position, with your legs and ankles uncrossed, and your hands and arms resting on your lap or by your sides. Since **you are in charge** of your own relaxation, you can adjust yourself now to find the most comfortable,

relaxed position for you.

EYE CLOSURE

Bring your full attention into the present moment, and into the space that your body occupies. As you continue to listen to the relaxing tones of my voice, I'd like you to look at a spot on the wall if you would, and keep your eyes fixed on that spot.

Any spot will do, and as you **do that now**, I am going to begin counting. You might

become aware that your gaze can become like tunnel vision as you continue to stare at that spot **over there**. I want you to open and close your eyes with each number I count. Each and every time that you open your eyes, keep them fixated on that spot as I count from 1 to 20. You will find that each time you close your eyes, they will want to **remain closed**. Each time you open them, it will be more and more difficult to do so, more difficult than the last time, much more difficult. And by the time I reach 20, or perhaps before, your eyelids will be **soo** heavy that they will remain tightly shut, and **you will go deeply into trance**. Beginning now.. one…your eyes are open, now closing…, two…open… and closed…, three… open and closed…your eyes are becoming very tired now, heavier with each closing…four. - …open….and closed…so much heavier than before… five…open. . . and closed…, so hard to open your eyes… six… so drowsy and sleepy that your eyes just don't want to open… seven…open and closed…just relax your closed eyes now as you instead **take a deep breath** and

become deeply relaxed…

PROGRESSIVE RELAXATION

You don't **have to close your eyes** to relax, so if you're in a place where you can do so now, your eyes can just as easily close…, if they haven't done so already. Just as **you are ready** to bring your full attention inside of yourself, preparing to use the full resources of **you're unconscious** mind and beginning to see more clearly with inner eyes, I wonder if you've noticed yet how much easier your breathing has become as you relax even more…

Because in a few moments you're going to be more relaxed than you've ever known yourself to be. I'm going to draw your awareness to certain parts of your body, and as you do so, I want you to just feel that part begin to…**relax and let go**…just feel the muscles relax. In order to help you to relax. I'd like to ask you to imagine yourself

sunbathing on the deck…of your very own luxury yacht. You can feel the sunlight warming every muscle, every cell in your body The sky is the most beautiful clear blue, and there are a few puffy white clouds..drifting lazily... across the sky, and as you listen to the lapping sounds of the sea and the whisper of the warm breeze, you are beginning to feel more and more relaxed. As you become aware of each part of your body now, you'll feel that part just begin to...**relax and let go.** so that in a few moments you will be more relaxed than you've ever known...

Starting with the forehead, I'd like you to feel all the little frown lines, all the little worry lines in the forehead, just seem to...**disappear**. The forehead smoothes out, feeling so relaxed, and you feel warm feelings of relaxation coming down now around the eyes. Now you may not have noticed yet.. how very heavy the eyelids are feeling now., so heavy that they don't want to open, and they may want to flutter a bit, but that's OK...just feel how warm and heavy they are... and as those feelings come down around the face, all the muscles in the facial area just begin to...**relax and let go**...

The warm, soothing feelings of relaxation come down around the mouth now, and all of the hundreds of little muscles around the mouth just start to relax.. so much so that the lower jaw can become heavy and the teeth can part. Your mouth may even open up a little bit with relaxation as continue deeper.. and deeper relaxed. Feel the tension easing now around the jaw and up behind the ears, so that all the little nerve endings behind the ears just seem to relax as you go deeper and deeper, even deeper as the sounds of the waves seem to lull you deeper and deeper

The relaxing feeling goes to the back of the neck now, down around the shoulders, so much tension seems to go to our shoulders, but now you feel the

shoulders just begin to relax...**and let go**...you can even feel them drop a bit...as the soothing sensations go to the backbone now, and as they go down the spinal column, it seems to spread out to the sides, so that every muscle, every nerve, every cell in your back just seems to relax… all the way down, all the way… **down** to the small of the back, and around the curve of the back…

This warm sense of relaxation comes into the backs of the thighs now, and,

and into the hollows of the knees, through the calves, into the heel, along the soles of your feet, and each and every toe just relaxes even more as you go deeper, deeper, even deeper, listening to the sounds of the sea as the yacht gently rocks you back and

forth…calm..very peaceful.., relaxed, the whole head and back area seem very, very relaxed…

Now you'll proceed with the rest of you, starting with the throat muscles, feel your throat muscles just start to relax. The relaxation comes down the front of the shoulders, down the upper arms, over the elbows, down through the forearms to the hands, as each and every fingertip relaxes more and more as you go deeper. . .and deeper. Feel the relaxation in the throat, in the shoulders, easing gently now into the chest, and all the muscles and organs within the chest area just begin to relax, continuing down, down into the abdomen, as all the muscles and organs within the abdomen seem to relax…relaxation spreading deeper now into the thighs, over the knees…more and more as you continue to go deeper, deeper, even deeper... calm… peaceful…and very, very relaxed…

I'm going to let you **enjoy this rest** for a moment, but when you hear me speak again you will continue to go down, peaceful and re-laxed imagine yourself daydreaming on that luxurious yacht, gently swaying back and forth, back and forth, drifting deeper and even deeper…

DEEPENER

So now I'd like you to allow your mind to daydream…to dream and float away from that scene. ,to another…and allow your inner mind to show you standing at the top of a fine staircase...carpeted in a thick, deep carpet in your favourite colour,, with ten steps leading down. There is a firm banister to hold onto and you feel safe and secure...with nothing to concern you. in a moment you will see yourself walking down the staircase as I++ count from 10 to 1, and as I count off each step down..you will go gently step down...deeper. . .doubling your relaxation with each step you take..

Begin now as I count... 10...doubling your relaxation going deeper... 9...deeper still...8...letting go of any remaining tension as you relax and go deeper...7... doubling the restfull sensations...6...aware now of the rhythm of your breathing and how slow its becoming...5.. each gentle breath relaxes you...and you can relax more with each breath you breathe...4...even deeper into a state of profound restfulness of mind..and body...3...doubling your relaxation going even deeper...2...the deeper you go, the better it feels...and the better you feel, the deeper you go... 1...almost all the way down now...ZERO... stepping off the bottom step and you can find yourself in a safe and special place...

SPECIAL PLACE

...a place that is comfortable and safe for you to be. .a place of safety and security where there is nothing to disturb you...just tranquility..and calm inner peace...you can imagine it to be any place you choose...perhaps you would enjoy the beach or the ocean with clean fresh air and warm sand...or perhaps the mountains with a crystal clear stream nearby. .or perhaps somewhere from your past that was safe, warm and totally secure...any place will do, so now imagine looking at this place through your own eyes...you are safe and there is no-one to disturb you. This is the most peaceful place in the world for you. Imagine yourself there and feel that sense of peace and well-being flowing through you now... enjoy these positive feelings and keep them with you long after this session is complete, for the rest of the day, tomorrow and all the days that follow. Allow these positive feelings to grow stronger and stronger, feeling at peace with a sense of well being, and each and every time that you choose to do this kind of relaxation, you **will be able to relax** deeper and deeper. Regardless of the stress and tension that may surround your life, you may now remain more at peace, more calm, more relaxed, and allow the tension and stresses to bounce off and away from you, just bounce..off... and away from you. And these positive feelings will **grow stronger** and stronger throughout the day as you continue to relax deeper and deeper...

THAT QUIET INNER VOICE

And as you continue to relax here…you can become aware of how little you need to be aware of…the sounds in the room sounds outside…each sound only helps to relax you even more deeply…each word that you hear is just a signal for you to become less and less aware of the importance of all that is unimportant here,..the exact meaning of words that are said or not said as I talk to you here… nothing bothers or concerns you as your conscious mind drifts off to a place which is comfortable and safe…and your unconscious… mind. . .takes on the responsibility for guiding and

directing your awareness...down...into your innermost self...aware now of that gentle connection.. communication with that part of you that is the essence of you…that knows all.., remembers each and every event that has served to shape and mould your unique and special personality a part of you that you really do hear as a quiet and calm voice from within…a voice of wisdom and of truth that is so often lost within the clamour and clatter of the world... the demands…the constraints.., the noise that is those who would have you bend to their will now hear that voice, still, quiet and calm...

but now clear as crystal...piercing through the fog of indecision and lack of confidence... unmoved and unaltered in its determination to give to you at all times... good advice..., wise answers and solutions **to all problems**...to the benefit of yourself and those who are special to you.

This is that creative and special part of you...that wise inner advisor that is always there for you with your benefit and your well-being always the prime consideration...a constant, etheric part...that is you and was you before there was awareness of this existence in this time...an invaluable friend that must be listened to .and you will listen, will you not?

And can you recognise now that value, that unique capacity and capability that is yours... has always been yours... and I really don't want you to know too much how good you can feel with that intense awareness of confidence in your ability **to make changes** and decisions in your life for yourself..no longer allowing others to manipulate you...to take advantage of you. you expect of yourself everything that is yours...that you deserve...that you are entitled to as a unique and special person.. aware of who you are aware of your own talents and special abilities...always that person who is at the forefront...always there with a valuable input to every situation...you listen and take note of what is important, and then you make a decision...you make your own decision, and you are comfortable in that.

I wonder if you can notice soon how others will come to rely on you to be the person that you are...confident and self-assured...an example to those who will admire you, as you allow those qualities so long hidden... to shine through from within.., to astound and confound those who would manipulate and control...you are your own person...proud and confident...**taking responsibility for your own life** and wellbeing...a true friend to your own inner advisor...that is you personified...

AWAKENING

So enjoy your special place for a few more moments until you hear me speak again...and when next I speak I will count... up from 1 to 5 and you can begin coming back to full consciousness, and you will come back feeling refreshed and alert as if you've had a long rest...come back feeling alert and relaxed...

When you hear the count of 5 you will come back to full awareness, feeling better than you've felt in a long time. I...getting ready to come back to full awareness now, feeling good...2...your mind is clear and your body is refreshed...3..looking forward to each and every day... 4...ready to open your eyes and to follow through everything you've learned here...and 5.. open your eyes, feeling wide awake now...alert and refreshed. Have a big stretch...smile. . . good!

Well done, and thank you."

This is an excellent trance induction and creates a deep trance rather quickly. Try it, it's fun. Alternatively, you can listen to me taking you through this exact hypnosis session on CD – just email me at enquiry@jonathanclark.org for a free copy of "Relaxation Self Hypnosis".

DEEPENING TECHNIQUES

Once they're deep in trance, give them instructions to stay there. In addition, there are a few other useful strategies to take them further down, some of which I used in the induction above...

- Peaceful scene – a guided visualisation takes the client through a tranquil scene in their imagination, perhaps a beach, or a secluded garden, or a clearing in the woods, with full sensory rich descriptions allowing them to drift off into their internal world. The same can be done by visualizing a candle flame and melting wax.
- The elevator – as the lift descends, the client can be counted

down many levels, "and the further down the elevator goes, the more deeply relaxed you become, and deeper into trance you can go…" Staircases, escalators, anything that goes up and down will work.

• Simple counting – "and as I count backwards from 10 to one, with each count you will be 10% more relaxed, and 10% less awake…"

• Arm catalepsy – suggestions to have the arm lift all by itself, so that when it goes back down all by itself, the lower your hand descends, the deeper you go…"

• Repeating the induction of trance, often called fractionation, deepens the trance. Typically, the more times a client is hypnotized, the deeper the client will go. If trance is induced several times in succession in a short period of time without allowing the client to fully wake up each time, the client will go deeper. This is my favourite method.

• Using embedded metaphors will deepen the client's trance. In fact, the more levels of embedded metaphor used, the deeper the trance which follows. Three stories told in succession, but none of them actually completed, seems to induce altered states quite nicely. See the chapter called "Stand & Deliver".

The subject is always in control, although if they have seen stage show hypnosis they may have fears about amnesia or acting in strange ways. They must learn to accept that their results using hypnosis are completely their results, and it is their ability to trust themselves and relax that determines the success of the session. The unconscious mind will never accept a suggestion that violates its values and ethics. Sometimes it is useful to suggest to oneself to do something uncharacteristic at the start of a hypnosis session, just to prove this point. "Now open your eyes and do a cartwheel across the room".

Deepening techniques may be required with a tense or highly conscious client, to help them to relax. Of course, a pre-induction discussion should always take care of these issues up front though.

IDEOMOTOR SIGNALS & PENDULLII

I once worked with a 16 year old girl with Endometriosis. During the appointment she embarrassingly admitted that she was worried that she was pregnant. So we asked her fingers, and they said no, and she wasn't.

What if you could ask the sex of a baby in the womb without having a scan? Its called psycho-physiological thought-reading. You can find lost items for instance.

Some people use a Pendulum, or a Pocket watch, necklace, ring on a thread, even a plumbers plumb bob. You see the mind runs the body, the Unconscious Mind controls the muscles, which means you can set up yes and no signals, and you can then go ahead and ask your Unconscious Mind to communicate with you, and it can answer you directly!

Some people think that Pendulums are too "New Agey". So you could use a swallow, a flush, or even better two fingers on the same hand, one for yes, one for no. We teach this technique fully on our Hypnosis Weekend. This comes from Lesley Le Cron 1964 – who coined the phrase Ideomotor Signalling. My Master Trainer David Shephard told me a great story about a car accident that we witnessed, where the driver of the car was thrown from the car and was bleeding on the roadside. So David kneeled down beside him and asked to speak directly with the man's unconscious mind, and the man's eyelids fluttered. He double checked that that was indeed the ideomotor signal by saying "if the eyelids flutter meant yes, they will flutter even more" and they did. So having established contact, he asked the man , or rather the man's unconscious, "Do you know what to do to stop the bleeding?" and the eyelids fluttered "yes". And the bleeding stopped. But then the man went into convulsions and David asked him "Do you know what to do to stop the convulsions?" and the eyelids fluttered "yes". And the convulsions stopped. The paramedics said it was David's ability to stop bleeding that saved the man's life. But as David said "It wasn't my ability to stop the bleeding, it was the man's unconscious mind"

Ask your unconscious mind for a signal for yes, and a different signal for no. If it's your fingers, you may need to give it a Kinesthetic awareness by moving it first. Hey, if you can lift and arm, **you can lift a couple of fingers**...

Remember when you were really small, and you knew the answer at school, what did you do? You put your hand up, didn't you? And when **you really, really knew the answer** and you **wanted to be noticed**, you would wave your arm in the air, wouldn't you? Now, if **you're all grown up** and at a posh restaurant, the staff are trained to **see clearly your signals**. You don't have to **raise the whole hand**, you just can **raise a finger** and they'll know **you're trying to get their attention**, won't they?

It's the oldest & wisest part of you, who's been doing all that work for so long, the part that runs your body, stores all of your memories, no one has talked to it directly........until now! It's bound to have a lot to say to you by now!

EXERCISE

Go through the following questions, answering all of the questions consciously, with your best considered answer. Then go back over them again, asking your unconscious mind to give you a clear yes or no signal, using finger signals or a pendulum....

DO YOU NEED TO....?
Feel safe.
Feel loved.
Be liked.

Be approved of.

Be punished.

Punish.

Suppress hostility.

Minister to others.

Serve others.

Be dignified.

Earn father's love.

Earn mother's love.

Get praise.

Be hurt.

Be respected.

Hurt others.

Have peace at any price.

Be alone often.

Notice any differences between what you thought was the answer, and what your unconscious mind knows....?

GENERAL HYPNOTHERAPY PARADIGM

Most Hypnosis books are full of specific scripts for specific problems. Rather than teach you a whole bunch of different interventions, here's the master template you can use with anything. It's actually more effective and gives the client more freedom to fix themselves in whatever way they need to. You ask the Unconscious Mind questions directly. You want straight Yes's. Whenever you get a No you've found something important and need to pursue it

1. Do you Know what to do to have this problem disappear?
   no - "what other resources do you need ? Run through Values and other states, and "imagine an infinite source of___ above the top of your head.."
   *Give me a clear Yes signal when **you have all the resources***

you need

2.   Is it possible ?

no - *"When did you decide that you could not ___ ? If you knew, was it after your birth ?"*

Treat as a Limiting Decision using Time Line Therapy

3.   Is it OK ?

no - *"I know that there's a part of you that thinks it can't _ "*

For what purpose would you not let this go now?

Get it's highest intention and ask

*"You know that you'd be more (intention) by **solving this now** wouldn't you? "*

4.   Are there any other problems you'd like to work on?

"Are there any other problems that you 'd like to clear up today?"

yes - go to step 1 no - go to step 5

5.   Give permission

*Thank it and acknowledge it, and assure it that client's Conscious mind gives it permission to **start immediately***

6.   How quickly can you start now? *Set up time periods*

Start *- When will you start ? Immediately ? An hour/day/week/ month ?*

Finish *-How quickly can you complete all the work necessary ? Will it take you an hour/day/week/month ?*

START NOW!

*BRING THEM OUT OF TRANCE

"In a moment I'm going to count... "

*DISTRACT IMMEDIATELY

This locks in the session and prevents the client's conscious mind from undoing all your good work.

POST HYPNOTIC SUGGESTIONS

You've probably heard about these - suggestions given in trance for the person to carry out after they come out of trance, to operate at a later time. A Post-Hypnotic Suggestion is a suggestion that activates and operates at a time after the induction of trance. The time of the activation of the suggestion can be minutes later or months later.

1. REQUIRES MEDIUM TO DEEP TRANCE:

A Post-Hypnotic Suggestion generally requires a trance which is at a medium to deep level.

2. MAKE THE SUGGESTION DIRECT & SPECIFIC:

While suggestions should, at first, be given in an indirect way, Post-Hypnotic Suggestions should be direct and to the point. This is the case with any suggestions given while the client is in deep trance.

3. TELL THE CLIENT WHAT THE TRIGGER FOR THE POST-HYPNOTIC SUGGESTION WILL BE:

E.G.: "Whenever you see chocolate or sweets...."

4. TELL THE CLIENT WHAT TO DO:

E.G.: "...you will feel an undeniable urge to look for food that is healthier and better for you"

5. TELL THE CLIENT WHEN TO DO IT:

E.G.: "...and you will do it immediately."

Suggest that next time they will go quicker and more easily into trance - that way your trance work with that person gets progressively better.

Give the client a suggestion that they will feel compelled to go to the gym, or eat salad with every meal, or take the stairs instead of the lift, or will remember all these hypnosis skills the next time they're talking to a client, or a friend who needs help…

They will demonstrate the new behaviour, and it's always a good idea to include the phrase "In ways that are safe, ecological and ethical".

It's also great fun at parties…

A CAUTIONARY TALE...

As I end this chapter, I would like to comment on the use (and misuse) of Hypnosis. When it comes to ethics, I like to think of it like this – only do with a client what you would want done yourself in their shoes. I could write an entire book on this subject alone (now there's an idea!) but for now let me say this. Technology has no ethics of its own. You can use a hammer to build a house, or something awful instead. The morals come from the wielder, the human being.

Newly trained students of hypnosis may have skills, but they also must have humility. Another downside from my NLP days was seeing newly certified Practitioners adamant that the methodology of modelling experts to quickly accelerate your learning, also somehow gave them wisdom and experience way beyond their station. WRONG! You may know a lot about hypnosis after a weekend training, but 2 days does not a hypnotherapist make! (Nor one book chapter!). You still have to build up your calluses and earn your stripes. I encourage you, if this chapter has whetted your appetite, to seek out further training. Go to a reputable body and enrol in longer hypnosis training. This is only the start, not the be all and end all.

You should also be made aware of another unfortunate occurrence in the hypnosis world – that of "The Hypnotic Seal". Certain unscrupulous individuals will include suggestions that **they** are the only person who can induce trance with **that client**, thus blocking any further inductions of hypnosis by any other hypnotherapist. Purported to protect the client, this in fact removes their choices and thus is not in their best interests. Again this approach tells you more about the therapist than the client.

Its far better to teach the client a trance-prevention technique which they can use if and when they choose to stop unwanted hypnosis, rather than limit their personal freedom.

Beware also the flamboyant advertising and hyped-up claims of 100% success rates or one hour guaranteed smoking cessation programmes. I don't know anyone who can guarantee that a client will stop smoking after one session of hypnotherapy – not me, not my Master trainers. There's usually a huge catch, like having to listen to a CD for 21 days straight afterwards else there's no money back. Tell me, how can you prove you listened to that CD every day? The unfortunate clients who fall for these shams usually then tell everyone Hypnosis doesn't work and that they still want to smoke. Worse, they're disappointed and usually £500 worse off…

One can make a quick buck in Hypnosis if one combines it with slickly written misleading sales rhetoric. Problem is they're doing no one any favours, and they're giving Hypnosis a bad name.

Then there's the Hypnosis Trainer who makes up a fictitious Institute, or calls themselves a Society, so they can run paper thin courses and charge people a fortune, handing them a certificate that's not worth the paper its written on. Ask me for my "16 Questions You Must Ask" report at enquiry@jonathanclark.org for more guidance on what to look out for.

Do I run Hypnosis Trainings then, I hear you ask? Yes I do – I include Hypnosis as part of my HGE Certification Courses. Look at the Events Calendar on my website for the next scheduled training. Students must first go through my 3 day Foundation Skills Training, so I can vet them and ensure that they have positive intentions and integrity. Only when I'm satisfied that they are trustworthy and honourable, will I teach them Hypnosis in person. And I'll share with them the same cautionary advice that you've just read here. Anyone not trained thoroughly in Hypnosis should consider a weekend course as *purely an introduction*.

There is one famous case in the UK of a household name stage show hypnotist who was sued for "causing a participant in the show to have a psychotic episode and subsequent mental illness". Firstly, note the cause and effect violation there. Secondly, that entertainer has been working closely with the creator of NLP for many years now. The risk of causing a mental illness using Hypnosis is highly unlikely, provided the Hypnotherapist uses common sense and sticks to these guidelines.

Health issues are another area that requires careful handling. It is illegal to claim that you can heal someone. See the Time Line Therapy and Health chapters for more information. Pain is a sign that something is wrong. Deal with the underlying issues, don't ask the pain to go away. It may be signalling that something critical is amiss, and to mask that signal could be a mistake.

Finally, as I conclude this section on careful management and cautious handling of people's heads and hearts, there is again the issue of control – the general public still believes that hypnosis is a form of mind control – that the hypnotherapist can suggest things to the client and they will automatically do them. Another big mistake. In some cases that would be great! Imagine no crime, no war, no self abuse, no cruelty. Unfortunately [or maybe fortunately], all hypnosis is self-hypnosis. No one has any power over you, unless you give it to them. The individual creates their own level of relaxation and trance, and will only accept suggestions that are in accordance with their own beliefs and values.

CLOSING BENEDICTION

So as we draw our chapter on the all-important science and art of Hypnosis to a close, ask yourself "how many metaphors are still open?" You'll need to come to my other events to hear them closed!! Or was that simply a suggestion? Only your unconscious mind knows....

****AND I HEREBY CANCEL ALL SUGGESTIONS THAT WERE GIVEN FOR DEMONSTRATION PURPOSES RELATING TO PRODUCING HYPNOTIC PHENOMENA – THOSE SUGGESTIONS ARE HEREBY REMOVED, AND I WOULD LIKE TO ASK THE UNCONSCIOUS MIND TO REMEMBER ALL SUGGESTIONS THAT WERE FOR THE HEALTH, GROWTH AND ENJOYMENT OF YOUR CONSCIOUS MIND, AND YOU KNOW WHAT THEY WERE............... WON'T YOU?****

AND SO BACK TO.........

So there I am in "so and so communications" trying to choose which one to buy. So we agreed on which category of mobile I needed. We talked vaguely about price, vaguely about size. Some of them you can even change the way it sounds. Some can even change colour........as you're using it. And I don't know if you already know how to do this or not, but you can store all of it in the memory – you simply recall it from the memory and then speak. That's what happens – its voice activated. You just open your mouth and speak, and the message goes through. That's what happens when you use the best, when you use an Erickson..............

So John's at the station, and now he's even more spaced out. How could this old machine, so old and dented and unused, hidden away in the dark, how could it speak such truths and say exactly the right thing? So he took a deep breath and stepped up..put his money where his mouth is, and out came the same gravelly deep voice

"Your name is still John, you still weigh 10 stone and you've just missed the 2:20 to Glasgow!"

"All learning, all behaviour, and all CHANGE, is unconscious"

12

WHAT IF THERAPY WAS QUICK AND PAINLESS – WHAT WOULD YOU WANT TO CHANGE ABOUT YOURSELF?

Let go of anger, sadness, fear, guilt & any trauma in your past in minutes, not years!

Let me introduce this powerful chapter with some concepts:

- *The essence of our being is love* – our Higher Self is a spiritual being, and as such believes in a higher order of thinking – truth, honesty, love, and forgiveness. Our physical bodies are merely vehicles with which we connect and interact, but sometimes we forget that and take things at a physical, tangible level only. We ought to remember our true nature, which is loving and kind and non-judgemental.

- *Health is inner peace, healing is letting go of fear* – our true measure of health is how mentally peaceful we are, despite our circumstances. To heal we must release our attachment to fear, thus increasing our inner peace.

- *We can let go of the past and the future* – all of the best philosophies and theologies on the planet talk about living in the here and now – if we did that we would be happy. To feel any anger or sadness or guilt we need to jump into the past. To feel anxious or fearful we must look into the future. Yet feelings of passion, fun, peace, and happiness are all present tense. Every minute we spend time travelling, we are blind to what's really going on right here. Yet the past and future exist nowhere but in our own minds. They are not real, they are just internal representations. Hence the old adage "The past is history, the future a mystery. Now is a gift, that's why its called the present". If the past is a source of pain, it's not the events themselves that hurt, because they are over. It's the afterimage of the events. And we can change that.

A BRIEF HISTORY OF TIME LINE THERAPY

1. ARISTOTLE - GREEK PHILOSOPHER IN 300 BC TALKED ABOUT "western minds represent time as a straight line upon which we stand with our gaze directed forward – before us we have the future, and behind us the past. The present is the point on which we are standing, the future is found on some point in front of us." According to Aristotle, we must represent time by the image of a line

2. WILLIAM JAMES, THE FATHER OF MODERN DAY PSYCHOLOGY, wrote in 1890 in his book "Principles of Psychology" "consciousness was like a string of bead like sensations all separate" and "time is but a saddle back with a certain breadth of its own, on which we sit perched & from which we look in 2 directions in time. Date in time corresponds to direction in space. We represent the actual time-stream of our thinking by a horizontal line"

3. MILTON ERICKSON – The world's greatest Hypnotherapist up until his death in 1980 – used hypnosis to age regress people and take them back to significant emotional evens in their past, so they could see them from a whole new perspective and let go of any old unresolved emotions. He had them look down at events from a distance & observe traumatic experiences from afar, and the emotions would disappear

4. In the eighties, Dr Tad James modelled Milton Erickson &

applied a therapeutic process to the concept of an internal memory storage system. The result was a collection of techniques, which produces long-lasting **transformation** very quickly - faster than what is currently called Brief Therapy. These powerful Time Line Therapy™ techniques are becoming the method of choice to make fast, effective, long-term changes in behaviour. Your "Time Line" is how **you unconsciously store your memories** or how **you unconsciously know the difference** between a memory from the past and a projection of the future. The Time Line Therapy™ process allows you to **work at the unconscious level** and release the effects of past negative experiences and change "inappropriate" programming in minutes rather than days, months or years.

5. TAD TRAINED DAVID SHEPHARD IN MID 90's
6. IN 1997 DAVID TRAINED ME
7. RIGHT NOW AND I'M TRAINING YOU!

HOW WILL STUDYING HGE AND TIME LINE THERAPY™ TECHNIQUES BENEFIT ME?

• Through using these techniques, your personal happiness and professional success will be much more consistent, and much more predictable.

• Your effectiveness working with others will be dramatically increased, and your ability to empower yourself for optimum results will be increased.

• You will be able to generate empowering emotional states within yourself at will

• Eliminate any negative emotions or limiting decisions

• Identify and change limiting beliefs

• Inspire yourself with a compelling future that will have much better chances of coming true

So why are you reading this chapter? Maybe you've had experiences in the past that to this day still bother you. Unresolved issues. Unfinished business…

You've already read about HGE and it's speed and impact. How would you like to be able to let go of the past quickly?

Perhaps you'd like to change some limiting beliefs that you have about yourself. To illustrate, finish the following sentences:

"I'm not _____ enough…"

"People are…"

"Life is…"

"I can't …"

"If only I'd……"

So did you uncover any limiting beliefs?

Or maybe you want to know how to set goals so they really do come true? Do you set goals? Or maybe you don't believe that goal setting works. I wonder when you decided that?

Time Line Therapy is especially valuable to Practitioners and Master Practitioners of HGE who want to add massively to their existing intervention toolkit, as well as any other helping professionals who want to have rapid, transformational techniques up their sleeves.

Maybe you've been to all of the seminars, listened to all of the tapes, walked on fire, broken arrows with your throat, and you're still less than perfect…?

We're going to learn how to do six things with Time Lines:

1. HOW TO DISCOVER THE TIME LINE
2. HOW TO DISCOVER THE ROOT CAUSE OF A PROBLEM
3. HOW TO RELEASE A NEGATIVE EMOTION LIKE ANGER OR FEAR
4. REMOVE A LIMITING DECISION THAT YOU'VE MADE
5. CHANGE THE TIME LINE ORIENTATION

6.   CREATE YOUR FUTURE

As you've probably already read in previous chapters, my thing was always Fear. I was the thin, specky kid with asthma and ulcers by age 16 from being so shy and timid.

My best friend in the late eighties was unemployed and on housing benefit, and he rented a room in my flat, which I rented in turn from a work colleague. One day I came home and he's hastily vacated the premises, owing me hundreds in rent and unpaid bills. I was angry, hurt and felt betrayed.

Some time later I helped set up a magazine business with some friends and we had a sort of "gentleman's agreement" with a professional journalist who knew the publishing industry. He basically stole it from under our feet, and I was left with the bills to pay. That left me angry, hurt and scared that it could happen again.

In relationships, my first girlfriend was everything I ever wanted at that age – I was in heaven. Six months later I caught her with a friend of mine. That was anger and betrayal again!

Are we seeing a pattern yet?

My brother had studied psychology, so I started reading about the mind and human behaviour. Later I would do correspondence courses, devour more books, and eventually stumble across motivational speakers and positive thinking. I learned how to think optimistically, set goals for my life.

Last year I set out to get five major outcomes, including my dream house, my ideal income and dream car, and I did…

Remember the movie "Back to the Future" – the Delorean time machine? Imagine if you could go back in time to make changes in your past history. What would you change?

And what about the future? If you could create it in advance, what would you install there?

Well, keep reading, because you're going to learn how to use your own internal time machine. As Richard Bandler once said, "It's never too late to have a happy childhood"

So let's start that journey right now. Take a blank sheet of paper, and split it into two columns. The first should be headed "What do I want to let go of?" and the second "What do I want to gain?"

Ask yourself – what would have to happen for this to be the most important book you've ever read in your entire life?

SOME TIME LINE THERAPY THEMES:

Have you ever done Gestalt Therapy? Inner child work? Past Life Regression? Primal Scream, Psycho Drama, or walking a time line? If you have, this is different.

Have you heard of Recovered Memory Therapy? Well this isn't that – this is Time Line Therapy. RMT requires that the client has to re-experience the trauma from the past all over again, and it doesn't always clear the emotions up. We do something different.

The body is holographic – neurotransmitters bathe every cell in your body, and these act as chemical messengers. In other words, every cell in your body knows what you're thinking and feeling at any given moment. If you're happy your eyelashes are happy. If you're sad your teeth are sad. And all of your memories are stored throughout the body, not just in the brain. Massage therapists know about this – they can even fell those little black bags of stuck energy cluttering up the body's neural pathways.

Time Line Therapy is content free therapy – meaning you can let go of issues without having to go deeply into all of the nitty-gritty and unpleasant detail. We don't need to know who did what to you and how often and why. All we need to know is the root cause of the problem, and how you feel about it now?

Imagine that I'm an engineer and I want to destroy a dangerous old bridge. I don't need to know the full history of who made it, how much concrete holds it together, the number of girders underneath it or the name and destination of every passenger on every train that ever went over it. I just need to know when was it built and where is the weak point that holds it all up. Does that make sense?

Two more concepts that make this form of brief therapy work every time:

- Play at a hundred per cent. You have to be willing to suspend disbelief and tell the truth, allowing yourself to fully let go of the past.

- Secondly, there's the issue of secondary gain. Sometimes a person has more to gain from keeping their problem, than in letting it go. It's what Dr Phil calls "payoff". Sometimes you have a vested interest in keeping your problem, because it gets you something. For example, being ill makes you significant. It works, but it's a costly way of doing it.

ELICITING THE TIME LINE

ALL EMOTIONS HAVE A TEMPORAL COMPONENT...

Have you ever thought of that before? Probably not. I know I hadn't. But think about it, to be angry it must be about something that *has happened*. Past tense. It's after the event. Same with sadness, and guilt. You get sad because you've lost something and now you're sad. You can only feel guilty after doing something wrong. Fear comes because you've seen this thing before and you know to be scared. The Big Four (Anger, Sadness, Fear and Guilt) are all about the past.

Now sometimes people say "That's not true! I could imagine the council building a motorway straight through my back garden one day and that would make me angry right now!". Hmmm, possibly. But to do that you have to make a picture in your head of that having happened....in the past. I rest my case.

ANXIETY IN THE FUTURE

It's the exception to the rule – you only get anxious when you don't know what's going to happen next. Or you don't know what you'll do if….. You can't be anxious about something that's *happened*. You could get anxious about repercussions, but they're in the future. Do you see?

Your brain stores time. You know the difference between something that has happened, and something that hasn't happened yet. You have to, or else you're in big trouble. You may end up hugging yourself all day long in a room with really thick wallpaper…

We all have seven intelligences – one of them is called visual/spatial. That's the intelligence we use to store memories. In other words memories have a location relative to your body. You see and hear verbal and non-verbal examples all the time when people say "Put it behind you" or they point somewhere as they talk about a past event. "I'm looking forward to it" or "Look back on it and laugh" are not just words. **They are coordinates in space.**

Think of your Unconscious Mind as a camcorder – it has a video record of every event that's ever happened in your life, and it's all stored at the unconscious level. But how do you find out how a person stores their memories?

ELICITING THE TIMELINE

"If I were to ask your unconscious mind, where your past is, and where your future is, I have an idea that you might say, "It's from right to left, or front to back, or up to down, or in some direction from you in relation to your body. And it's not your conscious concept that I'm interested in, it's your unconscious. So, if I were to ask your unconscious mind where's your past, to what direction would you point?"

(Always note all analogue behaviour in elicitation)

"And your future, what direction would you point if I asked your unconscious mind, where's your future?"

ELICITATION OF THE TIME LINE

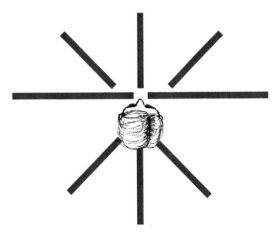

[Used with permission © Tad James & The Time Line Therapy Association]

NOTE: As you elicit the Time Line, make sure that you understand that however your client does it (how they organize the past and future) is perfect for your client. Make no value judgments about the organization of your client's Time Line until you find out if it works for your client.

If there are two or more Time Lines, say, "Which of these Time Lines would be the best to use to cause the most pervasive and long lasting change to occur?"

This elicitation works most of the time with almost every client. If that's still proving to be a challenge, carry on with another method:

1. Can you remember something that happened 1 week ago?
2. Good, as you do, can you notice where it comes from? (Alternatively, since some clients can't notice where a memory comes from, they "can notice where it goes to.")
3. Repeat the process for 1 & 2 for 1 month ago, 1 year ago, 5

years ago, and 10 years ago.

4. Now, repeat 1 & 2 for 1 month in the future, 1 year in the future, 5 years in the future, and 10 years in the future.

5. Now, ask the client, "Do you notice that this arrangement implies a line, or some linear arrangement of your memories?"

The arrangement may be linear or it may not. Allow your language and your behaviour to be non-directive so as to discover and not install the Time Line for your client.

The first elicitation is most conscious and quickest, the second is more unconscious & takes longer. Both work. Once you know where the time line is, it's time to get them to float above it (well, in their head at least!)

TEST FLIGHT

"Now, would you bring to mind the directions that you pointed to (or the memories of the past and future that you noticed). Do you notice that they imply a line?"

If no: "Well, could you notice that?"

If still no: "Is your past arranged by location, for example, where you lived?"

If yes: "How would it look if, for purposes of this process, it were stretched out in a line?"

(Remember Time Line Therapy™ is not *only* a visual process, it can be done visually or auditorally or kinaesthetically.)

"Good, now when I say line, I don't mean to imply only visual, because in a moment I'm going to ask you to float up above that line, and by float, I also mean as sounds floating on the wind, or floating in the bathtub, or visually. However you float up above your Time Line is perfect. So, can you just float up above your Time Line?

(If client is doing the process visually) "Make sure you are looking through your own eyes."

Now, remaining above your Time Line just float back into the past (pause). Are you there?"

"Good, float back toward now, and stop there (pause). Are you there? Good. Now, facing toward the future, float up higher and farther back into the past.

"And now, float out into your future (pause). Are you there?"

"Now, float up higher. Float so high that your time line seems like one inch long."

(pause)

"Good, float back to now, and float down into now and come back in the room." (pause)

"How was that?"

DISCOVERING THE ROOT CAUSE

As we've already discussed, the unconscious mind stores your memories like a string of pearls. In Time Line Therapy this is called a Gestalt.

Gestalt

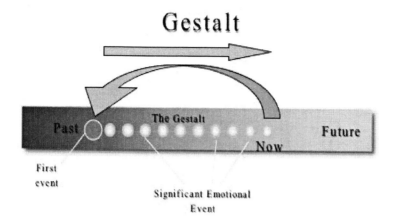

[Used with permission © Tad James & The Time Line Therapy Association]

I once had a client who was doing anger to the point of road rage. When we elicited the root cause he shouted out "THE BASTARDS SHOT ME THROUGH THE THROAT". I looked at his throat, no sign of any scar tissue. Then he said "I'm John F. Kennedy and the bastards shot me through the throat!". Now this guy was in his late thirties and this must have been the mid nineties, so by my calculations he couldn't have been JFK. But that's what we worked with, and the anger disappeared.

The Gestalt:

First   Significant
event   Emotional Event

Present Life - Root Cause Periods
0 - 7   Imprinting
7 - 14 Modelling
14 - 21 Socialization

[Used with permission © Tad James & The Time Line Therapy Association]

Now some people have a challenge with the ideas of past lives, or memories of being in the womb, or even further back. I don't care if your conscious mind doesn't believe in past lives or bloodlines, I don't even care if my conscious mind doesn't. It's what *your unconscious mind believes* that matters here, and if that's the answer that you get, then that's what you work with. Remember that the unconscious is symbolic, so it may just be giving you something to work with. Besides, let's face it, you'll never really know.

ELICITING THE ROOT CAUSE

NOTE: This section is done **before** client is above the Time Line. It increases unconscious trust and cooperation.

1. **Ask:** "Is it all right for your Unconscious Mind for you to release this (emotion or limiting decision) today and for you to be aware of it consciously?"

2. **Find the First Event:**
   "What is the root cause of this problem, the first event which, when disconnected, will cause the problem to disappear?

   If you were to know, was it before, during, or after your birth?

   -->**BEFORE:** "In the womb or before?"

   WOMB: "What month?"

   BEFORE: "Was it a past life or passed down to you genealogically?"

   PAST LIFE: "How many lifetimes ago?"

   GENEALOGICAL: "How many generations ago?"

   -->**AFTER:** "If you were to know, what age were you?"

NOTES:
- If client says "I don't know what the root cause is" then respond with "I know you don't, but if you did...take whatever comes up...trust your unconscious mind."
- If client says both genealogical and past life, work with the earlier one first, then the later.
- Ratify the change: Verify conscious acknowledgment of shift. When a major physiological shift occurs in the client, be sure to mention it: "That was a big one, wasn't it?"

- When you are eliciting the Root Cause for a Limiting Decision, note if the client is at Cause. If not, then ask for the Limiting Decision that caused the Limiting Decision in question.

So let's get in touch with the real issues at work here – we're here to learn how to let go of stuff that's held you back, and generally feel good more of the time. Imagine what it would feel like to have a past full of memories…that are either pleasant or neutral. How would that feel? How would you behave differently?

THE ROLE OF NEGATIVE EMOTIONS

This week alone, have you felt at any point at all:
ANGER
SADNESS
FEAR
GUILT
HURT?
And when you did, how did it feel?

THERE'S ABOUT 4 WAYS TO HANDLE YOUR EMOTIONS

1. You can try to ignore them – that's like getting a red light on the dashboard of your car. The message is to slow down, pull over and take a look under the bonnet. You wouldn't ignore it and keep pushing on, would you? Or worse, stick some black tape over it so you can't see it? I hope not, or else you might end up stranded on the hard shoulder, and you don't want that.

2. Secondly, you can try to not feel – repress your emotions, keep them stuffed under the carpet. Does that work? Is that healthy? Of course not. You probably know someone who has sat on painful emotions for years, and it's still in there,

festering. The Hawaiians called it "the thing that eats away inside"

3. Sometimes people wear their bad feelings like a badge of honour, compete with you and try to always upstage you. "Ha! You think you've got it tough, wait till I tell you...."

4. The fourth, and the best way to handle your feelings, is to think of them as helpful action signals. There's something to learn from them as they try to get your attention. They are focussing you, telling you that you're off the beaten path. Acknowledge that you've got strong emotions coming up, and learn from it. Get the gold nuggets – get the pearls of wisdom, the life lessons.

ANGER

The anger inside you isn't hurting the person you're angry at, it's hurting you. Be kind to your self and let it go. You always do the best you can with what you know at the time, don't you? The person you're angry at was doing the best they can with what they know, just like you. Anger has a message – someone has violated a rule or standard that you hold for your life. They probably don't know your rules. Your rules aren't necessarily the "right" rules

SADNESS

Act in a way that's positive, joyous and focus on what makes you feel good from now on. The message of sadness is that you think you've lost something – an expectation you had has not been met. They probably didn't realise the effect it'd have on you.

Maybe you need to tell people your expectations.

FEAR

Your unconscious mind knows many ways to keep you safe and raise your awareness so you can notice everything you need to notice to keep you safe. It knows how to protect you at any other time – sneezing, blinking when a bug hits your windscreen, arms go out when you fall, etc. Fear has a message – it's telling you that you need to prepare and get ready. Figure out what you need to do to prepare yourself mentally.

It's highest intention is safety and peace

GUILT

Live in accordance with your deepest values. Guilt has a message – you have violated one of your own highest standards, and you need to promise immediately to make sure you hold yourself to that standard in the future. It's driving you to take action to make a change. If you could do it again, how would you do it differently?

Have you ever had toothache so bad that eventually you go to the dentist, and as you sit in the waiting room, smelling the sterile smell of the surgery and hearing the high pitched whine of the drill, what happens to the pain? IT DISAPPEARS!! Why? Because you paid attention and did something about it. Magic formula.

Any time you've gotten emotional, angry, sad, whatever, did feeling that strong reaction actually help you deal with the situation? Or does it make it harder? What if you could learn how to let go of that emotion, in minutes not months?

For example

THE SALESPERSON WHO HAS FEAR

THE PERSON IN MOURNING WITH SADNESS

FALLING OUT WITH SOMEONE AND FEELING ANGER

THE END OF A RELATIONSHIP – HURT, OR FEAR OF COMMITMENT IN THE NEXT ONE

YOU BROKE YOUR OWN RULES - GUILT

So to recap – I recommend you find out where your Time Line is located, admit truthfully what negative emotions you've been storing up, and start getting to the root cause of each one and clear it out systematically. Let's look at the actual process of letting it go.

RELEASING NEGATIVE EMOTIONS NO 1

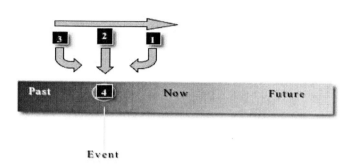

Event

[Used with permission © Tad James & The Time Line Therapy Association]

1. "Just float up above your Time Line, and over the past to Position #1, facing the past, and when you get there notice the event. Let me know when you're there"

2. "Now, float to Position #2 directly up above the event so you are looking down on the event. Ask your Unconscious Mind what it needs to learn from the event, the learning of which will allow you to let go of the emotions easily and effort-lessly. Your Unconscious Mind can preserve the learning's so that if you need them in the future, they'll be there." [1]

3. "Now, float to Position #3 so you are above the event and before the event, and you are looking toward now. (Make sure you are well before of any the chain of events that led to that event.) And ask yourself, 'Now, where are the emo-tions?'"[2]

4. "Float down inside the event, to Position #4, looking

---

1   See Notes about Learnings
2   Note: If the emotion does not disappear, then reframe.

through your own eyes, and check on the emotions. Are they there? Or have they disappeared! Now!! Good, go back to Position #3."[1]

5. "Now, come back to now above your Time Line only as quickly as you can let go of all the **(name the emotion)** on the events all the way back to now, assume position 3 with each subsequent event, preserve the learning's, and let go of the (**name the emotion**) all the way back to now. (When Client is done) Float down into now, and come back into the room." **(Break State)**

6. **Test:** (Client back at now.) "Can you remember any event in the past where you used to be able to feel that old emotion, and go back and notice if you can feel it, or you may find that you cannot. Good come back to now."

7. **Future pace:** (Client back at now.) "I want you to go out into the future to an unspecified time in the future which if it had happened in the past, you would have felt inappropriate or unwarranted (**name the emotion**), and notice if you can find that old emotion, or you may find that you cannot. OK?" Good come back to now.

3 THINGS TO CHECK AT POSITION # 3

1. MAKE SURE CLIENT IS IN POSITION #3.

(Indictor: Client is **really** feeling the emotions)

Tell client:

"Get up higher, and float farther back."

"Get high enough and far enough back until the emotion disappears,"

---

3   Note: When releasing sadness, hurt or fear: "Imagine an infinite source of love and healing above the top of your head. Allow it to come in through the top of your head, (from your Higher Self) and fill up your body, now, and overflow out your heart and fill up the 'you' in the time line until he/she is totally whole and healed."

2. BE SURE CLIENT IS BEFORE THE FIRST EVENT.

(Indicator: 90% of the emotions release.)

Ask client:

"Are you before the first event?"

"Is there an event earlier than this one? Go back before the FIRST one."

3. MUST BE TOTALLY AGREEABLE TO LET GO OF THE EMOTION.

(Indicator: Client says, "The emotions are not releasing.")

Ask client:

"What is there to learn from this event? If you learn this, won't it be better than having the old emotions? How can you get the same benefit that the emotions provided when you let them go?"

(Use this reframe or any other reframe on the **GENERAL RE-FRAMES.**)

NOTES REGARDING LEARNINGS

Learning's are not always obvious to the client. Especially where the client already has learning's, (s)he may not get any new or obvious ones. When you are aware of learning's they **should NOT be:**

- Negative (I wasn't strong enough…)
- Past oriented (that kept happening again and again…)
- Others (she shouldn't have said that to me…)

When you are aware of learning's they should be:

- Positive (I know how to stand my ground)
- Future oriented (I will be more aware)
- Self (I know how to ask for what I want)

GENERAL REFRAMES
USE IF NEGATIVE EMOTIONS DO NOT RELEASE

BASED UPON
1. LEARNING:

"What is there to have learned from this event, the learning of which will allow you to easily let go of the emotions? Won't it be better to preserve the learning's than the emotions? If you let go of the emotions and preserve the learning's you will have learned what you needed."

2. PROTECTION/SAFETY:

"The negative emotion of _____ doesn't protect you."
(If you're working with fear or anger, mention flight or fight)
"In fact negative emotions aren't safe for the body. Each negative emotion can contribute to the following types of health problems:

Anger	Heart attack, Heightened Cholesterol
Sadness	Weakened Immune System, Depression
Fear	Excessive stress, PTSD, Phobia
Guilt	Lowered healing energy
Conflict	Cancer

"Won't you be a lot safer if you let go of the emotions and preserve the learning's about taking care of yourself?"

3. PRIME DIRECTIVES:

"Not letting go of this emotion is in direct conflict with the highest Prime Directive of the unconscious mind, which is, 'To preserve the body.' This emotion, though getting results, does not preserve the body; it hurts the body. Wouldn't it be better to let go of the repressed emotion and get the same results in some other way?"

316

RELEASING NEGATIVE EMOTIONS NO 2

You would use this intervention with highly logical Academic types, or people who perhaps are not allowing themselves to feel the emotion. Or maybe you've run the first process and something still hasn't cleared. This technique will light them up like a Christmas tree...

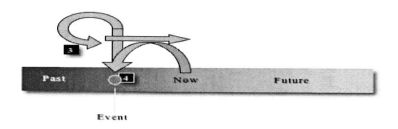

[Used with permission © Tad James & The Time Line Therapy Association]

PROCEDURE:

1. "I'd like to ask your unconscious mind to float up in the air, above your Time Line, into the past and down into the event—right into Position #4, and (pause) when you're there, notice the emotion that's present."

2. Float back up above the Time Line and go to Position #3, well before the beginning of the event, or any of the events that led to that event, and turn and look toward now. Ask your Unconscious Mind what it needs to learn from the event, the learning of which will allow you to let go of the emotions easily and effortlessly. Your Unconscious Mind can preserve the learning's so that if you need them in the

future, they'll be there." [1]

3. "Now where is the emotion? [2] Where did it go? That's right, it disappeared."

4. "Just float right down into the event and notice that the emotion has disappeared. Is the emotion totally gone! Good, come back up to Position #3."

5. "Now, come back to now, above your Time Line only as quickly as you can let go of all the (name the emotion) on the events all the way back to now, assume position 3 with each subsequent event, preserve the learning's, and let go of the (name the emotion) all the way back to now. (When Client is done) Float down into now, and come back into the room." (Break State)

6. Test: (Client back at now.) "Can you remember any event in the past where you used to be able to feel that old emotion, and go back and notice if you can feel it, or you may find that you cannot." Good come back to now.

7. Future pace: (Client back at now.) "I want you to go out into the future to an unspecified time in the future which if it had happened in the past, you would have felt inappropriate or unwarranted (name the emotion), and notice if you can find that old emotion, or you may find that you cannot. OK?" Good come back to now.

WHAT TO DO IF THEY FULLY ASSOCIATE?

Remember, it is not unusual for clients to associate into a traumatic memory during a Time Line Therapy™ Technique. There are other techniques that actually associate clients into traumatic events on purpose. Unlike these techniques, it is not the intent of Time Line

---

1 See Notes about Learnings.

2 Note: If the emotion does not disappear, then reframe.

Therapy to associate the client into a traumatic memory, however it is not unusual. If your client associates into an unwanted memory here is what to do:

1. "Where are you?" (If the client is feeling the emotions, the client is in the memory – in position 4.)
2. Whatever the client says, "Good, just get up above the Time Line so you are looking down on the event."
3. (Pause) "Are you above the Time Line?" (If no, then go back to #2)
4. If yes, "Good now make sure you are in Position 3. (Pause) Now, where are the emotions?"

Sometimes the Time Line Therapy™ Practitioner, although patient, has to be quite forceful or authoritarian in getting the client to get above the Time Line. Remember it is important for the client's comfort to get him or her out of the traumatic memory as soon as possible. While we say that negative emotions are good, it is also not good to hold on to the emotions. If the client remains associated it just strengthens the emotions.

5. If steps 1-4 do not work then stand up and clap your hands over the client's head and say, "Open your eyes and look up at the ceiling. Keep your eyes up." (With client's eyes open, go to step #2.)
6. If step #5 does not work, stand up and say to the client, "Stand up and walk with me." Then walk the client around the room at high speed while you do the Time Line Therapy Process while the client is walking.

WHY THE NEGATIVE EMOTIONS DISAPPEAR

THERE ARE 3 REASONS WHY THE NEGATIVE EMOTIONS DISAPPEAR

1. Psychological: (Reframe)

Based on the work of Leslie Cameron-Bandler in *Emotional Hostage*, 1987, and Alfred Korzybski, *Science and Sanity,* 1933, all emotions require time to express their meaning, so a switch in the temporal perspective reframes the emotion. The emotion is reframed, and so it disappears.

2. Metaphysical: (Illusion)

Based on the book *A Course in Miracles,* there is only one real emotion on the planet -- Love. All the negative emotions are derivatives of fear & are an illusion, so a switch in the temporal perspective shows the emotion to be the illusion it is, and it disappears.

3. Quantum Physics: (Non-Mirror Image Reverse)

Based on the work of Quantum Physics and Calculus, Position 3 is the Non-Mirror Image Reverse of the way the emotion is held in "now." So Position 3 is the multi-dimensional neurological opposite of "now." What happens is that this position acts like anti-matter, and the neurological boundaries of the emotion in the body get blown out -- they disappear.

CHANGING THE DIRECTION OF THE TIME LINE

While everyone's Time Line is different, there are two main possibilities, and most people will have characteristics of each. These are known as IN TIME and THROUGH TIME. Most people will be one, the other, or a combination of both. I've seen 'V' shapes, fireman poles, uphill struggles, downhill slides – anything is possible when you're dealing with people's internal storage of time. Note that your Time Line greatly affects how you perceive time, and any change in the location can dramatically change time for you. We do this on our live seminars. You might want to try it!

THE CLASSIC THROUGH-TIME TIME LINE:

Is left to right (or right to left).

Horizontal.

Reaches out about as far as the length of the outstretched arms.

Has memories which are about 4 inches high which are located just under the centre of the eye (horizontal).

Now is located in the centre.

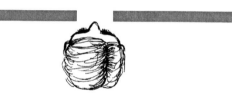

Usually very time conscious, their memories tend to be dissociated, i.e. they can see themselves in the pictures. Punctuality is vital to them, they like organisation, linear sequence and planning. They like closure and need to make clear decisions – the classic Judger.

The Classic In-Time Time Line:

Is front to back (or back to front).

Horizontal.

Stretches as far back as the original Time Line.

Has memories of a comfortable size, generally more than 4 inches.

Client is located in Now.

The In Time person on the other hand is in the here and now and may even struggle to think about the past. Memories tend to be Associated (looking through their own eyes, in it). Time keeping is not their strong point. Like to keep their options open and get anxious making decisions – the classic Perceiver.

NOTE: Any shift in the relationship between the body and the Time Line will have a profound effect on a person's personality, so make changes only after a thorough investigation, and a discussion with the client about consequences.

1. **Elicit the Client's Time Line.**

2. **Clean-up the past:** (Negative emotions and limiting decisions.)

3. **Check Ecology:** "Here are the consequences of shifting the Time Line (explain)... Is it OK with your unconscious mind to make this shift, and allow it to remain, and to be comfortable?"

4. **Rotate the Time Line:** "Now, just float up above the Time Line, right above now, and rotate your Time Line so that it is in the new desired direction (location), and tell me when you've done that."

5. **Reassociate:** "Good, now just float right down into the present, and organize your Time Line in the new way."

6. **Lock the Time Line into place:** "And you know the sound

that Tupperware makes when it seals? Just like that, lock it in."

7. **Test:** "As you think of it, will it be all right for your Unconscious Mind to leave the Time Line this way, and you be comfortable?"

8. **Future pace:** "Is there any reason in the future why you wouldn't be totally comfortable with this organization of your Time Line?"

ELIMINATING LIMITING DECISIONS

Imagine someone who, in their relationships keeps attracting the wrong type of partner. Or money. I once had a client who told me he could never earn more than £50,000. On investigation it turned out he'd heard a conversation on TV while in the womb. Imagine that! One female client of mine had self-esteem issues about being too "mannish"– she talked in a deep, macho voice and wore polo necks to her chin and jeans over her ankles, covering herself up as much as possible. On investigation it turned out that at aged 16 she climbed out of a swimming pool on holiday in Yugoslavia, and every lecherous old man in a mile radius leered at this girl in a bikini, and in that one moment her unconscious mind decided, "it's not safe to be sexy". As Tony Robbins once said, it's in your moments of decision that your destiny is shaped!

A LIMITING DECISION ALWAYS PRECEDES A LIMITING BELIEF

Event

[Used with permission © Tad James & The Time Line Therapy Association]

In doing Time Line Therapy™ Techniques, we will work mostly with eliminating the client's past Negative Emotions and Limiting Decisions. It is important to determine the difference between these two modalities of intervention. Generally anything that is not a Negative Emotion is a Limiting Decision. There are also some additional criteria for determining a Limiting Decision. You will work with a Limiting Decision when it is described as:

1. **Anything you can't feel:** If the description the client gives you is something, which when you "try it on" is something you cannot feel without hallucinating substantially then you are working with a Limiting Decision. "I just don't feel happy," for example, is a Limiting Decision.

2. **Negations:** As in the example above, anytime you hear a negation describing anything, which might be a Negative Emotion, you should be looking for a Limiting Decision. Examples include, "I'm not capable," "I don't feel loved," and "I can't make the kind of money I want."

3. **Comparatives:** Whenever you hear a comparison, such as "I wish I could make more money," treat it as a Limiting Decision. Comparatives include statements such as, "I have low self esteem," "I am not good enough," or "I want to feel better about myself."

4. **All Beliefs:** What is not obvious is that any time we have a Limiting Belief we must have Limiting Decision, which preceded it. Each time in the past when you adopted a Limiting Belief, a Limiting Decision preceded that acceptance. A Limiting Decision preceded even the beliefs that were adopted from other people. If a client says, "I don't believe I can do it," the Practitioner should say, "When did you decide that?"

5. **Physiological Issues:** Many issues that result in physiological symptomology have their roots in decisions. (This includes all physiological issues that look like dis-ease.)

6. **Accidents:** Many events in the client's past are the result of decisions that the client made which preceded the event. Even if this is not "true", when the client accepts his/her creation of a past "accident" then the client can un-choose the event and thus change his/her future.

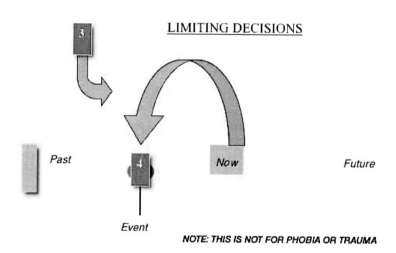

LIMITING DECISIONS

Past   Now   Future

Event

NOTE: THIS IS NOT FOR PHOBIA OR TRAUMA

[Used with permission © Tad James & The Time Line Therapy Association]

PROCEDURE

1. "I'd like to ask your unconscious mind to float up in the air, above your Time Line, into the past and down into the event—right into Position #4." (pause)

2. "Notice what emotions are present, and also note if you are aware of the decision that was made there, too." (If "No," say, "I'd like you to rewind the movie of your memory until you come to the time of the decision ... right now.") [7]

3. "Float back up above the Time Line and go to Position #3, well before the beginning of the event, or any of the chain of events that led to that event, and turn and look toward now. Preserve the positive learning's."

4. "Now where are the emotions? [1] And the decision, did it disappear, too? [2]

5. "Float down inside the event, to Position #4, looking through your own eyes, and check on the emotions. Are they there? Or have they disappeared! Now!! Good, & the decision too—it's disappeared! Good, come back up to Position #3."

6. "And come back to now only as quickly as you allow all the events between then and now to re-evaluate themselves in light of your new choices, and let go of all the negative emotions on those events, assume Position #3, preserve the learning's, let go of the emotions and allow each event to re-evaluate itself all the way back to now."

7. **Test:** "Now, how do you feel about that old decision (or belief)?"

8. **Future Pace:** "I want you to go out into the future to an

---

1 Note: If the emotion does not disappear, then reframe.

2 Note: Under certain circumstances, it may be necessary to install a decision. If this is desired, have the client float down into the event. Then have the client imagine making the new decision (associated), in a way that is in alignment with his or her outcome. Before leaving make sure the event is still associated.

unspecified time in the future that would be most appropriate, and imagine a time when something like this could happen again, and how do you react, OK? ... Good, come back to now."

PHOBIA MODEL

This is a particularly useful intervention, very quick and very effective. If the client has a particularly negative memory, this intervention will greatly reduce the intensity of the emotions, and if used fully, will neutralise them entirely, leaving the memory flat, neutral and balanced. Like ancient history in a very old scrapbook. Can you think of anything like that in your past?

This was called 'The Phobia Model' because it was originally developed to remove a phobic reaction e.g. insects, spiders, flying, whatever in minutes not years.

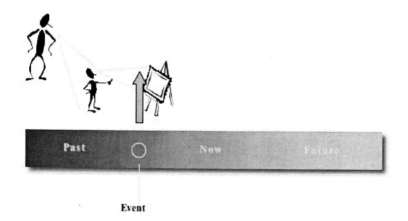

[Used with permission © Tad James & The Time Line Therapy Association]

PROCEDURE

(Use Negative Emotions #1, first. If that doesn't work, then use this page.)

1. (Optional) Establish a resource anchor. A tap on their shoulder perhaps, that brings them back into the here and now, safe and comfortable

2. Acknowledge one-trial learning and client's ability to learn. **You never forget to have this problem!**

3. Discover & scramble the strategy used for having phobia. How do they do it? When do they do it? Was there ever a time when they didn't?

4. Have them go back to the first event. Ask for the root cause using the normal procedure.

5. Make a movie theatre above the Time Line, and have them watch themselves in the front row (dissociated) watching a movie of their life, from the projection booth.

6. Run the movie forward in Black &White to the end.

7. Freeze frame at end, and white (or black) out.

8. Have the client associate into the memory and run it backwards in colour to the beginning.

9. Repeat steps 5 - 8 until the client can't get the feeling (K) back. (If you are deleting a memory, then repeat until the memory is not accessible — give appropriate instructions.)

10. Check ecology. If necessary, install a better more pleasant memory using other techniques.

11. Test and future pace. "Imagine a time in the future….?"

"THAT'S ENOUGH ABOUT THE PAST – LET'S LOOK INTO YOUR FUTURE!"

RELEASING ANXIETY

ANXIETY IS A FUTURE BASED EMOTION, where something might happen and you don't know what to do if it does. You're asking yourself "What if....?" questions.

This is probably the fastest and easiest technique I know!

Anxious about sitting examinations?

Job interview coming up and you're worried?

Have to do a presentation and scared it might go wrong?

Yearning to ask someone out but worried in case they reject you?

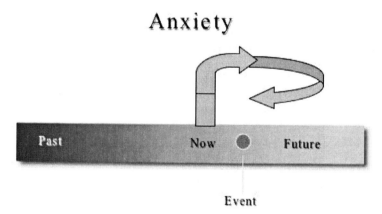

[Used with permission © Tad James & The Time Line Therapy Association]

PROCEDURE:

1. "Float up above the Time Line, and out into the future to 15 minutes after the successful completion of the event about which you thought you were anxious. Tell me when you're there."

2. "Good. Turn and look toward now, along the Time Line."

3. "Now, where's the anxiety?"[1]
4. "Come back to now."
5. If desired, test by having them think about what used to make them anxious, and notice that the feeling is emotionally balanced, or flat.

IDEAL FOR ONE OFF EVENTS THAT YOU KNOW ARE COMING UP.

Earlier in this book we took some outcomes through specific criteria and languaged them in such a way as to make them more achievable. Now let's stack the deck, and add to it the most powerful goal-setting technique on the planet!

CREATING YOUR FUTURE

We each have our own internal time machine, much like the one in HG Wells' movie. Remember the bathtub with the bingo wheel attached? Was that just a story? Or maybe you've seen the new version – did you know that many years later there was a remake done? Or perhaps you remember the movie series called "Back to the Future". Trancey title wasn't it? Remember when the mad scientist said "Your future hasn't been written yet Marty!"

Were these films just entertainment? Or is there a message here? I mean, what's a meta for?

Your conscious mind is the goal setter, but it's your unconscious that's the goal getter.

If you've ever set goals before, or visualised them in your future,

---

1 NOTE: If anxiety does not disappear, then reframe, "I know that there's a part of you that thinks it's important for you to have some anxiety to motivate you, and I agree that it's important for you to be motivated. The problem is that anxiety is not good for the body. Are there other ways that would be OK for you to motivate yourself, and let the anxiety go?"
Additionally, anxiety may be the result of fear, which has not been released. For a Presenting Problem of anxiety, always release fear first.

then your brain knows you want it and may mobilise all of its vast resources to get there. But if you have a picture and it's in your past time line location, what might happen? Your brain might think you've already had it. That's what happened to me. Or rather nothing happened, because I was sticking my future outcomes in the wrong location. Oops!

Now, if you were to place future wants into the location for your future, your unconscious mind then knows you're serious! This is what the Hawaiian Kahuna called "Make Luck Business"

I mean, everything that's ever happened is on your past time line, isn't it? And everything that will happen is on your future time line. So if you want to make something happen, there's only one place for it!

Putting a Single Event into the Future

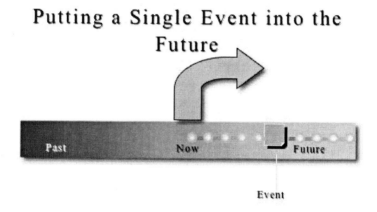

[Used with permission © Tad James & The Time Line Therapy Association]

STEPS FOR PUTTING A SINGLE GOAL IN YOUR FUTURE

1. Be sure the goal is stated so it is well formed. Use the keys to an achievable outcome in the earlier chapter of this book.

331

2. **Get the last step:**
   "What is the last thing that has to happen so you know you got it?"

3. **Make an Internal Representation:**
   A Visual representation, a clear picture of what you want to see
   Plus the Auditory representation, the sounds you'll hear
   And Kinesthetic representation, feeling how good it will feel

4. **Step into the Internal Representation — see it through your own eyes**

5. **Adjust the qualities of the picture**—Adjust them for the most positive Kinesthetic or for the most "real" feeling. Brighter, closer, louder.

6. **Step out of the Internal Representation — see yourself in the picture.**

7. **Take the Internal Representation and float above now.**

8. **Energize the Internal Representation with four deep breaths:** Have the Client breathe in through the nose, out through the mouth, and blow all the energy into the Internal Representation. Four Ha breaths.

9. **Float out into the Future:** Take the Internal Representation and float above the Time Line out into the future.

10. **Insert the Internal Representation into the Time Line:** "Let go of the Internal Representation and let it float right down into the Time Line.

11. **Notice the events between then and now re-evaluate themselves to support goal:** The Client may or may not have an experience of the re-evaluation, so we call it to his (her) attention.

12. **Float back to now.**

SCOPE OF PRACTICE

This is in no way a full and complete training in Time Line Therapy techniques. "Scope of Practice" relates what kind of interventions a practicing Time Line Therapy™ Practitioner should do and with whom. The answer to this question depends upon whether you are licensed or unlicensed.

An unlicensed practitioner should confine his/her practice to:
smoking,

weight loss,

stress reduction and

some performance enhancement issues.

If the practitioner intends to accept a client with issues that do not fall into these areas, then the practitioner should receive further training in Time Line Therapy® at the Master Practitioner level. In addition, the Practitioner should also get a written referral from a licensed person or should be under the direct supervision of a licensed person.

A Time Line Therapy™ Practitioner should definitely NOT perform outside the scope for which (s)he is trained and licensed.

Licensed Practitioner: A licensed practitioner may use Time Line Therapy™ Techniques for additional issues, provided that those issues are consistent with the practitioner's license and if the practitioner has received Time Line Therapy® Training at the Master Practitioner level.

ADDITIONAL CONSIDERATIONS

If the presenting problem or the personal history that you gather from the client indicates to you that the client is dangerous to self or others, then the client is beyond the scope of treatment by an unlicensed practitioner. Someone of this kind is best referred to a practitioner who is trained to handle clinical issues.

Under certain circumstances, highly traumatic or repressed material could indicate that if you are not trained in interventions that deal in this area, it would be best to refer the client to a practitioner who is trained to handle these issues.

A client who seeks treatment for a physiological and/or a life-threatening disease should be advised that such treatment is "controversial" and should be encouraged to get a diagnosis and referral from a Medical Doctor before proceeding. NOTE: It is not illegal to use Time Line Therapy™ Techniques for, say, helping to alleviate an ulcer or its symptoms. It is, however, illegal to claim to use Time Line Therapy™ Techniques to cure any physical condition.

Practicing beyond your Scope of Practice may result in de-certification by the Time Line Therapy™ Association.

Should you wish to be certified as a Time Line Therapy™ Practitioner then contact me and I'll refer you to Dr Tad James www.nlpcoaching.com.

We also have an entire Time Line Therapy™ training available as an eight CD set, in which you can hear all of these processes being demonstrated and explained fully. For details go to www.jonathanclark.org/products and look for the Time Line Therapy Weekend home study.

"Holding on to the past is like trying to not go to the toilet. It's easier just to go"

13

QUESTIONS ARE THE ANSWER

Questions: A Basic Tool in Your Communication Toolkit

The 'smart question' to ask is "Why am I looking at this chapter?" If the answer is to improve your ability to get more out of your meetings, interviews, negotiations, and communications with everyone at any level (internal and external to your organisation), this is the chapter to read by far. Ask and you shall receive; ask the right question(s) and you'll get what you want/deserve.

I remember it quite clearly. We had this really jerry-built rickety swing in the back garden, that my Dad had cobbled together. You know…. the kind of swing that judders at points normal swings don't! And I remember me sitting there – it's funny, because as you'll read about elsewhere in this book, the brain always uses the same picture (internal representation) every time you access the memory. You always get the same picture in your mind's eye. And there I am, sitting on this rickety construction, asking myself a question (silently, mind you). It was a question I'd often asked myself.

"Why does my mind keep feeding me bad thoughts?"

Now that's not a useful question. I'll talk about "why?" questions later to explain what I mean. But that's still not a well-formed quality question. And the reason I say that is because of the kind of answer it elicits.

"Because it wants to punish you and make you feel bad"

Now I still can't remember what it was I'd done to deserve a mental interrogation and metaphorical thrashing 24 hours a day, but it must have been some heinous crime!

I still think of that image to this day – it flashes up every time I run a workshop or training and we start talking about images in your head (don't worry, we all do it!). Personally, I think this is quite insightful for a ten year old. I may even have been younger.

By the time I was eighteen I'd developed a duodenal ulcer – I was so nervous and timid, I'd burned a hole in my intestine. All because I asked stupid questions all day long. Fear-creating questions. Worry. Anxiety. "What if...?" scenarios.

Now I also grew up watching a kid's television show called Blue Peter, and every day they would make or build something and show you how to build it yourself. Sometimes they even printed an instruction fact sheet that you could send away for. I found that fascinating, and I used to get these sheets and build the things that I really wanted. I'd also imagine I was on the show, with an audience, and I'd be teaching the imaginary class – presenting, building things, showing others how to. Do you see? It was my built in, genetic need to Coach. Now look at what I'm doing....

Whether it's a police interrogation, a therapy session, a new relationship, sales, exam papers, job interviews, whatever, questions focus the mind and are always answered. Aren't they?

See?

The most powerful way to direct your focus is through the questions you ask. Remember, the process of thinking or evaluating, is nothing more than the process of asking and answering questions. The challenge most people face is that they are not conscious about the questions they ask themselves.

QUESTIONS ARE THE LASER OF HUMAN CONSCIOUSNESS.

They concentrate our focus and determine what we feel and do. Think of questions this way: Imagine that your brain is the ultimate computer, and in that computer is the answer to any question you could possibly have.

Suppose you consistently ask yourself, "**Why do these things always happen to me?**" Your brain will search its database and take every possible form of input it's ever received - what people have ever said to you; what you've ever said to yourself; and what you've ever read, heard, or seen. Then, it will create an answer for you: "**They always happen to you because you are a loser!**" Right? That's why "why?" is rarely a useful question. Asking "why?" will get you a "because", and now you're using reasons, and now you're at Effect.

Whatever you ask yourself consistently, you will get an answer to. If you ask, "**How come I'm so lucky?**" your brain will search until it finds references to support the fact that you are lucky.

IF YOU ASK A BETTER QUESTION, YOU WILL COME UP WITH A BETTER ANSWER AND THEREFORE, A BETTER RESULT.

As we've already discussed, traditional time planning is based upon the question, "**What do I need to do today?**" If you keep asking yourself this question, you are undoubtedly going to feel stressed because most of us can't possibly achieve everything on our to-do list!

By changing the questions you ask when managing your life, you will immediately change your focus, gain access to new resources within yourself, and produce a better quality result.

All human progress is preceded by new questions.

It is by **questioning our limitations** that our **greatest strengths** are unveiled.

It is by **questioning conventional wisdom** that **new truths** are unearthed.

It is by **questioning our capacity** as human beings that this capacity **expands**.

WHY DO WE USE QUESTIONS?

Gather information we might not have gotten otherwise

Develop rapport

Key to unlock the client

Allow the client to go deeper inside to help clarify what the real issue is

Helps the client recognize how our emotions distort perception

Gets the client out of their head and moves them into their heart

Helps them hear what they need to hear

Keeps us focused

They demand answers

Questions stimulate thinking

Answers give us valuable information

They put us in control

Get people to open up

Lead to quality listening

Get people to sell themselves

WHAT EXACTLY IS A QUESTION?

According to the Oxford English Dictionary: "The action of inquiring or asking. The stating or investigation of a problem: inquiry into a matter. To inquire or seek after".

For our purposes a Question is the seeking of information and the directing and guiding toward insight.

WHAT CAN WE DO TO KEEP FOCUSED SO QUESTIONS COME FROM THE RIGHT PLACE?

• Stay in the present and be results oriented

• Listen without judgment.

• Not be attached to the outcome

• Stay focused on the "Who"

• Work from the assumption that our natural state is curious. (We almost unlearn our natural state of asking questions).

- Stay away from the "how to" and get to the point where you are almost nosy about the client.
- Creating a place for the client to see their own answer instead of giving them our answer (the "right" answer).
- Come from a real understanding that the present is perfect and there is no right way to be. This is a whole different level of un-attachment. We are not talking about self-discipline. We are peeling away to get to the curious state we all knew at one time as children and allowing ourselves to be ourselves once again. That natural way of being is the power we have as coaches. A tool for us is being childlike.

WHAT DO QUESTIONS DO?
- Make a person think
- Offer a possible new perspective
- Stimulate answers/possibilities
- May result in a greater focus about an issue.
- Push buttons
- Establish relationship between coach and client (How?)
- Honours client's intelligence-which in turn empowers. (They know the Answers)

WHAT ARE THE POSSIBLE RESULTS OF A WELL-ASKED QUESTION?
- Verify to the client and the coach that the client is brilliant and has the answers.
- Slow down automatic thinking and responses from the client.
- Client is required to think "out of the box".
- Awareness is being raised when stopped to re-think something
- Breakup current perceptions and patterns of behavior.
- Might breakup self-limiting assumptions.

- Allow/require the client to illuminate, clarify
- Stimulation of creativity
- Client feels empowered
- Move from seeing what's true to taking action

EXERCISE

1. Write some questions that you, or someone else, has asked you in YOUR life that has helped you move forward or understand something about yourself or a situation?
2. Create ten questions that contribute to or create relationship/build rapport.
3. Be conscious of how you are using questions this week. How many are you asking?

WHAT ARE SOME OF THE DIFFERENT KINDS/TYPES OF QUESTIONS?

As we become more experienced as a coach, and we grow as individuals, we will use more of these different types of questions. I am eternally grateful for my fellow students at CoachU who helped me compile these different categories. Thanks guys.

- Situational Questions: Stating a question to discover what is present/true now. What is clear for the client (and what is not)? This is the first step in discovering what the situation is. In this we listen for the second step, which are the symptoms of what is going on that may clarify the source.
- Inquiry Questions: Discovering what the client (or you) WANTS. What their objective is and what the Motivation (source) is of the want. For example, a person may have the Objective (want) to walk to the other side of the room to get a glass of water. The motivation (source) is thirst.
- Action Questions: How does the client (or I) get what they want? What action needs to be taken? What attitude/perspective needs

to change (shift) to create the desired results (solution)?

- Thought Provoking questions: questions that make a client "think" or "re -think" a perspective.
- Feeling questions: how does the situation/symptom/source/want relate to your emotional state or feelings. How is it affecting you?
- Why questions: used appropriately (not over-used), can peel away the layers of resistance or illusion in the way something is viewed or perceived: To get to the source of a block.
- Rhetorical Questions: Stating an observation as a question. To assist in further clarifying a situation, response, idea, block. Can have a right answer in mind and can use it to lead a client to what they think the answer should be. A truly effective rhetorical question has no answer to it before it is asked. You may think you have the answer, and if you are fishing for an answer, and you won't take the fish because you are attached to another answer then you can miss all the other fish (answers).
- Informative questions - helps gather more linear information
- Probing questions - sometimes you just have to go fishing
- Serendipity questions - chance intuitive questions
- Goal Setting questions - choices for self motivation
- Reality Checking questions - clarifying major distortions caused by opinions, judgements and perceptions
- Options Questions--various courses of available actions "What is to be done" questions.
- Focusing questions – Prioritizing
- Reflective Questions--questions that make a client "think" or "re-think" a perspective. For example

At the end of each month, review your progress.

1) What have I achieved this month?
2) Am I on track to meet my goals if I carry on in the same way?

3) Could I have done anything more / better / differently to meet my goals?

4) What is the big benefit of meeting my goals?

5) How can I reward myself for my efforts this month?
- Motivating Questions - Initiate stimulus to cause forward movement
- Discussion/Focus Statements: To move from seeing what's true to action. A question well asked is often the answer.
- Prompting/transformative questions
- What do you mean questions" (Question what the client means and what they think they mean).

EXERCISE

Create a list of questions that represent each of these types of questions.

Are there any more types of questions? Here are some ideas, collated from my colleagues on the Coach University Training Programme. I hope you'll find these useful and can dip into the appropriate type as and when required.

WHAT ARE SOME QUESTIONS THAT CONTRIBUTE TO OR CREATE RELATIONSHIP AND BUILD RAPPORT?
- How should I coach you now?
- Who are you becoming?
- Whom do you most admire that does what you'd like to do?
- How did you create that?
- What is one thing that you felt really good about over this past week?
- What's the one thing that would make the biggest difference in you life now?
- What's your belief about [money, success, etc] that may need to shift?

- When did you last create exactly what you wanted? What did you do to do this?
- Who do you need to be in order to HAVE what you want in your life?
- What would you like more/less of?
- Where is it you would like to be a year from now?

COACHING SESSION QUESTIONS

What sort of preparation is needed to coach brilliantly?

1) How well prepared am I for this call? (Mental Well being)
2) What is my motive for coaching? (Attitude Well Being)
3) What do I need to be careful of saying or doing on this call? (Awareness Well Being)
4) Who can this client become? What are their strengths? (Emotional Well Being)
5) What qualities do I want to radiate on this call? (Life Well Being)

Being Questions -- Ask the client who they are being

- Who are you being right now?
- Who would you have to be to get through this well?
- How proud of yourself are you now?
- Who do you remind yourself of?
- Is that really YOU?

INTEGRITY QUESTIONS -- TEST WHETHER THE CLIENT IS IN INTEGRITY

- Are you a person of your word?
- Where is your life out of balance?
- How would you feel if?
- How happy are you?
- What are you attached to?
- What are you running from?

- Where did that come from?
- Where are you sabotaging yourself?
- What does God say?
- How open are you, really?
- What gift(s) are you not being responsible for?
- What are you not being responsible for with that?
- What is the "should" in this situation for you?
- What stops you from always calling it as you see it?

SOLUTION QUESTIONS -- HELP THE CLIENT TO SOLVE THEIR OWN PROBLEMS

- And how do you intend to handle that?
- Who do you know who's gotten through that the way you want to?
- What is the first step?
- Coach's worst questions--create them on the call
- Yes and no questions--what's wrong with them?
- Why is a "why" question poor?
- How do we structure best and useful questions?
- What are the characteristics of these questions?
- Leading questions-useful or not?

PROMPTING QUESTIONS -- PROMPTING THE CLIENT INTO ACTION

- What is next?
- When will you do that?
- By when will you do that?
- What are the 5 steps to... (e.g.) become profitable within the next 30 days?

ENCOURAGE QUESTIONS -- ENCOURAGE THE CLIENT TO STOP TOLERATING

- Isn't there another way?
- What are you doing now in order to get something, rather than just getting that thing without having to go through all this?
- How much longer can you continue living this way?
- What are you tolerating?
- When will you give that up?
- Are you suffering about this? How so?
- What is the easier way?
- How much is this costing you?
- How would you like to be managed?

ENCOURAGING QUESTIONS -- ENCOURAGE THE CLIENT TO GAIN FRESH PERSPECTIVE

- Can you see what is beyond this problem?
- Can you see what is ahead?
- Can you see what you're building towards?
- Are you open to a completely different way of looking at it?
- Is it time to take a break and come back and look at this later?
- In which paradigm are you operating?
- Who told you that?
- Five years from now, what will have been the better decision?
- What will happen if you keep doing that for the next 10 years?
- For how long have you been doing that?

REMINDING QUESTIONS -- REMIND CLIENTS OF THEIR VISION

- What is your vision for yourself and the people around you?
- What are you really committed to underneath all of this?
- What do you really want?
- Is there a legacy you wish to leave?
- Are you really doing what you are built to do?

- What's worth living for?
- What are you building with that?

CHALLENGING QUESTIONS -- CHALLENGE THE CLIENT FOR MORE

- Can't you do better than that?
- Don't you have anything better to do?
- May I push you a bit here?
- How soon can you resolve that?
- So, what is possible here?
- What are you committed to?
- Do you mind if ...?
- Is this really in your best interest?
- Isn't this a familiar place for you?
- When will you stop that?
- Where did you stop?
- What is too big, even for you?

SAMPLE LIST OF VARIOUS QUESTIONS.

This is a general list, not in any specific category of question type.

1. If you knew you would not fail and time and money were not issues, what three things would you most like to have, accomplish, or work towards?

2. What are your special gifts? What is the one gift you'd feel great about orienting your life around?

3. What motivates you?

4. What are some of your healthy sources of energy?

5. What stops you?

6. What keeps you up at night?

7. What are the sources of energy that don't really serve you well or are actually unhealthy?

8. Are you willing to try new ways of doing things?

9. Where are you most irresponsible?

10. What are some professional or work opportunities you are currently not taking advantage of?

11. What is presently consuming your time that you wish you could eliminate?

12. How willing are you to do things the easy way or the simple way?

13. Who is in charge of your life? You or other people? Friends, peers, bosses, creditors?

14. Why have you hired me as your coach?

15. What are the 5 changes/actions to take in the next week to get you off to a good start in our coaching?

16. How will you know how effective our coaching has been?

17. How can I best coach you?

18. Should you be in therapy and be resolving something?

19. What one change in your life would make the biggest positive difference?

20. How willing are you to do whatever it takes to discover the highest and best of who you are?

21. What are you addicted to? (Alcohol, sugar, adrenaline, etc.)

22. If you lost your ability to earn a living this month, how long could you live comfortably on current savings?

23. Does your current income allow you to live the kind of life you want to lead? What needs to change?

24. Are you more engrossed in earning a living than designing a life?

25. What is your lifelong dream, starting NOW?

STRONG START

What do you want to talk about today?

TOLERATIONS

What are you putting up with?

Taking Stock / Where Are You Now?

What decisions did you make 3-5 years ago that got you to where you are now?

What are the improvements you wish to make in the quality of your life?

What needs to be different for your life to be perfect?

Where in your life are you compromising?

Where in your life are you denying your potential?

What do you want more of in your life?

What do you want less of in your life?

MOVING FORWARD

Today is the first day of the rest of your life. What are you going to do with this second chance?

What is the biggest opportunity you are currently not taking full advantage of?

What is holding you back from getting there?

STRUCTURE / PRIORITIES

What does your ideal week look like?

What does your ideal day look like?

RAPPORT QUESTIONS

Is this a good time to talk about....

Are you ready to be challenged?

What do you need from me during this time?

Can you trust me enough to tell me only truth?

Do you know that I want (...the most...) for you?

Unique Gifts and Talents

What do others say about your unique qualities, gifts and talents?
What is your special talent that you would like to orient your life around?

Creating Your Dream

What have you always wanted to do but have been afraid to try it, have thought about doing it but have held back, feeling uneasy and/or scared to?

Imagine that you received one wish from a genie. What ONE great thing would you dare to dream if you knew you absolutely could not fail?

What would be your dream if you had no limitations of any kind in your life?

What are your dreams?

What is your wildest imagination of what your life can be?

Life Purpose/Values/Vision/ Strengths / Qualities / Talents / Gifts / Uniqueness

What's your life purpose?

What activities do you get involved in (or did you use to get involved in) that put a huge smile on your face?

How long has it been since you were engaged in those activities? (Establishes that the person could be in a rut or out of synch with their life)

If you won/were given £10 million, what would you do with your life? (Will show their values and will allow them to think out loud about what is possible)

How do you define being happy?

What is your life really about?

What gives you a sense of meaning and purpose?

Looking back over all the things you have done in your life, what type of activities, doing what sort of things and in what sort of patterns give you your greatest feeling of importance, wellbeing, self-esteem? This is a key indicator of your greatest area of excellence.

Where would you like to be 1-2 years from now?

If I did exercise i.e.: if you did .... to what extent would this meet your values? Good for evaluating a number of options

How much of what you do fully expresses who you are?

What kind of behaviour have you been criticised for over the years? E.g.: talking too much? (This can trigger what they love).

Who are you jealous of? And why? (Can give interesting info about the types of people they admire/value as it shows what qualities the person stands for, you may nor may not need to ask this question depending on their initial answer.

What do you love?

What did you love to do as a child? Crucial to identifying our values as who we are authentically can then easily show up in the workplace.

What do you do like breathing?

What comes easy to you?

What kind of weaknesses do you have that could actually be strengths in the right setting?

What is your greatest gift?

What would it be like to get to the top of that mountain?

What is excitement like for you?

If this were perfect, what would your perspective be?

How do other people support you in your endeavours?

What is the greatest thing you can do for yourself?

What is one thing you can do today that would make your life different?

What part of yourself do you value/cherish most?

What needs to happen for you to stop doing this?

What is this about for you?

What's most important to you in life?

What would you most like others to know about yourself?

When do you feel at your best?

In what area would you most like to make a substantial contribution to changing the world?

You've been given the opportunity to represent your country in the Olympics. What's your role? (not necessarily an athlete)

Legacy

What would you like to be remembered for when you die? Are you living it now?

Goals

What are 3 really important things you would like to accomplish in your life starting now?

What would you like to see happen in one/three/six months time? And what are you prepared to do about it right now?

What would be a real stretch for you right now?

What specifically do you want?

What would you love to happen but you don't think is going to? (Ensure they give powerful answers to this question. Cleaning out their filing cabinet may indicate a resistance to what you are attempting to do with them.)

Career

What are the improvements you wish to make in your job/career/ work/business?

A Fun Exercise: Introduce yourself to someone lying through your teeth. You are an impostor. Describe who you are and your career. The truth will come through. If you were at a cocktail party, and you came as an impostor, who would you come as?

LIFE BALANCE

Do you feel that any part of your life is being lived at the expense of another part of your life?

Are you on the treadmill or are you actually having a life?

It takes 21 days of continuous effort to change a habit. Which one are you going to start on today?

Are you working to live, or living to work? Establish priorities that energise you.

MONEY

How did your parents/family treat each other regarding money? How does this affect your relationship with money today?

How did your parents treat you regarding money? How does this affect your relationship with money today?

What have you learned from your culture about money?

What is your first memory about money?

What are the money traumas you have experienced? What lessons did you learn form them?

What are your money successes? What lessons did you learn from them?

What is your greatest fear regarding money?

What's your belief system about financial success in life?

Do you have an action plan which focuses specifically on your finances?

Are you a spender or a saver? Would you re-evaluate your views on money from borrowing it to investing it?

How can you attract more abundance and monetary reserves without forfeiting
your lifestyle?

What three steps can you take to dramatically change your interaction with
money?

Where do you want your finances to be in ten years time and how do you plan
to get there?

What would "enough" mean?

How can you draw money towards you? or let it go?

What does it mean to be wealthy?

What are the improvements you wish to make in your financial situation?

SUPPORTING CLIENTS

How can I support you best?

How do you want to be supported?

RELATIONSHIPS

What are you willing to commit to right now?

What do you really want?

How would you need to attract the right person in your life?

Have you said all the things you need to the people in your life so that if they died tomorrow, there would be nothing left unsaid?

Do you spend enough time with the people who really matter in your life?

Who is the most important person in your life? (If it isn't you, how can you truly love or support anyone else?)

LEARNING

What do you need to learn next?

How can you learn from everything that happens in your life?

What are you pretending not to know?

What are you going to do differently with the insights you have about yourself (eg: someone who knows they over promise, procrastinate, love being unclear about what they want etc…)?

SPIRITUALITY

What does it mean to you?

When are you inspired?

When life gets at it's most difficult, what provides you with the most comfort?

Do you have an overall picture that is bigger than your work, relationships, money, etc.?

GETTING FEEDBACK - FROM OTHERS, FOR ME, FOR CLIENT...

What is the thing that springs to mind when you think of me?

What is the most interesting thing about me?

What do you consider to be my greatest achievement?

What is the thing you value most about me?

What should I stop doing?

What should I start doing and what should I continue doing?

Can you tell me how I am doing?

Is this working for you?

What has stood out for you most from this workshop/call.......why?

What value did you receive from today?

JOY / PLAY

What is one thing that you could start doing that would add joy to your life?

What things do you enjoy doing?

What is joy like for you?

GROWING AS A PERSON, GROWING THE WHO

Where are you most irresponsible in your life? (Gets them thinking and talking about themselves and makes them dig deep).

What are the improvements you wish to make in your personal character?

What are the improvements you wish to make on the inside?

Unblocking a Client

What answer would your heart give to that question?

What do you already know about this that you will find out in three months time?

When Stuck

If you were the coach, what would you ask me right now?

Encouraging Clients to Commit to Actions

What is / are your next step(s)?

How will you know when you have done it?

How are you going to do that?

When are you going to do that?

What is your next action step?

Do you really want to do that?

Getting More Commitment from Clients

Coaching is about commitment. As you are entering into a coaching partnership with me, are you prepared to do the things to make yourself truly successful?

Do you want to unlock and step into your full potential?

Are you ready to orient your life around what you really, really want?

What decisions are you willing to make today to create your tomorrow?

Who is in charge of your life, you or other people? (This is a powerful question and can by itself be used to bring a client on board to coaching. Can be challenging though!)

Do you believe that the best investment anyone can make is in themselves? (May help to create value in the coaching relationship, very important if someone's boss has decided they are going to have coaching)

Would you be willing to try some things that are totally new, different and maybe even outrageous?

What would it take to motivate you?

INCISIVE QUESTIONS

If you were to become the chief executive, what problem would you solve first, and how would you do it?

If you knew that you are vital to this organisation's success, how would you approach your work?

If things could be exactly right for you in this situation, how would they have to change?

If you were not to hold back in your life, what would you be doing?

If you found out that someone you love very much is going to die tomorrow, what would you want to be sure to say to them today?

If you could trust that your children would be fine, what would you do with the rest of your life?

If you knew that you are beautiful just as you are, what would change for you?

If you knew that you are as intelligent as your bosses, how would you present yourself to them?

If a doctor told you that your life depends on your changing the way you live, what would you do first for yourself? ·

QUESTIONS TO ASK A COACH ABOUT COACHING

What direct experience do you have regarding what I need to accomplish or resolve? Who else have you coached in a similar situation, and what happened with them?

If I was a client, what is the type of suggestions or strategies you would offer regarding what I've explained thus far about my situation?

What is your general philosophy or approach when it comes to coaching a client to become more successful?

What is your personal style? Aggressive or passive? Patient or driven?

What is your biggest strength, and why? How will it help me?

What do you not do well, or not want to do with me as a client? Why?

What are you hearing in how I've presented my situation or in how I am communicating with you? Any observations? Any changes I would need to make immediately?

Would you want to work with me? Why? How do you know?

What question should I have asked you that I did not?

Is there anything else you'd like me to know?

How much do you charge?

Am I required to sign up for a minimum amount of time?

How much advance notice for cancelling an appointment do you require?

If I feel that I need more than once-a-week coaching, how much extra does that cost?

What are you afraid of?

Relationship Questions

What is the one thing I do that most irritates you?

Exactly where on your body -- and how -- should I touch you so that you feel my love for you?

What is the common dream we have for our lives?

How willing are you to have a problem-free relationship?

What's the best part of being in a relationship with me?

GRATITUDE QUESTIONS

What would it be like to feel gratitude for every single moment of your life?"

What role does gratitude play in your life?

How aware are you of the blessings in your life?

How often do you stop or pause to say thanks?

How do you feel when you focus on this powerful emotion?

TYPICAL ROADBLOCKS ON THE PATH TO CLEAR COMMUNICATION

In his book "People Skills", Robert Bolton PhD listed thirteen roadblocks to communication between people, and you'll immediately see over the page which ones you tend towards. When problems arise, a person is stressed, or needs are not being met, these barriers tend to show up, and all are usually destructive. They tend to compound the problem, block the person's ability to access their own resources, create resistance and further drive the problem deeper down into the individual, making things worse. These can be chunked into three categories, and they are as follows:

JUDGING

Forming a value judgement about the other person, based on whether we agree with them or not.

1. Criticising – condemning or disapproving of the other person's approach and telling them so, as in a reprimand. "You chose to stay in the marriage, so live with it!"

2. Name-calling – putting the other person down or calling them a stereotype, giving them a label and no longer the individual.. "Typical New Age tree- hugging hippy crap!"

3. Diagnosing – like having dinner with an amateur psychologist, analysing the *real* problem. "You're just self-sabotaging to get attention cos you think he ignores you"

4. Praising evaluatively – telling the person how clever they are, often to control or manipulate them. "You're really good with language, I'm sure you can help me write this letter"

SENDING SOLUTIONS

Attempting to "fix" the problem

5. Ordering – instructing them in what to do next, being au-

thoritarian. "Control yourself and deal with it!"

6. Threatening – trying to control them with punishment or negative consequences. "You know what will happen to you if you just keep putting it off, don't you?"

7. Moralising – preaching about what *should* be done, the right thing to do. "You have to tell her how you feel – that's what I'd do"

8. Excessive/Inappropriate Questioning – using closed questions that elicit a "yes" or a "no", effectively ending a conversation. "You knew that would happen, didn't you?"

9. Advising – offering them a solution, thus undermining their ability to solve their own problems, and only looking at the problem superficially. "Then stop going and look for a new job if you hate it so much"

AVOIDING THE OTHER'S CONCERNS

Distracting the listener with statements that go off on a tangent

10. Diverting – distracting them with a different train of thought, often because they're uncomfortable with the way the conversation is going, or they want some significance themselves. "Speaking of love, that's a lot like my husband, but he's so considerate about it, he bought me this ring"

11. Logical argument – Using facts or rational logic and avoiding feeling anything, effectively creating distance between people. "You have three options to choose from, it's that simple."

12. Reassuring – Offering calming and cheering encouragement, thus sounding helpful but avoiding the emotional energy drain. "Everything happens for a reason you know"

AND FINALLY

Recognising some of these patterns and being annoying enough to "meta comment" on the other person's communication

13. Pointing out the other person's use of barriers – giving them a mini-seminar in communication styles! "Cheryl, come here and read this! You're number 9!"

THE META MODEL

Of course these roadblocks are generalised and are not useful in understanding that client's specific model of the world. To really enter the client's Deep Structure we need to borrow a tool developed from America's leading family therapist & couple counsellor Virginia Satir, now called the Meta Model.

The Meta Model recovers the deletions, distortions and generalisations in that client's map of reality, and gets right into the heart of the matter. The aim linguistically, is to get more and more specific and more precise. One of the great strengths in HGE is that we have the questions to ask, to cut through the chaff & to get into the real meat and bones of the matter. People tend to talk in really fluffy, general language. You ask someone "how's it going?" and they say "Fine". That doesn't really tell you very much. This model lets you cut through the surface structure of people's language and get into the real nitty gritty, so you can get to the heart of the matter within 2 or 3 sentences, with precision and elegance.

Imagine being able to talk to somebody and become like a living lie detector, because you can pull out information from them which they maybe didn't even know was going on inside. Now, in therapy that enables you to be able to get to the root cause of a problem very, very quickly. In Coaching or Negotiation or Facilitation it allows you to get into specific detail rapidly, cutting to the chase. It means you're understood more often, again increasing rapport, understanding and agreement. Wouldn't that be useful? Are you starting to see what all the fuss is about?

Use the Meta Model with Rapport, and I also suggest you build in softeners – after the client speaks, and before you respond using a Meta Model question, say something like

"Really? Wow. Tell me….." or "Interesting. Can I ask…" or "I'm wondering"

On the following page you'll see the left column with the different types of language patterns people tend to use. You read about these in the Presuppositions and Milton Model segments of this book, so they will look familiar. In the middle is the response – the specific Meta Model challenge for that pattern. The prediction is the end result of asking that question. So for example, your client says "I can't make enough money to get what I want"

That's a Modal Operator. You say "Really? Tell me, what prevents you? And what would happen if you could?"

In one sentence you'll uncover the block, and have them run a positive picture of their desired outcome. Hey presto! Linguistic magic!

"Silent" is an anagram of "Listen"

THE META MODEL

Pattern	Response	Prediction
Distortions		
1. **Mind reading:** claiming to know someone's internal state. Ex: "he doesn't like me."	"How do you know he doesn't like you?"	Recovers source of the info.
2. **Lost performative:** value judgments where the person doing the judging is left out. Ex. "It's bad to be disorganised."	"Who says it's bad?" "According to whom?" "How do you know it's bad?"	Gathers evidence. Recovers source of the belief, the performative, strategy for the belief.
3. **Cause-effect:** where cause is wrongly put outside the self. Ex: "you make me sad."	"How does what I'm doing cause you to choose to feel sad?" (Also, counter ex., Or "how specifically?"	Recovers the choice.
4. **Complex equivalence:** where two experiences are interpreted as being synonymous. Ex: "she's always yelling at me, she doesn't like me."	"How does her yelling mean that she..?" "Have you ever yelled at someone you liked?"	Recovers complex equivalence. Counter example.
5. **Presuppositions:** Ex: "if my husband knew how much I suffered, he wouldn't do that." There are 3 presuppositions in this sentence: (1) I suffer, (2) my husband acts in some way, and (3) my husband doesn't know I suffer.	(1) "How do you choose to suffer?" (2) "How is he (re)acting? (3) "How do you know he doesn't know?"	Specify the choice & the verb, & what he does. Recover the internal rep., And the complex equivalence

Generalizations		
6. **Universal quantifiers**: universal generalizations such as all, every, never, everyone, no one, etc. Ex: "he never listens to me."	Find counter examples. "Never?" "What would happen if he did?"	Recovers counter examples, effects, outcomes.
7. **Modal operators:** A. **Modal operators of necessity:** as in should, shouldn't, must, must not, have to or it is necessary. Ex: "I have to work hard." B. **Modal operators of possibility:** (or impossibility.) As in can/can't, will/won't, may/may not, possible/ impossible. Ex: "I can't tell him the truth."	A. "What would happen if you did?" ("What would happen if you didn't?" Also, "or?" B. "What prevents you?" ("What would happen if you did?")	Recovers effects, outcome. Recovers causes
Deletions		
8. **Nominalizations:** process words which have been frozen in time, making them nouns. Ex: "there is no communication here."	"Who's not communicating what to whom?" "How would you like to communicate?"	Turns it back into a process, recovers deletion, and ref. Index.
9. **Unspecified verbs:** Ex: "he rejected me."	"How, specifically?"	Specifies the verb.
10. **Simple deletions:** A. Simple deletions: Ex: "I am uncomfortable." B. Lack of referential index: fails to specify a person or thing. Ex: "they don't listen to me." C. Comparative deletions: as in good, better, best, worst, more, less, most, least. Ex: "that's expensive!"	A. "About what/whom?" B. "Who, specifically, doesn't listen to you?" C. "Compared to whom, what?	Recovers deletion. Recovers ref. Index. Recovers comparative deletion.

14

TIME FOR A CHANGE

How do you eat an elephant?

One bite at a time.

"An object at rest tends to stay at rest; an object in motion tends to stay in motion." -Sir Isaac Newton

"Things which matter most must never be at the mercy of things which matter least" - Goethe

If you keep doing what you've been doing, you'll keep getting what you've been getting. So if you want to get a different result, you're going to have to think about this differently

You've done time management seminars, you've probably got an awesome leather bound deluxe super-duper day timer system, maybe even a Palm Pilot, and you're still in a mess!

Technology will make your life easier and you'll have all this free time! Hah!

Traditional planning causes you to focus on one very specific question: What do I need to do? To-do lists can keep you busy, and checking off a series of tasks can provide the illusion of progress. But have you ever crossed off everything on your to-do list and still felt like you had not really accomplished anything? **There is a big difference between movement and achievement.**

I want to free you from your stress and to give you more choices, freedom, and certainty about what you can achieve and experience in your life.

This will literally train you to think in an entirely new way, causing you to focus on what's truly most important to you. When you are focused in this direction, you will begin to not only produce extraordinary results, but most importantly, you will experience an amazing level of personal fulfilment in the process.

INTRODUCTION

Time flies by when you're having fun, and it drags along when you're not. Now who set it up that way? However, the actual minute itself doesn't change, it's your perception of time that *changes on the inside.*

When you love what you're doing, time passes more quickly, and you get more of it done. Because it doesn't feel like a chore or like work, you are much more effective – you immerse yourself in it and cover a lot of ground in a short space of time.

This chapter is designed to give you several ways to use your time in a more effective way – not efficient, but effective. There's a huge difference as I'm sure you'll agree. My definition of efficient, is doing things competently and smoothly. Effective means doing **the right things, the things that have the most impact.** No matter how stressed you feel right now, no matter how pushed, you always find time to do what's important to you. Think about that for a moment. We don't do what we need to, we do what we want to. We can always **find time** for the hobby, friends or movie that we really want to see.

So we're going to start with looking at what's important to you. You must learn to control your focus, because what we focus on determines the direction in which we move. You always have a choice about where to focus.

WHY IS THIS IMPORTANT?

One of the best places to start is to ask yourself "**What are my roles and duties and what am I being measured on?**"

That's usually a good clue as to where to start, because ultimately you are being paid to fulfil a job description or set of responsibilities. And if you want to keep your position, you'd better be doing your duties.

This then tells you what is **important** in the long term, and what is **urgent** in the short term.

From there you can create a hit list of daily things you have to touch base with every working day. Have a daily routine where all of the major tasks get attended to at some point. That way everything keeps moving forward.

Think of the circus plate spinner – you can probably relate to this. The first thing he or she needs to decide is what size and weight of plates they can cope with.

Then you must discover just how many plates you can keep spinning in any one day.

Of course some are saucers, some are soup plates, some are big dinner plates. And they all make different sounds when they crash, so keep an ear open.

Most people can only handle 7 plus or minus two plates (Thanks to George Miller). Overwhelm usually occurs at about 10+

The best time management system for you, is one you design. So browse through this section and pick up the tools and techniques that you're drawn to.

There's a time-tested strategy for deciding what to do first. It's the difference between Urgent and Important

Urgent = time deadline, needs to be done now, other people want you to do it, fire fighting

Important = no real time limit, great for you long term, you want to do it, lasting change

This then leads you to 4 possibilities:

Important not urgent – Don't have to do it, but you choose to because it's meaningful to you, it's fulfilling.

Important and Urgent – Feel like have to be done immediately, and are really important, demanding.

Not important but urgent- grabbing your attention now but not very satisfying

Not important and not urgent – distracting yourself, medicating, escapism

The ideal would be working on those things that are *Important and not urgent*. Spend time on these and you'll reduce the amount of urgent things that come at you, cos you've anticipated them in advance and built in systems that prevent them occurring in the first place.

Now depending on your job description and the actual functions you perform, you may have a different outlook on what's urgent and what's important. If you're packaging overnight delivered goods then you'll spend most of your time dealing with urgent stuff. If you're in charge of company marketing strategy then you'll probably be dealing with long term logistics, which would be important. You might want to figure out what is a good percentage of your time to spend on *Important/not Urgent* given your job role. People who are stressed seem to spend less that 25% of their time on *Important, Not Urgent* tasks. Ideally I recommend you increase that to 40 – 70% of your time.

YOUR TIME HORIZON

In your job you need to consider a time horizon. Just how far out do you look each day. And how far out **should you** be looking? For someone working on a customer service desk, it is not much more than the next call. For a team leader it might be a couple of weeks. The higher up the management structure the greater the time horizon you need to be considering. A CEO might be looking 20 years ahead. There is also a shift from tactical to strategic thinking. Tactical is hour by hour, daily shop floor activity. Strategic is the long-term planning, logistics, supply, demand, pricing, marketing. Refer to the earlier chapter on the Hierarchy of Ideas. This means that Urgent takes on a different meaning at different levels in an organisation.

We must learn to categorise things so that we're spending the maximum time on the optimum activities.

If you find yourself getting overwhelmed by your list of things to do (and who doesn't have days like that?), try some of these strategies for regaining perspective and control.

1. DIARISE IT.

Instead of keeping one big ongoing list, write to-do items in your day-timer or calendar according to when you will do them.

2. GROUP IT.

Divide to-do items into categories (e.g. phone calls, errands, writing) so you gain momentum and save time by doing similar items together. That way you can do a batch of calls or emails all at once.

3. PRIORITISE IT.

Clearly identify the most important items on the list with stars, or arrange all items in order of their priority and work down from the top.

4. HIGHLIGHT IT.

Rather than crossing completed items off a list (which makes your accomplishments invisible), highlight items with a marker as you complete them. Focusing on what you've already done creates energy.

5. POST IT.

Write individual items on post-it notes and place on fridge or around work space. As you complete each item, crumple the slip with great glee.

6. 80/20 IT.

We usually get about 80% of our results from 20% of our work. Leverage your time and resources by concentrating on the 20% of items on your list that will generate the biggest impact.

7. PRUNE IT.

Many of the other 80% of the items can probably be safely ignored or delegated to someone else. Do so, and cross them off your list.

8. DIVIDE IT.

Keep a separate work list at work and personal list at home. Keep a separate short-term and long-term list.

9. PLAY IT.

Draw a visual playing board for to-do items and provide rewards for reaching certain targets. Make it a game.

10. TOSS IT.

Come to trust that whatever you are naturally doing is what is really most meaningful to you at that moment. Let go of everything else--the should's, the musts, the need-to's. It's a great way to live.

HOW TO GET MORE DONE IN LESS TIME

WHY IMPORTANT?

You're pushed for time and there's loads to do. You're probably feeling the pressure and you have a limited amount of time to do what's required. So how can you do it?

To get more done you could

- Multi task
- Do things to a lesser quality

- Get help
- Work faster
- Plan better

7 WAYS OF MULTI-TASKING

Multi-tasking is a very misunderstood activity. Most people claim to be multi-tasking, when what they are really doing is wearing themselves out trying to do too many things at once. Here are some tips for helping you multi-task effectively without burning yourself out.

1. Pair activities that require a lot of mental attention with those that require little or no mental attention.

2. Many people make the mistake of attempting to do two activities which both require mental focus at the same time. Multi-tasking works best when you pair an activity that requires your attention with another that doesn't. For example, you might read while peddling your stationery bike, or listen to audio tapes or CD's while exercising

3. Make a plan. Having a written plan for the things that I need to do helps me identify which things can be done at the same time. It also helps me see things that can be delegated, and things that will be more effective if done in a sequence. Before I learned to multi-task, I would run out in the morning and do two errands. Then I would run out at lunch and do another, then two more after work. Now I have learned how to map an effective route through town that will let me hit all of my errands efficiently and get them out of the way in one quick trip.

4. Make your waiting time productive. Never allow someone else to waste your time. Almost everywhere I go, I carry a small brief case. I carry reading materials, such as a magazine or book, note cards, bills and my cheque book, etc. Carry work related materials if you prefer - the latest proposal you

need to read, or a report that requires your feedback. When you are forced to wait because a client cancels an appointment, pull out something you can do to make your wait productive.

5. Leverage the time of others. Are you someone who feels that you have to do everything yourself? If you can get others to pitch in, the work gets done faster and, technically, you are doing more than one thing at a time. Remember, you do not have to do something yourself to know that you have completed the task. Delegate. Ask your spouse to take out the rubbish while you do the dishes.Ask your colleagues at work to help out with a project. Remember that asking for help from your friends or co-workers also implies a relationship in which you will at some time be the giver instead of the receiver. Hire. If you can afford it, hire others to do the work you hate or which you feel is not a good use of your time. This also provides an income for someone else. A good example would be hiring a housekeeper or a yard service. While they are cleaning your house or mowing your grass, you can be doing something else. Accept offers of assistance. When someone offers to do something, or help with something - let them! Unless you believe there are strings attached, accept any sincere offer of assistance... and be willing to reciprocate when appropriate. Group similar activities. It is important to me that I keep up with my friends and business associates. I have a group of business associates that all know and enjoy each other. Rather than schedule four separate lunch meetings, we will plan lunch or dinner as a group, and everyone catches up at the same time. Give your wallet and waistline a break. Unless you need to discuss something confidential or pertinent to only one person, try a group gathering.

6. Take advantage of technology. A portable phone or headset will allow you to pick up stuff around the living room while chatting on the phone. (A cordless headset will give you two hands free!) I work from home and will usually run the dishwasher and the washing machine while I am working. A website can be used to market your business, and even generate income while you sleep. Autoresponders keep your clients up to date.

7. Remember that some things deserve your undivided attention. You wouldn't want your surgeon watching TV while removing your appendix! Some things are so important that they require your full attention. Don't attempt to multi-task while praying, meditating, or sitting in church. Remember, too, that problems or issues at work or home will be handled most effectively if you will give them your complete focus.

TOOLS & TECHNIQUES

Five minute bursts – Mark Forster's "burst technique" from his excellent book "Get Everything Done…". It's only five minutes on the chosen task, and you must stop at the end of 5 minutes. Buy an egg timer or a stopwatch that will beep you when time's up. However, the unconscious mind won't stop – it'll keep working at it. So when you come back to it later on, you'll find you already have some momentum and you get off and running a lot quicker. It's like a search engine – you might switch to a different application, but the search is still going on and it will come back with results. Just like when you overhear a quiz show question and the answer escapes you…until an hour later while you're washing the dishes, and it pops right into your head.

Imagine using five minute bursts on a list of ten things. You might get a couple scored off, completed. You then start at the top of the list and do 10 minute bursts. Then 15, and so on. Try it – you'll love the results!

Keep an index card or page in your planner for each major person in your personal life, and every time something comes up that's related to them, capture it on their sheet. That way, next time you meet them or call them, you have everything you want to see them about on one page!

TWO MINUTE LIFESAVERS

"I barely have 2 minutes!" I hear you say. Great! What can you do in 2 minutes that will save an hour or more this week?

- Check for understanding at the end of each meeting ... "What is it you're taking away from our conversation?"
- Lead your e-mails with a clear request ("I need your action by Friday on...") and ask your team members to do the same.
- Did you or someone on your team blunder? Get the learning out of it and move on.
  Blame, guilt, and anxiety waste your time and energy.
- When your gut says no, stop your mouth from saying yes.
  Offer to consider it. Then see if you can reshape the idea so it makes sense to your head and gut.
- Stop the stupid stuff flying around your organization... cancel a useless meeting, ask your staff not to send chain e-mails.
- Diagram the problem.
  What are the separate parts, and how do information and consequences flow among them?
- Put your to-do's and promises in your Palm or note-book.
  Save your brain for thinking about your business. Let paper remember so you can forget
- When you're feeling stuck, find something to laugh about, take a quick walk around the building, or just sit and breathe. Break your state.
- Take a moment mid-day to remind yourself why you're doing

this work... picture what it is you're aiming to create for your company, your family, yourself.

• Speak the truth. It will save a lot of time. And it starts with you telling yourself the truth. Admit that it's not working.

A SIMPLE PROCESS TO FOLLOW

To help you understand that this system may take a little longer to master, but that this system will help you experience far greater results and tremendous levels of fulfilment.

It's all about Chunking – organising information into ideally sized pieces so that it can be used effectively to produce results.

Managing your time requires some kind of system, even if it's just in your head. Basing what you do day to day on the Outcomes that you want achieved. Chunking up to more abstract and more powerful concepts

This system causes you to focus first on what you **want** - *the results that you are committed to achieving in your life* - before you figure out what you need to **do**. You then design all of your activity around making progress toward achieving what you want. Simple 3 step formula – Outcome, Purpose, Action:

1. Always start with the Outcome. Ask yourself "What do I really want to happen? What's my outcome here?"

2. Know why you want that. "For what purpose? What will this get me? How will it make me feel when I get it?"

3. Do something. "What specific actions do I need to take to get this done?

THE MASTER SYSTEM

1. This step of planning is something most people are already familiar with - it's nothing more than quickly brainstorming anything you think you need to do. This doesn't need to be in any particular order. Simply type in the errands you need

to run, phone calls you need to make, projects you want to complete, etc. This "Capture" list will become the foundation upon which your plan is created.

2. What are the most important outcomes I need to produce today?

For what purpose? Why do I want this result? What will that do for me? Linking outcomes with values – the reasons why – the batteries for strategies

3. What specific steps do I need to take to get there? This step of planning is the process of turning your capture list into related chunks. To do this, you will look at your capture list for your day, week, or the project you are working on, and start to notice relationships between some of the items. Put things that are related together.

4. Which of these items are the 20% items that will get the 80% results? Highlight or asterisk these

5. Block out time in your diary to do these.

Notice that we don't start by asking "What do I have to do?" The secret is to focus on the end result, not all the steps to get there. Start with the end in mind. With a clear picture of what you want, imagine you have it now, and work backwards. What did you do to get there? If you get your result, but don't manage to tick off all your "to do" items, do you care?

1. Action Item 2. Action Item 3. Action item	Outcome	Purpose

Do you try to find time, make time, get time, buy time, squeeze more time into your day? Do you wonder how you'll get everything you need to done, in any given day? Do you suffer from "time-deficit disorder?" Is managing time a mystery to you? Well, you certainly aren't alone. Many people find their relationship to time a challenge. A vexing challenge. Many of us are walking around stressed and/or overwhelmed much of the time. There are no simple answers to creating space and time in your life. That said, you may want to try some of these suggestions as way to navigate through the time of your life.

EXERCISE

In normal hand writing, write your name in full.

Do this 10 times

Notice how long that took

Now write it again, but missing out every second letter

Do this 10 times

Notice the pattern – the second version took longer at first, even though it was half the amount of information.

Then ultimately it became quicker than writing your name normally.

This system is the same – initially it takes time to get into the groove, but over time you'll get quicker and quicker, and actually save time!

STRESSED AND UNDER PRESSURE?

I know that you have too much to do, and it's good to be a hard worker. As you read this you know it's time to slow down and get on top of things before they get on top of you. The fact that you came to this page means you're already managing your own emotions well. You may realise you have more resources than you thought you do. There's always things to do and you always have the resources to handle them. You could just take a deep breath and relax. Go on….. do it now. I'm watching you know. So just take a deep breath, and slow down.

That's better

As you begin to trust in this process of wonder that led you to this page, you can be relaxed knowing that we're here to help. In fact, you're in exactly the right place, aren't you? You may not know it yet, but you're already taking control. You're sitting here, reading these words, wondering whether you'll get everything done quickly, or slowly. Can you see what I'm talking about?

I was speaking with a friend the other day, who told me of a conversation she had had with a manager who told her about a session he'd had with a client who said that "it'll all get done eventually". In fact, this computer could tell a few stories, about touch typing, and what type you are, based on the way you touch the keys.

It may be impossible to get everything done – you might not have thought of that, and time doesn't allow the luxury. But you've got to think carefully about what to do next. You might prefer to use some of the tips below to help you, and then choose the first priority task.

It's mainly about your mental and emotional state!

Stress = too many chunks. Your 7 plus or minus two is full!

YOU'RE NORMAL!! You just need an effective strategy. This section has several. Read on.

BASIC BEGINNER KNOWLEDGE

When Emperor Hirohito of Japan travelled, his every day was planned down to the minute. One day, he was scheduled to meet with a delegation of monks and tour a local Buddhist temple for exactly ten minutes. The Emperor and his entourage entered the temple precisely on time, but the building was empty and the monks were nowhere to be found.

The aide responsible for setting the Emperor's schedule alternated between desperately searching for the missing delegation and making panicked excuses for their absence, but the Emperor simply stood in the centre of the room and said nothing. Exactly ten minutes later, the Emperor indicated that it was now time to leave. On their way out of the temple, Hirohito turned to his aide and said "I enjoyed that appointment very much - please schedule me another one tomorrow."

Here are some simple exercises you can use in the midst of a busy day or any time you wish to step more fully into the present moment and experience greater peace. Practicing them when you're not stressed makes it exponentially easier to benefit from them when you are. [With many thanks to Michael Neill.]

Count to Ten

"I have so much to do today, I will need to meditate twice as long."
-Mahatma Gandhi

Over the last few years, I have learned a simple method for instantly evaluating my current level of ease or stress:

How many breaths can I count before I freak out?

Here's how to do it.

With your eyes open or closed, begin counting your breaths, letting each complete breath (breathing in and breathing out) count as one. If you're at all stressed, you'll lose count before you get to ten (or give up because it's pointless and you've got a lot to do and people are staring and this is just stupid and you could get to ten if you really wanted to and... well, you get the idea). The sooner you lose count, the more stressed you currently are and the less effective you're likely to be.

To feel calmer, more centred, and become more effective in a matter of minutes, start over at "one" and carry on until you can get to "ten". Each time you lose count, simply begin again. (As a point of interest, the longest anyone has ever reported to me it took them to get to ten breaths was one hour and thirty four minutes! Lest this put you off, know that most people can get to ten (and feel calmer and more at peace) in less than five minutes.)

DOES THIS TASK EVEN BELONG TO ME?

It's all too easy to take on someone else's monkey – a colleague hands you a piece of work you asked them to do. You need to look it over, so you tell them you'll do that later and get back to them. Now you're working for them, and they're awaiting your update – you see how the roles have just switched? You just accepted responsibility for the project, and promised them a progress report. But it was their project in the first place! Do you see?

Quite simply, don't accept monkeys on your back unless the training of that particular monkey is part of your job description! If you do, you end up sending 2 signals

1} they can depend on you to solve all their problems

2} you don't think they're capable of solving it themselves

The more monkeys you hand back to your people, the more time you can devote to your people.

So make sure that the right things get done the right way, at the right time, by the right people.

DELEGATION

How often have you decided not to delegate because "it's easier to do it myself?" Delegation failure is usually the fault of the person who is delegating -- due to a lack of clear communication about what is required. Here are some tips to help you to start delegating, and to gain confidence in doing it.

Do what you do best, and get other people to do the rest

The art of delegation is anything but the practice of "dumping" responsibility off of your plate onto that of someone else. Delegation requires a vision toward maximizing your time and talents by focusing on the right mix of things to achieve your larger objectives. Here are some solid reasons for dealing out tasks that are best performed by someone else:

• Frees up your time and energy to perform at a higher level because there is less clutter.

- Lets you see more clearly what kinds of tasks or projects RE-ALLY could use your direct attention.
- Dispatches responsibility to others working in your immediate group and fosters team building.
- Make sure that the objectives of the responsibilities are clear and agreed-to in order to maximize buy-in.
- Lends a new dimension as to how things can be done.
- Cross-pollination can lead to interesting results!
- Builds others' skills and esteem.
- Lets others have a go at a task previously performed by someone else, most likely someone at a higher level in the organization. Delegating reflects trust in the other party's ability to perform.
- By appropriately delegating, you create for yourself a more professional, streamlined appearance to the outside world.
- Delegation reduces delay.
- Demonstrates an ability to manage with an eye toward getting tasks into action and not letting them wait their turn on an already-full plate.
- Creates greater efficiency if tasks are delegated to and performed by individuals with more expertise than you have.
- No need to spend time reinventing the wheel. There are outside vendors and consultants for just about anything. Be sure, though, not to overlook in-house expertise.
- Can help work to get accomplished on time.
- Sometimes an outside source is more dependable than we ourselves are at getting something signed, sealed and delivered! Consider automation as a form of delegation.
- Skilful delegation creates win-win situations for all involved.

Leveraging – what other resources do you have (outsourcing, software, other people) that would let you delegate, systematise or automate this task? For example, rather than posting a 500 letter mail shot each month, why not type one email and press "send"?

Do what you do best, let someone else do the rest

Delegate your weaknesses

Simplify – dump it, delegate it, automate it or systematise it

Just say no – don't take on other people's monkeys. Or tell them that if they want it done it'll be next week at the earliest. The item then goes on to next week's Capture list

Over respond: Ask yourself "What caused this to happen? And what caused that? And what caused that?" Ask yourself "How can I prevent this from happening again?"

List 10 things you can implement to prevent it happening again

Do the first one right now!

Notice who runs out of time first – you, or the person you're talking to. Who typically ends the conversation? Who is the first one to say "Listen, I need to go". Ideally it's them, because that means you have more time to spare than they do.

Never part company with a colleague until the next move has been decided, the next step, the appropriate course of action.

The dialogue must not end until it's clear who should do the next move. Only take on board what only you can do – delegate the rest

Make sure anyone else involved in a project comes to you with their recommended next move, but await your agreement on it.

Always set a date by which time you will check up on that project and establish where it's at, and set that date with your colleague before you go your separate ways.

WAYS TO SAY "NO" ELEGANTLY WHEN PEOPLE TRY TO CROSS YOUR BOUNDARIES

Many people have difficulty saying "no" and boundary invaders take full advantage of this difficulty. If a request or a question makes you feel uncomfortable, it is probably an attempt to invade your boundaries, even if the other person is not fully aware that this is what s/he is doing. If a straight-out "NO" is too difficult for you, try some of the following alternatives. (But also practice saying NO. It strengthens your boundaries.)

- I'm sorry but I don't feel right about doing that.
- If that's what you want, you're asking the wrong person.
- I realize many people feel fine about things like that, and it's not for me to judge them, but it just wouldn't work for me.
- What I did in the past is past. Now is now, and it's not right for me any more so please don't ask, because I won't.
- This is not an okay time. I'll let you know if I can spend time on it later.
- If you had let me know earlier we could have talked about, but it's just not possible for me now.
- I can see something needs doing, but it should be done by the person who caused the problem in the first place, not by me.
- It would be far more appropriate for you to do that yourself.
- Why would you want to know that kind of information about me?
- How would you feel if someone said something like that to your (wife, husband, daughter, son, etc)?

HOW TO BALANCE WORK & PERSONAL LIFE

To make it simple, we are going to divide your life up into two main areas: your personal life and your professional life. Within each of these areas of management, we are then going to decide on the specific categories you are going to consistently focus on and improve

Let's start with your personal life. What are some of the areas that you believe you must focus on and constantly improve in order for your life to be successful and fulfilling? Health, Money, Family, Personal Development, Relationships, etc

And in your business? Leadership, Accounts, Admin, quality control, new products, training, sales, marketing, etc

INTRODUCTION

TIME PLANNING

- **ensures that you are making progress and achieving balance in all the areas of your life that matter to you most.** By helping you develop a plan for your life before you ever start planning your time, this ensures that you are consistently making progress on what is most important to you. This prevents you from allowing yourself to live in reaction to the demands of the moment, or from focusing on one area of your life at the cost of another.

- **gives you a sense of purpose and fulfilment for your life.** Most people walk around unconsciously chipping away at seemingly random actions. In fact, many people have accomplished a great deal in their lives, only to reach a point where they start to ask themselves, "is this all there is?" Planning gives you a compelling reason behind all your actions-so that you are focused on the meaning and value it provides to your life.

- immediately **reduces stress,** helping you transform overwhelm into a sense of certainty you can accomplish what it is you want. Instead of having you focus on a huge list of action items (or "to-dos'), this system causes you to focus only on a smaller number of results or outcomes.

A METAPHOR

There is a story about a seminar leader who placed a large jar on a table. By the side of the jar he placed a bucket of gravel, a bucket of sand, a bucket of water, some sugar, and three big rocks. He then challenged his participants to find a way to fit everything on the table into the jar.

After numerous attempts, it became clear that the only way to successfully fit everything in was to start with the big rocks first. The gravel filled the gaps between the big rocks, the sand filled the gaps in the gravel, and the water filled the gaps in the sand. The sugar dissolved in the water.

When it comes to managing our time, it's pretty easy to get caught up in the daily gravel, ground down by the sand, and swept away by the water. What can be tricky is finding ways to put first things first - to prioritize the "big rocks" - those things in our life that matter most.

EXERCISES

Grab a piece of paper and three different coloured pens. Make a list of all the things that are in your life right now that take time and energy (examples: exercise, self care, relationship, children, hobby, coaching, job, etc.) After you've written those out use one colour of pen to number them 1 to whatever based on the amount of time you currently (or recently) have spent giving them your time and energy. Then take the second colour of pen and number them again based on what you SHOULD according to outside influences or internal limiting beliefs be spending time and energy doing. Lastly, take a moment to really get in touch with yourself and with the third colour pen number the items based on where you REALLY want to put your time and energy. What did you learn?

Try the Wheel of Life – look at the categories of your life that need constant attention, and score them between 1 and 10, 1 being terrible and on the inside of the wheel, 10 being perfect and on the outside of the wheel, and anywhere in between. If you fill in all the pies in the chart, or all the cheeses in the Dairylea box, you'll see which areas are tripping you up.

Goals Areas in Our Lives

IT'S GETTING STARTED THAT'S THE HARD PART – LIKE PUSHING A CAR. It's really hard to get it moving, but once you've overcome the inertia it's easy to keep it rolling.

COACHING OTHERS TO MANAGE THEIR TIME

From the section on Metaprograms we know there are two basic thinking styles: the Judger, who looks at the world, judges it, and tries to make it the way they want. And the Perceiver, who looks at the world, thinks that's the way it is, and who then goes with the flow. Which are you?

"If we were going to do a project together, would you prefer it to be outlined and planned out in step by step stages, or would you rather just dive in and go for the big picture?"

Judger (steps)--------------Perceiver(big picture)

Each of these thinking styles has their own thought processes:

Judger - I think you'd like a planned, orderly way to... make life adapt to them, everything planned. Clear cut categories and rules- demand closure. Lists and schedules, like to have this settled. Quick decision is required The right way to do this. Wants closure, organised, punctual.

We're going to give you a step by step specific system to follow
Perceiver - ..While at the same time remain flexible.. Adapt to life, do
what they feel.
 keep an open mind about this - avoid closure, difficulty deciding.
Spontaneity and freedom in life. Take life as it comes. Here and now,
lateness. We're going to give you a simple formula to run in your head
This is how to talk with each type, in person, or emails.

THE SOURCE OF "BUSYNESS"

There's a lot of things trying to get your attention aren't there? And if you don't make a conscious decision to control it, by deciding in advance what to focus on, you'll be sucked in by the demands of the outside world and end up living in reaction. There's usually 3 things trying to get your attention:

1. Other People's Urgent demands – trying to please others, their "monkeys on your back", their time pressure and deadlines, fire fighting.
2. Distractions – things that give you relief, escapism, quick fixes, counting the paperclips or cleaning the desk rather than make the calls.
3. Avoiding scary consequences – the pain that will result if you don't get it done

Its all about your emotional state. Stress is a fancy word for fear, of the consequences if something goes wrong. Stress comes as a result of running horrible scenarios in your head and asking yourself dumb questions like "What if this goes wrong, or what happens if I don't get it finished in time?". One Trainer told me that anxiety is your unconscious mind's way of getting you to focus on what you want....

TIME TIPS TO DIP INTO

Any Life management system needs to be visible, and consistent. You have to look at it ideally every week, preferably everyday. Life will try to tempt you astray – you need something to keep you "on path". Visibility is key. As Eurofighter pilot Chris Penrice says "Sight is life & speed is groovy".

A simple example would be to answer and reply to emails at a set time every day, for a set period of time every day. E.g. spend an hour on them at 11am.

Split your Email Inbox into different folders, for different projects or areas, so there's one for Sales, customer service, orders, whatever. You can set up rules in your software to automatically sort incoming emails before you even see it.

TOOLS & TECHNIQUES

Have a capture page that is where you write down any items, calls, communications or actions that you'll need to take action on. This page starts today, and anything you capture today will happen tomorrow earliest. In other words, you've got your plan for today – if it comes up at all, it'll be tomorrow or later before you act upon it. "Let paper remember so you can forget."

Top down system – plan your year, then plan your quarters, then your months, then your weeks and finally your days. Start with the end in mind, and work backwards from B to A. For some reason that temporal shift makes things much more achievable.

The 80/20 rule – 80% of your results will come from 20% of your actions, and only 20% of your results will come from 80% of your actions. So you should be focussing on the top 20% actions that get 80% of the results you want.

Think about modelling someone who does it well. Who at work seems to get everything done and still gets to go home at 5:00pm? How do they do that? What strategies do they use?

When is your most productive part of the day for what types of tasks? Use this knowledge.

Customise your own Time Management system. You will only ever really use what works for you, so create something that does.

When you think you need more time, you may actually need more space. When you are pressed for time, and not getting things done, it's easy to assume that you need more time...and sometimes you don't. Sometimes, it isn't just time we need for different projects, it's also needing space to have several projects in progress at the same time...without interfering with other projects, your life, or your business.

Leave out papers and work for several projects, without interfering with each other, so that you can come back to them and make progress with any of them, when you are ready to, when you want to.

Use these tips – implement one, work it for a week and judge by results. Then build in another. Before you know it you can have a simple life management system in place and get more done in a day than most people get done in a week.

"Doing a difficult task is like trying to push a car – it's hard to get over the inertia at first, but it's easy once it's rolling"

15

WHERE PERSONAL DEVELOPMENT GOES TO DEVELOP

Glad you could get to this chapter. Now you may have read the chapters on subjects like rapport or presenting skills before, but next I want to tell you about something that you probably won't have heard anywhere else. I'm going to show you a model which when I first saw it, sitting where you are, it was like a bolt out of the blue. So keep your eyes peeled, because you're going to see yourself in what I'm going to illustrate here

I want to spend the next few pages showing you something that blew me away when I first saw it, something that explains a lot about your life, who you are and where you're going, and also where you've been.

Have you ever done some work on an aspect of your life, and yet certain stuff still seems to hang around? Like, you try and boost your relationships area, yet you still keep meeting the wrong type? Or you enhance your wealth area and yet your money situation is till crap a year later. Has that happened to you? Well part of that is to do with Astrology, and part of that is to do with your own "personal evolution" – by that I mean where you are in your personal development...

The very fact that you're reading this is significant. Only certain people come to a book like this. And certain people wouldn't be seen dead in a book like this. (Maybe that's not the right choice of words but you know what I mean...) Have you ever wondered why that is? Ever noticed that you do some work on yourself – you raise your own standards, or make a resolution, or promise yourself that you'll never do that thing again…. and yet it comes back to haunt you? Is it just me, or have you also experienced that?

Ever worked somewhere for a while, and gradually thought that you've outgrown it, or you just don't get on with their co-workers anymore? Have you ever looked back at some of the stuff you've done in the past and wondered, "What the hell was I thinking?" If you're a helping professional, who works with people's "stuff", wouldn't it be useful to have an idea of what direction to move your client in? Sometimes you get a client and quite frankly, you're not totally certain what to do with them.

Anthony Robbins says "People's lives are a direct reflection of the expectations of their peer group."

Your peer group are the people you spend time with. You adapt to them, to keep their love and connection. You bend to fit them. You become like the people you associate with.

You'll have three choices:

1. lead them and hopefully they'll follow
2. stay & let them pull you down, or keep you static
3. leave the peer group

Tony said "if your expectations are higher than theirs, they'll try to pull you down to theirs". They don't want to lose you. To grow and evolve, Tony suggests you team up with people who will stretch you. Love your family, choose your peer group.

Dr Claire Graves (who was a man by the way) was an American Sociologist in the fifties. He said that the things that are important to us move and "change, as we grow, and our notions of what we want and what we don't want change too." We move up a structure (like a ladder) stage by stage. There are no rules about how fast we go, or how far along it, but we are always moving… He studied societies all the way back to the birth of Christ. However, he never wrote a single book on this. Grave's system didn't have enough levels to explain some of the people that we meet in life, so Dr Tad James expanded upon it, bringing it up to date. Subsequently it has gained greater popularity and even had an overhaul when it became known as "Spiral Dynamics". I also wish to thank Jim Morningstar PhD for his further contribution to this awesome model.

Spiral Dynamics is simply a model for "mapping" how we as humans evolve and tells you where you've been, and where you're going. Frustrated by the multitude of conflicting theories about human behaviour, Graves was determined to pin down what made humans do what they do. He spent decades working on this, looking at a wide range of sources. The results will feel familiar and instantly recognisable. Canada's MacLean Magazine reporting on Grave's work in the late 1970's called it "The Theory that Explains Everything."

Jim Morningstar described Graves as "a professor at Union College in New York, who died relatively unknown in 1986. Like many geniuses who are perfectionistic, he never published his complete work. That is because he was always discovering new refinements and exploring new horizons such that he saw his work as never complete. Also like many geniuses, the publishing and application of his work was later accomplished by his students. Two such enterprising followers, Beck and Cowen (1996), coined the term Spiral Dynamics and applied its principles to social change. They were hired by the government of South Africa, for example, to assist in the transition from apartheid. The theory has been successfully applied to the areas of social welfare, education, business management and marketing. My interest is in the area of psychotherapy and consciousness growth. It helps me select which healing approach is appropriate with which individuals, under which circumstances. It makes obsolete questions like what is the best form of government or best system of education or best form of therapy. But more than this, it indicates what is most likely to be effective with whom and when."

THIS APPLIES TO INVIVIDUALS - GROUPS - FAMILIES – A COMPANY - SOCIETY – A COUNTRY, AND SHOWS UP ESPECIALLY IN RELATIONSHIPS. Conflicts such as he's a hard driven worker trying to make a living, she's a meditating housewife trying to save the whales. "Why doesn't he care about the whales?" she cries. "The whales? Give me a break – I'm trying to pay the mortgage!"

Let me tell you what I've observed every time I've taught this idea. As we go through this, you'll start off understanding and following this model really easily. Then you'll gradually realise where you are right now. The point at which you struggle to understand this model tells you where you've reached, and where it loses you altogether, or you go "Nah, that's rubbish!" is well outside your present position.

Let us review the thirteen levels of consciousness as we know them to date. No one level is better than another. Countless humans have lived happy and fulfilled lives at each level presumably because they came here to address the lessons that level had to offer. These lessons tend to come around again and again, but with increasingly expanded awareness as we grow. Beck and Cowen use colours rather than numbers for each stage.

EVOLUTION LEVEL 1

SPIRAL DYNAMIC COLOUR

"BEIGE , the colour of the Savannah grasslands 'Survivalistic' 1st Awakening"

BASIC THEME

Do what you must just to stay alive

CHARACTERISTICS
· Uses instincts and habits just to survive
· Distinct self is barely awakened or sustained
· Food, Water, Warmth, Sex, and Safety have priority
· Forms into survival bands to perpetuate life
Survival Oriented   Living alone grubbing for roots and berries.
No associations. Homeless people. Basic drives of food and shelter.
Eat when you're hungry.

COACHING THEM
You won't get clients at Level 1. Help at this level would be CPR or intravenous feeding. All assistance is here directed toward keeping the individual breathing

GAIN
Safety in numbers – form associations and get into tribes.

PASSIVE/ACTIVE
Active/expressive

THEME FOR EXISTENCE
React naturally to imperative physiological needs so as to reduce the tension of them. No concept of cause and effect

PROBLEMS OF EXISTENCE
Achieving stability of imperative Psychological systems.

WHY IS A GOOD IDEA A GOOD IDEA?
Because it has to be in order to survive.

EXAMPLES

The first peoples, newborn infants, senile elderly, late-stage Alzheimer's victims, mentally ill street people, starving masses, bad drug trips, and 'shell shock.'

EVOLUTION LEVEL 2

SPIRAL DYNAMIC COLOUR

"PURPLE , the first basic dye colour used, 'magical' 2nd Awakening The Clan"

BASIC THEME

Keep the spirits happy and the 'tribe's' nest warm and safe. Mystical spirits, omens, signs. Wise elders and Shaman protect the nest. Rely on customs, elders, magic or shaman to find safety and security for the people, and their spirit realm. Kinship.

CHARACTERISTICS

· Obey the desires of spirit beings and mystical signs. Consult Tarot & palm readers, psychic or faith healers, horoscope phone lines and other Shaman
· Show allegiance to chief, elders, ancestors and the clan
· Preserve sacred objects, places, events, and memories – mysticism & fate
· Observe rites of passage, seasonal cycles, and tribal customs

Notice their inclusion of "guardian angels." Lessons at this level return, I believe, in level eight which is the threshold of where we are now as a planet.

Tribal Oriented   Safety in numbers. Collect together in tribes and the strongest became chief, so give up individuality to serve the chief's wishes. Chief decides your actions. That's up to the Chief - I have no control, no choice. Time measured by seasons, they feel it kinaesthetically, so they may be latecomers cos they work with events, not clocks. Magic, superstition and spirits very prevalent here. Realise that there are other tribes, animals and spirits that will attack you, so you set out in heroic fashion to kill them first! Dependent on others but don't want to admit it.   Usually very creative in music and art. NOBODY WINS   Missing a sense of inclusion. Love to be a quiet team member. Dependence.

COACHING THEM

Help at level 2 involves classical conditioning procedures because they intervene at the human brain stem level. Background anxiety from birth is the underlying condition of most humans on earth. Rebirthing literally reconditions trauma to the breathing mechanism which verbal therapies cannot reach. Rare type, won't meet these guys much, but prevalent in relationships: people who are otherwise at different levels, but play level 2 in their relationship. Use metaphors, stories. Be rigid with timekeeping. Be kinesthetic. They come to you wanting to be led.

LET GO OF

LET GO OF BEING A VICTIM

GAIN

UNDERSTANDING [self, others, their roles) TO GET TO NEXT LEVEL

PASSIVE/ACTIVE

Passive/reflective

395

THEME FOR EXISTENCE

Live in accordance with established tribal ways. Bonding together. Animalistic and tribalistic. Sacrifice self for the ancestors or the customs.

PROBLEMS OF EXISTENCE

Achieving basic safety in a non-comprehended world which seems full of spirits. The world is a threatening place full of spirit beings and mysterious forces.

WHY IS A GOOD IDEA A GOOD IDEA?

Because our honoured chieftain says it is so.

EXAMPLES

Belief in guardian angels and Voodoo-like curses, blood oaths, ancient grudges, chanting and trance dancing, good luck charms, family rituals, and mystical ethnic beliefs and superstitions. Strong in Third-World settings, gangs, athletic teams, and corporate 'tribes.'"

EVOLUTION LEVEL 3

SPIRAL DYNAMIC COLOUR

"RED 'Impulsive' colour of blood, hot impulsive energy 3rd Awakening"

BASIC THEME

Be what you are and do what you want, regardless. Powerful urges and impulses. Immediate gratification & conquest. Spontaneous and colourful. BLING! To the victors the spoils

CHARACTERISTICS

• The world is a jungle full of threats and predators

- Breaks free from any domination or constraint to please self as self desires
- Stands tall, expects attention, demands respect, and calls the shots
- Enjoys self to the fullest right now without guilt or remorse
- Conquers, out-foxes, and dominates other aggressive characters

Aggression Oriented [Rambo]. The warrior or predator. Instant pleasure, immediate gratification. Fun at any cost. Sex, power, domination, control over others. Charm is a weapon to be used. Macho, hard hitting, sexy, respect. Usually some of the young ones in the tribe start to strike out on their own. To hell with anyone else - I need this and I need it now! Loners. FIREPOWER. Iran in late 1980's. No respect for anything but aggression. Kill or be killed. Sack on the spot. Dog eat dog world. Always sleep with your gun. Old West Gunfighter "I am the law." Noisiest group in society, very aggressive. Low grade manipulators. Call in a favour I'm owed. Slowly becomes the rights of kings, benefits of rank. No responsibility for their actions, at effect. It's not their fault. Guilt free. Great business start ups. Can't control their urge to spend money. I HAVE TO WIN/YOU-HAVE TO LOSE SEXUAL ABUSE Scarcity outlook. Can't accept who they are, therefore feel hurt. *Dependence*

COACHING THEM

Helping techniques at this level include operant conditioning procedures, "shaping" behaviour or reconditioning phobic responses. Again these are precognitive interventions and address deep level habit patterns, e.g. addictions, and fears e.g. phobias. Reward them, or show them how to achieve. Unwilling to plan, so plan with them. Give them tasks with deadlines, and punish failure. Show them how to get out of the mess and make them look good. You'll be expected to pay for any favours they do for you, so avoid that until you know the price you'll pay. Coach towards level 4 (Blue). Be edgy & stick to your agreements & boundaries

LET GO OF
LET GO OF HURT & REJECTION

GAIN
ACCEPTANCE OF SELF TO GET TO NEXT LEVEL

PASSIVE/ACTIVE
Active/expressive

THEME FOR EXISTENCE
Express self for what self desires regardless of the consequences lest one feel ashamed. Ego driven and exploitive. The Powerful Self. Be as tough as you can be and count only on yourself when the chips are down, so you can fight off the aggression of others. Live for today!

PROBLEMS OF EXISTENCE
Awareness of existence as an individual; how to live against the fact of death. Power driven, hostile world where your strength as an individual keeps you alive.

WHY IS A GOOD IDEA A GOOD IDEA?
Because it suits ME right here, right now

EXAMPLES
The 'Terrible Twos,' rebellious youth, frontier mentalities, feudal kingdoms, James Bond villains, epic heroes, soldiers of fortune, 'Papa' Picasso, wild rock stars, Atilla the Hun, William Golding's 'Lord of the Flies,' and Mighty Morphin Power Rangers. Die Hard, The Terminator, Rocky, Fast 'n Furious

EVOLUTION LEVEL 4

SPIRAL DYNAMIC COLOUR
"BLUE 'Purposeful' Looking upwards to the heavens in faith, 4th Awakening" Truth Force

BASIC THEME

Life has meaning, direction, and purposes with predetermined outcomes. There is one right way to be through discipline & morality. Guilt based sacrifice as rightful authority dictates. The just earn the reward.

CHARACTERISTICS

- One sacrifices self to the transcendent Cause, Truth, or righteous Pathway
- The Order enforces a code of conduct based on eternal, absolute principles
- Righteous living produces stability now and guarantees future reward
- Impulsivity is controlled through guilt; everybody has their proper place
- Laws, regulations, and discipline build character and moral fibre

At this level more coordinated functioning between the sub cortical forebrain and the brain stem along with an abundance of adrenalin makes the avoidance of punishment a very powerful motivating factor. It is said that if there are no aversive consequences at this level, there is no learning. At this level I first learn to avoid punishment and am rewarded later. Delayed gratification is actually a great advance in our civilization over the Atilla the Hun quest of immediate gratification of the previous level. Guilt, penance, expiration confession are all important steps in development. But if this has been inflicted too harshly or dogmatically, it hinders later growth

System Oriented [The Loyalist] Gunfighters live long enough to get old. How come? What happens when you die? System oriented. This created the American Government/Catholic Church/Communist Party. Sacrifice self for the good of the system, or for salvation later. Benefits/gold watch on retirement, or in the afterlife. Russia/China 1990. Caste system, classes in society. Dominated by guilt. Incest common here. I'm not OK, but you are OK. I WIN/YOU LOSE I'M TOTALLY GUILTY; I'M A SINNER. Unending struggle. *Dependence*

COACHING THEM

They believe there's only one right way to live and it's theirs – their faith, rules, dress codes, moral standards, social positions, rankings. Discuss outcomes but let them design the "how to". It's futile to attempt to persuade them that there's another model of the world. They like to strive and progress up the ranks in the hierarchy. They understand guilt & expect to feel it, so deliver chastisement if they fail to perform. Like sameness, regular safe employment and salary. Like pension schemes. Give them an agreement and rules to follow. Get them to sign an agreement with you. Send them testimonials, your qualifications, certificates and any recognised bodies you belong to.

LET GO OF

LET GO OF GUILT & UNWORTHINESS

GAIN

FORGIVENESS TO GET TO NEXT LEVEL

PASSIVE/ACTIVE

Passive/reflective

THEME FOR EXISTENCE

Sacrifices the desires of self now in order to get reward later on in some other realm. Belief in the one truth that answers life's mysteries, and provides an authority figure to dutifully obey. Absolute order. Live for salvation later.

PROBLEMS OF EXISTENCE

Reasonable order in a world of seeming chaos; how to live in a world of threat and want. Desperately need purpose and order in life to give it meaning and to feel secure.

WHY IS A GOOD IDEA A GOOD IDEA?

Because it conforms to the rule of Law

EXAMPLES

Rev. Billy Graham, Frank Capra's 'It's a Wonderful Life,' Puritan America, Confucian China, Hasidic Judaism, Dickensian England, Singapore discipline, codes of chivalry and honour, charitable good deeds, the Salvation Army, Islamic fundamentalism, Garrison Keillor's 'Lake Wobegon,' Boy and Girl Scouts, patriotism.

EVOLUTION LEVEL 5

SPIRAL DYNAMIC COLOUR
"ORANGE 'Achievist' Glowing like the hot steel from the furnace 5th Awakening"

BASIC THEME

Act in your own self-interest by playing the game to win. Compete to succeed, by learning the best ways to win. Image and status. **Strive Drive.** Every man for himself in the rat race.

CHARACTERISTICS

- · Change and advancement are inherent within the scheme of things
- Progress by learning nature's secrets and seeking out best solutions
- Manipulate Earth's resources to create and spread the abundant good life
- Optimistic, risk-taking, and self-reliant people deserve their success
- Societies prosper through strategy, technology, and competitiveness

Materialist Oriented - Entrepreneur [Achiever] Industrial revolution – science will solve the world's problems. Man seeks to conquer the world not by force or manpower, but by learning it's secrets. The Have's and the Have Not's. Envy and respect if successful, but not liked. Transition for USSR in early 1990's. Free enterprise. It's what built America. Business gurus. My dad worked there for 50 years and all he got was a gold watch - stuff this! Junior bosses who can't delegate. I'm going to set up my own business! Raped the Earth, strip mining, deforestation, polluted atmosphere, and eroded ozone layer. Biodegradables that won't. Ever. Pampers will never disintegrate. Oil spillages. I want to run the show myself. Reluctant leader. I have to make it all happen. Heavy stress due to expectation. Lots of modal operators. Sacrifice fun, life is really serious. Noone tells me what to do. Do what it takes. Feelings of inadequacy, don't feel good about myself. Working hard to make it all happen - experience frustration when it doesn't. START TO PLAY WIN/WIN. Companies: 1980's hard driven, £££ oriented. Companies want to recruit level 5 Salespeople. Perfectionists in a relationship – partner must be happy all the time, or else something must be wrong. Need to set goals. Have a fixed idea of how it should be, and trying to make it happen. (That's why TM in the 60's evolved loads of people, as did Feminism and

Women's Movement) Short on empathy. You have to earn it & you can, if you do the work. Like to win and pose. Chase & win in relationships. *Independence*

HOW TO COACH

Psychoanalysis grew out of helping people transition from the prior Saintly System (4th Awakening) to this more cognitively reliant Pragmatic System. The authoritative doctor allowed guilt-ridden patients to bring their libidinous id (level 3) out from the Victorian rule of their superego (level 4) and be guided through the rational ministry of their ego (level 5). In the 5th level we see the introduction of many cognition therapies which teach us to think rationally to a better life or to communicate more clearly to improved family systems.

Slick, punchy, demanding thinking. Striving to attend elite positions and win competitions. Money, designer everything, success & achievement are the buzzwords. Victory, mastery & glory. Porsches. You'd better look well off, and have glossy brochures. Tell them who you've coached. Strong entrepreneurs wanting clever solutions. They want big tasks and high goals. Live on motivational tapes, books and seminars. Usually stressed, fatigued and suffer IBS or ulcers as wealth more valued than health. Get them exercising & eating healthily by quoting successful people who do both. Link health club to networking. Recommend expensive, healthy restaurants. Tony Robbins has a dietician & chef. Experiment with change and entrepreneurial alternatives to reach goals for the betterment of self and others.

LET GO OF

LET GO OF UNFULFILLED EXPECTATIONS

GAIN

TOTALLY LET GO & GO WITH THE FLOW TO GET TO NEXT LEVEL

Level 5 people love things and use people. They need to learn to use things and love people.

PASSIVE/ACTIVE

Active/expressive

THEME FOR EXISTENCE

Express self for what self desires but in a rational, calculating way without feeling shame or guilt. Materialistic, the enterprising self seeking out the good life. If it isn't broke, break it and make it perform better.

PROBLEMS OF EXISTENCE

Reasoned knowledge leading to control of the physical universe. How to conquer threat and want. They sense the possibility of change and the opportunity to improve.

WHY IS A GOOD IDEA A GOOD IDEA?

Because it serves my plans and objectives

EXAMPLES

The Enlightenment, 'success' ministries, Any Rand's 'Atlas shrugged,' Wall Street, Rodeo Drive, The Riviera, emerging middle classes, the cosmetics industry, trophy hunting, Chambers of Commerce, colonialism, TV infomercials, the Cold War, DeBeers diamond cartel, breast implants, fashion, J.R. Ewing and Dallas, Donald Trump.

EVOLUTION LEVEL 6

SPIRAL DYNAMIC COLOUR
"GREEN 'Communitarian' Peaceful ecology 6th Awakening"

BASIC THEME

Seek peace within the inner self and explore, with others, the caring dimensions of community. Consensus opinion with benefits for all members of the community. All should benefit equally.

CHARACTERISTICS

- The human spirit must be freed from greed, dogma, and divisiveness
- Feelings, sensitivity, and caring supersede cold rationality
- Spread the Earth's resources and opportunities equally among all
- Reach decisions through reconciliation and consensus processes
- Refresh spirituality, bring harmony, and enrich human development

Group & Cause Oriented [Involver] California touchy-feely psychologists. Seen as pacifistic wimps to everyone in levels 1-5. Ecology. "The best for all concerned, for the greater good" Laid back. Save the whales. Ban the Bomb. Anita Roddick, Body Shop. Group hug. Thanks for sharing. Belonging, being accepted by others, harmony, knowing your inner self. Group consensus, everyone has a vote, we'll all have an equal say. Social acceptance is more important than progress. Save the whales probably hasn't. Ban the bomb never did. Touchy-feely psychologists are being replaced by HGE Practitioners. Exhibit covert control – make them do it my way, therefore missing trust. Give up your suit and tie for another uniform that's just as pervasive – beads & tie-dyed T-shirts. The person you married is expressing your unconscious. WIN/WIN Level 6 Businesses don't work: too much emphasis on feeling good and not enough results. Some people not pulling their own weight. The system is supporting some people who should, perhaps not be supported. True communication begins here – you can start to tell your truth as you see it. Love, peace & harmony are the only ways to live. Need to balance commercialism with community values. Wants to fit in and may suffer to keep friends or colleagues happy. They're good at reaching group agreements and keeping the peace, and will easily attack you if you cross them or make them feel unfairly treated. Good intuition and interpersonal skills, often therapists. Always trying to rescue others. Often taken advantage of by others. Voluntary work or protest groups. Companies: Cooperative - everyone has a say – all shareholders *Independence*

HOW TO COACH

At the sixth level there is more integration between lower appetitive centres and higher cognitive processes. People learn here through observation of others rather than having to make all their own mistakes. This yin (adapt self) level recognizes the authority of the peer group. The advent of group therapies and consciousness raising groups is especially meaningful at this level. The therapist is not looked to as the authoritative answer giver. Solutions come more from group process.

Want to work with you in a mutually beneficial way. Tell them what causes you support to deepen rapport. May need to improve their appearance and dress sense – get them an image consultant.

LET GO OF (COVERT)CONTROL

GAIN

PEACE(which is what they really want)/FAITH/TRUST TO GET TO NEXT LEVEL

PASSIVE/ACTIVE

Passive/reflective

THEME FOR EXISTENCE

Sacrifice what one desires now in order to get reward now in the form of acceptance by and approval of others. Sacrifice self so all may prosper in unity. Join together, share your truth and work towards the group goals.

PROBLEMS OF EXISTENCE

Comprehension that human subjectivity is a reality not a myth to be cast aside; how to live in a world of abundance for human wants. Human problems demand collective action to reach vital social goals.

WHY IS A GOOD IDEA A GOOD IDEA?

Because we have reached consensus on it

EXAMPLES

John Lennon's music, Netherlands' idealism, Rogerian counselling, liberation theology, Doctors without Borders, Canadian health care, ACLU, World Council of Churches, sensitivity training, Boulder (Colorado), Green Peace, Jimmy Carter, Dustin Hoffman in 'The Graduate,' animal rights, deep ecology, Minneapolis-St Paul social services, the music of Bruce Cogburn, Ben & Jerry's Ice Cream company

EVOLUTION LEVEL 7

SPIRAL DYNAMIC COLOUR
"YELLOW 'Integrative' Solar energy and life force 7th Awakening" The integrated being.

BASIC THEME
Live fully and responsibly as what you are and learn to become. Think about the long term big picture.

CHARACTERISTICS
*   Life is a kaleidoscope of natural hierarchies, systems, and forms
*   The magnificence of existence is valued over material production
*   Flexibility, spontaneity, and functionality have the highest priority
*   Knowledge and competency should supersede rank, power, status
*   Differences can be integrated into interdependent, natural flows

Functional Flow [Choice Seeker] Yes we need ecology (level 6) and we also need someone to be in charge & get results (level 5). Integrates all the previous levels. The first wave of a quantum leap. Results oriented. Global thinking. Seek choices. Can adopt previous Level traits if need be, at will. Anyone can run the system as long as they know more than I do. Otherwise, forget it. Moving beyond roles, but still looking for results. Missing partnership, even though they have trust. Seeking commitment, truth or integrity. Not getting anywhere near what they deserve in terms of rewards. WIN/WIN (Therapists should be here). There's all this stuff you're supposed to have been doing but never did e.g. a hobby you never took up, a dream you always dreamed of. Still searching for a sense of truth and integrity. The Tragic Hero – doing all this work and not being fulfilled. Companies: Leader with direction - WIN / WIN - Self-actualised people who have their own values satisfied. Well read in a variety of subjects. Loves information, learning and gaining knowledge. Independent, doesn't really care about what others think, but is interested in modelling. Well developed self esteem based on applied knowledge, not ego. Value personal freedom. *Independence*

HOW TO COACH

The seventh level marks a new tier in the spiral of human consciousness, coming from a being motivation rather than a survival mentality: i.e. valuing one's being rather than doing to survive. Learning here is more with the whole person than any one part or parts of the brain. Gestalt techniques and those which bring into play non-verbal and non-linear processes often open the door for guidance from other dimensions of our being. Like specific outcomes/projects and seek support & knowledge. Recommend they consult experts. Get them to acknowledge their own successes but keep praise to a minimum. Offer only what is asked.

LET GO OF

LET GO OF ROLES & DUTIES (work, partner, husband, wife) Just be you.

GAIN

COMMITMENT TO GIVING & RECEIVING TO GET TO NEXT LEVEL

There is also a need at this level to reconnect with a sense of what's bigger than you – spirituality, the Higher Self, the Super Consciousness, the Creator, whatever you want to call it. To grow and evolve beyond level 7, people need that spiritual connection. That's why for me personally, after learning NLP and Hypnosis, the next path was Huna (and you'll see why in the next chapter).

PASSIVE/ACTIVE
Active/expressive

THEME FOR EXISTENCE
Express self as self is inclined but not at the expense of others. Live according to internal principles to find the most effective ways to be by gaining broad knowledge.

PROBLEMS OF EXISTENCE
Restoring ecological balance disturbed by the knowledge accrued; how to restore a disturbed universe. Interconnected living can be threatened by outside influences.

WHY IS A GOOD IDEA A GOOD IDEA?
Because it is the most functional approach

EXAMPLES
Carl Sagan's astronomy, Peter Senge's organizations, Stephen Hawking's 'Brief History of Time,' W. Edwards Deming's objectives, Paul Newman's version of stardom, chaos theory, appropriate technology ,eco-industrial parks (using each other's outflows as raw materials), early episodes of TV's Northern Exposure, Fel-Pro, Inc. (a gasket manufacturer), Fred Alan Wolf's 'new physics', Deepak Chopra's 'Ageless Body.'

EVOLUTION LEVEL 8

SPIRAL DYNAMIC COLOUR
"TURQUOISE" The Holistic Being. **The blue planet as seen from space 8th Awakening"**

BASIC THEME
Experience the wholeness of existence through mind and spirit, leading to global balance. Sacrifice self so all life can continue.

CHARACTERISTICS
- The world is a single, dynamic organism with its own collective mind
- Self is both distinct and a blended part of a larger, compassionate whole
- Everything connects to everything else in ecological alignments
- Energy and information permeate the Earth's total environment
- Holistic, intuitive thinking and cooperative actions are to be expected

Inspirational. Unconscious heavy stress. True leader, but reluctant to lead a society that expects them to. Need for privacy, reluctant to be famous. Gives up niceness to become more natural - previously installed level 4 shame, embarrassment & guilt dropped away. Nudity is comfortable, sense of sexuality. Relates better to nature. Aliveness, everything is delightful. People are giving to you. Start to go with the flow. No more need for goal setting - goals become more universal. Personal inspiration. Fritz Perls called this "You've lost your mind and come to your senses" Martyrs *Interdependence*

HOW TO COACH

This is our cutting edge. People at this level register a different physiology, often different from others, i.e. less core anxiety and operating from a different level of being. Helping at this level entails not doing something to change someone, but being them as you both change. This requires a commitment of total being and removal of all illusions of separation. It is imperative that we reach a critical mass of being at this level to tilt the balance of world consciousness. Breath is the thread, which runs through the physical, emotional, cognitive and metaphysical systems and brings them together as no other element can. It is only through breath that love and light can transform the beings of this planet.

LET GO OF

LET GO OF SOCIAL EXPECTATIONS Need to be able to receive graciously

GAIN

LET GO & BE A LEADER TO GET TO NEXT LEVEL

PASSIVE/ACTIVE

Passive/reflective

THEME FOR EXISTENCE

Sacrifice the idea that man will never know what it is all about and go on living. Need a coordinated and holistic approach to global problems.

PROBLEMS OF EXISTENCE

Truly accepting the reality of ever broadening realms of consciousness; how to live when having, but never really knowing life. Become attuned with all life forces to address the problems which jeopardise the future.

WHY IS A GOOD IDEA A GOOD IDEA?
Because the living system ultimately benefits

EXAMPLES
Theories of David Bohn, McLuhan's 'global village,' Gregory Stock's Metaman, Rupert Sheldrake and morphic fields, Gandhi's ideas of pluralistic harmony, Ken Wilber's 'Spectrum of Consciousness,' James Lovelock's 'Gaia hypothesis,' Pierre Teilhard de Chardin's 'noosphere.'

This is usually where Spiral Dynamics ends. Dr Tad James(one of my Trainers) expanded this list to include another 5 levels:

EVOLUTION LEVEL 9

"CORAL 'New Energy' Life beneath the ocean surface 9th Awakening"

BASIC THEME
Vision state - acknowledged as King, Queen or Shaman.

CHARACTERISTICS
Visionary. Begins to move into leadership happily. An artist at the highest level. Provide healing symbols in society, affecting the world. Power begins to dawn and so comes the fear of it. Lots old past fears in your life come back to haunt you. Lots of power now, but you can still lose. Suspect that there are "entities" that can attack you. Missing the true power. Must remember there's a higher power in charge and you need to remember that *Interdependence*

LET GO OF

LET GO OF FEAR OF POWER

GAIN

FEEL THE POWER & BE IT !! TO GET TO NEXT LEVEL

PASSIVE/ACTIVE

Active/expressive

WHY IS A GOOD IDEA A GOOD IDEA?

Because its coming through me from the source

EXAMPLES

Certain celebrities. Certain musicians. Certain members of the Royal Family. Luke Skywalker. Neo in The Matrix

EVOLUTION LEVEL 10

"TEAL 'spirit and life connect' Power 10th Awakening"

BASIC THEME

Mastery

CHARACTERISTICS

Mastery One or more talents that are "alive". Begin to tap into and feel the power. If they can accept/receive the power they'll evolve. Power is a real issue. Fully realise & "get" that Perception is Projection. You create your own reality. *Interdependence*

LET GO OF

LET GO OF FEAR OF SHARING THE POWER

GAIN

To the extent that you accept, receive and share the power, you'll transition to the next level.

PASSIVE/ACTIVE

Passive/reflective

WHY IS A GOOD IDEA A GOOD IDEA?

Because it just is

EXAMPLES

Neo in Matrix 2: Reloaded

EVOLUTION LEVEL 11

BASIC THEME

Enlightenment [Cosmic Consciousness]

CHARACTERISTICS

As described by the Maharishi Yogi. Experience the absolute unchanging, infinite world. Dichotomy between this and the real world. Can astrally project.

LET GO OF

Let go of all limitations.

PASSIVE/ACTIVE

Active/expressive

WHY IS A GOOD IDEA A GOOD IDEA?

Just because

EXAMPLES

Neo in Matrix 3:Revolutions

EVOLUTION LEVEL 12

BASIC THEME

Enlightenment [God Consciousness]

CHARACTERISTICS

Dichotomy has now become a range, and you can switch between both. Sadness comes up because there's nothing else out there. It's all one reality.

PASSIVE/ACTIVE

Passive/reflective

WHY IS A GOOD IDEA A GOOD IDEA?

Just be…

EXAMPLES

Beyond me at my current level!

EVOLUTION LEVEL 13

BASIC THEME

Being of Light

CHARACTERISTICS

Enlightenment [Unity Consciousness]. Everything is fully integrated. It's all one reality.

GAIN

Vibrate at such a high level that they disappear

PASSIVE/ACTIVE

Active/expressive

WHY IS A GOOD IDEA A GOOD IDEA?

Just…

EXAMPLES

The Aumakua in Huna. Possibly the Incas, the Aztecs and other beings that are here but we can't see them…

Think of this like a game of snakes and ladders. At each level, there is stuff you have to let go of to move up. There's also, however, new things to learn before you get there. And it is possible to slide back down, even after you've moved on. So how do you move up the ladder? Do personal development work, learn and study, start being creative, really start to trust your intuition. Get emotional issues cleared up with therapy, counselling or Life Coaching (I do all 3 – ask me for a session). I use the phrase "Awareness is Progression". This is why "when the student is ready the teacher appears" (and vice versa). If you combine this with the concept that Perception is Projection, then as you grow and evolve, you create a teacher at a level higher than you to pull you ever upwards. Does that make sense? Yet until you evolved up a level, they weren't around…

You can also be at different levels in different contexts – so you might be a striving, driven business person at level 5, but at home be a charitable, giving hippy. People who go for therapy tend to be between levels 3-7. Above that, they tend to be self sufficient. There's a Passive/reflective quality in the even numbered levels, and an active/expressive quality in the odd numbered levels.

Dependence at lower levels. Independence is slightly better. Interde-

pendence – satisfying each other's needs and values

This is just a model, and like any model, it's only one way of looking at things, but I've found it very useful. How could you use this information? What level is your partner at? If you mentally labelled everyone you know, what might you find out?

In a company or a business, how could this model be useful when understanding relationships between colleagues, or between management and staff? Now you know about it, you'll always remember what I showed you here. So now you're more aware....guess what that does for your evolution...Awareness is Progression.

I have a home study programme on CD which explains each of these levels in full, and we now have a written test which elicits the level **you're actually on**, not the one *you wish you were*. For full details, email me at enquiry@jonathanclark.org.

Dr Claire Graves also said "Questions we wrestled with were never solved, we merely learned new coping strategies. We may never have actually solved them, they merely became irrelevant. What are some of the things you've learned to cope with, or around, that you never actually cleared....

As Jim Morningstar put it: "We must address and successfully solve the challenges at that stage of growth. In tribal life, for example, I must learn the customs and rituals of my clan and glean the advantages they bring. Then, there must be some dissonant stimulus to my current belief system that attracts me. In the Saintly system (Level 4), for example, I begin to notice those who are not waiting till the hereafter to enjoy their rewards, and who do not seem to be immoral people to me. Fourth, I must get insight into how I could live differently than in the prevailing system, envision myself in a new life as it were. And fifth, I must then overcome the barriers, inner and outer, that the current system has to my growing beyond it. I have to do the work, in other words."

As we progress, we reach plateaus then often seemingly regress before we grow further. There's a great metaphor in the Buddhist philosophy I believe, that says we need to sink deep into the pit of despair so we can bounce back up and reach the new ceiling. If we are growth oriented, we can operate within any belief systems only so long, till we reach a point of moral crisis. In Level 5 for instance, I may no longer believe that just accumulating more goods or money is truly fulfilling to me. I may seem to be left without moorings then I cannot subscribe to my old beliefs, but I do not have a fully integrated new set yet. I've lifted my foot off one rung in the ladder, but haven't reached the next one yet.

"This is when we often see people in therapy. They are looking for help in making sense of an expanding universe (to them it may seem disintegrating). Some people get stuck in these dips for years or perhaps lifetimes. During this period I search often through old forms of doing and explaining life. In the end, these will not suffice and I reach a point of behavioural crisis. At this point, I hit rock bottom, really let go and start to put together a new life based on the new principles I am learning. Given the success of this integration, I reach a new plateau and spend time there mastering this level and the challenges it brings."

"Each system incorporates the one before. We can always go back to and use the strengths (or weaknesses) of a prior system when called for. In a crisis I may revert to "more primitive" forms of behaviour which may be entirely appropriate or even life saving. I may not say "excuse me" or take a vote before going to get the fire extinguisher in an emergency."– Jim Morningstar

Everyday we hear all of these arguments in the media, from government, protest groups, parents, big business, the church, even your Dad shouting at the TV – materialism is either great, or greed. Technology is a blessing, or a curse. There are those who deserve their success because they worked hard, or they must have screwed someone over to get it. Ecology is either humane, or terrorism in disguise. Poverty is either caused by laziness and lack of discipline, or through oppression by economists. Who's right? Are you one of them, or one of us? And does that depend on your home address? Technology will make your life easier. Really? Kids that can't do basic arithmetic in their heads, but spend their teenage years glued to a play station

Fortunes have been sunk into charities, relief and aid. Good works have been carried out. Yet there's still poverty, violence and disease. Is it just me or did the New Orleans Hurricane disaster look more like a military coup than a rescue operation?

Hypno Genetic Evolution work as a holistic technique has been able to do what few other methods have done, namely to bridge all the systems of personal growth and open the neurology for higher levels of evolution. In other words, this planet is evolving. We as a race are developing. But be careful not to label yourself, or others. Remember that these are transitional, not absolute steps. You will be on different levels of thinking depending on the context. That's why sometimes you get a personal problem that you can't seem to fix, and you hear yourself saying "If this was a work issue I'd have solved it by now!"

Just because a country evolves from level 4 righteousness to level 5 consumerism, doesn't make the one true path invalid. That old level will remain as the level 5 spreads throughout the economy, media, religion and popular culture. Don Beck Ph.D describes this as the Russian Doll analogy [a doll within a doll].

There will probably always be level 3 terrorists, protestors and activists attacking the level 5 corporations. The holy orders of level 4 will continue to defend their noble cause from the level 3 anarchists that smash their windows, as well as the level 5's who want to develop the church hall into a shopping mall. Meanwhile the level 6 environmentalists will hold up their placards and banners as the bulldozers roll towards them... And on the weekends, the level 5's who want the shopping mall will go on a spiritual retreat and sit in the sweat lodge laughing at the protestors.

What do you have hanging from your car's rear view mirror? A rabbit's foot or furry dice? A cross, or the latest sat nav system? Or maybe a dream catcher, maybe even a hologram? Or maybe you no longer need a car…

As Michael Talbot said in his book "The Holographic Universe", "We are indeed on a shaman's journey, mere children struggling to become technicians of the sacred."

"You need to challenge yourself to improve and get better. If you don't, life will!"

16

THE SECRETS OF HUNA MAGIC THAT THEY DIDN'T WANT YOU TO KNOW

Aloha!

We're going to explore some of the ancient teachings of old Hawaii – get our hands into some real hands on concepts you can take away and use after this book is closed. We're going to be talking about Spiritual growth, healing and psychology in an art that was rich in language, song and legends. Now Huna's not for everyone – some people see it and are turned off by the "s" word – spirituality. So it can be a tricky subject to look at. I'd like to show you some ancient ways that I've looked into and I've certainly had my horizons expanded as a result, and I hope you'll have the same insights.

These concepts are easy to learn, and easy to use in daily life. There are some gems here that you'll find nowhere else. So lets begin, and the best way to begin is to begin at the beginning…. And so let's begin in the ancient way with a chant. In Hawaii the highest compliment you can pay someone is to write a song for someone, or better, sing a song to them…. This is a traditional chant to the goddess Laka, and it says:

Oh goddess Laka
O wildwood bouquet, O Laka
O Laka, queen of the voice
O Laka, giver of gifts
O Laka, giver of bounty
O Laka, giver of all things

I greet you with love.

The Initiation Chant: "E Laka E"

E Laka e

Pupu we'uwe'u, e Laka e

E Laka i ka leo

E Laka i ka loa'a

E Laka i ka wai wai

E Laka i na mea a pau

Ano ai ke aloha e

WHAT IS HUNA?

Huna was once part of the original teachings of the people of the earth. But there was a concerted effort, as you will see, to bury this information. It will probably intuitively seem right, feel familiar and just make sense.

If you're an old hand in these types of esoteric studies, I'm sure you'll find things that feel familiar. You're also going to discover some things that are brand new to you. Like all esoteric study, Huna was an exploration of the nature of mankind and the universe. The Kahuna, the Huna practitioners, developed a science of psychology and medicine that was capable of healing most ills of the people at that time. Mental illness was virtually unknown in Hawaii. The Kahuna school of La'au Kahea taught that we had a Conscious Mind, and an unconscious mind, a concept that the West only cottoned onto when Freud was a lad.

I first came across Huna on an NLP Practitioner Course, where our Trainer was also a master of Huna. He taught an introductory morning class on this subject, and I was fascinated......there I was on a course. Listening carefully and learning all about an ancient and esoteric art, and I was about to see something that made a huge impact on me. There was another student on the course who had dislocated his shoulder, and he had his arm in a sling. Apparently it had been causing him a lot of pain, and he asked David, the Trainer, if he could use Huna to help him. So as we watched, David asked the student:

"Do you know what it is that you want to let go of?"

"And do you know how you'd like to be instead?"

"Is it totally OK with your Unconscious Mind to make these changes today?"

"Let me know when it's disappeared"

Then he did something like this:

He breathed in through his nose, and out through his mouth four times, with the out breath long and extended. At the same time he made a hand gesture towards the student, moving his hand in a series of concentric circles, then as if he was pushing those circles towards the guy.

And the arm relocated back into its socket. With a crunch and a click, it snapped right back into place........and the guy got rid of his sling! And I thought......**I want to learn how to do that!**

So Huna put some things together for me – I'd spent years doing martial arts, meditation. I've always liked music, drumming, singing and dance. These are all present in Huna. I spent years learning state of the art psychology like Hypnosis and Neuro Linguistic Programming. I also studied and taught Feng Shui, the ancient art of placement and energy. I use numerology and Japanese astrology for prediction and certainty – again these are all present in Huna. It's like the source, the master system. I read loads of books. Attended many trainings. I recently studied with Kahuna, masters of Huna on the big island of Hawaii, and I go back at least once a year to continue my studies...

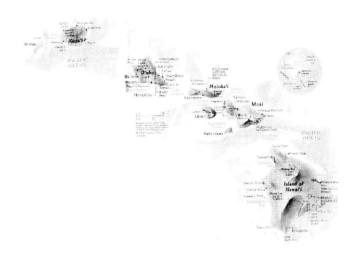

Now I was trained in the western education system, so I had to translate these ancient concepts back into that system so I can share them easily with you, in a way that makes them easy to pick up and use. The presentation of this information in this book is by no means a traditional presentation of Huna – the wisdom and knowledge is ancient, but the presentation is modern. Which reminds me of a story....

Tad James and I in Hawaii (Tad's the one with the tan!)
My Huna teacher Tad James tells a story of a Hawaiian boy, a

member of the Polynesian voyaging society, a group who sailed a canoe with no navigation except the stars over a great distance. He did Tad's Huna intensive training. Tad told a story about a wise man, a Kahuna, travelling on the Hawaiian coast. They'd stop and pick up special people, including a bearded, ancient one with staff, the stereotypical Gandalf figure. The young man was steering, and the wise old man said he was using Huna "the way you steer the ship, communicating with the ocean. You don't know this now but you're going to be taught Huna, but by a non-Hawaiian". Soon after that he ended up hearing a Tad James audiotape and attended Tad's Huna training in Hawaii...which is where I've just been.....

And in my study of Huna, I came across another, fascinating tale...

"At some point in time, long before the rise of Atlantis, a race of men came to this solar system from a group of stars now known as the Pleiades. Some landed on the Earth and others on another planet that no longer exists. The men who came from the stars fled catastrophe, and on Earth they intended to find peace. It was a long time in coming, however, because they found other men there already, remnants from a previous civilization that had fallen apart. They also found intelligent dinosaurs, and many battles for territorial control ensued.

"At last most of the starmen settled on a continent in the Pacific known today in legend as Mu. They called themselves the People of **Mu**, but others called them Manahuna or Menehune, 'the people of the secret power,' because of their advanced technology and psychic powers. They were a small people, pygmy-like by modern standards, and very industrious. Their knowledge was Huna, a fundamental philosophy for successful living. Once they felt securely established, they began to teach this knowledge to the men of Earth. Because many different languages were spoken and because their own was partly telepathic and difficult to learn, the teachers of Mu created a new language that was simple to learn. This language was structured to contain the Huna knowledge within it in a way that would ensure its survival for as long as the language remained in use. Today we know this language as Polynesian, and traces of it are found all over the world.

"Men came to the continent of Mu to learn, and Mu also sent missions of teachers to other parts of the world to set up schools of various types. A fair amount of inter marriage took place between the Mu people and their neighbors, resulting in children who carried on the genetic abilities and memories of their star-born parents.

"Gradually, those who studied with the Mu became organized into three different orders, each one practicing the Huna knowledge with a slightly different emphasis. Using English terms, they could be called the Intuitionists, the Intellectuals and the Emotionals.

"Generally speaking, the Intuitionists developed into what we would call mystics, metaphysicians and psychologists or psychotherapists. The Intellectuals became the equivalent of scientists, technicians and engineers. The Emotionals were more concerned with political, economic and athletic activities. All three made use of trained psychic abilities in their work, and each group taught and practiced various forms of physical healing.

"Now it is a basic part of Huna philosophy that every human being has psychic abilities. The orders trained people in their conscious and disciplined use. Nevertheless, there were people on Earth before the arrival of the Mu who could use these powers at will, and there remain people today unconnected with the orders who can use them in the same way.

"For many centuries things were going well on Earth and a world civilization was in the making when the Mu made a fatal mistake. For quite awhile they had maintained contact with their brethren who had settled on the other planet in the solar system, but eventually they turned all their attention on Earth and left the others to themselves. Then there came a time when desperate calls for help came from the sister planet. The people there were on the verge of destroying themselves and quick intervention was needed. Unfortunately, the Earth Mu had grown complacent and didn't want anything to disturb their peace, so they closed their ears to the pleas and tried to pretend it didn't concern them. In this they acted contrary to their own philosophy.

"With nothing to stop them, the people of the other planet created more and more terrible weapons of destruction to use against each other until the final, awful moment came. They reached a point where they blew their whole planet apart in a mighty cataclysm that rocked the solar system. The complete disappearance of an entire planet caused an immense imbalance, which the forces of nature sought to correct. In so doing, the orbits of the remaining planets were disrupted and the effect on Earth was devastating. Our planet was tumbled into a new orbit a little further from the sun, and the stress of the change caused intense volcanic and earthquake activity. Old lands sank beneath the seas in some places and new lands rose in others. The toll of death and destruction was indescribable.

When some semblance of stability returned, the survivors looked out upon a new Earth. The continent of Mu was no more. Only scattered islands remained in a vast and empty ocean. Around the world, people reverted to primitive survival and began the arduous climb toward civilization again. In many places the Mu were blamed for what had happened and they had to go into hiding to escape persecution. These lonely, scattered groups gave rise to later stories of magical "little people' found in almost every culture. The orders they created continued without them, except for rare contact by a very limited number of adepts.

"Other civilizations rose and fell. Among them was brilliant Atlantis, which almost achieved world domination before, in lesser imitation of Mu, it tore itself apart in a war that sent it to the bottom of the ocean. Meanwhile, the tradition of Huna was carried on by small groups who clothed the teaching in the culture of their locations. The majority of these lost contact with one another, but they continued to teach and heal and train. In some cases they were able to keep the simplicity of Huna intact, and in others distortions entered to the point that the fundamental knowledge was virtually lost, and good practices were carried on with a false understanding of their nature.

"After the disruption caused by the fall of Mu, survivors in the Pacific Basin, whom we now call Polynesians, gathered at two places to rebuild their societies—Samoa and the Society Islands. Among them were members of the three orders who acted as priests, healers and technical experts. Only the Intuitionists maintained contact with their colleagues in the rest of the world. Slowly, they built their technology up to the point where they could build great sailing vessels capable of carrying a hundred people or more, and they set off to explore what remained of Mu. For the most part, they stayed within the rough boundaries of the old continent, making only occasional forays into bordering lands.

"The group that successfully ventured the furthest outside of those boundaries was the Maori, who settled in New Zealand. The name Maori means 'the true people' or the original inhabitants, and refers both to their origin from the old continent of Mu (as mixed descendents of the star race) and to the fact that they were the first people to settle the new lands they discovered. They soon lost touch with the other Polynesians, and except for memories in old chants and songs the two groups forgot about each other until Western explorers brought them together again.

"Another group, following ancient navigational information contained in traditional chants, struck north from Tahiti and the Marquesas to land and settle in the Hawaiian Islands. The first island they landed at was Kauai, oldest of the main islands, and there they discovered some of the original Menehune people, whom they also called the Mu. These Mu were very shy, but not unfriendly, and were sometimes helpful to the newcomers. They had stone temples and waterways and were experts at irrigation and building fishponds. (To this day there are stoneworks and temples that resemble Inca architecture). For many years the two peoples got along fairly well together and there was considerable intermarriage. It was this last point, however, that led the king of the Mu to make a harsh decision. He saw that if the intermarriage continued the Mu would disappear as a separate people, so he decided that they would have to leave. Tradition says that one night all the Mu departed from the north end of Kauai, but no one knows how or where they went.

At first the three orders of Kahuna in Hawaii were on an equal basis and commerce continued between Hawaii, Samoa and Tahiti. In the thirteenth century A.D., though, a power-hungry Kahuna of the order of Emotionals came from Samoa, ostensibly to help a reorganization of the Emotionals of Hawaii. In a short time he succeeded in gaining religious and political control of islands, with the result that contact between Hawaii & the rest of Polynesia came to a halt; the building of the great sea-going vessels was stopped; the navigational and astronomical schools were abandoned; the people became subject to a religion of superstition and restriction. The Intellectual order suffered the most and much knowledge was lost. The Intuitionists were forced into hiding for the most part, and many Emotionals turned increasingly to distorted practices. For six hundred years the people of Hawaii were subject to harsh rule, psychic terrorism and much social turmoil. By the time Captain Cook arrived, all the islands were engaged in war. The idyllic nature of Polynesian life was largely a myth perpetuated by foreigners who couldn't see below the surface.

"Throughout all of this, a small group of Intuitionists maintained telepathic contact with the rest of their order around the world, and were content to work behind the scenes for the good of mankind. Now the times have changed, and because of the rapidity of communication, the expansion of consciousness in much of the world, and the growing understanding of alternate realities, it is felt that the knowledge of Huna needs to be spread as far and wide as possible."

But of course, that's just a story….

SO THIS IS HUNA

There is no one right school. In fact there's a Hawaiian saying:

"A Ohe Pau Ko Ike I Kou Halau"

which means:

"Think not that all wisdom is in your school" –including this one, by the way. I love that phrase. I'm not saying this is the right way, the only way. It's just one model, and we certainly don't have all the answers. But it does work…

There are numerous ways to express the same thing. Sometimes people get caught up in their philosophy, getting almost righteous about it and that's always bothered me. People try and tell you the real reason why something is the way it is. According to whom right? And in the process of putting this book together I'm trying to stay true and to honour the original teachings.

Any training in esoteric studies should increase the positive character traits in the student. I think we'd all agree with that? It should bring increasing balance of the mind. What is the point of achieving a connection with the creator and infinite possibility, if you lose your rationality, livelihood, possessions and friends? The result should always be balance. You have 4 aspects to your personality – physical, mental, emotional and spiritual – any esoteric study should balance all of these. If not, there's something wrong…

The Huna author Laura Kealoha Yardley said that "The key to becoming a strong, self-contained Kahuna means creating an inner balance so strong that nothing in the external material world or the internal spiritual world can throw one off centre without the individual being aware of it and possessing the ability to re-establish that balance at will. The reason for this is that balance is not a static state that, once achieved, remains forever. Balance is ever changing, constantly shifting and rearranging itself in order to be established. There is no such thing as static balance. Therefore, in order to experience balance, a Kahuna must learn to constantly shift and rearrange himself or herself according to the exterior world he or she is experiencing. And experience is the key."

And no real teacher would ever withhold knowledge from anyone who was worthy to receive it. On the other hand, he or she cannot accept as a pupil someone who would misuse that knowledge or betray that trust.

HUNA TIMELINE

Huna is an ancient science, maybe going as far back as 33,000 BC. It was centred on a continent, which no longer exists – all that seem to remain are the mountain peak chain of islands called Hawaii. It was a system of personal development, healing and spiritual discipline known by everyone. Called the Order of I'o, it honoured men and women equally. Nothing was a secret. Nothing was taught formally. It was just "How it was". In Hawaii it was called Ho'o mana – to make mana, or life force energy. All mana comes from one source – the I'o. This is the Huna that I'd like to share with you.

In 325 AD there swept around the planet a wave of patriarchal systems, which took over and overthrew the old balanced systems. There was a real concerted effort in western Europe to remove the ancient systems. Most dictatorships take all the sacred knowledge, covet it and then burn the books, outlawing the use of such sacred wisdom by the masses. In western Europe there was Wicca, or witchcraft. The Holy Inquisition conducted by the Church killed hundreds of thousands of people. Spain had 50% of its population wiped out. Did you know that? The India tantra system was challenged by a new system called Vedanta. North America had the medicine man. In Australia there was the Aborigine Kundela, or dreamtime walker.

We're going back to 750 AD, when Kahuna Pa'ao came from Tahiti (which means "somewhere other than here") not necessarily the physical location. He actually came from Samoa, and brought with him priests and warriors. He installed his style of Huna, the order of Ku. The order of Ku introduced a number of taboos, rules, or Kapu. A kapu place would be signposted with a pair of crossed sticks topped by a ball of white cloth. Reminiscent of a pirate skull and crossbones. Also introduced human sacrifice, a practice that was never part of the Huna tradition.

The original teachings in Hawaii were concealed in the chants, and in the Hulahula (the Hula dances)

1700 The creation chant of the Kumulipo compiled by the Kahuna Keaulumoku

1778 Captain James Cook arrived – the first ever western contact on the island. Hawaiians thought he was the god Lono (god of agriculture), because the tall masts and sails of the British ships looked like the poles and banners used in ceremonies dedicated to Lono. So 10,000 Hawaiians turned out to welcome him. Then he left for America.

1779 Cook returns and lands in a sacred location dedicated to Lono (coincidence?) and has to pretend that he is indeed a god. Leaves after a few weeks. Cook is forced to return a week later with a broken mast, tempers flare, hostages are taken, Cook is bludgeoned and stabbed to death on the beach at Ka'awaloa Point on the Big Island

More Europeans visit the islands and hear tales of the Kahuna powers – telepathy, clairvoyance, healing by touch, walking unharmed over burning lava, exotic ceremonies and chants, the practices of massage and herbal medicine.

1819 The King's high priest, Hewahewa, had a vision of a powerful God and his representatives landing on the shores of Hawaii. The priest worked on the mind and willpower of his King, Kamehameha. King Kamehameha 6th ended the order of Ku, by sitting down and eating with women, an act which was Kapu, forbidden. Thereafter, a whole series of forbidden acts and laws were broken, leading to a period of temple burning, statue destruction and lawlessness

In 1820 the Christian missionaries from Boston arrived in Hawaii, exactly where the priest Hewahewa had predicted – they had a different model of the world from the natives, and tried to do away with original teachings. They found much that they couldn't understand, and much which directly challenged their own beliefs. So they changed many things, even the Hawaiian language, "to save the heathen from the pit of darkness"

The priest had brought many sick and lame people for the new god to heal – of course the missionaries could not do that, so Hewahewa realised he had wrongly interpreted his vision and he had urged the destruction of the old order of Ku for nothing! Hewahewa means "the crazy one who failed to recognise something"

1820 Laws passed to make Hula banned, against the law to dance that lewd dance until 1895. It worshipped Hawaiian gods such as Kane, the creator, Lono god of harvests and Ku god of war, which were obviously pagan gods and so should be suppressed.

Once again the new priests brought their new gods, and the original teachings were buried even deeper. The missionaries began to do away with the old "superstitious ways." In 1820, they passed the first of the laws designed to eradicate the ancient teachings:

Section 1034: Sorcery — Penalty, Any person who shall

attempt the cure of another by the practice of sorcery, witch-craft, *ananna, ho'opiopio, ho'ounauna, or ho'omanamana* or other superstitious or deceitful methods, shall, upon con-viction thereof, be fined in a sum not less than **one** hundred dollars or be imprisoned not to exceed six months at hard labor. There is also another section of the law which classes the kahuna with bunco men and defines him as one pos-ing as a kahuna, taking money under pretense of having magical power, or *admitting* he is a kahuna. For this the fine goes up to a thousand dollars and a year in prison."

— Long,1948

So, in a Pacific Island nation influenced by American Missionaries, the people were disallowed from practicing their original teachings

1881 Dr William Tufts Brigham comes to Hawaii and becomes curator of the Bishop Museum

1917 Max Freedom Long comes to Hawaii and studies Brigham's work. Brigham told him "I've been waiting for you for forty years". Witnesses and successfully accomplishes fire walking, records many cases of spontaneous healing, controlling the weather, calling sharks to the beach and other exploits, yet never learns how the Kahuna do these things

1920 Hawaiian Homes commission act demands that 50% Ha-waiian blood required to own land, a house or an acre

1936 Max Freedom Long publishes his first book "Recovering the Ancient Magic"

1941 Island of Kaho'olawe seized for use as a bombing range by the US military, despite the fact that it has 2,000 archaeological sites on it

1948 Max Freedom long publishes "The Secret Science Behind Miracles"

1953 Daddy Bray arrested in downtown Kona for chanting just like we do on Huna courses.

1959 Hawaii became a US state

1976 Pius Mau Piailug navigates a 62 foot canoe replica 2,600 miles from Hawaii to Tahiti without charts or instruments

1979 Freedom of speech in US – against the law to chant in Hawaiian until 1979 when native American religious freedoms act passed.

1983 Hawaiian language begins to be spoken and taught in schools again

1985 "The Battle of The Bones" began – Ritz Carlton resort proposed on a Hawaiian burial ground on the island of Maui

1989 last set of laws repealed – hence not heard about much. Max freedom Long, and Serge King are the only real authors. Otherwise unheard of. At last Hawaiian kids can be taught how to speak Hawaiian in Hawaii

A wave of transformation started about 1989, when the political male dominant system (communist) unravelled. There's change.....
occurring...The old schools are struggling to survive...

1993 President Clinton signed into law what has become known as the Apology Bill (Public Law 103-150). The document offers "an apology to Native Hawaiians on behalf of the United States" for using U.S. naval forces to invade Hawai'i and depose Queen Lili'uokalani in January 1893.

1994 Island of Kaho'olawe returned to state control so it can be restored

March 2003 I studied Huna with real live teachers of the ancient ways on the big Island of Hawaii. I have studied with people who know the ancient chants, the Hula, the healing techniques and the knowledge, because it is in their lineage, in their blood, in their cell memory.

What I'm about to share with you is not secret, it was illegal!! To even be talked about.

It's traditional not to call oneself a Kahuna, since a) it was illegal and b) it's best to let one's works speak for themselves. There are probably not more than 25 genuine Kahuna in Hawaii today – the genuine Kahuna have either retreated completely from society or no one realises who they are or what they can do. In Kona people searched for years to find one, even though Uncle George, one of the greats, lived on the last street out of Kona (near the hotel where we did our training).

NOW I'm passing on some of what I learned to you, and it's my pleasure.

King David began to revive the ancient dances, which came real close to being wiped out. No major cities had any Hula masters still alive. Uncle George Naope's family had preserved the dances and chants. There is a revival of alternative teachings, universal re-evaluation of life, balance, spirituality. The information is available to anyone who is willing to tune in and listen….would you agree with that?

These original teachings are returning, cos the planet's in a time of need. Huna remained pure because Hawaii is so remote. These teachings have been waiting for a time when mankind was ready to understand them again, a time when they are needed. A time when the consciousness of the people would be at a high enough level to accept and comprehend…. Some even say that the youth in Hawaii are the prophesised 7th generation – those who will recapture the knowledge of the Ka Po'e Kahiko, the People of Old.

SO WHAT IS HUNA?

Definition of word "Kahuna"

Ka	the light
Huna	secret, spiritual, concealed knowledge or wisdom protected like a treasure
Kahu	honoured or high servant who takes charge of persons,

property or knowledge

Na   calm, centred, balanced

Anyone with specialised knowledge, PhD, a Jedi Master. Someone who protected a state of calmness and balance. Keeper of the calm, centred state. There were all types of Kahuna – in politics, government, planting, fishing, child birth, negotiation, farming, canoe building, navigation, tiki (statue) carving. The areas we're interested in here include:

La'au Lapa'au	doctors of medicine, herbal healers – the first people on record to have performed an autopsy
La'au Kahea	Literally "We call the medicine" - psychologists, faith healers
Kilikilo	prediction, divination, runes
Na'auao	mystics

Kahuna Kapihe in 1850 said:

"E iho ana o luna. E pii ana o lalo.

E hui ana na moku. E ku ana ka paia."

Which means:

"Bring down that which is above by means of the light.

To ascend take from darkness into light that which is below by means of light

This will transform the spiritual energy as it flows from the source and integrates(all inside you), giving peace."

That's an interesting statement – "E hui" means to make one of all the islands. To integrate all of the parts of your unconscious mind. Similar to a technique we do in HGE.

"This will affect you profoundly, and change your life bringing illumination, and you will feel the delightful supreme fire." —Kapihe (Kahuna, 1850 Kona, HI)

Another description:

"That which is above is like that which is below, and that which is be-

low is like that which is above." — Hermes Trismegistus states the Law of Correspondence in the emerald tablet, 1500 AD or so.

Do you know what that means? It means there's no difference between you and the rest of the universe. Western schools teach objective thinking, so its OK to rape and pillage the planet, have acid rain, erode the ozone layer. In ancient times the belief was that you were one with the universe. It's western man who believes otherwise. We are connected to other people, and the land, and the planet.

"And 144 (thousand) light warriors with their shields balanced, respecting all paths as leading to one shall come to the planet in her time of need and teach the teachers." — Hopi Indian Legend.

So Huna was the secret teaching behind all other secret teachings. 80% of the content has never been published in writing. Originally it was called Ho'o mana.

Ho'o = to make

Mana = Energy, Chi, Ki, Life force = empowering yourself.

Everything you do requires energy, and the more energy you have, the longer you will live, and the more you can do with your life. It's all about making connections with sources of Mana, and we're going to do that in this section. Now that may sound weird and "out there" to you, but there are corresponding systems that you already be familiar with:

Having a Higher Self/Guardian Spirit— Native American, Hermetic(western Europe) and alchemy

4/5 Elements-	Alchemy, Hermetics, Egyptian Magic, Tantra, Western and Japanese astrology
Entering the Dream Time (Moe Uhane)-	Native American, Maori in New Zealand, Aborigine in Australia.
Herbs in Healing-	Native American, Chinese, etc.
Energy Healing-	Philippines psychic surgery, Reiki, Chinese Acupuncture

Numerology-	Cabalah, Pythagoras, Japanese astrology, numbers and their vibrational essence
Astrology-	Most systems use the stars and planets to predict
Chanting -	Native American, Aborigine, Maori, Tantra

Of course these should all correspond if they all came from the same source...? Now is the time for the revival of ancient teachings – a shift is occurring...

So let's begin with a couple of core concepts that are at the heart of Huna.

HUNA'S PROCESS OF EVOLUTION

There's a big picture description of what Huna is really about. Would you would like the big picture? This kind of gives you the larger frame, into which everything else we cover in this chapter will fit.

To begin with, we have several bodies, all connected together:

Physical body people – driven by basic drives, not very evolved

Some are Physical + Emotional, so they feel a lot but aren't very intellectual

Some are Physical + Mental, but not emotional, so they dissociate from feelings

Ideal is to develop them all – have a healthy physical body to live in, understand and feel emotions, have a developed intellect and focus, and be connected to a spiritual power that's bigger than you. As we grow up and get older, each of the bodies evolves with us, doesn't it?

HUNA CODE OF FORGIVENESS

There are 3 words in Hawaiian translated as the word "sin"

HALA — To miss the path, To err by omission, failing to do something that needs to be done. An error of judgement. (Also: Repressed, denial, avoidance, feeling sorry for .... sadness, guilt not enforcing your boundaries)

HEWA — to go overboard. To do to excess. Can and ought to be rectified.

(Also: Excesses, obsessions, addictions perfectionism, anger, hate, revenge)

But neither of these were classed as a real sin, because the only real sin was to consciously and knowingly hurt another human being.

'INO — To do intentional harm to someone with hate in mind.

Leads to the boomerang effect, where the bad karma comes right back at you

(Self-harm, self-Judgment, self-deprecation)

You may like to think of how these categories apply in your life so far.

Then we move onto what to do about it:

1. "E iho ana o Luna, e Pi'I ana o lalo"
2. Bring to light all material that is Hala, Hewa or 'Ino and then release it using some sort of therapy, be it Time Line Therapy, HGE, Hypnosis or Higher Self Therapy.
3. Balance the male & female energies in the bodies - Balance Yin and Yang
4. Train the neurology so it can be aware of the higher vibrational energies, by expanding the consciousness though meditation, breathing and chanting.

THE 3 SELVES

You probably know that you have a conscious mind, don't you? The part of you that answered - that was it! Did you know that you also have an unconscious..........mind as well? And you may also realise that you have a Higher Self too.

Let me ask you a quick question:

1. Who are you?

      What labels do you have?

      What kind of a person are you?

2.   Is that who you think you are?

3.   Is that all you think you are?

4.   Aren't you more than that?"

5.   What are you that's not (the previous identification)?

      I want a verbal answer here.

6.   And beyond (the word elicited in #5), is that all you are?

      How much more are you than that?

      "You do know you are more than that, don't you?"

7.   How do you know?

      You're more than just a Conscious Mind

      Conscious Mind – thinks, I am

      Unconscious Mind – feelings, I feel. Runs your body, beats your heart, the "body/mind"

      Higher Conscious Mind also, with different functions

THE THREE SELVES

INNER EXPRESSION Inside the person		OUTER EXPRESSION Outside the person Tikis (statues)
Aumakua	Higher Con Mind	Kane Uncarved upright stone, formless
Uhane	Con Mind	Lono Eyes closed – no experience of outside world Tall headdress – lofty imagination Not touching ground – no connection with material world
Unihipili	Uncon Mind	Ku Eyes partially open – filters outside world Short headdress – not very creative Streamers touch ground – full contact with material

The Boston Missionaries who arrived on Hawaii in 1820 decided that the local islanders couldn't think as deeply or as logically as they could, so obviously they were heathens. Unfortunately they didn't realise that there was no incidence of mental illness on the islands prior to the missionaries arrival.

The Conscious Mind is the one you think with, and the Hawaiians called it Uhane, which means soul or spirit. It's that logical, reasonable part of you, the one who says "I am…, or I think…"

The Unconscious Mind was called Unihipili, the seat of our emotions, runs your body, makes your heart beat, continues to breathe, blinks your eyes, digests your food, repairs cuts. How much do you **trust your Unconscious Mind?** The Kahuna taught that **learning to trust your Unconscious Mind was the first step to mastery.** The Unconscious has certain functions, which we'll call the Prime Directives, and these are to be found earlier in this book.

Then there are the 4 bodies, which we discussed earlier in this book:

THE FOUR BODIES

FORMATION OF THE 4 BODIES

The four bodies mature at different times in your life. The Emotional body develops between 18 and 22, the Mental Body between age 28 and 32, and the Spiritual Body between 38 and 42. Most people experience big shifts in their identity during those periods as the body activates and grows. How about you? These are huge learning curves, and we may or may not optimise that body's development at that time. A friend of mine called this an AFOG (another F*****G opportunity for growth).

The spiritual body activation is often called a "mid life crisis". Unresolved emotional issues come up, and if they are cleared, all is well. If not, men may find problems with relationships, expressing intimacy, and family values. This can lead to heart disease if unresolved. In women, who they are and what they want comes up. If resolved, the life shocks will spill out and she'll become very expressive. If blocked, it can cause thyroid problems.

Again, all the more reason to learn HGE, build your energy and clear out any unresolved issues.

ENERGY

Mana is life force energy. It's called Chi in China, Ki in Japan, Shakti or Prana in east Indian system. The hypnotist Mesmer called it "animal magnetism". Huna was originally called Ho'o mana – the Hawaiians said there was only one real difference between someone who was dead and someone who was alive – one has energy, or mana. And only one's breathing…

Really simple, and really profound. But then, profound things are really simple. Like that last sentence.

Anything that adds life – is good. Anything that takes away life/decreases aliveness is bad. So some days you have tons of energy and you race to work. Other days are heavy gravity days, when you look over the quilt, the sun is too bright, the sheet wraps itself around your ankle and you just slide slowly back into sleep…

So begin now to pay attention to the energy in your body. The Huna diet book would be one page: Eat it and have low energy, stop eating it. Eat & energy up? Eat more!

What is your energy doing inside you? How is it feeling inside of you?

You see low levels of mana leads to sickness and dis-ease, and premature ageing. Most esoteric studies taught that if life force energy was low or depleted, or maybe stuck and stagnant, ultimately that would lead to physical dis-ease. High levels of mana leads to empowerment and health, youthfulness and longevity. Imagine sending mana up to the Higher Self, and then having it come back down into the Unconscious Mind, turbo charged. Like rocket fuel.

Then there's the ancient Hawaiian chants. Why chant? Why not let them die? Because they won't, they remain alive. As in Sanskrit the sounds of the chants invoke the essence of the content. Language captured the spiritual essence in every word. When I first heard chanting in Hawaiian, it unnerved me. Really. There was something primal, old and powerful about it. The second time I heard it, I felt physical pain. (Energy blockage that I later cleared up). The words hold the vibration. Paul Goodwin, a doctor in Alaska, says we have 10 to the power of 10 to the 11th neurological connections in our nervous systems. That's more than all the grains of sand all over the planet. More stars than in the visible sky. Yet only 1 tenth are active in the neurology. What do you think the other 90% are for?

Chants make new neurological connections to expand your neurology, and your consciousness. So why not chant in English? Well, English is a mental language. All airline chat is English. Did you know you can't fly in Arabic? – the concepts are not there. English is like Computer language – its easily stored on a PC in a small space.

People tell me the Catholic mass in Latin had a completely different feeling from English. The energy changed dramatically when it changed to English. Like Hebrew, and Greek, ancient languages capture the essence, and Hawaiian is one of, if not the oldest. In Hawaiian there are 7 consonants

H K L M N P W and 5 vowels. English has 22 consonants.

When the Missionaries arrived, they were wearing tall hats, long woollen trousers, dark coats and long underwear, because that was the way one dressed. The natives wore a lot less. Clearly they were inferior and were far less spiritually aware! So a lot of Huna knowledge was hidden in the chants, dances and stories. When the missionaries couldn't accept the basic idea that the Hawaiian ancestors had come from another planet, how on earth could they be trusted with even more sacred teachings?

I've included a chant in this chapter and the English translation too. This chant is used in a Hula festival –it's the entry chant when the Hula dancers come onstage.

HO'OPUKA E-KA-LA MA KAHIKINA

Ho'opuka e-ka-la ma ka hikina
(me) Kahua ka'i hele no tumutahi
Ha'a mai na'i wa me Hi'iaka

(me) Tapo laka ika ulu wehiwehi
Nee mai na'i wa ma ku'u alo
Ho'i no'o e te tapu me na'ali'i e
E ola makou a mau loa lae
Eala, eala, ea. A ie ilei ie ie ie.
He inoa no ma ka hikina
(A chant to invoke the dawning of enlightenment)

People often ask "Is Huna a religion?" I think there are some fundamental differences. The author Max Freedom Long put it this way:

In religion one worships a supreme being, picturing it usually as a man, one fears him, so one prays to him for favours, bribes him with sacrifices, worships him and obeys his imagined laws. In Huna, you loved (not worshipped) the Higher Self, a totally trustworthy parental spirit and a part of you, which lays no laws on you, in a relationship of mutual love and respect. There were no books, no religion, no philosophical needs, no salvation, and no hell. Now which sounds more appealing?

All knowledge was traditionally kept in the church. In ancient times all sacred knowledge was kept in the religions. My definition of a religion is that it's ritualised spirituality. In Huna the La'au Kahea were pysychologists - Mental disease was virtually unknown in Hawaii. The Hawaiian Kahuna La'au Lapa'au healers are on record as having performed the first autopsy. I don't believe that Huna is a religion. Think of it this way. In Hawaii there is Hiiaka (a goddess). But what are gods and goddesses? Merely a personification of an energy pattern. Hurricanes have women's names, but that was sexist, so Hurricane Roy was named. It's an energy pattern with a name. You have healing energy inside you – you can make neurological connections so you can heal yourself inside.

HA BREATHING

Let's re-learn how to breathe. Before doing something in Hawaii, the native Hawaiian took a breath to get in touch with their energy. Then the white folks arrived on Hawaii, and in fact they didn't breathe first, they just went straight into the activity. Hawaiians went "they don't breathe!"

Rather simply, the Hawaiians looked at the difference between someone who's alive, and someone who's dead. What's the difference? One has energy, one doesn't. Oh, and when they die, they stop breathing. Therefore, there must be a link between life force energy, and breathing. So many of the ancient teachings on the planet taught breathing techniques.

The words "Ha" and "ole" mean breath and without, and to this day white people are called "haoles". So here I am, a Scottish haole, writing about Hawaiian secrets.

There's a legend: a sailor arrives off the boat, asks a native "Where do you live?" He answers "Ha Wai I".

The first ships landed at Captain Cook – amazing eh? How did they know to land there? (Just kidding). So they sail to another island and ask another native the same question – and got the same answer "Ha Wai I". Is this place called Hawaii? Yes! So they named it. All the islands are called that. But they missed the point – it's not just a place in the Pacific.

Ha = breath Wai = water, Mana, Life Force I = supreme

What the Native was saying was "I live in the supreme life force that rides on the breath". It's a place inside you where all your energy resides. You can get in touch with it anytime. You don't need a metal pyramid, or a headdress, or crystals. You can stop – take a deep breath in through the nose, and breathe out while whispering the word "Ha". The Out breath should be twice as long as in breath.

In ancient China this was known only by the Emperor and royal family – teaching it outside the Royal Court was rumoured to be punishable by death. This is Ha breathing – calming, centering, increasing your energy.

It's late, you're at work, and you're wilting. Don't drink more coffee – just breathe. Long day at work , you're going out at night - breathe. You get home and your dog has ate your sofa – breathe! The Kahuna would do that in a group, for up to 6 hours at a time! Fill the entire lung, and the belly goes **out** on in breath, just like a baby breathes. There's probably stale air down there that hasn't moved in years!

Try that right now:

Then the middle part of the lungs

Then the top of your lungs, up under your shoulders

Now the entire lung

If dizzy, yawning or hyperventilating, just stop and relax and get comfortable again

Ha breathing opens up your neurology, makes you alert, calm, and energised.

Imagine a rain barrel of water (energy) over your head, and you're squeezing it into your body through an eye dropper

First a chant for opening up the breathing apparatus – just read the chant out loud as best you can and notice what happens inside you....

PA KAMAKANI

Ai, Pa Kamakani na'ue ta lau oka niu

Ai, Ai, Ai,

Pa kamakani na'ue ta lau oka niu

Ha'a Ka Pua kou wale ike kula

Leha Ka maka oka manu ai Pua Lehua

Ha'u ka waha oke ka huli'i Kanahele

Li ta i'o o ta'auhelemoa la

Eala Eala ea.

Kahiko ula ka lama ika pali

0 Kihekihe ka-ua-ke nana aku

Na'ue ia e ua wale mai no

Kiki'i ka ua nana ika lani

Hiki ta haili o pua i ka'u pea la

Eala, Eala ea.

A ie ilei ie ie ie.

He inoa no Ka'auhelemoa

A chant in the honour of the continuously falling fine rain, rising up.

EXERCISE

Now try 5 minutes of Ha breathing.

HAKALAU - CHANGING CONSCIOUSNESS AT WILL

Bothered about limiting decisions or bad events in your past? We talked about Hakalau, or peripheral vision, in the presenting skills chapter in this book. It allows you to expand your awareness & your consciousness. "Hakalau" means focus in and spread out at the same time – how can you do that? It's a form of peripheral vision – where you more attention on the peripheral than the focussed.

In all traditions Kahuna (learned ones) or Shamans can access expanded states of awareness quickly. A Trance state – focussed, expanded and alert. In most cultures they used a hallucinogenic drink, root, or smoke. I like Hawaiian Huna because they believed in being self sufficient, and not to rely on such props. It's also healthier!

Would it be useful to be calm? Need some way of staying externally focussed, so you don't internal dialogue yourself crazy? Would you like to be able to learn more, and more quickly? If there was a way to make negative emotions vanish at will...you'd at least be curious to try it out, wouldn't you?

This is the active meditation of the Kahuna – "To stare at, and to allow to spread out"

Foveal vision is the sharp search light focus that you have when you look at something. Peripheral vision is everything else that's blurry. Now when you're in Sympathetic (Stress) mode you'll be in Foveal (focussed) When you're in Parasympathetic (Relaxed) mode you'll be in peripheral, staring at the sky or gazing distantly out of the window. Relaxed, receptive, externally focussed.

"Na" as in Kahuna means calm, centred, quiet. Other cultures used mildly hallucinogenic substances, or rattles and drums to induce trance. Anything that's rhythmic will do that. In Hawaii it was thought best to be self-sufficient, and not to rely on external props, be able to just go into the state at will. This technique can be a real eye opener! The steps are almost identical to Patanjali's description in the Yoga Sutras

1. Ho'ohaka: Just pick a spot on the wall to look at, preferably above eye level, so that your field of vision seems to bump up against your eyebrows, but the eyes are not so high as to cut off the field of vision. Slightly upward, 45 degrees preferably. That's the way you start this, after a while you won't have to do that again.

2. Kuu: "To let go." As you stare at this spot, just let your mind go loose, and focus all of your attention on the spot.

3. Lau: "To spread out" Notice that within a matter of moments, your vision begins to spread out, and you see more in the peripheral than you do in the central part of your vision. Notice you can begin to pick up information in the peripheral

4. Hakalau: Now, pay attention to the peripheral. In fact, pay more attention to the peripheral than to the central part of your vision.

5.   Ho'okohi: Stay in this state for as long as you can. Notice how it feels. As you do it for a while begin to notice the giggly, ecstatic feelings that bubble up from inside. It seems to be impossible to feel a negative state in this state

Kahuna spent most of their lives in this state. Certainly when outdoors in nature – they'd see small movements in the woods, the water, in the air. On the ground.

Here's the challenge – once you're good, you can get into state in a matter of seconds, and notice how far out 180 degrees on either side you can see. Get in touch with it, pull it around all the way behind you….. Like Radar, all the way behind you. Your awareness fills the entire room . You may not sense it visually, you can begin to feel the energy patterns as though you saw them, all the way around you. That's why it was so important – one becomes totally connected to your environment. This is the process. Expanded awareness - bring your eyes down, but stay in that state of Hakalau

Once you've got that, move around yet stay in that state. Stand up, walk around, staying in hakalau, walk normally. As you turn keep connected to what's around and behind you. Try this for five minutes. When you feel you can keep that state well, come back & sit down.

Use this all of the time, until it becomes automatic. The more you do it the easier it is to let go of negative emotions. Many Shaman won't actually make eye contact with you cos it could interfere with their state (actually you should be able to look someone in the eye and still be in Hakalau)

Let's extend this, and meditate on the light.

MEDITATION ON THE LIGHT

There is an old Hawaiian legend that says when the Creator was creating earth, there were not enough Higher Selves to go around.

Each Higher Self needed was like a small seedling of light and they came across space to here. This chant is designed to recreate that within ourselves. The chant No Luna E Kahale Kai

Last word is Pele, the goddess of the volcano in Hawaii, also Kundelini energy that travels up your spine. There are no snakes in Hawaii. The word Puna, or "spring" is also a code word for the Kundelini energy rising up over the head

NO LUNA E KAHALE KAI

Ai, No luna e ka hale kai o ka ma'alewa

Ai, Ai, Ai,

No luna e ka hale kai o ka ma'alewa

Nana ka maka e moani nui ka lehua la

Ho'ohihi kai o maliu mai

I kua e la ka lehua ila ila la

Eala eala ea, llaila hoi*

Ho po'e ka lehua kiekie ia la

Maka u ka lehua i ke kanaka la

Lilo a ilalo e hele ai ea la eala ea

Ilalo hoi

0 keaau ili ill nehe i ke kai

E ho'olono I ke ka'i la o puna la ea

0 puna I ka ulu hala la

Eala eala ea Kaiko'o puna e

A ie ilei ie ie ie.

He inoa no Hi'iaka ika poli ao Pele

Hiolani, or meditation on the light, is a very deep meditation used by the Kahuna to increase their ability to focus, as well as enter a deep, calm, meditative state. You can experience a time of thoughtlessness, or silence inside. No internal dialogue.

An ancient chant says "let the light radiate from its source from the heavens above to me here below, first I roll my eyes up and right, then up & to the left, then I lift my eyes straight up & I open up the heavens and the fine misty rain of light begins to flow to me – it brings me the skills that I need, the supreme vision and the mana"

Hio = to lean upon

Lani = the heavens

This technique stimulates the 3rd eye, the Pineal gland

HIOLANI

1. OKu'u: Find a comfortable place to sit - in a chair or upright on the ground will do. Darken the room, or cover the eyes so that no external light gets in. (This is important, at least the first time you do it.)

2. Ha: If you wish, begin by doing 5 to 15 minutes of Ha breathing as described above.

3. Ka'a: Roll the eyes up and to the right, then up and to the left, and then straight up to the heavens. Focus the eyes, without strain, as if looking up at the sky, on the space between the eyebrows. (You can roll the eyes up even more if it is comfortable.) Remember the kinesthetic (feeling) of Hakalau, and take that into meditation with you. Be comfortable. This is where you will see the light.

4. Kala: E iho ana o luna. As you look up to the space between the eyebrows, focus on the light. Pay attention to the light, let the light come to you, welcome the light. Watch the light. (If as you begin, you do not see the light easily, just press lightly on your eyeballs pushing them up and inward. Hold for the count of 5. Then let go, and watch the light.) It can be any colour, and will probably start dim, getting brighter.

5. Kuu: "To let go." Now, just let go and watch the light. If there are other thoughts, and light is still there, that's OK. If you've forgotten to pay attention to the light, just bring your attention to the light. Let the light come to you – welcome

the light

6. No'o: At the same time, meditation; concentration on the light. No'ono'o: Thought, reflection, thinking, meditation — to think, reflect, meditate, concentrate on, and consider the light.

EXERCISE

Do that exercise, then write down your experience.

Patanjali's Yoga Sutra's mention "From meditation on the light in the head, comes knowledge of things which are subtle, hidden or far distant". Practice this and you'll be able to go into an altered state more and more rapidly. It permanently expands your consciousness, and increases your ability to focus and concentrate – as you go up in HGE you learn that **energy flows where attention goes**. It also increases your ability to visualise – to see clearly, inside...

Now what happens if you're trying to grow and evolve, but you have some energy vampires around you, or you're hanging onto past hurts? Huna teaches a process to deal with that...

HO'O PONO PONO

Means "To make right" – double up the "Pono" in Hawaiian means to make **doubly right**. This is a process where you align with and clear up relationships with people in our lives. The Huna belief is that we all carry within us as Parts of us that represent all of the significant people in our lives. Ever talk to someone in your head as if they were here? Then that's what they're talking about.

What if they're not supporting us in our growth & evolution? If you're trying to heal, or help someone else heal, you need your energy. What if you're connected to people who are draining you? Imagine invisible connections with people. Or even co-dependent relationships, where it's important to make them stand on their own two feet. Massage therapists, or any therapy in fact. Think of all the connections they'd make with all of their clients. Energy can't be destroyed, it can only change form. So if you help clear out somebody's stuck energy, it has to go somewhere. And if you're a personal growth enthusiast, chances are you are clean and evolved. Great place for the client's stuck energy to climb into…

Cut connections at the end of each day is the advice here. Or if you run long training courses. Student/teacher relationships should be empowering connections. All groups must die eventually – group psychology teaches that. Cut the connections. At the end of my Practitioner & Master Practitioner courses we run this process. People's ideas of you can keep you stuck. Doubting Thomas's – you come home after a transformational seminar & they burst your bubble. Or worse – do you hate anyone – want revenge on anyone? You've despised them for years – have they noticed? The more you hate them the more you carry them with you. You bind people you hate to you as much as if you loved them. Negative emotions connected to any other person binds them to you

The field around your body is sticky – the Hawaiians called it "Aka". The aura sticks to people you touch. You might see energy connections between us, made up of Aka.

Everything you've ever touched, you're still connected to! Imagine that! Every person you touch, or who has touched you. Strong emotions make the Aka connection stronger, and you can do it over distance – strong thoughts connect you. It doesn't even need touch!

Remember siphoning in science at school? Energy flows from one person to the other, back & forth. So if you have tons or energy, it flows to them. If you're tired, you steal from them. The quality of energy affects you also. Ever felt drained after being with someone? They took your energy! Or ever been in an "icky" part of town – leaves you tired, down. This is the basis of Feng Shui – energy being connected with places, and objects. In some cases you may feel like you've picked up a thought form from someone – in the three etheric bodies. Thoughts are things. Powerful thoughts can get in and attach to you. Some people call this possession. This process is for that.

A famous Kahuna was on her death bed and she told her students "I want you to let me go, if you mourn and grieve about me you could hold me here and I want to go."

So here's how to do the process of Ho'o pono pono. Alternatively you can get this process, and all of the other Huna techniques discussed in this chapter, on the "Introduction to Huna" CD set.

Construct a stage in your minds eye, below and in front of you, so you're looking down on it. You'll invite people up onto the stage, then imagine an infinite source of love and healing, healing them up quickly. You forgive them, they forgive you. Now I know that some people don't deserve your forgiveness – know what I mean? You bind people to you with your hate of them through the Aka. You're holding them to you. The highest form of revenge is indifference – so what? So I recommend you run this process. You decide who to forgive. Your unconscious mind will bring appropriate people up on stage. You're going to have a discussion which basically asks "Are you totally willing to support my magnificence and my connectedness with Higher Self today?". If they say Yes = send them off, thanks a lot. If they say No – stay on the stage. That question will help uncover your intention, or your perception of theirs. What kind of energy do you want to stay connected to? Dodgy bars, or sacred places? Then you'll cut the aka connections, and we'll close with a chant which brings in a lot of healing energy

EXERCISE

START WITH 5 MINUTES OF HA BREATHING
Get comfortable
Free your mind of other thoughts

Construct a small stage in your mind upon which we will bring certain people

The first is your parents – your mother & father

And the question to ask is "Are you willing to totally support my magnificence & my experience of my connection with higher self today?"

If the answer's yes, give them a hug, thank them

If the answer's no, ask them to remain on the stage

Next are your children, if you have any

➡

Next are brothers & sisters, or anyone who acted as that

➡

Next aunts & uncles & cousins

➡

Next current friends

➡

Next old friends, childhood friends

➡

Next is Ex's – ex girlfriend/boyfriend, husband, wife

➡

Next is teachers, mentors, bosses and ex-bosses – anybody like that

➡

Then co-workers and colleagues

➡

Anyone no longer alive

➡

Anyone else who your unconscious mind now suggests should be there – anyone who's not supportive, anyone who you have incompletes with, unresolved issues.

The people still on the stage are meant to be there…

Imagine an infinite source of love and healing above the top of your head. Allow it to come in through the top of your head, (from your Higher Self) and fill up your body, now, and that you become totally whole and totally healed & then allow it to overflow out your heart and fill up the people on the stage, until he/she is totally whole and healed

As soon as you get a sense that they are totally healed, which happens rather quickly..have a discussion about forgiveness. Have them say what they need to say, you say what needs to be said

As simple maybe as "I forgive you, do you forgive me?"

Whatever needs to be said....

Somewhere along the way some of them may just disappear, some may float off, you may be able to see the aka connection between the two of you, cut it and draw the nearest end back inside of you

If they are not forgiving you, then your Unconscious Mind is not letting go of them, and I'm not asking you to forgive them, that person, I'm asking you to forgive the part of you that's them......... forgive yourself ultimately

Continue the flow of love and healing

Heal yourself at the deepest level, integrate and become one

Make sure as they float off or disappear, cut that aka connection with them

If you've already finished just remain in a calm, centred state...... and we'll conclude this with a chant

Imagine an infinite source of love and healing above the top of your head. Allow it to come in through the top of your head, (from your Higher Self) and fill up your body, now, and that you become totally whole and totally healed & then allow it to overflow out your heart and fill up the people on the stage, even the negative thought forms, until he/she is totally whole and healed

You do deserve forgiveness, because at your ultimate you are simply a being of energy

This is a great way of clearing Negative Emotions that are related to a particular person – so it makes a good intervention. Is this real?

Of course not (nodding).

You're forgiving the part of you that is them, not them. We're asking you to forgive yourself. Sometimes people will call you up or mention it to you, at exactly the point where you sever the connection. The connection then gets remade in a way that supports both of you.

If you've already finished just remain in a calm, centred state......and we'll conclude this with a chant

As the legend goes in ancient times there were no healing traditions before the Kahuna, no traditions of anyone healing anyone else, there came from Tahiti (anywhere other than here) a group of healers called Alaneo who taught the Hawaiians how to heal, which became the healing techniques of ancient Hawaii. This chant asks them to return now, to revisit us and to bring their healing energy again.

"He kanaka loa
he kanaka poko
He ui-aa-he alaneo
A na maka
pa I ka lani
Malu ka honua
Ia kama uhili e
Hee nei Ku
I ka moe au
a ke Kahuna"

The alaneo taught the Hawaiians to heal. When the alaneo left one by one they returned to Tahiti, somewhere other than here, and when the last 4 Alaneo left, as a reminder to the people, that each person has healing power in and of themselves, the last 4 Alaneo turned themselves to stone. And even today on Koheu beach at Waikiki on the island of Oahu, people come from all over the world to visit the alaneo stones, and are miraculously healed.......by their own power.

"He kanaka loa
he kanaka poko
He ui-aa-he alaneo
A na maka
pa I ka lani
Malu ka honua
Ia kama uhili e
Hee nei Ku
I ka moe au
a ke Kahuna"

PERCEPTION IS PROJECTION

One of the first major teachings of magic is to get away from the beliefs that society has taught you. Now it's not easy to go against the trend. It's far easier to remain plugged into the Matrix. So let's unplug you some more...

Modern science is still dominated by Newtonian Physics, which says we are separate from our universe. People continually demand "Prove it to me!". If you can prove it, it's valid. "I'll believe it when you prove it to me". Unfortunately, with the phenomenon called "Research Bias", you can always find proof that something is true, or false, depending on your bias.

That's funny, because just over a hundred years ago people went by Faith. Faith = belief, or "our experience proves it". The men who started Quantum Physics now regret ever doing so. They say that if you don't find Quantum Mechanics appalling, then you don't understand it. String Theory now talks about there actually being 36 dimensions. We can only currently perceive four. Maybe you're reading this book right now and laughing at the outdated theories in it!

Kristin Zambucka said in her book "The Seed" : "Though I may travel far I will meet only what I carry with me, for every man is a mirror. We see only ourselves reflected in those around us. Their attitudes and actions are reflections of our own. The whole world and its conditions has its counterpart within us all. Turn the gaze inward. Correct yourself and your world will change."

Go back and look at the HGE communication model. Here's the argument. The world is your creation – even if it's not true, you'd better believe it. Everything in the Universe is you! Your Universe is yours! There's nothing outside of you that isn't you. You filter everything as it comes in, but what if it works the same way on the way out? What if your body is like an overhead projector, and the light streaming out is your energy. Your model of the world is the acetate, and what shows up on the screen (your reality) is exactly what's written on the acetate.

The Hawaiian belief was that every night, when you go to sleep, your Higher Self comes down into your Physical Body and collects all of your wants, needs, desires, hopes, dreams….and fears, dreads, anger, sadness, fear, guilt, hurt and limiting beliefs, and then creates your future for the next segment of your timeline. That explains why people keep getting very mixed results! Guess what happens if you clear out all of the negative emotions and limiting beliefs using Time Line Therapy?

You're projecting holographically in 360 degrees, all of the time! You filter 2 million bits of information per second down to 134 per second, and leave bits in that fit your map of the world. Remember that the 5 senses are just electrical interpretations in your brain. You don't experience raw data, you experience your interpretation of the data. So what's real? Anything that has substance? Your thoughts have no substance. Are they real? What's the sound of one mind clapping?

So ask yourself, the people in your world – are they happy? Angry? Have money? In good relationships? Are they like you? Could it be that they are just grey silhouettes, until you look at them, when you project a hologram over them of how you *expect* them to look and behave. You see, a person can't behave in any other way than the way you believe they will. So expect the best. As Virginia Satir, America's leading Family Therapist once asked:

> *"With whom am I now having the pleasure?*
> *You, or my picture of you?"*

Your world is a projection of you. Quantum Physics says that reality is relative to the observer. Every person creates a unique world which can never be 100% identical to that of another. Observation changes reality – just by being present, you alter the course of events.

Everything in your world is there for your learning, so that you can control your future!

Remember the Neurological Levels model from the start of this book:

Neurological Levels

NEUROLOGY

LANGUAGE

- SPIRITUALITY
- IDENTITY
- BELIEFS
- CAPABILITIES
- BEHAVIOURS
- ENVIRONMENT

SYMPATHETIC/PARASYMPATHETIC NERVOUS SYSTEM

IMMUNE SYSTEM Defence

AUTONOMIC NERVOUS SYSTEM Blood pressure, heart rate, digestion

SEMI CONSCIOUS REACTIONS

CONSCIOUS ACTIONS

REFLEXES Peripheral Nervous System

FOR WHAT PURPOSE? Higher Self, Mission, Why I am here, what's bigger than me?

WHO? Who I believe I am, Value

WHY? X means Y, what I believe is true

HOW? Skills, strategies, How prog it seem, what I'm capable of

WHAT? Habits, what I usually do

WHERE? When? Surrounds, results, geography

Imagine yourself standing at the top of this pyramid, looking out at your world. Your sense of why you're here (indeed your Higher Self) will affect and shape your purpose and drive, and therefore your future. That purpose and drive will affect your sense of self or identity, thus determining what you believe, what you're capable of doing and ultimately your external environment, house, bank account, relationships, everything. Doesn't that make a lot of sense?

Evil can only exist if it exists in your mind, and only what you allow. If you feel like a victim you are probably victimising someone. If you feel like you are being manipulated, you are probably manipulating. People who act as caretakers for others may be avoiding taking care of themselves. What you see is who you are. The people in your life are a barometer of your experience of life. The significant people in your world are a reflection of your internal state

HOW WE CONSTRUCT REALITY
- We create what we observe.
- We observe with our minds.
- Observations are measurements.
- Measurements transform nothing into something.
- We make measurements through our language.

"Reality are those myths that we haven't seen through yet" – Alberto Villoldo, Ph.D.

A Kahuna wouldn't do a healing if there was someone present who didn't believe, or was there to prove it didn't work (and if there was, that was the Kahuna's projection). So they'd go home and work on themselves, asking "For what purpose did I create a doubter or sceptic? Where am I doubting myself?". As inside, so outside. Everything you love about your partner is you. And everything you hate about them is you also. There is a theory that we marry our Unconscious Mind and blame all our unresolved stuff on them. You can't see something you're not. The more energy you give it, the more you'll find it. "Energy flows where attention goes".

What's more, for you to perceive something in someone, it has to exist in you. Perception is projection. So it's not them, it's you. What you observe is an aspect of you. Heal it in you and it vanishes outside. You did not consciously choose to create this problem, but you may have unconsciously. And your unconscious mind has only positive intentions for you in everything that it does.

One of the biggest challenges I've had to overcome was to accept the following truth – whenever I see a person displaying a trait that drives me nuts, that's also the trait in me that I haven't accepted yet. Whatever they do that bothers me mirrors something that I haven't yet come to terms with, in myself or in someone from my past.

For example, I remember sitting on a bus listening to an acquaintance telling tall stories to entertain the other passengers, and I was seething inside, infuriated by his need to be significant. It was months later when I realised that I was jealous of the attention he was getting.

As Joseph Campbell said, "If you don't learn it, you end up marrying it". If you don't get the learning's, it just keeps coming back, bigger and worse than before. And better to get it at the unconscious level, than just the mental level. Think about that – what are some of the repeating patterns that you keep generating for yourself, over and over again? The arguments, the health patterns, money hiccups, betrayals, upsets. Make a list of three patterns that you've noticed repeating in your life.

Now what's the common denominator? You are!

You know, if your cars keep breaking down one vehicle after another, maybe it's not the cars that need fixing – maybe it's the driver...

And if you're getting smart with this, just remember you can't say someone else is projecting their stuff onto you, because they're still *your* projection!

CLEANING UP YOUR PROJECTIONS

Go easy on yourself! It's focussing you on what you want, it's perfect!

A psychologist will work on the last time the pattern repeated. An HGE practitioner wants to find the first time it happened, when the imprint was created in the first place. Clear that and it'll never happen again.

Apply to self – where else am I doing this?

I've created a projection of….

Now - What do I need to learn from this, such that if I clear it, this will never happen again?

How can I prevent this from happening again?

What's the need in you that's unmet at the moment?

Clear any negative emotion with Higher Self Therapy, Time Line therapy, or Hakalau

GET THE LEARNING

Clear Limiting Decisions with Higher Self Therapy or Time Line Therapy

GET THE LEARNING

Do Ho'o Pono Pono

Test & Future Pace – Is it bothering me?

Dwell on the new outcome

The highest form of revenge is indifference

Let it go so you no longer "get plugged in"

What if you really could create what you want – what would you ask for? Your thoughts are law in your universe. Taneo Sands Kumelae said "The people you hate, you bind to you as much as if you loved them". If you notice it, you're projecting it right now. If its unresolved, it'll keep coming back until you get the learning's.

"If you don't pay with attention, you pay with pain"

A Little Black Bag opens up – ask yourself "What is the learning I need to get right now to let this go?". Oh and by the way, there's usually another set at a higher evolutionary level, so there's always more to clear. The lesson of life is Physical Emotional Mental Spiritual. You deal with a problem on one level, but later in life it comes back, at another level. So a physical problem you had years ago may return, but this time it's from a spiritual challenge. Something you clear may come back again on a different level. We need to keep evolving and growing in that direction.

You achieve a new state of consciousness, then stuff comes up to be handled. The next time a major issue returns, look at the opportunity – go where the resistance is

You can't clear it out if you don't know its there. Awareness is Progression.

It's like a Xmas tree with fairy lights on it, but the room is dark and the lights are off.. You have to put the lights on before you can see where all the lights are, so you can unravel it safely from the tree. Light up the Xmas tree first. We talk about that in my Master Practitioner courses – you have to get the client fully associated into the problem before you attempt to blow it out. In reframing, you ask them to restate the problem just before you reframe them. It's like in computers, you have to highlight the file before you press delete.

OK, so let's look at the third self, the highest and best of any person, and what it does.

PRIME DIRECTIVES OF THE HIGHER CONSCIOUS MIND

Let's look at the Prime Directives of the Higher Self, or Aumakua. That's a grab bag term for any parental spirit – ancestors and any gods. Your higher self, the higher mind of mankind. Manao Iaau was another name, and it has many roles. Once again thanks to my Huna teacher Dr Tad James for the following:

1. Guardian Spirit (over the individual). As in Native Americans who believed that you were not connected with your Higher Self at birth, you had to go through a ceremony to connect – they dipped you in water. Hmm, sound familiar? Baptism?. It was a "Totally trustworthy parental spirit". The Hawaiians believe you are connected but may not experience it. It's like you're up there looking down on yourself, wondering "I wonder if Jonathan's going to wake up today?" You are connected, you just need to learn how to communicate with it.

2. God Spirit in the individual. Your way of relating to the source of all creation, God, I'o

3. Connection/communication with higher self makes everything OK - everything the way we want it. That's the basis of Western high magic -

4. Totally balanced male and female energy. Yin & Yang, assertive male energy and totally nurturing female energy. Plato mentioned a time when we were both.

5. An expression of man and woman's own perfection.

6. Our connection to the higher realms of creation, above Higher Self and God

7. Represents the process of evolution in Huna. Shows us the way we're developing

8. Has the power to recognize causes (source of events) of events that happen in our lives in the now. Direct knowl-

edge of Past Lives comes from the Higher Self

9. Has the power to remove complexes, fixations and false identifications. Can clear up psychological ailments

10. Has the power to produce attainments (Sanskrit siddhis, etc.) including ESP, clairvoyance, clairaudience etc.

11. Has the power to know, predict and affect the future. Creating Your Future process in Time Line actually works with Higher Self, that's why we Ha breathe in that process to energise the Internal Representation

12. Doesn't make mistakes. If you're worried about making mistakes, operate from the Higher Self and you can only do right

13. Higher Self cannot interfere with conscious mind's free will (it must be asked). It can't intervene unless you ask (through prayer)

14. Is all forgiving, because we are all one. All knowing and all seeing. It thinks you're perfect the way you are

15. Conscious mind has free will to deny Prime Directives of Aumakua (and just might do it).

CONNECTEDNESS

Go back to 3 minds diagram earlier in this book. Draw a line between Conscious Mind and Unconscious Mind. Draw a connection between the Higher Self and the Unconscious Mind. So to connect with the Higher Self, it's not a Conscious process. It's an unconscious process – you have to experience it, it's beyond words. HGE teaches you how to connect with Unconscious Mind. That's the first step. This is the next. Draw raindrops from the Higher Self flowing down to the Conscious Mind. In Hawaii that's called the Ka'au Helemoa, the fine rain that blows off mountains in Hawaii & you feel it, but your skin is dry. Think of it as energy that rains down from the Higher Self. Trust & honour & love your Unconscious Mind, because it holds the connection to Higher Self .

What prevents connecting with your Higher Self? There are only 3 reasons

1. Negative Emotions like Anger, Fear, Sadness & guilt
2. False identifications – identity crises, who am I?
3. Aka connections with other people that would prevent you from getting there.

These all act like sewage in the pipes, blocking the connections.

HIGHER SELF CONNECTION

This is the highest process one can do in Huna. First do some Ha breathing to generate energy, then connect with Higher Self . You'll have your arms outstretched, standing up. Ha breathing should be done for 10 minutes in sets of 4. then you'll imagine sending an Aka cord up 1/3 of the way each time – imagine a small piece of rope or silvery thread, a wisp of smoke, purple, silver or white coming out of your third eye, throat, heart, any chakra. You'll build energy in the N'au (solar plexus), then send it up. Do that 3 times till the Higher Self is directly above your head.

Visualise it as a ball of light like a 3' diameter dandelion seed. The Aka cord connects with Higher Self and then you'll bring the Higher Self down and inside, merging together inside and then you'll meditate for about 15 minutes

Take off your shoes

Turn off any bright lights

Find a place to stand in with room to have your arms outstretched

You'll sit down to meditate after this process

Slightly bend the knees so they're not locked

Arms extended with palms up

You'll actually be able to feel your Higher Self directly above your head, shortly…

4 ha breaths

drop arms

notice how your energy has risen

Next set of 4 force the air out on the "Ha"

Rest

Feel the energy building

Next set of 4

Next set of 4

Let that energy really be building now

Next set of 4

{repeat for 10 minutes}

Reach up over your head, directly up above your head. Move your palms back and forth and you may notice a tingling, or heat, a pressure, or energy directly above you. It might be quite big, it may be smaller. At some point you'll begin to feel the tingling of the Higher Self directly above you. If you move your hands in and out you'll actually be able to feel your Higher Self.

Next set of 4 Ha breaths

Building the energy to send it up

Relax, feel the energy rising up inside

With next set of 4 we'll be sending an Aka cord up 1/3 of the way

Next set of 4 send the aka cord 2/3 of the way up to the Higher Self

Next set of 4

Send the aka cord all the way up , fully extended all the way up now

Allow the aka cord to fall back on and connect with the Higher Self

Next set of 4

Send your mana up the aka cords up and into the HS

Next step is to ask the Higher Self to come right down inside, all the way down inside and merge with the Conscious Mind and Unconscious Mind & the Higher Self to merge and become as one

Whenever you're ready sit right down and meditate
Now your communication with your Higher Self will come...
in many different ways. You may see pictures or sights, visuals that
remind you of your connection. Some will hear sounds, voices or a
conversation – so **go ahead and listen, really listen..** You may even
feel feelings or sensations, perhaps hot or cold, tingling...inside
As we close this meditation, we'll end with an ancient chant to the
Higher Self

KE WELINA MAI NEI KE KINO O LALO
Ai, Ke welina mai nei ke kini o lalo
Ai, Ai, Ai,
Ke welina mai nei Ke kini o lalo
Na hoa o ka uka naheleo puna
Akahi ka noho o ka ua I kaukahi
Noho Kane i ka papa i lohia
A lau o kalohelani a pi'i lani la
eala, eala, ea.
Ua ma'ona o Kane i ka awa
Ua kau ke keha i ka uluna
Ua hi'olani i ka moena
Kipa 'ia e ke kapa a ka noe
Ka ho'opa'a kai a kinilau la
eala, eala, ea.
A ie ilei ie ie ie
He inoa no Kane.

A chant in the honour of the One Creator in the Hawaiian sys-
tem, Kane.
Take a couple of Ha breaths
Come on back into the room
Welcome back

Just notice whatever it is that indicates your connection with Higher Self.

Write down your experience of that process, and especially any learning's that you may have received from your Higher Self

[NOTE: Once you have connected with your Higher Self consciously, you can learn how to ask your Higher Self to come down and remove any negative emotions, limiting beliefs or decisions directly out of your neurology, at any time. This is the quickest and deepest form of therapy I've ever seen. If you are interested in learning how to do this for yourself, contact us for details of our trainings.]

TANEO SANDS KUMELAE

Ever worked on an issue over and over and it still hasn't cleared up yet? Want to practice real magic?

Sometimes the Conscious Mind needs some kind of ritual to go through, to give the Unconscious Mind permission to heal itself, or make a change. Taneo Sands Kumalae was a Kahuna who was born in Hawaii, trained in Hawaii, lived much of her life in New York City, and died in New York in 1980. If we **are** right, she was of the Kumalae family of great Kahuna. Although I never met her, I have been greatly influenced by her work. I received her teachings directly from one of her students, and include them here because of the simplicity and the beauty of her philosophy. We offer this to the great Kahuna Taneo Sands Kumalae — *"Amama"*.

There are certain laws in magic. Anything that resembles or reminds you of someone or something can be used to affect it/them. You get what you focus on, so focus on what you want. Everything that exists can be symbolised. That symbol can be changed. Changing the symbol changes the reality.

Think back to the four bodies diagram in the beginning of this book. The closer to the physical world you get, the heavier the matter and the less consciousness or energy it has. Whereas, the closer to the Spiritual Body you go, the less matter it has but the more consciousness or energy it has. Compare the bumper of your car with a Pentium 4 microchip. One is dense and heavy with one function, the other is tiny and fragile, with thousands of functions.

Taneo Sands Kumalae taught her students a number of basic techniques that were designed to produce results in the nonmaterial, metaphysical universe. Some of these techniques were basic, and I can share them with you.

THE BASIC AHI (FIRE) RITUAL:

1. Take a sheet of paper. Write on the page a question about something from which you wish to be free. E.g.: Why can't I be free of self- sabotage? (Never put a person's name in the question.)

2. Answer the question, free association from your Unihipili (Unconscious Mind). Fill up the paper.

3. Take a match, and burn the paper. Watch it burn. Hear the fire. Smell the smoke. Feel that you are burning the obstacles.

4. Take the ashes, throw them in the ocean. (You may flush the ashes down the toilet if no ocean is available).

Taneo Sands advised regularly making an exhaustive list and practicing in the areas of love, health, material and self-expression.

Another Ahi (Fire) Candle ritual, for concentration of focus

1. Light a candle
2. Watch the wax drip down
3. Concentrate on the flame. Draw the energy and the flame into you
4. Have the energy of the flame empower your intention for _____ (outcome)
5. Send the energy up to the higher self

6.   When done, do not blow the candle out. Put it out with your fingers

THE BASIC HONUA (EARTH) RITUAL:

1.   Be aware of something you want to change (or heal) in your life.
2.   Get a piece of molding clay. Knead it; as you do, become one with the clay; and then make a shape that represents the issue or problem with the clay. Be in Hakalau. Let your Unihipili do the work. Free associate. Associate the problem into the clay. Look at it when done. (Alternatively, the Kahuna used a number of sea shells or small stones.)
3.   Destroy the image. Get rid of it. Pound the clay out — hard!! (If using sea shells or stones, just shake them up, or rearrange them.) Let your Unihipili do the work, unconsciously.
4.   Immediately reshape the clay. Make a **new** shape that signifies the new desired state or condition. Recreate the clay in a symbol of the new state or condition — how you want it to be.
5.   Keep the new shape until the outer world changes. Put new shape where you can see it regularly.

THE BASIC WAI (WATER) RITUAL:

1.   Rub your hands together - seven times.
2.   Place them on your solar plexus. Very Calming!
3.   Hold your hands over a cup of water. Let Mana flow into cup.
4.   Say out loud, "This cup of water is now filled with the Mana — the life force to heal (me/client's name).
5.   Pass it to the left 7x if you're in a group. Or do this 7x if alone
6.   Either you or your client can drink it!

ALOHA

Lots of people use the word "Aloha" in Hawaii, in fact it's a well known word now throughout the world, but do you know what it really means? "Alo" means space, and "ha" means? That's right, breath. "Hello, come, share my space, share my breath"

Daddy Bray (1889 – 1968) the great Kahuna said "In order to be a Kahuna one must know the secret teaching of Aloha"

Its an acronym, and each letter has its own thought:

A - "ala" watchful alertness. Enlightenment, which starts at the unconscious level. Bring in the Light. Everything outside of you started on the inside. Is my behaviour leading me to Spirit, or is it short circuiting me back towards matter? You will be tested often, so choose the light. You don't know you're incorruptible until you're tempted. Defend your boundaries lovingly. Use Huna for good. Be in Hakalau. There's a right time and a right place - look around before doing Huna. Is now appropriate? If so, here? Can they handle what you're about to say? The more you know the less you say. The less you know the more you talk. So be wise - shut up. The wider your mouth is open the harder it is to hear. Once you know who you are, the less you'll have to show off. If someone's trying to impress you, say "what's that?" & feign ignorance. You don't need to be interesting, you need to listen.

L - "lokahi" working with unity. Become "pono" with everyone in your world, starting with yourself!. Congruent, no conflict inside, aligned. Internal conflict scatters your energy. You can't lie to your own unconscious. The more you evolve the more you become one. The more you evolve the less people you can talk to about it. Anything less than 100% support is sabotage. Talk to the person you have a problem with. To forgive and not to forget, is not to forgive at all. Cut connections with people who slow you or pull you down.

O - "oiaio" truthful honesty. Speak your truth & do it elegantly.

To yourself first. Your needs, your boundaries. Create a safe space to speak your truth first. Hold nothing back. Every 1% held back is 1% sabotage. "Kuka kuka" - talk it out, say what needs to be said. If you're playing a role or putting on a face, you're not pono.

H - "ha'a ha'a" humility. You're replaceable. Admit that you're not perfect and don't have all the answers. The more you tell people how important you are, the less you listen. Keep your judgements to yourself. It'll take you a lifetime to become God in your universe, so who are you to judge someone else? Be willing to learn from anyone. If you play power games you'll always have competition. You are not less or more than anyone. We are all seedlings of light - see through the mask, the persona. "See the light, not the light shade". Give it away - share the knowledge. The more you share your knowledge, the more you'll receive back. Underpromise & overdeliver. See the seedling of light, the Higher self in everyone, but don't let them screw you over either. You can't give up your ego until you let it out. You can't surrender until you feel safe, yet when you totally surrender you are safe.

A - "ahoniu" Patient perseverance. Nothing seems to happen for ages, then a Quantum Leap! It'll take longer than you want it to – get used to it. It's probably a lifetime commitment. You have no say over other people's karma - stop telling them what's right. The right time and place will show up. If the conversation is necessary, the occasion will arise and that person will open the door.

These are the characteristics of the Hawaiian people, and certainly the suggested code of conduct for a Kahuna.

As it clearly states in the book "The Kybalion" by the Three Initiates, written in 1912,

"The possession of knowledge, unless accompanied by...action, is like the hoarding of precious metals – a vain and foolish thing. Knowledge, like wealth, is intended for use". If you don't use what you've learned in this book, and every other book you've ever read, then you're suffering from "Mental Miserliness". Knowledge will cover a lot of ground, but it won't cultivate any of it. It's what you do consistently that counts. Remember that.

CONCLUSION

It's been a great honour for me to share this information with you. It's an honour to be passing on some of the teachings of ancient Hawaii. One of the things Daddy Bray, the great Kahuna who died in 1968, said

"Don't believe in me just because I'm sitting up here"

There are many paths, just as there are many teachers, and many teachings. There are many sources of light – the sun, the moon and the stars. All the teachers are teaching the same thing. All the paths lead to the same place. All paths lead inside you....to your connection with your authentic self ...who you are. And if I've stretched your boundaries and your beliefs in any way, then I really have done my job well.

If you want to hear the chants being chanted, or you'd like me to take you through Ho'o Pono Pono or Hiolani, you'll find all of these Huna processes are available on compact disc on 2 Home Study programmes – a beginning level and an intermediate level. They, like all of the Home Study programmes I offer, are available at www. jonathanclark.org/products. Or perhaps you'd like to attend a live training and really experience the esoteric levels of HGE in person. Full information of upcoming events will be on the same website.

By way of completion I'll share with you one final chant

**Ai noho ana keakua I ka na...helehele
I alai 'ia e-ke ki ohu ohu e-ka ua koko
O na kino malu-i ka lani**

Malu e hoe
E ho'o ulu mai ana o Kane I kona kahu
'Owau 'owau noa.. ua Ike a..

As you go on your way, may our timelines cross again…

"If you're not using Huna, you're trying too hard"

YOUR HOMEWORK....

"What, there's homework?" I hear you cry.

Hey, you'll like this homework. I want you to watch some movies. These are all movies that contain elements of, or references to, the principles of HGE. Now as any of my students know, I'm a bit of a movie buff. People think I sit at home and just watch DVD's and videos all day. I don't, but give me time...

These are simply good films that illustrate a point, or have a message behind them, or leave you thinking "hang on, wait a minute..." and in my opinion, it's a good film that does that. I present to you, for your delectation and delight...

THE MATRIX TRILOGY

The ultimate illustration that the universe is your projection. Watch as Neo goes through Practitioner, Master Practitioner and Trainer training over three movies.. Notice that the lead female role is called Trinity (Conscious, Unconscious, Higher Self). Neo says initially "I don't like the idea that I'm not in control of my life". Morpheus points out that "real is simply electrical signals interpreted by your brain". Humans are being farmed for energy (Mana). The mind has trouble letting go, and once freed you need training. You have to let it all go – fear, doubt, disbelief – free your mind. Not everyone is ready to be unplugged and many of them are so hopelessly dependent on the system that they will help to defend it. Ignorance is bliss. As a species human beings define their reality by suffering and misery. "This is all about evolution" we're told. And there's a difference between knowing the path, and walking it.

In "Reloaded" Morpheus has obviously used Time Line Therapy, as he says he's "fearless, not because of what lies before him, but what lies behind him". There are so many gems here, they've spawned a whole internet religion! Two of my favourite lines "Everything begins

with choices" and "Denial is the most predictable human response"
Watch the scene with the Architect when he uses Milton Model language patterns.

EQUILIBRIUM

Intriguing sci-fi movie set in a future where it is illegal to feel emotions, else you've committed a "sense offence". What a dilemma when the lead police officer has to condemn his own wife and partner, then starts to feel about it. This movie shows us what will happen if the Cerebrals take over!

DONNIE DARKO

Cult classic already, it's a quirky film about cause and effect. Maybe I should change my name to Jonathan Ross?

THE WIZARD OF OZ

Ah, the classic screen gem with those seriously disturbing flying monkeys! But the whole dream sequence thing, seeking the courage and heart to be who you want to be, the Wizard himself getting carried away – full of great messages. We're not in Kansas anymore Toto....

PLEASANTVILLE

You have to watch this to get it. I'm saying no more.

STAR WARS EPISODE ONE: THE PHANTOM MENACE

Qui Gon states that "your focus determines your reality". Loads of hypnotic language patterns being used by those Jedi Knight Kahuna. The Jedi spot potential early and take the youngsters away to train them, just like in ancient Hawaii. And remember that "Fear leads to anger, anger leads to hate, and hate leads to the Dark Side"

STAR WARS EPISODE TWO: ATTACK OF THE CLONES

Ben tells Anakin "Be mindful of your thoughts – you're focussing on the negative" Anakin lacks humility ("ha'a ha'a") and is instead cocky and arrogant. Yoda cautions against becoming too sure of yourself. Look for the scene where a youth tries to sell Obi Wan "death sticks" (cigarettes) and instead goes home to rethink his life. Dex reminds Obi Wan that the Jedi know the difference between knowledge and wisdom.

STAR WARS EPISODE THREE: REVENGE OF THE SITH

Yoda teaches Anakin "Train yourself to let go of everything you fear to lose" – practically identical to an exercise we do on our Master Practitioner courses! Count Dooku loses both hands, Mace Windu loses one, as did Anakin, as will Luke. Is there some kind of hidden meaning there that I'm missing? Note that Grievous's ship is also called "The Invisible Hand". Look out for the scene where Darth Sidious shouts about one of Tony Robbins' books. The Supreme Chancellor says "All those who gain power are afraid to lose it. Even the Jedi." This film is a stark warning to those who suppress their anger… then again, it's just a metaphor…

STAR WARS EPISODE FOUR: A NEW HOPE

Watch Vader using Blamer while Leia Placates. This film inspired me to learn hypnosis in the "These aren't the droids you're looking for" scene. Obi Wan feels the aka connections severed as Alderaan is destroyed. Han Solo at level 5 evolution, the Jedi at level 6. Ben evolves to level 13 when Vader strikes him down. Obi Wan trains Luke to let go of his conscious self – "the eyes can deceive you – don't trust them".

STAR WARS EPISODE FIVE: THE EMPIRE STRIKES BACK

Jedi can sense other Jedi's presence even over vast distances (aka cords?). Watch Yoda's wanton curiousity when he meets Luke, and his comments about Luke's "lack of patience and his habit of dreaming about the future all the time, not paying attention to where he was or what he was doing. Jedi must have the deepest commitment, and a serious mind." Note also that Yoda's training regime starts with the physical body. In the sinister cave there's a great metaphorical dream sequence for going down into the deepest, dark part of the unconscious mind and confronting his deepest fear & unconscious symbology. Luke asks "What's in there?" Yoda replies "Only what you take with you". Yoda tells him "You must unlearn what you have learned" and the classic line "Try not. Do or do not. There is no try" (Reasons vs. excuses). "Luminous beings are we, not this crude matter" (Higher selves in physical bodies). When Yoda demonstrates his powers, Luke exclaims "I don't believe it" The Jedi replies "That is why you fail". Also look for the scenes where Luke can send a thought form to his sister, as well as predict visions of the future.

STAR WARS EPISODE SIX: RETURN OF THE JEDI

Now a fully fledged Jedi, Luke can merely gesture and people respond, or use hypnotic language patterns to deliver embedded commands. Obi Wan (now level 13) tells Luke "You'll find many of the truths we cling to depend greatly on your own point of view. Again, as in all of the films, we hear about the Jedi's ability to foresee the future. Luke tells the Emperor "You're confidence is your downfall". The film ends with Obi Wan, Yoda and now Anakin all evolved to level 13 (or am I taking all of this just a bit too seriously?)

THE VILLAGE

I watched this movie on a British Airways flight in March 2005 as I flew to Hawaii for the fourth time. Talk about "The Map is not the territory"?!! This is a wonderful example of the principle of Perception is Projection, where a small community of peace loving pilgrims live in constant fear of danger from outside. I won't spoil it by telling you why, just watch it.....all the way to the end....

WHAT THE #$*! DO WE KNOW?

Now this is the ultimate movie that backs up everything in this book, as well as every complementary and alternative practice on the planet. At last we have quantum physicists outlining such ideas as Cause & Effect, Perception is Projection, the Mind Body Connection. Remember, "the more you fire the more you wire!" Neurology, perception shifts, it's all here! This film has a great tagline........

"It's Time To Get Wise!"

17

SO WHAT NOW?

There's one last question I'd like to put to you now that you've read this whole book (and I assume you have read it, you aren't cheating by flicking through to this end page are you, cos if you are – GO BACK TO PAGE 1 AND READ IT PROPERLY!)

>Ahem<

So here's my question:

WHAT ARE YOU GOING TO DO WITH THIS MATERIAL?

Every year I have the opportunity to work with hundreds of people – salespeople, educators, managers, Coaches, professionals, entrepreneurs and more – and I've learned that in any group of people who attend a seminar or training course, only a small number of the attendees will actually ever do anything with the material they've just learned.

Now I can't imagine NOT using these techniques, but then that's why I do what I do. But what about you? Will you be one of the few who will walk your talk, or will you be one of the many and fumble your stumble?

IT'S WHAT YOU DO CONSISTENTLY THAT COUNTS!

**Knowledge will cover a lot of ground,
but it won't cultivate any of it.**

You can't have a bath once and be clean forever!

**True understanding =
Intellectual knowledge + experiential results**

The people who live successful, balanced, fulfilling lives are those who take action and apply the principles in this book. Be action oriented. Systematically and relentlessly apply the powerful techniques and methodologies in these pages that make that kind of life attainable and enjoyable. My greatest hope is that you will now take what I've shared with you and use it. You can have everything in life you want as long as you persistently and consistently chip away at it. Go out now and learn how to run your own emotions, have more people like you more often, help others evolve along the way and enjoy the journey. Live by the secret Hawaiian code of Aloha.

Go to www.jonathanclark.org/bodyquotient and complete the on line assessment of your 4 bodies. Then download the free guidance booklets, each containing advice on how to develop the bodies, as well as a gift certificate redeemable against any of my products and services.

Realise one thing – the only thing that can stop you – is YOU! And you can only have three excuses why you're not getting the results you want. Limiting beliefs, Ineffective Strategies, and Negative Emotions, and there's a solution to all three of those in these pages, so you have NO EXCUSE!

Master your own emotions, be friends with your unconscious mind, and connect with your Higher Self. Improve your physical body. The majority of people are being carried along, obeying their environment and having more and more of their choices made for them. They are vulnerable to manipulation, seduction, suggestion and end up being moved around like involuntary chess pieces. Applying the principles of HGE offers you the freedom to make your own choices, control your impulses and emotions, create what you want for yourself, and become a chess master yourself.

And please do email me or write to me, and tell me how things are different after applying this material, or maybe we'll meet at a live event someday and you can tell me how you've changed. Till then,

Take care,

18

SPREAD THE WORD!

Did you enjoy this book? If you did, I want to ask you to help me tell other people about it.

I bet you have an email list of friends and contacts. Would you consider sending round a 'group email' about this book and its contents?

Post messages about it on web forums and message boards!

Mark your copy so people know it's your property, and leave it in any 'common area' where you work, play or meet other people. It could be quite a conversation starter!

Got friends or contacts in the media? Tell them about this book. They might get a good story, article or feature out of it! (I am easily contacted via my website and am happy to do interviews.)

Do you contribute to a magazine? Why not write a short review of the book, and mention how to order a copy?

Are you a student or teacher? Maybe this book could be a 'set text' for a course module, or provide the basis for some interesting research and practical social experiments!

THANK YOU!

Jonathan Clark

www.jonathanclark.org

19

WHO'S JONATHAN CLARK?

There are numerous active NLP Practitioners, Master Practitioners, NLP Trainers, Life Coaches, Speakers and Firewalk Leaders that all have one thing in common – Jonathan trained them.

Jonathan is the Founder & Developer of HGE. He's also a Certified NLP Trainer trained by Tad James and David Shephard, and has been doing NLP for 14 years. The bulk of that was one-on-one therapy and group-workshops, which means he has a lot of experience dealing with NLP in the real world, dealing with real people, with real problems, real concerns and real aspirations. He didn't just do a course one day and thought it would be a good idea to reproduce it. He didn't just read a book, and he is not just newly certified. In fact he's been certified by 3 different NLP training companies, and is certified by the American Board of NLP.

He has given public talks and private consultations for the best part of 14 years. He has taught these skills in household-name kind of companies and is often asked to come and do seminars and trainings for household-name firms. He still has a full therapy practice in Glasgow and a full life-coaching practice, as well. He's been interviewed on local radio-stations. His work has been featured by BBC Scotland, by the channel STV2, in the Sunday Post, Sunday Mail and the Glasgow Herald.

The Anthony Robbins YES Group in Glasgow was originally

launched and run by Jonathan way back in 1995.

Jonathan is also a professional Life Coach. He was trained and certified over three years by Coach University in the States founded by Thomas Leonard, which is probably one of the longest-running if not THE first life-coaching companies on the planet. He recommends Coach University over and above any other life-coaching companies, because they seem to have the definitive, comprehensive model on how to do that. If you're going to model a good Life Coach, then go to the company that's been here the longest, who consistently turn out elegant and exquisitely skilled coaches.

Jonathan started his first self-employed business when he was 19 years old, and to this day teaches that a new start-up, especially in a service professional industry like Coaching or Therapy, can make a profit in month one.

He is also a qualified Financial Adviser. He spent a number of years in financial planning and financial services advising people on what to do with their savings, investments and pensions. That comes in handy. It also exposed him to the world of sales and all that kind of thing, which generally is a source of references of what not to do. However, it did emphasis regulation and governing bodies, which Jonathan firmly believes in.

Also, he's a Master Practitioner of Time-Line Therapy, personally trained and certified by Tad James and David Shephard. Time-Line Therapy is a particular technique devised by Tad James, which enables you to let go of emotional traumas very, very quickly – in minutes, in fact, not years. It also enables you to create things that you want to happen in your future, and to change things that have happened to you in your past, or change the effect that they have on you. Jonathan is a full member of the Time Line Therapy Association.

Jonathan is also a Master Hypnotherapist, a registered and certified Hypnotherapist and has used hypnotherapy with hundreds of clients in his therapy practice over the last 14 years. He's currently working on a Bachelor's degree in Clinical Hypnotherapy, because a lot of HGE techniques go hand-in-hand with hypnosis techniques, because a lot of them came from hypnosis originally. We certainly have a lot of HGE people who are learning hypnosis, and a lot of hypnotherapists who are learning HGE. The two go hand-in-hand, and he can teach you both.

ANCIENT SECRETS AND MODERN WISDOM

For 10 years Jonathan has practiced Feng Shui, often called "the ancient art of placement", which is based on the belief that the way you lay out and organise your space has a great effect on the internal and external results in your life. Now, whether you believe in it or whether you don't - the fact is, an organised system in a neat office works more efficiently and effectively than a cluttered one. People whose houses are cluttered tend to have cluttered minds as well. As within so without. If your house is a mess, then usually your finances are a mess. So, whether you look at it from an esoteric point of view, or whether you look at it from a purely common sense point of view, there are aspects that work. Many ancient teachings and ancient philosophies have certain core concepts that keep showing up time and time again, and Feng Shui is one of them.

Another one is Hawaiian Huna. Huna is rumoured to be the source of the majority of other esoteric disciplines, such as Chinese Medicine, Energy Healing and Shamanism. Jonathan has been initiated on a live volcano in Hawaii by Huna Masters **5 times**, and has been granted permission to teach the healing, spiritual and shamanic discipline of Huna. He's currently also studying towards a PhD in Esoteric Studies.

And he also holds full membership of the Association of NLP, the British governing body for Neuro Linguistic Programming. Jonathan is a full member of the ANLP and fully adheres to their guidelines on regulation and code of ethics.

He's taught classes and workshops as a lecturer in three Scottish colleges, and is regularly asked back to talk to the Entrepreneur Course at Strathclyde on how to set up in a private practice that's profitable from month to month. In fact, one of his seminars teaches you exactly how to do that, how to set up a service-based professional practice, such as therapy or life coaching, starting from zero and earning a profit within your first month.

Previous clients that Jonathan has worked for include professional footballers, Morgan Stanley, Barclays Stockbrokers, Virgin Cinemas, Hilton Hotels, Marriott Hotels, Texstyle World, Decorum, Laura Ashley, Waterstones, Slaters Estate Agents, Share, and Paisley & District Chamber of Commerce.